Strategic Human Resource Management

The last few years have brought fundamental changes to the business environment. Borderless economies now exist and no business organisation can afford to ignore the international dimension. A strategically managed human resource function within a company is a key part of making a business successful, and this foundation textbook analyses the current theories on both sides of the Atlantic. It recognises that human resource management should be central to corporate strategy, rather than hived off into a separate personnel 'ghetto'.

Divided into four parts, the book covers theoretical perspectives; strategic human resource foundations; strategic human resource managment integration; aspects of strategic human resource management in action. The authors have selected case studies which will help students to assimilate the essential points concerning strategic human resource management.

This student-friendly book will advance understanding of the evolution that is taking place from personnel management to strategic human resource management, and is designed around current courses in human resource management and strategy.

Olive Lundy is Senior Lecturer in Human Resource Management at the University of Ulster. **Alan Cowling** is Professor and Head of the Centre for HRM Studies at Middlesex University Business School.

Strategic Human Resource Management

Olive Lundy and Alan Cowling

ROUTLEDGE

London and New York

First published 1996
by Routledge
11 New Fetter Lane, London EC4P 4EE

Simultaneously published in the USA and Canada
by Routledge
29 West 35th Street, New York, NY 10001

© 1996 Olive Lundy and Alan Cowling

Typeset in Garamond by
J&L Composition Ltd, Filey, North Yorkshire
Printed and bound in Great Britain by
Clays Ltd, St Ives plc

British Library Cataloguing in Publication Data
A catalogue record for this book is available from
the British Library

Library of Congress Cataloguing in Publication Data
A catalogue record for this book has been requested

ISBN 0–415–13603–2 (hbk)
ISBN 0–415–09989–7 (pbk)

Contents

**Part IV Aspects of strategic human resource management
in action**

Figures

Tables

Exhibits

Introduction

In the recent past the human factor has moved, from the wings to centre stage in the organisational arena. It is safe to say that never before has the contribution that human resources may make to organisational success been the subject of such scrutiny. Taking pride of place among reasons as to why this has occurred is the fundamental change that has been occurring in the business environment and which is predicted to continue into the future.

The key word is globalisation. Increasingly, organisations are viewing their market areas as global rather than domestic or even foreign. Every corner of the world has become a potential source of raw materials, labour or new market for products and/or services (Khambata and Ajami, 1992). It is a world of increasing uncertainty but one presenting many challenging opportunities for those organisations that can maintain effectiveness and efficiency while becoming both flexible and adaptable (Taoka and Beeman, 1991). The trend is towards borderless economies, (Hodgetts and Luthans, 1991), examples of expansion being: the European Community; unification of Germany; 'glasnost' and 'perestroika' in Russia and, the impact of the latter on other eastern European countries. The United States and Canada have eliminated trade barriers while Mexico and others south of the border may become part of this trade area. Japan and Korea and other east Asian countries such as Singapore and Taiwan and perhaps China (particularly after the absorption of Hong Kong) may create a further geographic region for trade. It is projected that by the middle of the 1990s other regions, such as India, the Middle East and Africa may also be of importance.

At present and in the foreseeable future no business organisation can afford to ignore this international dimension. Competition has become the name of the game. Porter (1990) has pointed out that to sustain competitive advantage an organisation must have a commitment to improvement, innovation, and change. Important sources of these qualities, that cannot easily be replicated by competitors, are superior human resources and technical capability. Employees should be recruited with care, treated as permanent rather than dispensable, seen as a source of continuous improvement in productivity and, trained, on an ongoing basis, to support more sophisticated competitive advantages. Outstanding competitors should serve as benchmarks and motivators and a visionary leader should create an atmosphere in which organisational change is both normal and expected.

Progressive management, tuned to this perspective, will wish to engage the intelligence, expertise and commitment of its employees in achieving the organisation's strategic aims and to this end will create a learning organisation which continuously transforms itself in each part of its value chain of activities (Pearson, 1992). Problems, among many organisations, in achieving speed of response, flexibility in structure and capacity to transfer technology, have been attributed to failings in organisational culture. A global competitive culture will contain integrating values, mechanisms and processes that permit an organisation to manage constant change (Rhinesmith, 1991).

This scenario in which employee involvement and commitment are actively sought and valued is in sharp contrast to the dominant and widespread one based on the principles of scientific management and epitomised by Fordism, although latterly (Starkey and McKinlay, 1993), the Ford company has also been espousing the newer approach. There is, in fact, a viewpoint (Beer and Spector, 1985; Walton, 1985), that this movement from 'control' to 'commitment' represents a paradigm shift in management thought. However, such conclusions emerge as propositions derived from research originating in the United States and are a reflection of mainly piecemeal interventions by a number of organisations as they have responded to their competitive environment in particular, but also to the need to curb union power and, accommodate the expectations of a workforce more highly educated and experiencing better social conditions than in the past.

. It is against the above background that this book is written. Its origins start at another point however. It commences with a deep and persistent seam of literature dating back at least twenty years which is highly critical of the personnel management function's contribution to the organisation. According to this literature, for example, (Drucker, 1968; Watson, 1977; Legge, 1978; Rowland and Summers, 1981; Fombrum et al., 1984; Purcell, 1985; Rhodes, 1988; Schuler, 1990) the function is weak and its effectiveness diminished because it is locked in a non-strategic administrative role, conflict is endemic in its relationship with line management due to blurring of the staff/line responsibility for the management of people and, as it has failed to develop a sound theoretical base, it has been prone to make piecemeal prescriptive 'best practice' interventions which, too frequently, have been irrelevant to the needs of the organisation. Recurrent advice offered to the function is that reversal of fortune will only come about when it takes advantage of an increasing incidence of employees becoming significant issues in terms of the achievement of organisation strategy and actively seeks the involvement of the function's activities at that level. The snag, however, in proffering such advice, is that there is no theory, and subsequently no guidance available, as to how such strategic integration might be achieved in reality. Models and frameworks, which are American in origin, do begin to appear (for example, Beer et al., 1984; Devanna et al., 1984; Schuler and Jackson, 1987) and these are representative of the origins of a search for a concept of strategic human resource management.

This book draws, in the model that it presents, upon a research project designed to explore the theoretical development of the concept of strategic human resource management. In one important strand of the investigation there was focus on the strategy concept because it was felt that the personnel management function is insufficiently aware of the nature of that senior managerial area. In another, equally important strand, effort was made to understand the state of theoretical development within the field of personnel management. Intriguingly, literature searches appear to suggest that two simultaneous evolutions are occurring within these two distinctive areas of management, convergence of which might help to bring into existence the proposed concept of strategic human resource management.

There is an apparent evolution from personnel management to use of the term Human Resource Management, referred to in the literature as HRM, which seems to be a reflection of (a) a growing 'planning' orientation and, (b) piecemeal interventions, also strategic in orientation, and, seemingly, in the main, stemming from the control versus commitment movement referred to in the discussion of environmental change at the start of this introduction. The evolution gains momentum as the focus turns to finding the theoretical basis of a concept of strategic human resource management. The evolution within the strategy concept reflects over-emphasis on strategic planning and neglect of strategic implementation. The case is made that issues of implementation (organisation's internal capability) should be an integral part of the formulation process and that there is a requirement for an evolution from strategic planning to strategic management of both formulation and implementation phases. Clearly implementation is mainly to do with the human side of the organisation and, as the focus has shifted to issues of its link with strategy, interesting views have begun to emerge as to how human resources may provide the organisation with distinctive competences in its search for competitive advantage. The trigger which led to this reappraisal of the strategy concept was, perhaps not surprisingly, the growing turbulence in the business environment.

Reflection on these evolutionary trends leads to the proposition that the drive for the strategic integration of personnel management/HRM might be met with the complementary need for

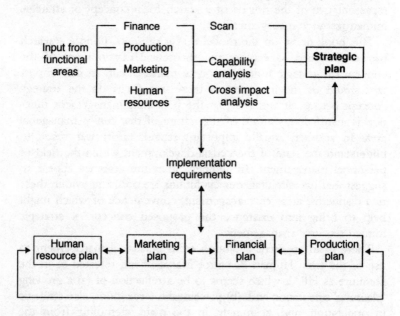

Figure 0.1 Strategic management

attention to the human side of the strategy process. The model of strategic human resource management presented in this book, see figures 0.1 and 0.2, is built upon this assumption. The model and its underlying perspectives is intended as a guide to thinking about the process and for research purposes.

Figure 0.1 represents the strategic process within a functional

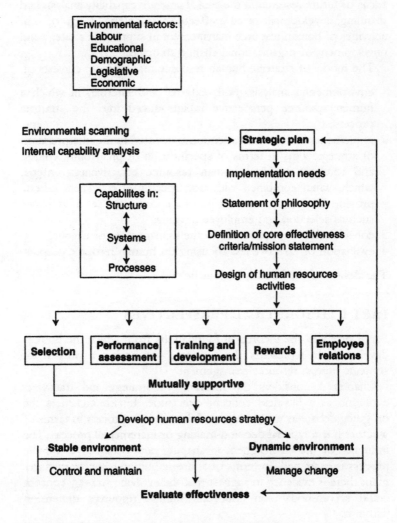

Figure 0.2 Strategic human resource management

organisation. This is chosen because of the concern with the integration of the human resources function into the process. However, the principles underlying the process may be applied to any size of organisation, including public and privately owned.

Figure 0.2 incorporates important areas of attention intended to further understanding and development of the concept of strategic human resource management and which will continue to be the focus of future research in the area. These are capability analysis and planning, development of core effectiveness criteria, design of sub-activities of human resource management in support of strategy and development of organisational change strategies.

The model of strategic human resource management consists of:

1 environmental analysis (both external and internal) in which a human resource perspective is introduced into the strategic process;
2 implementation in which attention is devoted to the interpretation of strategic aims in terms of specification of philosophy, culture and resultant required human resource effectiveness criteria, which, when combined with task specific effectiveness criteria provide the basis for the design of a coordinated set of activities such as selection and employee rewards;
3 consideration of approaches to the management of change;
4 evaluation of effectiveness focusing on human resource outputs.

The design of the book is set out below.

PART I THEORETICAL PERSPECTIVES

Part I provides the theoretical foundations from which the book is developed. It represents the rationale for having a process of strategic human resource management.

Chapter 1 considers the meaning of strategy and traces its evolution as a business concept over time. It also considers the on-going debate as to the nature of the strategic process in terms of whether it is a rational decision-making or incremental process. The influence of the environment in shaping new perspectives on the process is examined. In terms of strategic human resource management there is evidence to suggest that the evolving strategy concept could accommodate an important human resources dimension within it.

In chapter 2 the organisational status of the personnel management function forms the background against which HRM is seen to evolve. The debate as to its precise meaning is reviewed. The evolution continues with signs of the emergence of strategic human resource management with its focus on integrating the human resource concept with strategy. The perceived need for this integration is the driving force in pursuit of this link. A model which encapsulates the function is derived from a synthesis of both strategy and HRM literature and provides the foundation for this book. Its functioning is explained in the remainder of the book.

PART II THE FOUNDATIONS FOR STRATEGIC HUMAN RESOURCE MANAGEMENT

Using the elements of a definition of strategy as a framework, chapter 3 explores its constituent elements of leadership, effectiveness and the strategy process of formulation and implementation. Whilst acknowledging the significance, in the process of formulation, of the leadership and effectiveness concepts, judgement on their utility must be tempered by the conclusion drawn from the literature that they are in need of greater conceptual development. Finally, an overview of strategic management as it is currently practised, and including its various tools and techniques, is provided.

The view taken in chapter 4 is that decisions on structure are strategic decisions. While structure has, historically, been viewed as following strategy, it may also be the deciding factor in motivating an organisation to follow a specific strategy or even drop an anticipated new one. Put simply, there is no 'one best way'. This perspective is in opposition to the best traditions of 'scientific management' and, for that matter, the teachings of the 'in search of excellence' approach to structural design. There are key contingency variables of organisation design and the choice of variables must be considered from the standpoint of the overall corporate strategy being pursued. However, the dominant western management approach to organisation design based on hierarchy, power and authority, dies hard, although, increasingly, many pressures, not least Japanese competition, are bringing home the need to develop flatter, more participative structures and more flexible patterns of work and job design.

Chapter 5 addresses issues of culture, strategy and change. Key factors of consideration when an organisation engages in strategic analysis are whether (a) current strategic attainment is being enhanced by an appropriate organisational culture and/or (b) there is the internal capability, in terms of culture, to engage in new strategic direction. Culture, with its intention to link organisation mission with the human resources dimension of the organisaton, in terms of the transmission of required values and behaviours, is a powerful tool and, as with structure, its implementation brings in its wake the management of change. The meaning of culture is explored in both organisational and national terms and various models for the management of change are examined, including the Japanese process of Kaizen. In a link with chapter 3, the 'transformational' potential of the leader in relation to culture change is considered. Finally, the political nature of change comes in for scrutiny.

Chapter 6 considers an evolution from manpower planning to HR planning, in which an 'operations management' oriented approach to planning for people, based on assumptions of a stable environment, has acquiesced to the need for the flexible, responsive approaches of the renamed 'HR' planning, geared to assumptions of a rapidly changing environment. The important difference between the old and the new approaches is a reduction of emphasis on quantification and measurement in favour of an orientation towards establishing processes to motivate and lead people in the pursuit of strategic aims and to put a value on their contribution.

An overview of manpower planning models and forecasting tools is provided. The chapter goes on to focus on the managerial level of organisations and considers whether career planning is an anachronism or a strategically oriented approach to succession planning and management.

PART III STRATEGIC HUMAN RESOURCE MANAGEMENT ACTIVITIES

Part III provides state of the art understanding and perspectives with which to utilise human resource activities in support of strategy.

In chapter 7 the selection process is defined as being the process by which an organisation recruits new entrants, inducts new employees (in the sense that this constitutes a period of probation) and chooses those for promotion, transfer or severance. It is seen that the link with strategy is not well developed. Scanning of the organisational environment, in a general sense, reveals many strategic issues capable of influencing strategic selection and the implications of these are considered. Some thought is given to the application of the tools and techniques of the SM process to selection and, while such application is in its infancy, it is seen that some progress is being made in efforts to match the product life cycle, portfolio analysis and generic competitive strategies with strategies of selection.

The perspective of the chapter is that an ineffective selection process will undermine the value of any attempted link with strategy and it is seen that issues of central concern deal with questions of reliability and validity. These concepts are reviewed in relation to various selection instruments, in particular, the interview, testing and assessment centres. The chapter concludes with discussion of a framework to guide the practice of strategic selection.

Chapter 8 on strategic training and development acknowledges confusion over terminology and an attempt is made to bring the concepts of education, training, development and learning together within one overarching concept.

The external, and particularly, the economic/political dimension of education, training and development cannot be escaped. A historical perspective on these spheres of activity highlights significant issues, helps explain the constraints and also opportunities they present to organisations, and in consequence, underlines their strategic significance.

At the organisational level an assessment is made of the state of practice in the area of training and it is found that current models of the process contain no direct link with strategy. Strategically, the process is in need of development. Its main underpinning principles, that of learning theory and evaluation, whilst requiring attention to issues of reliability and validity, have much to offer strategically.

Also, in the chapter, current approaches to linking training and development to strategy are considered. The developing concept of organisation learning is explored and an assessment is made as to its potential contribution to securing alignment between organisation strategy and appropriate human resource education, training and development activities. Finally, the role of performance appraisal in strategic training and development is examined.

Chapter 9 is concerned with strategic reward management. Increasingly, reward management is a primary issue for management, firstly, because rewards to employees are an important element in organisational costs and therefore strategic and, secondly, it is now, more than ever before, being recognised that there is a link between employee motivation and the achievement of an organisation's competitive advantage, in terms of securing employees' commitment to the pursuit of strategic aims and from willingness to adapt to change. Reward management, with its roots in motivation, is therefore an important aspect of HRM capability in terms of formulating and implementing an organisation's strategy.

The theoretical scope of a reward strategy is reviewed and its links with performance appraisal are examined. It is seen that performance management has emerged as a progression in the history of performance appraisal and that it is overtly linked to the strategic mission of the organisation. The pros and cons of a performance related pay system are considered.

Strategic employee relations, in chapter 10, takes the position that HR strategy should, as far as possible, merge the needs of the organisation with the attitudes and aspirations of employees. In order to enhance this concept of mutuality, organisations must understand the various frames of reference within the context of which managers and their subordinates must coexist. It is seen that differing frames of reference, (unitary, pluralist and radical) influence both the ideological relationships that exist within an organisation and the interaction between these relationships and the organisation environment. From this perspective it is possible to view the organisation/employee relations' climate in terms of militancy v. acquiescence, individualism v. collectivism and, the extent to which a collective orientation has been translated into a collective organisation.

In the light of these insights, the employer should take account of employee beliefs, attitudes and orientations when formulating and implementing HRM strategies. At issue is the extent to which there is employee participation in its various guises, such as collective bargaining or autonomous work groups. A number of approaches to participation are discussed. Finally, conflict and its management, another issue of central importance to employee relations, is explored.

It seems that the reality of organisational employee relations is that employee perspectives and those of other organisational stakeholders are not taken sufficiently into account in strategic issues. The importance of 'empowering' people is emphasised.

PART IV ASPECTS OF STRATEGIC HUMAN RESOURCE MANAGEMENT IN ACTION

The cases in part IV complement the text. They provide the reader with opportunity to reflect on the linkage between theory and practice. Questions relating to each case promote the analysis of strategic issues.

Final points in this introduction are:

1 It is emphasised that this unfolding concept of strategic human resource management is in an early phase of development. Further research will bring change and additional synthesis of its disparate areas.
2 The model of strategic human resource management is intended for use as a guide to thinking and acting strategically in this field.
3 Chief executives will obtain insights into the process and hopefully bring their strategic know-how to bear on the further development of strategic human resource management.
4 Managers, at various levels will obtain a clearer view of the line management role and the relationship with the human resource function. They, too, have much to offer from their perspectives, in terms of the future development of strategic human resource management.
5 Human resource specialists will, it is hoped, use the model and the theoretical perspectives presented, to, creatively, advance ways and means of contributing to strategy formation and the translation of strategic decisions into action in human resource terms.
6 Students, from undergraduate to postgraduate level will draw from this book according to their needs. Students taking undergraduate modules will gain an overview with which to understand this area of management and perhaps be motivated to study it further. Higher level students will study it in detail.

The authors hope that the book will advance understanding of the evolution that is taking place from personnel management to strategic human resource management and, as a consequence, contribute to the theoretical and practical development in this field.

REFERENCES

Beer, M. and Spector, B. (1985) 'Corporate transformations in human resource management', in R.E. Walton, and P.R. Lawrence, (eds) *HRM Trends and Challenges*. Boston Mass.: Harvard Business School Press.

Beer, M., Spector, B., Lawrence, P.R., Quinn Mills, D. and Walton, R.E. (1984) *Managing Human Assets*, New York: Macmillan.

Devanna, M.A., Fombrun, C.J. and Tichy, N.M. (1984). 'A framework for strategic human resource management', in C.J. Fombrun, N.M. Tichy and M.A. Devanna (eds) *Strategic Human Resource Management*, New York: John Wiley & Sons Inc.

Drucker, P. (1968) *The Practice of Management*, London: Pan.

Fombrun, C.J. Tichy, N.M. and Devanna, M.A. (1984) *Strategic Human Resource Management*, New York: John Wiley & Sons.

Hodgets, R.M., Luthans, F. (1991) *International Management*, New York: McGraw Hill.

Khambata, D. and Ajami, R. (1992) *International Business Theory and Practice*, New York: Macmillan.

Legge, K. (1978) *Power, Innovation and Problem-solving in Personnel Management*, Maidenhead: McGraw-Hill.

Pearson, G. (1992) *The Competitive Organisation*, Maidenhead: McGraw-Hill.

Porter, M.E. (1990) *The Competitive Advantage of Nations*, London and Basingstoke: Macmillan.

Purcell, J. (1985) 'Is anybody listening to the corporate personnel department?', *Personnel Management*, September: 28–31.

Rhinesmith, S.H. (1991) 'Going global from the inside out', *Training and Development*, November: 42–47.

Rhodes, D.W. (1988) 'Can HR respond to corporate strategy', *The Journal of Business Strategy*, 2: 57–58.

Rowland, K.M. and Summers, S. L. (1981) 'Human resource planning: a second look', *Personnel Administrator*, 26: 73–80.

Schuler, R.S. (1990) 'Repositioning the human resource function: transformation or demise?' *Academy of Management Executive*, 4:3: 49–60.

Schuler, R.S. and Jackson, S.E. (1987) 'Linking competitive strategies with human resource management practices', *The Academy of Management Review*, 1:3: 207–19.

Starkey, K. and McKinlay, A. (1993) *Strategy and the Human Resource: Ford and the Search for Competitive Advantage*, Oxford: Blackwell.

Taoka, G.M. and Beeman, D.R. (1991) *International Business*, New York: Harper Collins.

Walton, R.E. (1985) 'Towards a strategy of eliciting employee commitment based on policies of mutuality', in R.E. Walton and P.R. Lawrence (eds) *HRM Trends and Challenges*, Boston, Mass: Harvard Business School Press.

Watson, J. (1977) *The Personnel Managers: A Study in the Sociology of Work and Employment*, London: Routledge and Kegan Paul.

Part I

Theoretical perspectives

Part I examines the nature of a link between the strategy and human resource management processes. Review and analysis of the relevant literature uncovers the conceptual evolution occurring within these processes. On the strength of insights gained it is possible to find support for a rationale for a new concept of strategic human resource management.

These theoretical foundations provide the basis for a proposed model of strategic human resource management which becomes the focus for exploring the nature of the concept in the remainder of the book.

Chapter 1

The concept of strategy

INTRODUCTION

The term, Strategic Human Resource Management, conveys the sense of human resource management in a strategic context. In order for this to take place there has to be some connection made with the strategic process through which the aims of an organisation are managed, that is, its strategic management. In this chapter the state of development of the strategic process, which, at present, culminates in the concept of strategic management will be considered. The anticipated outcome of the strategy process is to win in the face of the competition. It will be seen that the military roots and battle analogy of the concept are still influential in the process. Awareness is created of the scope of the field of research in relation to strategy, and progress in this sphere is evaluated. Against a background of ever accelerating environmental turbulence, the process of strategic management emerges from an evolution of earlier, more simple systems for managing business planning. How should the many changes in the concept be interpreted? Looking ahead, are there aspects of the concept, in its current state of development, which can accommodate a linkage with human resource management?

THE STRATEGIC CONCEPT

The subject of strategy . . . falls a long way short of an established discipline, characterised by a widely accepted organising structure and a growing body of empirical knowledge. Indeed the strongly commercial orientation of the strategy business itself conflicts directly with this. The tradition of scholarship demands that each author should explain carefully how his contribution relates to all that has gone before; the dictates of profit suggest that each consultant should dismiss as bunkum the theories of his rivals and proffer his own nostrums as the one true solution.

(Kay, 1993: 358)

The above commentary conveys well the nature of the perplexity to be experienced in trying to reach some understanding of the current state of knowledge of the strategy process. While the roots of strategy, in its military sense, reach far back into history, there is general agreement (for example Ansoff and McDonnell, 1990; Grant, 1991; Faulkner and Johnson, 1992) that its study, in a business sense, has been more prolific in the past thirty years than at any earlier time. There is also acknowledgement of the fact that the concept has evolved, particularly in the past ten years, from a situation during which strategic planning was the main focus of study and application to one which has witnessed the broadening of the planning concept to the process now known as strategic management. As will be seen there are important insights to be gained in more fully examining both the origins and more recent developments in the strategy concept.

Definition

A dictionary definition of strategy conveys its military orientation. Strategy is:

The art of war, generalship, especially the art of directing military movements so as to secure the most advantageous positions and combinations of forces.

A strategem is:

An artifice, trick, or manoeuvre for deceiving an enemy.

A strategist is:

A military commander.

The Latin root of the concept is to be found in the words, *stratos*, meaning army and *agein*, meaning to lead.

Interpretation of the above definitions suggests a leader, directing the movements of an army and engaging in actions to out-manoeuvre the enemy. Applied to the business organisation, the definitions suggest the chief executive (or main decision-makers) engaged in leading the organisation in a direction and in a manner intended to secure competitive advantage over competitors in pursuit of the organisation's mission. Using this definition five key elements in strategy can be discerned:

- leading,
- positioning the company,
- deploying resources,
- securing competitive advantage, and
- being successful in the environment specific to each organisation.

These elements may be further categorised into three main areas:

1 The strategic process. Planning and implementing (Positioning the company, securing competitive advantage, and deploying resources).
2 Leadership. (Actions of the individual/s who direct the company.)
3 Organisation effectiveness. (Securing success in a specific environmental context.)

As will be seen, this definition is utilised in modelling the processes of strategic management and strategic human resource management in chapter 2. It also provides the framework for discussion of strategic management in chapter 3.

A definition from Faulkner and Johnson (1992), which would gain general support in the literature, quite closely reflects the above fundamental analysis of strategy. In their view strategy is concerned with the long-term direction and scope of an organisation. It is crucially concerned with how that organisation positions itself in its environment and in relation to its competitors. Strategy is concerned with establishing competitive advantage by taking a long-term perspective as opposed to tactical manoeuvring. They pinpoint also a dilemma of leadership, in the management of strategy, in that while managers may well be familiar with the term strategy and with discussing strategy, many find it 'extraordinarily difficult to manage its implementation', a hint here of a central part of the basic rationale, as will become apparent later, for the evolution from strategic planning to strategic management, namely recognition of the neglect of and the general lack of skill in strategy implementation which was detracting from the effectiveness of strategic achievement.

The military analogy

The military roots of the strategic concept, as conveyed through historic information, are to be found as far back as prehistoric times, for example the actions of Philip and Alexander at Chaeronea in 338 BC when they fought to rid Macedonia of influence by the Greek city states. One function of the earliest historians and poets was to collect the lore of successful and unsuccessful life-and-death strategies and convert them into wisdom and guidance for the future. As societies became larger and more complex strategic concepts were studied, codified and tested until a body of principles emerged. These were ultimately distilled, by various writers, to form sets of maxims regarding strategic behaviour (Quinn, 1988). (A very interesting analysis of the battle of Chaeronea and some modern analogies are to be found in Quinn's paper.)

Quinn suggests four dimensions of formal strategy, derived from these military origins, which effective strategies should contain. Firstly, there should be information on the goals to be achieved, policies which guide or limit action, and the major action sequences or programmes that are to be accomplished. Secondly, strategies should be developed around a few key concepts and thrusts, which give cohesion, balance and focus, and there must be coordination of action to support the intended thrust/s. Thirdly, as strategy deals with the unpredictable and even unknowable, it is necessary to build a proactive posture, of sufficient strength and flexibility, that the organisation can achieve its goals despite the impact of external forces. Fourthly, an organisation should have a hierarchy of mutually supporting strategies, each complete of itself, but shaped as a cohesive element of its next higher level. Quinn suggests certain criteria which define a good strategy. Strategic goals should be achieved by directing organisation effort through clear decisive objectives. The organisation must maintain the initiative. A reactive posture will reduce morale and commitment and surrender the advantage of timing and intangibles to opponents. The organisation must work out what its distinctive competencies are and concentrate its resources at the place and time where these can make a difference. The strategy must ensure flexibility by having reserve capabilities, planned manoeuvrability and capacity to reposition. The strategy must have coordinated and committed leadership. It must contain the element of surprise to attack exposed or unprepared opponents at unexpected times. There must also be security, that is, the strategy must secure resource bases and all vital operating points. This is achieved through having an effective intelligence system which will avert surprises. It must have the full logistics (services and equipment) to support its major thrust/s. It must make and use coalitions that extend the resource base of the organisation.

Quinn sees the military battle analogy in, for example, the business organisation that, '. . . first probes and withdraws to determine opponents' strengths, forces opponents to stretch their commitments, then concentrates resources, attacks a clear exposure, overwhelms a selected market segment, builds a bridgehead in that market, and then regroups and expands from that base to dominate a wider field'.

Quinn's analysis of strategy's military origins conveys the image of a very 'deliberate' and 'rational' cognitive process in which strategy is 'purposively' goal-directed, around several key concepts and strategic thrusts. A 'hierarchy' of strategies supports the main strategic aim and 'implementation', in the shape of policies and programmes of action, facilitates the achievement of strategy. An intelligence system is used for 'surveillance and analysis' of an unpredictable, even unknowable environment. The strategic position is 'proactive', 'flexible' and geared to take the 'initiative'. There is focus on 'distinctive competences' and the development of 'capabilities' so that the organisation may manouevre and reposition. External 'coalitions' will be availed of where these will enable the organisation to secure its strategy. These concepts are very much in mainstream strategic thinking and as will be seen reach their most coherent form in some models of strategic management, particularly those which view the strategy process as a formal and rational one.

THE STATE OF RESEARCH INTO THE STRATEGY CONCEPT

There are two subfields of strategy research (Chakravarthy and Doz, 1992). Strategy 'content' research considers the strategic positions of an organisation and conditions for their optimum performance under varying environmental contexts, examining such aspects as organisational scope (the combination of markets in which the organisation competes), competitive action within individual markets, and positioning the firm in relation to its environment. Strategy 'process' research is concerned with how a firm's administrative systems (structure, planning, control, incentives, human resource management and value systems) and decision processes influence its strategic position. It is concerned to understand how effective strategies are shaped, validated and implemented within the firm. It is interested also to understand how the organisation modifies its systems and processes both in response to environmental changes and through its own proactive actions. Each subfield is supported by different disciplines. Strategy 'content' research has a base in economics and decision-making theory and has a very rational orientation. It deals with the interface between the firm and its environment. Strategy 'process' research draws on sociology, organisation theory, behavioural decision theory, political science, psychology, and ethics. It deals with the behavioural interactions of individuals, groups, and/or organisational units, within or between firms.

There is some suggestion however (Schendel,1992; Pettigrew, 1992), that the separation of research into these two fields is a false dichotomy. Both areas have causal links with performance. Good strategy must be created, able to gain winning positions and capable of being implemented. The challenge then is to use administrative process to shape or develop good strategy, and then go on to develop those processes necessary to use the strategy to operate the organisation. It is unlikely that it would be possible to have good strategy without knowing how the administrative processes both find and use strategy. Researchers, are beginning to ask more dynamic research questions which are crossing the boundaries between the two areas. In, for example, the analysis of strategic change, there would appear to be strong advantages to be gained not only from linking process to content but also from exploring simultaneously the links between the context, content and process of change together with their interconnections through time.

The concern in this text is with the 'process' dimension of the research, that is, the formation of strategy and its implementation within the organisation. One of the first issues of note is that there is significant debate as to the optimum way to form strategy.

The strategy formation debate

The debate is dominated by two distinctive schools of thought, although others are also referred to in the literature. One view is that strategy is formed through a formal and rational decision-making process and another is that it happens through an informal incremental process in which managers rely upon experience and intuition.

In an early work which continues to be influential, Quinn (1978) explores the concept of how business strategy is formed in practice and concludes that organisations, when they make significant changes in strategy do not necessarily use a rational-analytical approach. The processes used to arrive at the total strategy are typically fragmented, evolutionary and largely intuitive. His concept of 'logical incrementalism' acknowledges that although the rational-analytical approach is excellent for some purposes it does not sufficiently allow for the psychological, power and behavioural relationships which contribute to the formation of strategy. Quinn has endeavoured to accommodate both phenomena within his perspective on strategy. As will be seen, the concept of incrementalism has become a major issue in the research literature relating to strategy formation.

The rational planning approach

Mintzberg (1990), a leading figure in the debate, provides a critique of the rational planning approach. He identifies three prescriptive schools of thought in which strategy formation is developed by conceptual design, formal planning, and analytical positioning. The first of these, the design school of thought, is the most entrenched. Its basic framework underlies the other prescriptions, and as a consequence, it has had great impact on how strategy and the strategy-making process are conceived in practice and in education and research. See figure 1.1.

The model places primary emphasis on appraisal of (a), threats and opportunities in the external environment (which leads to the identification of key success factors), and (b), strengths and weaknesses in the internal organisation (which permits the identification of distinctive competences). Emphasis is also placed on understanding the values and social responsibilities of management. Analysis of these elements leads to creation of options. This is followed with evaluation and choice of strategy, which is then implemented. The premises which underpin this model are that strategy formation should be a controlled, conscious thought process, the responsibility of the Chief Executive, and kept simple so that it can be held in

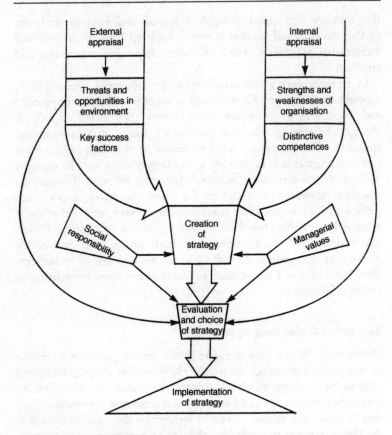

Figure 1.1 **Basic design school model**
Source: Mintzberg, 1990

one mind. The strategies which emerge should be unique (a process of creative design, tailored to the individual organisation and built on distinctive competences), fully formulated (a grand strategy), and explicit and preferably articulated (the loss of confidentiality is a necessary evil). Finally, formulation of strategy is distinct from implementation in that there has been a rational process of diagnosis, prescription and action.

Mintzberg considers that the rational approach has denied itself the opportunity to adapt. It is dogmatic and overly simple. It promotes thought independent of action. How can an organisation, in focusing on strengths and weaknesses to identify distinctive competences, ever be sure whether a competence will be a strength or a weaknesses? The promotion of the approach that structure follows strategy (based on Chandler's 1962 research) does not hold up in that the assessment of strengths and weaknesses is an input into strategy formation and structure is an essential element in the internal organisation. By articulating strategy, for the purpose of staying on course, the organisation is denied flexibility.

The incremental approach

Mintzberg's concept of 'crafting' strategy is in stark contrast to the formal planning approach, Mintzberg (1987). Strategy formed through the latter approach is based on thinking and reasoning. Crafting strategy is completely different. The concept of craft evokes traditional skill, dedication, perfection through mastery of detail. There is a sense of involvement, intimacy and harmony which has been developed through long experience and commitment. 'Formulation and implementation merge into a fluid process of learning through which creative strategies evolve.' In Mintzberg's view the crafting image captures the reality of the process by which effective strategies come into being, while the planning image 'distorts this reality and in doing so misguides organisations that embrace it unreservedly'. Mintzberg, in research into how strategies are actually made as opposed to how they are, prescriptively, supposed to be made, has concluded that strategy is needed as much to explain past actions as to describe intended behaviour. If strategies can be planned and intended, they can be pursued and realised or not realised. A pattern of action, that is, realised strategy, should be discernible. When strategy is portrayed as a deliberate process it suggests thinking before action. However strategy can form as well as be formulated. 'A realised strategy can emerge in response to an evolving situation, or it can be brought about deliberately.' Strategies that appear without clear intentions are emergent strategies. Mintzberg thinks that deliberate strategy pre-cludes learning while emergent strategy fosters it but precludes control. Learning must be coupled with control. Effective strategies combine deliberation and control with flexibility and organisational learning. The organisation manages the environment by handling periods of stability and revolutionary change, that is, convergence and divergence. In his view the strategist is a pattern recogniser and a learner who manages a process in which strategies and visions can

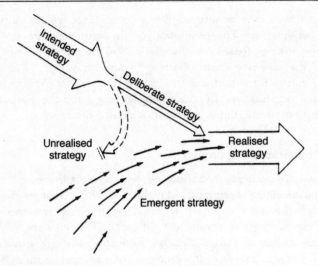

Figure 1.2 **Deliberate and emergent strategies**
Source: Mintzberg

emerge as well as be deliberately conceived. Figure 1.2 demonstrates Mintzberg's view of deliberate and emergent strategies.

Table 1.1 demonstrates Mintzberg's classification of strategies which range from deliberate to emergent.

The debate with regard to the nature of strategy formation continues. Ansoff (1991) condemns Mintzberg's analysis as being methodologically unsound on a number of counts, not least that he moves from description to prescription without offering any evidence that the prescription will work. In Ansoff's view the 'emergent' approach is unsuited to the continuing high levels of turbulence in evidence in the environment and could even endanger the survival of the organisation, because by the time the 'emergent' strategists had brought a product/service to the market, they could find that they had been preempted by more foresightful competitors who had planned their strategic moves in advance. The model is based on extrapolation of the past although managers are never totally sure or unsure about the past and formulate strategy precisely because they are partly unsure. Use of the organisational learning concept of 'trial and error' ignores the rational model of learning which is a legitimate alternative. The 'emergent' strategy model is a valid prescription for organisations operating in environments in

Table 1.1 Classification of strategies

Various kinds of strategies, from rather deliberate to mostly emergent

Planned strategy: precise intentions are formulated and articulated by a central leadership, and backed up by formal controls to ensure their surprise-free implementation in an environment that is benign, controllable, or predictable (to ensure no distortion of intentions); these strategies are highly deliberate.

Entrepreneurial strategy: intentions exist as the personal, unarticulated vision of a single leader, and so are adaptable to new opportunities; the organisation is under the personal control of the leader and located in a protected niche in its environment; these strategies are relatively deliberate but can emerge too.

Ideological strategy: intentions exist as the collective vision of all the members of the organisation, controlled through strong shared norms; the organisation is often proactive vis-à-vis its environment; these strategies are rather deliberate.

Umbrella strategy: a leadership in partial control of organisational actions defines strategic targets or boundaries within which others must act (for example, that all new products be high priced and at the technological cutting edge, although what these actual products are to be is left to emerge); as a result, strategies are partly deliberate (the boundaries) and partly emergent (the patterns within them); this strategy can also be called deliberately emergent, in that the leadership purposefully allows others the flexibility to manoeuvre and form patterns within the boundaries.

Process strategy: the leadership controls the process aspects of strategy (who gets hired and so gets a chance to influence strategy; what structures they work within, etc.), leaving the actual content of strategy to others; strategies are again partly deliberate (concerning process) and partly emergent (concerning content), and deliberately emergent.

Disconnected strategy: members or subunits loosely coupled to the rest of the organisation produce patterns in the streams of their own actions in the absence of, or in direct contradiction to the central or common intentions of the organisation at large; the strategies can be deliberate for those who make them.

Consensus strategy: through mutual adjustment, various members converge on patterns that pervade the organisation in the absence of central or common intentions: these strategies are rather emergent in nature.

Imposed strategy: the external environment dictates patterns in actions, either through direct imposition (say by an outside owner or by a strong customer) or through implicitly preempting or bounding organisational choice (as in a large airline that must fly jumbo jets to remain viable); these strategies are organisationally emergent, although they may be internalised and made deliberate.

Source: Mintzberg, 1988

which strategic change is incremental and the speed of change is slower than the speed of organisational response. It is a valid description of poorly performing firms in discontinuous environments, and a valid descripiton of the behaviour of a majority of not-for-profit organisations. The debate with regard to the formation of strategy continues (Mintzberg, 1991; Gould, 1992) with no resolution of the issues raised in sight.

Variations on the rational and incremental approaches

1 A generic strategy perspective

Whittington (1993) identifies four generic approaches to strategy formation, illustrated in figure 1.3.

The four approaches differ along two dimensions, namely, the 'outcomes of strategy' and the 'processes' through which it is made. The vertical axis relates to the degree to which strategy produces profit-maximising outcomes or permits other possible outcomes. The horizontal axis provides for the extent to which strategy formation is deliberate or a result of 'accident, muddle or inertia'. Whittington identifies four generic approaches to strategy, each containing certain basic assumptions. The axes are continua and each generic approach accommodates various perspectives on strategy and it is possible that particular perspectives will overlap from one quadrant into another.

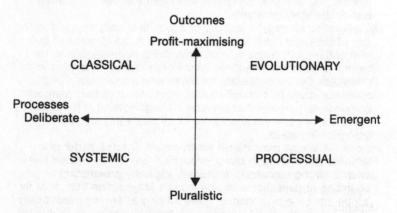

Figure 1.3 Generic perspectives on strategy
Source: Whittington, 1993

In the 'classical' approach, strategy is described as a rational and deliberate process based on analysis and calculation. A basic assumption is that it is possible to master both internal and external environments and decisions taken through this process will lead to long-term success.

The 'evolutionary' approach, which views the 'classical' approach as often irrelevant because of the unpredictability of the environment, contains a paradox. The dynamic nature of the environment means that long-term survival cannot be planned for yet, only organisations that have a profit-maximising strategy will survive. Competitiveness ensures only the survival of the fittest. Managers can only ensure that the fit between strategy and environment is as efficient as possible. They are not in command of the situation.

In the 'processual' approach, the same conditions are recognised as in the evolutionary approach. 'Processualists', however, do not hold to the Darwinian theory to the same extent. Bounded rationality (managers are unable to consider all factors in a situation, reluctant to engage in unlimited searches for relevant information, biased in their interpretation of data and prone to accept the first satisfactory option that presents itself) ensures that strategy emerges 'more from a pragmatic process of bodging, learning and compromise than from a rational series of grand leaps forward'. Moreover competitors are affected in the same way, that is, no-one is likely to know what the optimum strategy is.

The 'systemic' approach, is not so pessimistic about people's capacity to develop and carry out strategies but the objectives and practices of strategy depend on the social system in which strategy formation occurs. Strategists may deviate from rational planning and profit-maximising quite deliberately because their social background or culture may produce interests other than profit. The 'systemic' perspective considers that the environment can be manipulated to secure the aims of the organisation and that it is not only evolutionary profit-maximising organisations which survive.

Whittington tends towards the systemic perspective. The growth of international competition has rendered the objectives and contexts of organisations much more complex than can be accommodated by the simplicities of profit maximisation and perfect markets. Organisations will vary greatly in the ends and means of strategy depending on the social groups that dominate a particular context. In a pluralist environment history and society are influential forces in shaping competitive strategy. Whittington feels that the strategist must make a fundamental strategic choice as to which perspective on human activity and environment most closely fits with his or her own personal perspective on strategy. Clearly, Whittington's generic approaches to strategy suggest that the two major archetypes of strategy current in the literature are not mutually exclusive systems. His focus on outcomes expands the choice of goals beyond that of profit and the potential processes are gradations on a continuum from rational to accidental. The generic perspectives serves to concentrate attention on the assumptions underlying each of the approaches and may offer useful frames of reference to advance research in this area.

2 An organisational dynamics perspective

Stacey (1993) suggests that the nature of assumptions held by management is central to advancing research into the strategy concept. Managerial strategic action is initiated from a basis of shared paradigms or cognitive models through which the world is experienced and understood. He classifies the 'conventional wisdom', based on assumptions about the dynamics of successful organisations, into three approaches: 'rational' planning; 'one best way' based on study of excellent organisations and contingency-based configurations. Stacey says that in practice, managers claim to use some combination of these three approaches to strategy. He fears that the approaches do not work as well as they are intended to with their failure being linked to their basis in what he terms the 'stable equilibrium' organisation paradigm which has the perspective that success is linked to regularity, stability, harmony and consensus within an organisation and that the future is predictable. This concept of organisation dynamics is out of touch with the reality of a changing world. Organisations that build on their strengths eventually move along trajectories that take them to states of either instability or stability. In both states they ultimately fail because they do not innovate. Innovation would require management to adopt a new paradigm.

Stacey draws extensively on the theory of chaos to explain how the dominant paradigm is intrinsically unsuited to perhaps the majority of organisations in today's turbulent environment. See exhibit 1 for a summary of the relevant elements in chaos theory.

Exhibit 1.1 Chaos theory

The theory of chaos holds that there are three feedback states which govern the dynamics of a nonlinear system. Nonlinearity occurs when some condition or some action has a varying effect on an outcome depending on the level of the condition or intensity of the action. Negative feedback loops compare the outcome of previous action to some desired outcome and the discrepancy is fed back into the system to guide future action so that the discrepancy is reduced or disappears. This takes the system towards a state of 'stable equilibrium'. While negative feedback controls a system according to prior intention, positive feedback produces explosively 'unstable equilibrium' where changes are amplified, putting such pressure on the system that it eventually runs out of control. Finally, when a nonlinear feedback system is driven away from stable equilibrium towards unstable equilibrium it passes through a third feedback state of 'bounded instability'. In this border area feedback flips autonomously between the amplifying conditions of positive feedback and the damping conditions of negative feedback to produce chaotic behaviour which has the effect of pulling the system in opposite directions. In this area neither of the forces can be removed but are endlessly rearranged in different yet similar patterns. In the border area patterns of behaviour are generated that are irregular and unpredictable but which have an overall hidden qualitative pattern. These are properties of the enviroment and are independent of the system. In this bounded area, which is far-from-equilibrium, the system automatically applies internal constraints to keep instability within boundaries. Figure 1.4 demonstrates a computer simulation of patterns of events in the area of bounded instability. It represents the outcomes from a mathematical equation which has generated stable and unstable effects depending on the parameters introduced. The black area represents stable sequences and the white area shows unstable sequences. The border area between the two is not clean-cut but has the properties of bounded instability described above. Up until some twenty years ago these properties were unknown to scientists. The theory of chaos has been explored in many fields such as meteorology, medicine and, comparatively recently, the human organisation.

Source: Stacey, 1993

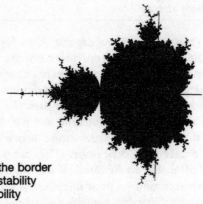

(a) Mapping the border
    between stability
    and instability

(b) A closer look
    at the border

Figure 1.4 Maps of stability and instability
Source: Stacey, 1993

The implications of chaos theory for organisations are: today's dominant paradigm is based on negative feedback loops and the state of stable equilibrium may be unsuited to the majority of organisations; organisations contain all three feedback states; dynamic nonlinear feedback systems generate completely unpredictable behaviour at a specific level over the long-term which is therefore inherently unknowable; an organisation must maintain itself in the border area if it is to innovate and renew, and therefore, forecasting activities could turn out to be 'fantasy activities'. Stacey says that companies which succeed will be able to sustain contradictions. On the one hand they need to achieve a state of coherence, centralisation, tight central control and synergy in the organisation's configuration, while, on the other hand, they need to achieve states of decentralisation, differentiation, rivalry and variety. Without the latter qualities they will be unable to innovate and transform. They need to introduce a process of organisational learning in which these forces can be synthesised in order to create more complex forms of strategy and structure. The conventional wisdom with its emphasis on order and stability, management by objectives, planning and incremental changes simply focuses on doing better what companies already do well. A new paradigm will recognise the non-equilibrium nature of innovative organisations and the tension between destruction on the one hand and creativity on the other. Stacey prescribes a process in which an organisation has the choice to practice both 'ordinary' management which pulls the organisation towards order, control and the status quo of the existing paradigm in order to achieve current strategies and 'extra-ordinary' management which uses social and political forces to pull the organisation in a direction which threatens the existing paradigm in order to achieve innovation and change.

Is strategic planning worthwhile?

A final strand of research into the strategy concept has dealt with the extent to which organisations have found utility in the application of strategy formation processes. The conventional wisdom has been the main focus of study. Ansoff and McDonnell (1990) report on research by Ansoff *et al.*, in 1970 in which they investigated the relationship between performance and the growth methods (mainly mergers and acquisitions) used by large US organisations in the period 1947–66. They concluded that firms which did plan tended to use these plans and to exhibit deliberate and systematic acquisition behaviour. On all relevant financial criteria, planners significantly outperformed the nonplanners. Not only did planners do better on the average, they performed more predictably than nonplanners. Ansoff *et al.* say that since this study several others have arrived at much the same conclusion.

Powell (1992) has reviewed studies dating back to 1970, since when there had been a rapid expansion in the use of formal strategic planning but his findings are not as positive as those of Ansoff *et al.* Having reviewed studies which explored the financial performance consequences of the use of tools, techniques and activities of strategic planning, he has concluded that the studies were 'confusing, contradictory and impossible to reconcile'. These problems were attributed to methodological flaws such as failure to account for key contingency variables, incomplete and unreliable planning measures and, small sample sizes. However, the more rigorous the methodologies employed, which he concedes have become more so over time, the portent for the process has not been favourable in that correlations between strategic planning and financial performance have tended towards zero.

Stacey (1993) suggests that if excellent companies have mastered the prescriptions of the conventional wisdom it should be reasonable to expect those companies to remain successful over long periods of time. However, of the 43 excellent companies identified by Peters and Waterman in 1982, only one-third could be included in the sample after five years. The companies identified, in a UK context by Goldsmith and Clutterbuck in 1984 had met with much the same fate. Moreover, the rankings of the Fortune 500 and *Financial Times* top 100 companies change dramatically over a five-year period. Stacey's review indicates that the impact of environmental turbulence is the usual reason proffered by companies which failed to master strategic management over the long term. His remaining findings were similarly bleak. Greenley in 1986 was unable to find a connection between the existence of formal planning and superior performance in UK organisations. In a survey of large UK organisations, Goold and Quinn in 1990 found that only 15 per cent of those having formal planning systems used these as templates against which to monitor strategic action. Japanese companies, it would seem, do things very differently. It appears, according to Argenti in 1984, that only 20 per cent of them ever practice long-term planning. Hamel and Prahalad in 1989 found that the relative success of the Japanese organisation is linked with a superior model

of strategy in which they do not attempt to adapt to the environment but rather create core competences and build market share.
Hampden-Turner in 1990 describes Japanese managers as being
more comfortable with dilemmas and paradoxes than Western
managers. Nonaka in 1988 describes how Japanese managers deliberately encourage the instability of counter-cultures within the
organisation whilst Western counterparts strive towards more and
more conformity.

In this review of research into the strategy process it has become
apparent that the state of development of the concept raises
important questions but does not generate conclusive answers.

THE RISE OF STRATEGIC MANAGEMENT

Strategic management has been evolving from the original concept
of strategic planning. The reasons for the emergence of strategic
management and for problems with introducing it into the business
organisation are best understood by taking a historical perspective
(Ansoff and McDonnell, 1990). Although written in a US context,
the chronology of events appears to be similar for other developed
capitalist countries. It is important to this and subsequent discussion
of their work to understand the concept of environmental turbulence which they use. Turbulence has two dimensions: (a), the
changeability in the environment which is characterised by the
degree of novelty of challenges, and (b), the speed with which the
challenges develop. In the analysis which follows, as the turbulence
level increases management systems have been developed which
have been correspondingly more sophisticated.

Historical perspectives on the emergence of strategic management

1 The changing industrial environment

At the onset of the industrial revolution entrepreneurs created
production technology, surrounded it with organisation technology
and developed market share. Competition was perceived as an ability
to dominate or absorb the competition. This period was followed by
a mass production era. The application of technology, including
managerial techniques made it possible to progressively reduce
unit costs. The marketing concept was one of producing standard
items at the lowest possible price. The immediate environment

offered ample opportunities for growth. Attention was focused on achieving a highly efficient process.

The 'production' mentality resulted in a set of management perceptions, attitudes and preferences. Government interference was minimal. From the 1930s and into the 1950s in the US there was the onset of the 'marketing orientation' characterised by more differentiated products, exemplified by the historic divergence in marketing approach between Ford (offering a standard product) and General Motors (offering a customised product). There were power struggles within firms and resistance from some who saw the shift in focus, from the tried and tested efficiency approach, as costly, time-comsuming and psychologically threatening. Many firms stagnated, however a concept of total marketing emerged which combined market and production perspectives and this prevails in most progressive firms up to the present day.

By the mid 1950s the pace of change was accelerating and organisations were faced with new challenges. There was rivalry for market share in a highly competitive market. Internally there were struggles for increased productivity and more efficiency which could be facilitated by greater automation. This shift was unrecognised or resisted in many organisations. Such a shift required new perceptions and skills and many existing managers felt threatened. There was often a gap between the behaviour of an organisation and the imperatives of this new environment, such as the quality of working life demanded by a more affluent workforce. These stages were layered one upon another.

In the 1980s competition intensified through internationalisation of business, scarcity of resources and the acceleration of technological innovation. This continued into the 1990s with a further escalation in environmental turbulence, for example, the emergence of Japan as a global power, the economic development of the pacific basin countries, the emergence of a united Europe, and the continuing rapid growth in new technologies. Ansoff and McDonnel suggest that the increasing frequency and diffusion of change makes it more difficult to anticipate in order to plan. These conditions of change are expected to continue into the twenty-first century.

2 The changing focus of managerial systems

Up to the 1950s it was feasible to use a managerial system in which performance was controlled by reviewing past performance. See

Change-ability	1900	1930	1950	1970	1990
Unpredict-ability of the future	Familiarity of events				
	%Familiar ,%Extrapolable,%Familiar discontinuity,%Novel discontinuity,				
Recurring	• Systems and procedures manuals			**Management by control**	
	• Financial control				
Forecastable by extrapolation	• Operations budgeting • Capital budgeting • Managment by objectives • Long range planning			**Management by extrapolation**	
Predictable threats and opportunities	**Management by anticipation**		• Periodic strategic planning • Strategic posture management		
Partially predictable opportunities	**Management flexible/rapid response**		• Contingency planning • Strategic issue management • Weak signal issue management		
Unpredictable surprises			• Surprise management		
Turbulence level	1 Stable	2 Reactive	3 Anticipating	4 Exploring	5 Creative

Figure 1.5 Evolution of management systems
Source: Ansoff and McDonnell, 1990

figure 1.5 which demonstrates the evolution of management systems and its relationship to environmental change.

During the 1950s long range planning was introduced as the means of assisting organisations to deal with expansion and future competitive challenges. In long range planning the future was expected to be predictable through extrapolation of historical growth. By the 1960s strategic planning had been invented to meet growing environmental uncertainty in which extrapolation of past trends could have unwelcome consequences for the organisation. Strategic planning provided an approach through which organisations could anticipate and respond to environmental change. Change, although rapid, was still manageable. The first step in strategic planning was to analyse the organisation's environment in order to identify threats and opportunities. Such surveillance produced the potential gap which existed between past extrapolation and future scenarios. The next step was to undertake a competitive analysis through which the organisation could identify the improvement in performance which might be gained from changes in competitive strategies. If an organisation was engaged in a number of business areas, a process of strategic portfolio analysis would enable the prospects in business areas to be compared one against another which would permit priorities to be set and strategic resources allocated.

An organisation could work towards its present business potential or could undertake a diversifation analysis followed by a decision as to whether or not to change strategic direction.

Strategic planning, in the early stages of its introduction into organisations, did not fare well. Usually introduced by an enthusiastic chief executive, the technique was poorly understood by managers who were expected to engage in it. This and the fact that new strategies could be slow to take effect caused resistance to its implementation and apparently even attracted attempts to sabotage it. Its critics labelled it a poor technique, which even in cases where it was successfully introduced, did not improve organisational performance.

Ansoff and McDonnell contend that resistance to strategic planning was not due to it being a poor technique but rather to the fact that the conditions for its implementation were missing from organisations. They have used findings from Chandler (1962) to explain the difficulties encountered by strategic planning and suggest that these can be counteracted through the introduction to organisations of a broader concept of strategic management.

3 The need for strategic management

Chandler studied four of America's most successful organsiations: DuPont, General Motors, Sears and Standard Oil. He examined how the organisations responded to major discontinuities in their environments. This was followed up by a study in 40 other organisations which demonstrated the same pattern of results. Others replicated Chandler's findings in studies of European organisations. Organisations, it appears, resisted change by refusing to recognise it until it made an impact on performance. New strategic responses were recognised and developed by trial and error over as long a period as 10 years. With new strategy installed, expected profits were slow to materialise in spite of considerable competitive efforts in the market. Management eventually concluded that the problem was not that the strategy was bad, rather there was a mismatch between organisation structure and strategy. This encouraged reorganisation. However, the new structure created problems because management lacked the skills and knowledge required to perform new roles, information systems no longer fulfilled the needs of the new roles, and the old reward system did not encourage the actions required by the new strategy. These shortcomings were discovered and remedied piecemeal. The period of adaptation could take a further 10 years. The formation of new strategy and its implementation could therefore take as long as 20 years.

Ansoff and McDonnell contend that while reactive unguided Chandlerian process may have been the best way to adapt to environmental discontinuites in the early twentieth century, it is too slow for the last quarter and for the foreseeable future. A reactive organic adaptation could leave organisations one cycle behind the external reality. They argue therefore, that while strategic planning was invented to deal with the first Chandlerian gap, that is, the relationship between the organisation and its environment, strategic management (which more fully brings the internal organisation, including a process for managing change to bear on the strategy process) is required to deal with the second Chandlerian gap, that is, ensuring that the organisation has the capability to pursue its strategic choices. The authors' model of strategic management is reviewed later in this chapter.

Modelling the strategic management process

This need for expansion beyond concern primarily with strategic planning has been recognised by others who have subsequently offered models of a strategic management process (for example, Sharplin, 1985; Boseman *et al.*, 1985; Comerford and Callaghan, 1985; Bowman and Asch, 1991). These prescriptons, of which there are two main groups, configurations and models of strategic management, are reviewed to demonstrate the nature of the field past and present.

Configurations

The configurations link specific organisational elements to strategy formation. See table 1.2.

Table 1.2 Elements in configuration models

Authors	Elements
Galbraith and Nathanson (1978)	Strategy, structure, processes, rewards, people
Waterman, Peters and Philips (1980)	Strategy, structure, systems, style, skills, staff, shared values (culture)
Stonich (1982)	Strategy, structure, human resources, culture, management processes

Galbraith and Nathanson (1978) believe that organisation effectiveness would be obtained if there was successful achievement of congruence (fit) between strategy and certain organisational elements. The organisation, in moving from one strategy to another would be required to manage strategic change in order to disengage, realign and reconnect all of these elements. Waterman, Peters and Philips (1980), referred to earlier in the chapter, suggest seven interconnected elements. Organisations concentrate on strategy, structure and systems but tend to neglect skills, style, staff and culture. There is no hierarchy among the variables with each having the potential to be critical to effectiveness. Stonich (1982) suggests five interrelated elements, which must all be managed together. A contingency perspective will emphasise whichever of the above elements are most relevant, at any one time, to the strategy chosen by the organisation.

Models of strategic management

There are also, in the literature, models entitled strategic management which have broad components of formulation and implementation. Sometimes control is added as a separate component and in some cases it is found under implementation.

The formulation process mostly follows a rational planning pattern, that is, environmental scanning, analysis of threats and opportunities, generation of strategic options, etc. The elements in the implementation process however, as table 1.3 demonstrates, vary as much as those in the configuration models.

All of the authors emphasise the importance of implementation. It

Table 1.3 Elements within the implementation phase of strategic
management models

Authors	Elements
Sharplin (1985)	Structure, policies, directives, resource commitment, leadership, motivation, power, politics
Boseman et al. (1985)	Structure, human resources, rewards, culture
Comerford and Callaghan (1985)	Structure, human resources, rewards power
Thomas (1988)	Structure, culture, functional policies, organisation development
Ansoff and McDonnell (1990)	Structure, management skills, management mentality, culture, power, systems
Certo and Certo (1991)	Structure, culture, management skills

is critical to an organisation's success, even its survival. The importance of achieving fit between strategy and implementation variables is stressed. All of the models include the concept of control and may be summarised as including standards, performance, measures and evaluation. The models utilise an open systems perspective and there is emphasis on a contingency approach to linking strategy to the internal competencies of an organisation.

Synthesis of models

When the elements in both the configurations and the implementation phase of the strategic management models are considered, it can be seen that, as well as there being a variety of elements, there is also a mix of broad concepts, such as systems, and the more specific such as culture. Further analysis of the models reveals that structure is common to all and human resources and culture are elements in seven and six respectively. The remaining elements are mentioned singly, although some could be merged perhaps because of their similarity for example, incentives/rewards, power/politics. A rationalisation of the elements could be achieved by using the abstract terms of systems and process in table 1.4.

It will be noticed that, in temporal terms, the configuration

Table 1.4 The elements of strategic
management implementation

Structure	
Systems:	Human resources
	Policies/directives
	Performance measurement
	Rewards
Processes:	Change management
	Organisation development
	Culture
	Motivation
	Politics

models precede the strategic management models. If the concept of strategic management has evolved to a large extent because of weaknesses in the capability of implementing strategy, then these configurations appearing in the implementation phase would seem to be a necessary part of an evolution towards refinement of the strategic management models. Attention, in future research, should be turned to analysing the reasons for differences in the models in order to gain insights into these implementation configurations. To this end the use of the generic terms of structure, systems and processes offer a convenient framework.

The Ansoff and McDonnell model

Finally, in this examination of the rise of strategic management, account is taken of a strategic management model from Ansoff and McDonnell (1990). Emphasis is given to the model because of the nature of the seminal work by Ansoff in the field of strategic planning and strategic management. He claims to be the first to introduce the term and concept of strategic management into the literature. Ansoff's model incorporates a number of components: strategic planning; strategic posture management, and real time issue management.

One of the basic principles of strategic planning when it was first introduced was that an organisation's ability to move into a new business area was tied to its capability to perform successfully in the area. One of the key strategy selection criteria, therefore, was to match new strategy to the historic strengths of the organisation by means of analysis of strengths and weaknesses. It became apparent that there were several difficulties with this, for example, historic strengths often became weaknesses and an obstacle to change.

Strategic posture management was developed to deal with this problem. It contains two elements. First, capability planning which introduces a process for assessing if the organisation has the capability to achieve new strategy in (a) its functional areas, for example, marketing or production, and (b), its general management. While functional capability is fairly widely understood, general management capability is new and designed for the model. It consists of five mutually supporting elements: qualification and mentality of the key managers; culture; power structure; systems and organisation structure, and capacity to do managerial work. Processes have been developed for assessing strategic capability in relation to these dimensions and for designing implementation capability plans. Second, systematic management of resistance to change takes place during implementation of strategy and capability plans. Processes have been developed to facilitate the management of change.

Real time issue management consists of strategic issue management; weak signal issue management; and surprise management.

Strategic issue management involves continuous surveillance of environmental trends, estimation of the impact and urgency of trends, and presentation of key strategic issues to top management. Issues are classified into four categories: highly urgent; moderately urgent; non-urgent; and false alarms. The resolution of issues is monitored by top management and the list of issues and their priorities are kept up-to-date. Issues can also be divided into strong signals (concrete enough to permit the formation of plans for response) and weak signals (imprecise early indications). Over time weak signals may become strong signals. Once the turbulence level passes 4, (see figure 1.5) the time to respond to a weak signal has reduced. At high turbulence levels, therefore, it may be necessary to respond when signals are weak.

Strategic surprise management means that the issue has arrived suddenly and unanticipated, it poses novel problems, failure to respond would cause financial loss or opportunity cost, and the response is urgent and cannot be handled quickly enough by the normal channels. Ansoff and McDonnell have devised a system, 'a strategic task force network' for handling strategic surprises which is derived from a study of military surprises, as well as histories of response to surprises which have hit business organisations.

Ansoff and McDonnell say that in the 1990s different organisations will be required to deal with continually changing challenges. There can be no single prescription for future success which will apply to all organisations. This situation presents two key issues: each firm will be required to diagnose its unique pattern of future challenges, threats and opportunities, and then, must design and implement a unique response. They have proposed a 'strategic success hypothesis' which they have gone some way towards empirically validating and which should help guide future research. The hypothesis states that an organisation's performance potential is optimum when three conditions have been met. These are:

- aggressiveness of the firm's strategic behaviour matches the turbulence of the environment;
- responsiveness of the firm's capability matches the aggressiveness of its strategy;
- the components of the firm's capability must be supportive of one another.

CONCLUSION

What is the practising manager to make of the state of the strategy concept? Whittington (1993) has calculated that there are thirty-seven books in print bearing the title strategic management.

> Most are thick tomes, filled with charts, lists and nostrums, promising the reader the fundamentals of corporate strategy . . . nearly all contain the same matrices, the same authorities. . . . There is a basic implausibility about these books. . . . If there was really so much agreement on the fundamentals of corporate strategy, then strategic decisions would not be so hard to make.
> (Whittington, 1993: 1)

Having reviewed the literature it is difficult to disagree with the above comments. It is possible to add to it. All the signs are that strategic decisions are not only hard to make, they are also very difficult to put into practice. At present, as the review of strategic management texts reveals, the majority of them are based upon the conventional wisdom. It is essential therefore for the manager to be informed by the criticism relevant to any particular approach. In responding, however, there is always the danger of throwing out the baby with the bath water.

There are a number of issues of significance. The basic meaning of strategy is important. It is a military analogy applied to the business setting. If the term is to continue to be applied then it is inescapable that there must be recognition that it is about competing and trying to win, or in other words, trying to be 'effective' in strategic terms. It has goals which relate to specific environmental situations. It is a cognitive and human process in that dimensions of both leadership and those who are led are a part of the concept. Intrinsic, also, is the sense of engaging in action to achieve the goals. The basic concept is about a strategy of war and its achievement, which in business terms, translates into strategic management.

This suggests that the over-emphasis in research into strategy content has been one-sided. While there still may be a case for pursuing research into content and process separately, there is also a case to be made for a part of the research activity to be devoted to examining the totality of the concept.

Another issue relates to how to interpret the claims for sovereignty or otherwise of the various schools of thought about strategy formation. Again the research is one-sided, there have been mainly studies, and less of these in recent years, to determine if the strategic planning process has pay-off in terms of organisation performance. Overall the results have not been positive. If, as some claim, the rational process is a waste of time, this would have to be balanced with research findings that prove another approach is preferable. Mintzberg's emergent strategy, Whittington's systemic approach, Stacey's views on organisational dynamics, and Ansoff's concept of strategic management are all avenues which should be pursued in terms of research before a particular paradigm is swept aside in favour of any other.

Discussion of paradigms crops up time and again in the literature. It is important that the meaning of the concept and its place within the development of theory is understood in order to evaluate literature findings and of course in order to pursue research.

Grant (1991), having reviewed the criticisms of the rational approach to strategy-making in his text on strategy analysis, has chosen to, as he puts it, 'follow the "planning" rather than the "crafting" approach advocated by Mintzberg', not because he regards planning as necessarily superior to crafting or from any wish to downgrade its essential elements but because he believes that strategy development is a multidimensional process which must involve both rational analysis and evolution through implementation and experience.

[W]hatever process of strategy formulation is chosen as most appropriate and whatever the emphasis between analysis and implementation, there can be little doubt as to the importance of systematic analysis as a vital input into the strategy process. Without analysis, the process of strategy formulation, particularly at the senior management level, is likely to be chaotic. . .

(Grant, 1991: 28)

Stacey, drawing on the literature in the field, has gone some distance in combining stability and instability in his concepts of 'ordinary' and 'extraordinary' management, and in doing so provides a stimulating perspective on the respective places in the field of strategy of the rational and incremental schools of thought. Ansoff whose work, extending back over 25 years, is seminal in the field has, with McDonnell, produced a concept of strategic management that takes to an advanced level the accumulated knowledge in the rational school of thought regarding strategy, whilst also trying to deal with the effect of environmental turbulence on the ability to 'realistically' plan. This has been achieved by the design of planning and implementation cognitive software that insists on the imperative of matching environmental turbulence with sophisticated management approaches and techniques.

Ultimately, it is hoped, that research will point to the best synthesis to be gained from the various issues raised in the literature into the strategy concept. This will present a better basis for the design of models than exists at present. It is essential that the practising manager be informed of the issues and makes choices regarding the strategy-making process which seem to best suit his/her organisational requirements.

Finally, are there any promising signs that the strategy concept, in its current state of development, offers potential for a link with human resource management? A confident 'yes' is the response. The grounds for this are as follows:

- Environmental turbulence is leading organisations to recognise the importance of human resources to the competitive performance of the organisation. As has been seen in this chapter, turbulence is a central element in the strategic process.
- The cognitive, and therefore human, nature of the strategy process has been continually emphasised, for example, the centrality of managerial paradigms, the management of change and discussion of organisation dynamics. A claim can therefore

be staked for the human resource dimension of the strategy process.

• It has been put forward that strategic management has evolved, to a notable extent, because the capability to pursue novel strategies was not sufficiently attended to and, implementation capability was similarly neglected. The human dimension pervades these processes.

The next chapter will take up the human resource management dimension and consider the emergence of a concept of strategic human resource management.

REFERENCES

Ansoff, H.I. (1991) 'Critique of Henry Mintzberg's "The design school: reconsidering the basis premises of strategic management"' *Strategic Management Journal*, 12(6): 449–61.

Ansoff, H.I. and McDonnell, E. (1990) *Implanting Strategic Management*, Hemel Hemstead: Prentice Hall International.

Ansoff, H.I., Avner, J., Brandenburg, R., Portner, F. and Radosevich, R. (1970) 'Does planning pay? The effect of planning on success of acquisitions in American firms', *Long Range Planning*, 3(2).

Argenti, J. (1984) 'Don't let planners meddle with your strategies', *Accountancy*, April: 152.

Boseman, G., Phatak, A. and Schellenberg, R.E. (1985) *Strategic Management*, New York: John Wiley & Sons.

Bowman, C. and Asch, D. (1991) *Strategic Managment*, London: Macmillan Education.

Certo, S.C. and Certo, J.P. (1991) *Strategic Management: Concepts and Applications*, Singapore: McGraw-Hill.

Chakravarthy, B.S. and Doz, Y. (1992) 'Strategy process research: focusing on corporate self-renewal', *Strategic Management Journal*, 13: 5–14.

Chandler, D. (1962) *The History of American Industrial Enterprise*, Cambridge, Massachusetts: M.I.T. Press.

Comerford, R.A. and Callaghan, D.W. (1985) *Strategic Management: Text, Tools and Cases*, Boston: Kent.

Faulkner, D. and Johnson, G. (1992) *The Challenge of Strategic Management*, London: Kogan Page.

Galbraith, J.R. and Nathanson, D.A. (1978) *Strategy Implementation: The Role of Structure and Process*, St Paul, Minnesota: West.

Goldsmith, W. and Clutterbuck, D. (1984) *The Winning Streak*, London: Weidenfeld and Nicolson.

Goold, M. and Quinn, J.J. (1990) *Strategic Control: Milestones for Long Term Performance*, London: Hutchinson.

Gould, M. (1992) 'Design, learning and planning: a further observation on the design school debate', *Strategic Management Journal*, 13(2): 169–70.

Grant, R.M. (1991) *Contemporary Strategy Analysis: Concepts, Techniques, Applications*, Oxford: Blackwell Publishers.

Greenley, G.E. (1986) 'Does strategic planning improve performance?', *Long Range Planning*, 19(2): 101–9.

Hampden-Turner, C. (1990) *Charting the Corporate Mind*, New York: Free Press, Macmillan.

Hamel, G. and Prahalad, C.K. (1989) 'Strategic intent', *Harvard Business Review*, May–June: 63–76.

Kay, J. (1993) *Foundations of Corporate Success: How Business Strategies Add Value*, New York: Oxford University Press.

Mintzberg, H. (1987) 'Crafting strategy', *Harvard Business Review*, July–August: 66–75.

Mintzberg, H. (1988) 'Opening up the definition of strategy', in J.B. Quinn, H. Mintzberg, and R.M. James (eds) *The Strategy Process*, Englewood Cliffs, NJ: Prentice Hall International.

Mintzberg, H. (1990) 'The design school: reconsidering the basic premises of strategic management, *Strategic Management Journal*, 11: 171–95.

Mintzberg, H. (1991) 'Learning 1, Planning 0: Reply to Igor Ansoff', *Strategic Management Journal*, 12(6): 449–61.

Morden, T. (1993) *Business Strategy and Planning: Texts and Cases*, Maidenhead: McGraw-Hill.

Nonaka, I. (1988) 'Creating organisational order out of chaos: self-renewal in Japanese firms', *California Management Review*, Spring: 57–73.

Peters, T.J. and Waterman, R.H. (1982) *In Search of Excellence*, New York: Harper and Row.

Pettigrew, A. (1992) 'The character and significance of strategy process research', *Strategic Management Journal*, 13: 5–16.

Powell, T.C. (1992) 'Strategic Planning as competitive advantage', *Strategic Management Journal*, 13: 551–8.

Quinn, J.B. (1978) 'Strategic change: logical incrementalism', *Sloan Management Review*, 1(20): 7–21.

Quinn, J.B. (1988), 'Strategies for change' in J.B. Quinn, H. Mintzberg and R.M. James, (eds) *The Strategy Process: Concepts, Contexts, and Cases*, Englewood Cliffs, NJ: Prentice-Hall International.

Schendel, D. (1992) 'Introduction to the Summer 1992 Special Issue on "Strategy Process Research"', *Strategic Management Journal*, 13: 1–4.

Sharplin, A. (1985) *Strategic Management*, Singapore: McGraw-Hill.

Stacey, R.D. (1993) *Strategic Management and Organisational Dynamics*, London: Pitman.

Stonich, P.J. (1982) *Implementing Strategy: Making it Happen*, Cambridge, MA: Ballinger.

Thomas, J.G. (1988) *Strategic Management: Concepts, Practice and Cases*, New York: Harper and Row.

Waterman, R.H., Peters, T.J. and Philips, J.K. (1980) 'Structure is not organisation', *Business Horizon*: June.

Whittington, R. (1993) *What is Strategy and Does it Matter?*, London: Routledge.

Chapter 2

The emergence of strategic human resource management

INTRODUCTION

In the previous chapter, it was found that a number of relatively recent developments in the strategy concept are highlighting a significant, and previously largely unacknowledged, human dimension within it. This human orientation suggests a powerful rationale for promotion and development of a concept of strategic human resource management as a process through which the human resource management of the organisation would be linked to strategy.

The purpose of this chapter is to explore the human resource literature in order to see what light it throws on the development of the concept. It will be seen that it has emerged in the US, apparently as the most recent phenomenon in an evolution which commenced with personnel management and moved on to human resource management, the latter being commonly referred to in the literature as HRM. HRM has made the transition, to a more limited degree, into UK practice, where it has aroused considerable academic debate, not to say confusion, particularly in relation to comparisons made between it and traditional personnel management in its UK setting. There is also examination of the research relating to strategic human resource management. The concept is in an early stage of development. The various approaches taken to conceptualise it are examined. Finally, both the strategy and human resource literatures are synthesised to suggest models of strategic management and strategic human resource management which will be utilised to guide research into the development of theory and to inform practice. These models provide the framework for the development of the remainder of the book.

PERSONNEL MANAGEMENT – A FUNCTION IN DECLINE?

A starting point for understanding the emergence of the concepts of HRM and strategic human resource management is to consider the proposition that they have evolved to replace personnel management. Examination of the literature suggests the main dimensions of such transition.

Criticisms of the personnel management function

There is evidence of long-standing criticisms of the function. A widespread perception is that it lacks strategic relevance because it performs a mainly administrative-type role (Drucker, 1968; Watson, 1977; Legge, 1978; Rowland and Summers, 1981). It is in an uneasy relationship with line managers because human resource management is a dimension of all managerial roles. The seeds of its problems are traceable to its origins in the Industrial Revolution when a combination of factors led to the fundamental and by now, historic division between employer and employed, that is, trades unions and collectivism versus management and its various control mechanisms. The introduction of the welfare worker (the precursor of the personnel specialist) into organisations was viewed by many trade unionists as a cynical managerial control tactic (Sheehan, 1976b; Watson, 1977; Lawrence, 1985).

The function is beset by another major weakness, derived from its failure to develop a sound theoretical base, which is manifested in a tendency to introduce piecemeal prescriptive text-book interventions as a cure for organisational ills. Such prescriptions have been, too frequently, experienced by management as out of context with the aims of the organisations and therefore irrelevant (Legge, 1978). Furthermore, use of certain tools and techniques in these interventions, such as the interview, performance assessment, job evaluation, occupational testing have failed to demonstrate validity and reliability and this creates yet further misgivings about its theoretical rigour.

Advice to become proactive

The most recurring piece of advice given to the function, as the means of solving its problems, has been to become proactively engaged at a strategic level (Legge, 1978; Hunt, 1984; Alper and Russell, 1984; Devanna *et al.*, 1984; Anthony and Norton, 1991). There has been continuation during the 1980s and into the 1990s of a voicing of concerns about the function's seeming decline and even demise (Farnham, 1984; Purcell, 1985; Storey and Sisson, 1990; Storey, 1992). Recent research findings suggest evidence of a shift in responsibilities for many aspects of personnel management away from the function and towards line management (Brewster and Smith, 1990; Storey, 1992). On a more optimistic note there are reports, in the literature, that increasingly, there are challenges in the environment which will create opportunities for the function to develop a more strategic role. A rapidly changing environment for business has been resulting in globalisation and a need for competitiveness which, in turn, has been causing management to bring a new focus to bear on how human resources are organised and managed (Drucker, 1988; Kanter, 1989; Farnham, 1990; Schuler, 1990; Porter, 1991; Reinmann, 1991).

THE STATE OF RESEARCH INTO STRATEGIC INTEGRATION

Exhortations for the personnel management function to become involved at strategic level may sound impressive, however the reality is that theoretical and applied perspectives on how to achieve strategic integration are in their infancy. Two concepts emerge in a search of literature in pursuit of the goal of strategic integration. These are HRM and strategic human resource management and they are discussed below in terms of (a) the evolution from personnel management, and (b) their current state of development.

The concept of HRM

1 *A perceptible change in terminology*

The concept is American in origin. Literature, from the early 1970s documents the appearance of HRM as a replacement for personnel management and describes a change in the function's boundaries, essence and objectives (Miller and Burack, 1981). In HRM there is emphasis on integrating human resource planning with the strategy of the organisation and this marks a fundamental change from an older 'maintenance' personnel management model defined by

Burack and Smith (1977), as being characterised by 'Taylorism, control, efficiency, low cost and containment of conflict'. However, as examination of the literature demonstrates, it would be wrong to think that a sudden switch occurs in which the term personnel management is replaced by HRM or that a clear divergence in meaning emerges between the two. Both terms are united in a text, entitled *Personnel and Human Resource Management* (Schuler, 1981). In a footnote to their 1982 text entitled *Human Resource Management*, Foulkes and Livernash refer to the different terms in the literature and indicate that the terms are being used 'synonymously' by them and with 'no fundamental differences in meaning' being intended. There is also, which is interesting in terms of the apparent trend noted in the previous section, a conscious linking of the personnel management function with the line role in terms of their shared responsibilities for human resource management. By the mid-1980s the term personnel management is less prevalent. Klatt, Murdick and Schuster (1985), in a text entitled *Human Resource Management*, define their concept as covering all activities by both line and personnel managers. Fisher, Schoenfeldt and Shaw (1990), in a text entitled *Human Resource Management*, echo much the same sentiments. The human resource manager is in 'a value-adding partnership' with line managers and by their combined efforts they contribute to organisational goals. However, in a new departure for such texts, they include a penultimate chapter on strategic human resource management in which, using a rational planning model of formulation and implementation, they discuss human resource practices, strategic issues and options in relation to grand corporate strategies.

2 The Harvard contribution

A major contribution towards understanding the HRM concept has been made at Harvard Business School, firstly in 1980 through the introduction of a human resource management syllabus for the first time into year 1 of the MBA programme, and secondly, in 1984, through a research colloquium in which academics and business managers considered the future character of HRM. The syllabus was a 'synthesis of the organisation behaviour/development, labour relations and personnel administration perspectives' of the teaching group, among whom there was conviction of the growing strategic importance of human resources as a source of competitive advan-

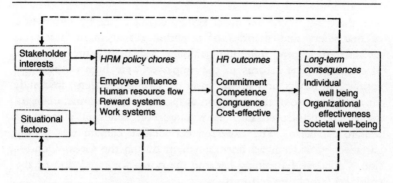

Figure 2.1 Harvard analytical framework
Source: Beer *et al.*, 1984

tage (Beer *et al.*, 1984). Their 'Harvard analytical framework' for HRM illustrated in figure 2.1, is a 'broad causal mapping of the determinants and consequences of HRM policies'. It has components of 'Stakeholder Interests', 'Situational Factors', HRM Policy Choices', 'HR Outcomes' of commitment, competence, congruence and cost-effectiveness, and 'Long-term Consequences' in which are included organisational effectiveness, individual and societal well-being. Situational factors and stakeholder interests act as constraints on HRM policies and can also be influenced by these policies. HRM policy choices affect immediate organisational HR outcomes and also have an effect on long-term consequences. The map illustrates an open systems perspective in that HRM policy choices can affect each of the other components and be affected by them.

A historical perspective

In one of the outputs from the 1984 research colloquium, Lawrence (1985), taking an historical perspective, suggests that the balance of influence between employer and employed has shifted over time in response to the phases of industrialisation, resulting in five different human resource systems. The 'craft' system was characterised by mutuality of interest between the mastercraftsmen and employees. With trade expansion came the 'market' system and new pressures on the mastercraftsmen from merchant capitalist to reduce prices which forced a reduction in labour costs which was often achieved through hiring unskilled labour. The increased conflict coincided with the onset of the 'technical' system characterised by automation of machinery and theories of scientific management based on division of labour, minimum training and management control mechanisms. The returns to the employer were high output, low conflict, flexibility and in the early days of the system, low staff turnover because of the attraction of high wages. Personnel management was introduced into many large companies in a form of welfare capitalism. The expected cooperative climate was greatly curtailed by widespread unemployment during the Great Depression. Collective bargaining became the norm for regulation of the employer/employee relationship.

When the market changed to one requiring customised, high quality goods, the 'technical' system was too inflexible to respond. Changing expectations of a better educated workforce were also challenging the motivational assumptions of management that bargaining for high pay was sufficient return for boring dead-end jobs. Another pressure on the 'technical' system was that industry-wide settlements could increase labour costs to the extent that companies would be vulnerable to foreign competition. One response to these problems was the 'career' system, the dominant pattern of HRM in the US today. It was initiated by the developing Electronics industry, which was rapidly expanding into international markets. Its key features are recruitment to positions having clear duties and rights, each of which are linked to a career ladder, long-term employment, with lay-offs only as a last resort, seniority and merit are taken into account in decisions regarding employee flows and rewards, employees are non-union and their right to express grievance is protected and work organisation consists of loosely structured groups of technically related positions reporting to a supervisor. In this system it is possible to establish a single homo-geneous work culture in which adversarialism and its costs are reduced and flexibility is increased. While there have not been major problems with the 'career' system, Lawrence suggests that there may be some in store, in particular the effects of severe depression when this causes lay-offs.

Awareness of the problems associated with both the 'technical' and 'career' systems has led organisations to experiment with a 'commitment' system which draws on a variety of experiences, such as American programmes of job enlargement, British socio-technical planning, the quality of work life approach, gain-sharing experiences, European work councils, Japanisation, quality circles

Table 2.1 'Policy characteristics of the 'control-based' and 'commitment-based' HRM systems

Policy area	HRM System	
	Control-based	Commitment-based
Job design principles	• Sub-division of work • Specific job responsibility • Accountability for specific job responsibility • Planning separated from implementation	• Broader jobs • Combined planning and implementation • Teams
Management organisation	• Top-down control and co-ordination • Management prerogative • Status symbols • Hierarchy	• Flat structure • Shared goals for control and co-ordination • Status minimised
Compensation	• Fair day's work for fair day's pay • Job evaluation • Individual incentives	• Reinforcing group achievements • Pay geared to skill and other contribution criteria • Gain-sharing, stock ownership, profit sharing
Assurance	• Labour a variable cost	• Mutual commitment • Avoid unemployment • Assist re-employment
Employee voice	• Unionised (Damage control, bargaining, appeals process) • Non-union (Open door policy, attitude surveys)	• Mutual mechanisms for communications and participation • Mechanisms for giving employee voice on issues
Labour management relations	• Adversarial	• Mutuality • Joint problem-solving and planning
Management philosophy	• Management prerogative • Management's exclusive obligation to shareholders	• Emphasis on claims of all stakeholders • Fulfilment of employee's needs is a goal rather than an end

Source: Adapted from Walton, R.E. (1985)

and life-time employment policies. Pivotal to the 'commitment' system are processes for ensuring multi-level employee representation and for organising work to increase employee involvement. The 'commitment' system marks a shift in societal values away from traditional authority and compliance. It is an attempt to replace the control orientation which has characterised the earlier systems. Its radical difference lies in that it aspires to promote mutuality of interest between employer and employee through altering the

Table 2.2 New assumptions about the management of people which underpin the 'commitment-based' HRM system

Assumption	Philosophical shift
1	Organisations are open systems with effectiveness defined as being successful in achieving a fit between its various components and between the system and its environment. There is a change of emphasis towards linking HRM with strategic planning and developing a culture that supports this and away from piecemeal interventions in response to specific problems.
2	People are capable of growth in terms of skills, values and commitment if and when the work environment encourages this. People therefore are social capital rather than variable costs.
3	There is a long-run coincidence of interests between all of the various stakeholders of the organisation. This requires a shift form a climate in which self-interest dominates.
4	Power equalisation is a key factor in encouraging openness and collaboration among stakeholders. This is in contrast with the old assumption that there must be managerial control to enhance power and efficiency.
5	Open communication builds trust and commitment. Instead of adversarial relationships there is encouragement of mutuality of interest between employer and employed.
6	Employees will be motivated and the organisation more effective if they work towards organisational goals that they accept as legitimate.
7	People who participate in defining problems and solutions will become committed to the new results from the process of participation. This is in contrast to hierarchical control from the top.

Source: Adapted from Beer and Spector (1985)

relationship by increasing the autonomy, responsibility and influence of employees at all levels. The common thread of the new policies is first to elicit employee commitment and then to expect effectiveness and efficiency to follow as secondary outcomes (Beer and Spector, 1985: Walton, 1985).

The 'control' and 'commitment' systems contrasted

Table 2.1 demonstrates Walton's views on the contrast between the two systems and their differing human resource management policies. Beer and Spector's research in both old and new industries in the US indicates that the 'commitment' model tends to differ in focus between the two, with old (unionised) organisations focusing on labour costs, productivity, quality, and dealing with adversarial relations, and the newer (non-union) organisations concentrating on attracting, satisfying and motivating highly skilled professional employees. In their view the 'commitment' model is a transformation which has its basis in a new set of assumptions. Table 2.2 indicates the nature of the philosophy underpinning these assumptions.

3 Industrial Relations in transition

The above views are complemented by research conducted by Kochan, Katz and McKersie in 1986 which points to a transformation in American industrial relations brought about by environmental changes, with organisations modelling themselves on the successful non-union companies and the Japanese system of management, McKersie (1987). The objective of the research was to understand the changing nature of the industrial relations system in the United States using case studies, surveys, and systematic analysis of industry data. The study, extending over a five year period, centred on the private sector, especially manufacturing industries which had been experiencing many economic pressures. Table 2.3 illustrates a framework intended to assist in thinking about the changes which the research suggests are taking place. The framework consists of a matrix in which three tiers of industrial relations at strategic level, collective bargaining level and shop-floor (operations) level, are described in terms of the characteristics of each level in relation to three industrial relations systems: 'traditional', 'non-union' and 'transition'.

Table 2.3 Overview of alternate systems of industrial relations in the US

Level within the firm	Traditional IR	Non-trade union	Labour relations in transition
Strategy	Managerial prerogative	Managerial prerogative	TU and workers have access to business decisions
Employment relationship (plant or group)	Wages out of competition, protection of worker rights	Compatible wages and fringes, and appeal systems	Decentralised and continuous bargaining Employment security and profit-sharing
Operations (shop floor)	Job control	Commitment and quality of work life	Teams, pay for knowledge, and flexibility in rules as well as in use of new technology

Source: McKersie (1987)

The traditional system has held sway in the United States for the past fifty years. It reached its peak in the mid-1950s with approximately 35 per cent of the workforce organised by unions and with substantially larger fractions in most manufacturing industries. Since then the decline has been steady and more recently, rather steep. At present the rate of unionisation is under 20 per cent. The essential feature of the system is that unions are able to take wages out of competition in many sectors. Wages are protected against inflation through a cost of living clause in the employer/union agreement. Collective bargaining takes place on a regular basis with long-term agreements, usually of three years' duration, resulting in stable and predictable labour costs. At strategic level, the unions have very little power and management is mainly left to manage. At workplace or operating level, industrial relations is characterised by 'job control unionism', in which detailed agreements specify rules for the allocation of jobs and workers. Such allocations are usually based on the principle of seniority. A formal system of regulation with a grievance procedure ending in binding arbitration ensure protection for workers and significant roles for shop stewards and local union officials.

   In the 1950s, 1960s and for most of the 1970s the traditional system worked well in a situation in which markets were expanding and there was, for the most part, absence of foreign competition. Productivity increased, profits were satisfactory and wages were increased on a regular basis. Around the 1960s many companies, for example Proctor and Gamble and General Electric, whenever new operations were being established, began to design them so as to make unions unnecessary. This non-union system for organising employee relations drew heavily on the concepts of HRM. The non-union system occurred mostly in newer industries which were able to use growth and the establishment of new facilities as the basis and opportunity for designing new human resource systems.

The strategic tier of the system was similar to the traditional system. At middle level, grievance systems were introduced with the full array of fringe benefits as in traditional union contracts and with the payment of market or above market wages, companies hoped that employees would be convinced that unions were unnecessary. The operating level represented the most interesting point of departure from traditional unionism. Companies in the lead with this new system of industrial relations introduced teams with facilitators rather than supervisors and emphasised extensive participation by operating level employees. The aim of this 'commitment' approach was that the companies would gain productivity and quality and the workers would gain job satisfaction and a high level of involvement.

The research findings suggest that by the early 1980s a repositioning began to take place in industrial relations. Traditional industries found themselves under severe economic pressures, caused by many factors, for example: increased imports, deregulation of many sectors, and increased domestic competition from non-union, better performing plants. In addition, given the prominence of the Japanese threat in many industries, attention was focused on the Japanese system of industrial relations and methods of organising work. The traditional system began to be modified. Changes have taken place at the various levels. At the collective bargaining level there is concession bargaining with new items on the agenda such as employment security and gain sharing. There is substantial decentralisation of contract negotiations from the industry to the company level and bargaining is taking place on a more continuous basis rather than following the pattern of a master negotiation every few years. At the workplace level there is a great deal of experimentation with some type of quality of work life. This might include, for example, quality circles, productivity task forces, joint labour–management committees. The concepts of flexibility and the ability to adapt to a changing environment on a continuing basis are key features of the new system. At strategic level, unions, as yet to a limited extent, have been brought into a formal role, such as representation at board level or involvement through briefing sessions and receipt of key information about the business outlook.

The researchers conclude that a transformation is taking place, although they are unwilling to prescribe just what shape it will ultimately take. Two main scenarios are suggested. It may be that the union sector will continue to decline and the non-union sector will continue its steady growth, or, it may be that a new system of industrial relations will emerge and unions will begin to attract new members. This latter system, however, would require new roles and skills for union leaders as well as for key management, particularly at middle and supervisory levels.

It would seem clear, therefore, that some fundamental changes have been wrought in the management of the employment process.

4   HRM – the UK context

'Personnel management' is the term in common usage in the UK and there is an industrial relations background of entrenched adversarialism. When HRM appeared on the UK scene in the mid-1980s and associated as it was with a particular set of practices and a seemingly new approach to managing human resources based on individualism, involvement and commitment, it created an enormous amount of debate and much confusion as to what it meant.

It might be just old wine in new bottles (Armstrong, 1987). Its novelty perhaps lay in that it was oriented towards management needs and represented the discovery of personnel management by chief executives (Fowler, 1987). The differences between personnel management and HRM remain 'confused and confusing' (Miller, 1989). Storey (1989) notes that the term has become very topical. 'As a set of interrelated practices with an ideological and philosophical underpinning, it appears to align closely with prevailing ideas of enterprise, and the freeing-up of managerial initiative.' However, while there is great interest in the phenomenon, the literature has, he suggests, by no means caught up with the demand for knowledge. 'There is a lacuna in theoretical and conceptual discussion (for example, on the meaning, distinctiveness and significance of HRM) and hard empirical data (for example on the extent of its application across organisations and its pervasiveness and impact in those organisations which profess to practice it).'

As Keenoy (1990) has pointed out, it arrived on .the UK scene, 'seemingly fully-formed'. In the rapidly growing literature what stands out, he says, is a series of puzzles and contradictions, for example, HRM seems to be in conflict with personnel management in that the latter operates within a pluralist perspective while HRM requires a unitarist framework, and personnel management is tactical while HRM is strategic. Yet as HRM and personnel management are both directed towards the most effective use of people, how can the two be in conflict? Keenoy suggests that they are complementary rather than mutually exclusive. A human resources policy may be unitarity or pluralist depending on both circumstances and strategic choice. Keenoy raises a number of other important issues, for example, the tension between the HRM aim of maximising the economic return of labour and the aim of increasing employee commitment, participation and involvement; the validity of the assumption that HRM is a coherent and universalistic set of practices; the variety of forms of HRM which appear to exist, and ethical questions which HRM raises for the personnel specialist.

Guest (1987, 1989, 1991) has sought to address this issue of whether there is a fundamental difference between personnel management and HRM. Central to it is a set of HR outcomes or HR policy goals: strategic integration, commitment, flexibility/adaptability and quality, each of which are necessary to secure organisational outcomes of job performance, problem-solving, change, innovation, cost effectiveness, and low levels of turnover, absence and grievance. The HR outcomes are achieved by using systems of organisation/ job design, management of change, recruitment, selection, socialisation, appraisal, training, development, reward systems and communication. Guest also places the assumptions and beliefs which he discerns as characterising personnel management and HRM into categories of control and compliance respectively. He is engaged in research which is intended to develop measurable criteria against which to explore the extent to which his model of HRM may be present in organisations and if it is, what its impact is. He perceives problems with the HRM concept. There is, for example, no evidence that commitment and flexibility will contribute to organisation effectiveness although he concedes that the potential might increase if these are part of an integrated HR strategy.

Guest is dubious that the HRM concept will usher in a new orthodoxy in the management of the employee/management relationship in terms of good practice arguing that there are many pressures that the .concept may not survive, such as competing theory and practice, a growing influence of European rather than American values, increasing turbulence which argues against one best way being feasible.

This question of the distinctiveness of HRM also receives attention from Legge (1989). Are there substantive differences between HRM and personnel management? If differences exist, what are their significance? Legge compares, using US and UK texts, normative definitions of personnel management and HRM.

She concludes that there is not a great deal of difference between the two. Both sets of definitions express a need to integrate HR practices with organisational goals, emphasise the responsibilities of line management within the process and attach value to the contribution and development of individuals.

Legge detects only three differences. While personnel management is aimed mainly at non-managers, HRM emphasises the development of the management team. In HRM the line role has a central responsibility in employment matters. It is business-led and focused on the bottom line. In personnel management the line role is largely concerned with implementation of employment procedures. In HRM, unlike personnel, culture is viewed as an important activity for senior management. Legge comes to the conclusion that HRM is more strategic than personnel management and might well represent, as she puts it, 'the discovery of personnel management by chief executives'. She feels, however, that there are problems with the goals of the HRM model. The more strongly, for example, an individual employee is committed to a particular set of skills, the greater the tendency there will be towards inflexibility and thus loss of adaptability. There could be a similar tension between goals of individualism and collectivism. HRM's focus on the individual may be at odds with effective team-working. A strong culture with 'unobtrusive, collective controls on attitude and behaviour' can mediate these tensions. In other words, individualism must be within the bounds of the collective culture. Legge perceives a series of paradoxes within these goals. She suggests that HRM is a reflection of the rise of the 'new right'.

In Britain, 'personnel management' evokes images of do-gooding specialists trying to constrain line managers, of weakly kowtowing to militant unions, of both lacking power and possessing too much power. Our new enterprise culture demands a different language, one that asserts management's right to manipulate and ability to generate and develop resources.

(Legge, 1989: 40)

Storey (1992) thinks that much of the debate, as to the meaning of HRM, has been at cross-purposes because it is often not clear whether prescriptive, descriptive or conceptual models are being used. As a consequence, some discussions have been very confused. In most current accounts of what HRM 'is', it is unclear how these have been arrived at and seem simply to have been asserted. The main approach in the UK to date has been to classify features of HRM and compare these with personnel management. While this may contribute towards clarification of meaning, a danger, to be avoided, is that an 'idealised' version of HRM may be compared with 'a practical lived-in account of the messy reality of personnel management'.

Storey (1993) distilled the literature on HRM and categorised this under what he discerned to be four key aspects: a particular constellation of beliefs and assumptions; a strategic thrust to the management of people; the central involvement of line managers; and 'levers' to shape the employment relationship. In total there were 27 points of difference identified in relation to these categories and these were then contrasted with characteristics of 'personnel and industrial relations'. See table 2.4. Using the classifications, Storey conducted research in fifteen mainstream UK organisations with the aim of assessing the extent of change which might be occurring in the management of labour. His findings, summarised in exhibit 2.1, reveal that many of the features of HRM were present in the organisations although there was no sign of a coherent theory of HRM.

Exhibit 2.1 HRM in mainstream UK organisations

- Beliefs and assumptions

   Line managers at all levels demonstrated HRM-type thinking, notably in terms of language used, a business-needs outlook and awareness of organisation culture.

- Strategic aspects

It was difficult to establish signs of linkage between strategy and HR practices. There was evidence of a considerable number of management initiatives, the sources of which were usually consultants or emulation of other organisations. Examples were devolution of responsibility to 'mini-business' managers, increased systematisation in selection/appraisal, performance-related pay, management development, quality circles and team-briefings. The initiatives seemed to be piece-meal with no evidence of clear strategic intent.

- Line Management involvement

There was widespread recognition that line managers are crucial for the delivery of new HR initiatives. It was also clear that many such initiatives had originated outside of personnel, having been devised and driven by key line and general managers. Zone or area managers were being created with responsibility for production, maintenance, supply, quality, process engineering and HRM. This seemed to denote a retreat from Taylorism and bureaucracy towards the concept of a single boss and assertion of management prerogative and was seen to have as much to do with removing the restriction of staff specialists as with disengaging from collective labour agreements. Line managers seemed confident with approaches to management development, partly, it was thought, due to belief in transformational leadership.

- Key leavers

These were enhanced communications, team working experiments, performance-related pay, harmonisation, and training and development.

The organisations:

- Austin Rover ● Bradford Metropolitan Council ● British Rail ● Eaton Ltd ● Ford of Britain ● ICI ● Jaguar ● Lucas ● Massey Ferguson UK ● The National Health Service ● Peugeot-Talbot ● Plessey (Naval Systems) ● Rolls-Royce Aero Engines ● Smith & Nephew ● Whitbread Breweries

Source: Adapted from Storey, 1993

Table 2.4 Twenty-seven points of difference

Dimension	Personnel and IR	HRM
(A) Beliefs and assumptions		
1 Contract	Careful delineation of written contracts	Aim to go 'beyond contract'
2 Rules	Importance of devising clear rules/ mutuality	'Can-do' outlook: impatience with 'rule'
3 Guide to management action	Procedures	'Business-need'
4 Behaviour referent	Norms/custom and practice	Values/mission
5 Managerial task vis-à-vis labour	Monitoring	Nurturing
6 Nature of relations	Pluralist	Unitarist
7 Conflict	Institutionalised	De-emphasised
(B) Strategic aspects		
8 Key relations	Labour–management	Customer
9 Initiatives	Piecemeal	Integrated
10 Corporate plan	Marginal to	Central to
11 Speed of decision	Slow	Fast
(C) Line management		
12 Management role	Transactional	Transformational
13 Key managers	Personnel/IR specialists	General/business/ line managers
14 Communication	Indirect	Direct
15 Standardisation	High (e.g. 'parity' an issue)	Low (e.g. 'parity' not seen as relevant)
16 Prized management skills	Negotiation	Facilitation
(D) Key levers		
17 Selection	Separate, marginal task	Integrated, key task
18 Pay	Job evaluation (fixed grades)	Performance related
19 Conditions	Separately negotiated	Harmonisation
20 Labour– management	Collective bargaining contracts	Towards individual contracts

21	Thrust of relations with stewards	Regularised through facilities and training	Marginalised (with exception of some bargaining for change models)
22	Job categories and grades	Many	Few
23	Communication	Restricted flow	Increased flow
24	Job design	Division of labour	Team work
25	Conflict handling	Reach temporary truces	Manage climate and culture
26	Training and development	Controlled access to courses	Learning companies
27	Focuses of attention for interventions	Personnel procedures	Wide-ranging cultural, structural and personnel strategies

Source: Storey, 1993

The majority of managers, especially personnel managers, stressed how industrial relations had come to assume a very low placing in their list of concerns and priorities. The scope of issues covered by joint regulation had narrowed considerably. Bargaining had moved closer to a form of joint consultation. There was a shift away from industrial relation's procedural devices, such as, job evaluation and negotiated pay and towards individualised contracts and performance-related pay. Shop stewards were seeing their numbers and influence decline. Storey found evidence of what he has termed 'dual arrangements' within the organisations, in which the established trade union approach and new approaches and initiatives in labour management relations were being run in parallel.

A major problem with the HRM debate is that, for the most part, it has not been informed by the changes in human resource management which have been taking place in the UK context or by the historical evolution occurring in the US, although recent academic writing and research has begun to remedy this.

As has been seen, the US had the advantage of a well-established and wide-ranging forum on developments in human resource management. The various environmental pressures with which it had to contend also served to bring HRM issues into the forefront. The employment debate in the UK, when HRM appeared in the mid-1960s, was largely to do with union power. At the same time environmental pressures, similar to those in America, were beginning to mount. In a climate of recession and the increasing globalisation of business, the conservatives, under Thatcherism, were emphasising competitiveness, entrepreneurialism and minimal interference in business affairs. They were also intent on curbing trades union power. Research, highly critical of the UK's quality of training and poorly targeted education in relation to its main competitors (Handy, 1987; Constable and McCormick, 1987), led eventually to sweeping changes in the national education and training infrastructure. All of these circumstances served to focus attention on failure to effectively utilise human resources.

There were other influences that could have informed the discussion on the nature of HRM. There was, for example the promotion of the quality of work life concept by the Work Research Unit for a period of over twenty years, and the focus on managing people promoted by the Department of Trade and Industry in preparation for entry into the Single Market. There were also HRM practices being introduced into industry by multinationals from the US and Japan, see for example, Garrahan and Stewart (1992) and Starkey and McKinlay (1993) and their accounts of HRM in the Nissan and Ford plants, respectively. The message from the 'In search of excellence' companies and the British equivalent were making an impact on management at this time, (Peters and Waterman, 1982; Goldsmith and Clutterbuck, 1984). This was followed by the quality movement.

The concept of strategic human resource management

1 Human resources – a strategic issue

Another term also began to make an appearance in the US literature in the early 1980s – strategic human resource management. As a starting point a case is usually made for a pro-active HRM presence at strategic level on the basis of criticism of the functional role in terms of perceived weaknesses and/or evidence of environmental pressures which demonstrate the strategic nature of human resources (for example, Nininger, 1980; Miller and Burack, 1981; Gehrman, 1981; De Santo, 1983; Kaufman, 1984; Frohman and Frohman, 1984; Ondrack and Nininger, 1984; Kanter, 1983, 1989; Redwood, 1990, and Schuler and Walker, 1990).

Nininger (1980), for example, in a study for the Conference Board of Canada which had the aim of examining how organisations should be thinking about the role and management of human resources in relation to overall organisation strategies, identified various environmental challenges relating to human resource management which organisations must deal with in the 1980s. He suggested that organisations which succeed in linking strategy and human resource planning will also be effective in meeting such challenges. With the assistance of senior human resource executives in ten organisations, seven principles were identified as being important to the effective integration of human resources with strategic planning and management. In subsequent research, Ondrack and Nininger (1984) have used the principles to explore, through case study research, the extent to which strategic human resource management was present in organisations. The principles are summarised in exhibit 2.2. An important part of their findings is the key role they attribute to the chief executive on the grounds that human resource issues were becoming so important to the strategic plans and operations of the organisation that they require attention at the highest level.

Exhibit 2.2 The seven principles

Each principle should be read with the following preamble: Effective human resources management, in the context of overall business planning and management, is facilitated to the extent that:

1 There is an overall corporate purpose and that the human resource dimensions of that purpose are evident.
2 A process of developing strategy within the organisaton exists and is understood, and that there is explicit consideration of human resource dimensions.
3 Effective linkages exist on a continuing basis to ensure the integration of human resource considerations with the organisational decision-making processes.
4 The office of the chief executive officer provides the climate for integrating human resource considerations to meet the needs of the business.
5 The organisation at all levels establishes responsibility and accountability for human resource management.
6 Initiatives in the management of human resources are relevant to the needs of the business.

7 It includes the responsibility to identify and interact in the social, political, technological and economic environments in which the organisation is and will be doing business.

Kanter (1983), also suggests that organisations need a process of strategic human resource management to help them deal with the rate of 'strategic surprises', which generate needs for flexibility and innovation. Organisations need to develop a culture which harnesses creativity and enterprise. She indicates what steps an organisation should take to introduce the process of strategic human resource management into practice.

Kanter (1989) emphasises that competitive pressures are forcing organisations to adopt new flexible strategies and structures and would appear to suggest that strategic human resource management is being practised but is perhaps not well enough thought out. Many of the strategies and structures, she says, are familiar, for example, acquisitions and divestitures aimed at achieving more focused combinations of business activities, reductions in management staff and levels of hierarchy, and increased use of performance-based rewards. Others are less common but have a profound effect, for example, horizontal ties between peers are replacing vertical ties as channels of activity and communication, corporate staff and functional departments are being asked to take on a more strategic role through greater cross-departmental collaboration, the organisation is buying formerly internal services from outside supplies, forming strategic alliances and supplier–customer partnerships that bring an outside influence on internal policy and practice. Such changes are intended to enable organisations to become leaner, less bureaucratic, more entrepreneurial. Little attention, however, has been given to the reality of managerial work in such organisational changes. There are issues relating to power and motivation which cause dilemmas.

Schuler and Walker (1990) say that the 1980s has been a time of more rapid and dramatic changes than any other recent period. Many of these changes, for example, demographic shifts, heightened competitiveness, changing work patterns and employee needs and more complex technologies have significant implications for human resource management.

2   The need for a concept

Much of the literature provides evidence that strategic integration is not well developed and advances reasons why to achieve it would be beneficial to organisations (Devanna *et al.*, 1981; Rowland and Summers, 1981; Beer *et al.*, 1984; McEwan *et al.*, 1988; Miller, 1991; Anthony and Norton, 1991). That there is breadth of support for strategic integration is indicated by findings that 92 per cent of a survey of USA opinion leaders (university faculty, leading consultants, managers and human resource specialists) felt that human resources were a major factor in organisation success and recommended certain key changes in HRM practice. They advocated an increase in the input of human resource considerations at strategic planning, an attitude of treating employees as assets, more participation and greater involvement for employees; effective and open communications, less rule-oriented policies and practices, better training and career development opportunities, rewards and recognition tied to performance and less adversarial labour–management relations (Alper and Russell, 1984).

In a British context, the designers of a programme (sponsored by the Manpower Services Commission and the National Economic Development Office) for chief executives, directors and senior managers in British companies, aimed to promote a philosophy of 'People – the key to success', which in the government's view was a concept not widely accepted in British boardrooms. Despite the facts that the idea of people as an integral segment within the formulation and implementation of business strategy is not new, that a number of large companies such as IBM, Polaroid, Marks and Spencer and Matsushita Electrical have consistently regarded their employees as a major resource, that a number of authors in academic circles have stressed the need for people to be included in the strategic equations and business plans and, it has been shown that people are part of the formula for achieving and maintaining competitive advantage, people issues tend to be ignored, except when they become a problem. Companies must choose the best strategic alternatives, position themselves in the right target market segments with the right range of products at the right price. People in the company must be mobilised to produce the product or service at the right quality, on time and every time. People must therefore be considered a factor of equal importance to finance, marketing, production, etc. in the business planning equation.

Such an approach will require the development of managers and employees who possess a variety of skills and who have the ability to work flexibly, a sense of involvement in the affairs and future of the organisation, the ability to adapt and the capacity to change. These qualities are summed up as competence, commitment and capacity for change. The key factor is the capacity for change because it integrates the effects of improved competence and commitment to achieve and maintain competitive success. In a predicted turbulent business environment all organisations will need to change and adapt in some way (McEwan *et al.*, 1988).

3 Models and frameworks of strategic human resource management

There is also literature which proposes models and frameworks to describe the process. Baird *et al.*, (1983), taking the example of a divisionalised organisation, propose a model for strategic human resource management which has its basis in a rational strategic planning process. The corporate mission is shown into which flow environmental influences (for example, technology, economics, demographics and competition) and cultural influences (philosophy, values and beliefs). From the mission the corporate strategy is formulated. A series of business units have two-way information flows into the corporate strategy and the flows come from inputs from marketing, finance, production and human resource management. The outcomes from this are corporate functional strategies for each of the functional areas including a human resource strategy. They stress that the model is applicable to any organisation type. They also use the marketing and finance concepts of competitive advantage, product life cycle and portfolio mix and demonstrate how to apply these to the development of strategic human resource management strategies.

Devanna *et al.*, (1984) view strategic human resource management as part of the solution to two issues: declining worker productivity and the declining rate of innovation in industry, and believe that 'more effective systems for managing human resources . . . will lead to increased effectiveness in organisations'. They present frameworks as aids to conceptualising strategic human resource management. A basic framework for strategic management illustrates an organisation being influenced by political, economic and cultural forces. The process has interactive elements of mission

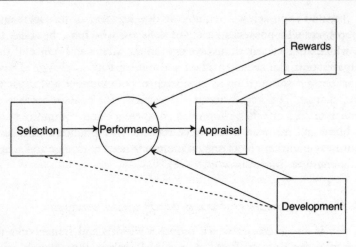

Figure 2.2 The human resource management cycle
Source: Devanna *et al.*, 1984

and strategy, organisation structure and human resource management. See figure 2.2.

There is a one-way flow of data from the environment to the organisation and a one-way flow from mission and strategy to organisation structure and HRM. There is a two-way flow between organisation structure and HRM. Within the HRM element they present a cycle of practices in which selection is linked to performance which is linked to appraisal. Appraisal is linked to both development and rewards which are both linked in a feedback loop to performance.

In a further framework they provide a description of four HRM systems of selection, appraisal, rewards and development at different stages in an organisation's growth cycle. Organisation systems are typically designed piecemeal and so there is often incompatibility in the sub-system. The critical managerial task is to align the formal structure and the human resource system so that they drive the strategic objectives of the organisation. They discuss the underlying assumptions about employee motivation which, they say, are present in the design of organisational human resource systems and which range from self-motivation to punishment avoidance. They recommend that management include the following such considerations in developing a human resources philosophy: the nature of the psychological contract, the extent to which there is participation in decision-making, whether there is internal promotion as opposed to recruitment from the external labour market, and the extent to which there is emphasis on individual versus collective or group work organisation.

A contingency approach

Some of the literature takes a contingency approach to proposals for a strategic human resource management model (for example, Miles and Snow, 1984; Ackermann, 1986; Baird and Meshoulam, 1988; Lengnick-Hall and Lengnick-Hall, 1988; Kidd and Oppenheim, 1990).

Miles and Snow suggest that organisations pursue a generic strategy and that they develop a structure and human resource management process which matches the chosen strategy. From research evidence they identify a number of generic strategies. The 'defender' has a narrow and relatively stable product-market domain. The 'prospector' continually searches for product and market opportunities and experiments with potential responses to emerging environmental trends. The 'analyser' operates in two domains, one relatively stable in which it operates routinely and efficiently, and the other changing, in which it operates in an innovative way. The key question for organisations is how to reduce, if not eliminate, the lag between the emergence of new strategies and structures and their appropriate HRM processes. They have classified as 'reactors' organisations in which there is inconsistency between strategy and environment or in which there is poor alignment between strategy, structure and processes.

Lengnick-Hall and Lengnick-Hall offer a typology by which to explore what they perceive to be the two dimensions of strategic human resource management, namely organisational goals and the availability/obtainability of human resources. The typology relies on three assumptions: that the choice of strategy has not been made, that the management of human resources should contribute directly to strategy formulation and to strategy implementation, and that as strategic conditions vary, the fundamental questions that must be addressed also vary because strategic issues reflect strategic contingencies. Conditions that influence what types of questions should be asked are not the same contingencies that determine the answers to those questions. The questions which are asked primarily reflect organisational outcomes and environmental threats and opportunities. These issues vary with bottom-line expectations and prior organisation choices. The answers to these questions depend heavily on organisational strengths, weaknesses, and culture, and its ability to implement change. Both asking the right questions and making acceptable choices are necessary for sustained high performance. The basic features of their typology are arranged in a 'growth/readiness' matrix. Corporate growth expectations are a proxy for the goals of the organisation. Organisational readiness measures the obtainability of human resources skills, numbers, styles, and experience needed for strategy implementation. Readiness is a proxy for implementation feasibility and indicates how well resources meet the needs of the situation. The four quadrants of the matrix: expansion, development, productivity and redirection, represent four conditions under which organisation strategy and they recommend, human resource strategy should be formulated. Evolutionary forces, such as industry and product maturation, apply pressure to move the strategic situation from left to right (from high readiness to obsolescence) as technologies and strategies change. In most industries, technological change makes current skills or techniques less competitive over time. Industries also change from a focus on marketing and research and development in emerging industries to a focus on production and manufacturing in more mature industries. Evolution also moves conditions from top to bottom (from high growth expectations to lower growth goals) as markets become saturated and as new competitors enter the marketplace. As industries and products mature, growth becomes less feasible because there are fewer opportunities, because these are more expensive and because market share must be taken away from competitors. The strategic choice and human resource management characteristics of each quadrant are described. Movement from one quadrant to another results from an interaction between environmental conditions and organisational choice. The authors suggest a contingency approach in which organisation choices influence the rate and direction of organisation life stages.

Ackermann hypothesises that HRM strategies follow business strategy and will contribute to organisational effectiveness and efficiency measured by criteria such as productivity, labour costs and behavioural indices such as turnover and absenteeism. Fifty three German and 27 Austrian organisations took part in survey research which enabled a factor analysis to be undertaken of a number of variables describing human resource policy decisions. The result was a four-factor classification of HRM strategies: development, control, administrative and scanning. A 'development' strategy has emphasis on training and development. There is considerable use of planning and heavy reliance on internal resourcing of staff. A decision that external recruitment is desirable is followed by intensive search and selection activities. A 'control' strategy utilises performance-related pay systems linked to training and development. HR tools of job descriptions, job evaluation and selection are not emphasised. In an 'administrative' strategy, HR planning has a short-term orientation with heavy reliance on external recruitment. All other HR activities receive less emphasis. A 'scanning' strategy utilises labour market scanning both internal and external. Extensive use is made of attitude surveys. There is reliance on monetary incentives and the application of rigorous selection procedures. Ackerman, utilising the Miles and Snow typology of generic strategies, also found that among the 80 organisations, 20 identified themselves as defenders, 13 as prospectors, 38 as analysers, one as a reactor and eight as hybrids, (a combination of generic types). Correlations of generic strategy and choice of HRM strategy supported the hypothesis that HRM strategy follows business strategy. The findings indicated that:

• Defenders prefer the administrative strategy
• Prospectors prefer the scanning strategy
• Analysers prefer the development strategy
• Hybrids prefer both the development and scanning strategies

Ackermann makes the point that HRM should be the subject of planning and decision-making in the interests of the organisation and employees. The realisation of this would take HRM into a more advanced stage – a stage of strategic human resource management.

Baird and Meshoulam propose a model, consisting of dimensions of external and internal fit, for developing and implementing human resource management strategies. They have drawn on literature relating to the stages of organisational development to design a stage model and corresponding HRM responses (the external fit dimension) which they have sought to verify through interviews with managers and HR professionals in 20 organisations ranging in size from 2,000 to over 300,000 employees. They also conducted in-depth historical analyses in four organisations. Their growth model has five stages: initiation, functional growth, controlled growth, functional integration and strategic integration. They propose that human resource management must pass through the stages of organisational development in sequence. Each stage incorporates and builds on the previous stages. They further propose (the internal fit dimension) that strategic components of HRM, which they identify as management awareness, management of the function, portfolio of programmes, personnel skills and information technology, must (a) fit with and support each other and (b) fit the stage of organisation development. These two fits interact and must be managed simultaneously. Baird and Meshoulam propose a HR strategy matrix, which describes each HR component in terms of the stages of organisation growth. The matrix may be utilised to draw an organisation's HR profile which will contain implications for HR practice.

Kydd and Oppenheim conducted case study research in four organisations (considered to be successful competitors in their respective industry as well as reputed to have excellent management of human resources), in order to determine how they linked their strategic direction and goals to the planning of their human resources. The research first looked at the formal human resource policies as stated in formal policy documents and by human resource managers and executives. It then examined these formal policies through the eyes of the middle level managers. Having compared the formal policies with actual practice they were able to describe how four diverse yet successful firms have taken virtually the same set of formal policies and adapted them differently based on different environmental conditions and different corporate strategies. Based on the four case studies, they propose a two-dimensional contingency framework which offers guidelines as to how certain HRM practices should be implemented to gain competitive advantage. The first dimension is based on the environmental turbulence that an organisation faces. The second dimension is based on whether or not an organisation's key competitive thrust is to be an innovator. An organisation's position on each of these dimensions predicts what its approach will be to HRM issues.

Another group of researchers focus specifically, in their various frameworks and models, on the concept of competitive advantage. Schuler and MacMillan (1984) suggest that if an organisation can capture the control of strategic behaviour in the industries in which it competes it will gain competitive advantage and its competitors will be placed in a reactive role. By effectively managing key human resource management practices of planning, staffing, appraising, compensating, training and development, and union-management relationships, the organisation would be able to attract and retain qualified employees who are motivated to perform and there will be outcomes of greater profitability, low employee turnover, high product quality, lower production costs and more rapid acceptance and implementation of corporate strategy. They propose a matrix of 'strategic thrusts' (cost/efficiency and product differentiation) and 'targets (self, customers, distributors and servicers, and suppliers). The targets represent upstream and downstream activities as well as the organisation itself. An organisation can reach backward or forward to help shape the human resource management practices of other organisations as well as changing its own practices. The thrust-target matrix provides the organisation seeking competitive advantage with eight options which, when matched with appropriate human resource management practices, will enable it to launch a strategic advantage.

Schuler and Jackson (1987) focus on Porter's framework of competitive strategies: innovation, quality enhancement and cost reduction and consider what employee role behaviours would be needed to pursue each. Each role behaviour is presented in two dimensions, for example, highly repetitive, predictable behaviour and highly creative, innovative behaviour. The findings are then considered in terms of what the implications would be for each of the human resource management practices of planning, staffing, appraising, compensating and training and development. The human resource management practices are arranged in a typology with a menu of choices being suggested in relation to each area of practice, with each choice being presented on a continuum, for example, under planning the suggested choices are: informal/formal; short term/long term; explicit job analysis; implicit job analysis; job simplification/job enrichment; and low employee involvement/ high employee involvement. Each competitive strategy is then defined in terms of a matching human resource management strategy.

Schuler (1992) proposes the 5-P model of strategic human resource management, see figure 2.3.

As will be seen, the model is uni-directional from the top downwards. At the top is 'Organisational strategy' in which strategic business needs are identified and specific qualities are assigned to these. Two components, 'Internal characteristics' (culture and nature

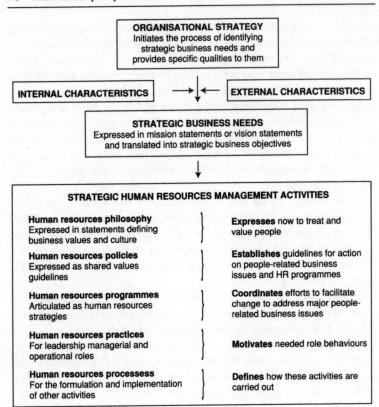

Figure 2.3 The 5-P model of strategic human resource management
Source: Schuler, 1992

of the business) and 'External characteristics' (the state of the economy and critical success factors in the industry) flow into the process and enables business needs to be defined and expressed as mission statements. Business objectives are articulated and flow into the 5-P component enabling human resources management philosophy, policy, programmes, practices and processes to be established.

Without exception all of these frameworks and models are American in origin. In the UK a major research programme has been taking place at the University of Warwick (e.g. Hendry and Pettigrew, 1986; Sparrow and Pettigrew, 1988a, 1988b; Hendry and

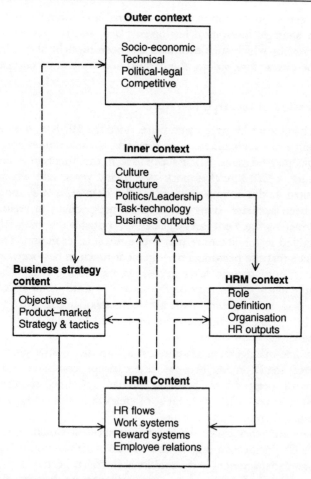

Figure 2.4 Strategic change and human resource management
Source: Hendry and Pettigrew

Pettigrew, 1990). The field of HRM is viewed as a range of factors affecting the employment and contribution of people, judged against criteria of coherence and appropriateness. In a series of case studies since 1985, the researchers at Warwick have built in-depth cases of business and human resource change. They have developed a framework, illustrated in figure 2.4, which explores the dynamics of HRM practices and business strategy as they have evolved over a period of time – usually 15–20 years – in some detail. The model also permits investigation of the external and internal context in which strategic innovation has taken place, and is sensitive to the processes by which such evolution has been brought about, including the interactions among the context and content of change.

Discussion of research literature

The changes which have taken place since the 1970s in the field of personnel management are quite dramatic. Some comment on these changes may be made. The issues raised in the 'function in decline' literature, which stretches back over many years, and which was presented at the commencement of the chapter, would appear to have been accurate. If new theoretical perspectives in relation to personnel management can be gained it is possible that the problems highlighted in the literature may move towards resolution. There is evidence that the personnel management function has been operating at a non-strategic level in the organisation. Strategic human resource management may be the means to finally alter that. If its theoretical development expands then this should provide the knowledge base and the different professional emphasis needed by the function.

The line-management relationship is intrinsic to strategic human resource management because the concept combines line and functional perspectives. Strategic human resource management, therefore, may offer a means of resolving this long-standing dilemma inherent in the function.

There are other issues worth consideration. It would seem that, from a US perspective, a good case can be made for concluding that personnel management in its traditional form has been evolving to a process identified as human resource management. In particular the Harvard model and writings demonstrate the nature of the evolution. It incorporates a strategic orientation, environmental awareness, a multiple stakeholder perspective, and standard personnel management practices. It has a strong managerial perspective and in many ways the new practices have been management's pragmatic response to its changing environmental context. It is suggested that HRM's underlying philosophy represents a new paradigm to replace the traditional control paradigm. The approach contains a strong organisation behaviour/organisation development orientation. There is attention to gaining employee motivation and commitment. Extensive use is made of new forms of work organisation. Initially, HRM developed in some large organisations keen to experiment with new approaches. These organisations tended to be committed to not having unions. An interesting perspective on personnel management and human resource management may be gained by considering Lawrence's historical analysis of HRM systems. Both the 'craft' and 'market' systems would have been eclipsed by the appearance of the 'technical' system before personnel management as a functional activity, described by Lawrence as a form of 'welfare capitalism', entered the organisation. There was therefore a line management relationship and tradition already in existence. The function was from its inception associated with managerial control and the development of unions. HRM's development, in organisations committed to no unions, attracts some claims that it was and is a union-busting tactic. It is also worth noting that historical analysis has suggested that the five systems described were linked to varying environmental conditions. This places strong emphasis on the need to recognise the contingency-based properties of the current 'Commitment' system. While its likely endurance is unknown it is important to take account of the probable strength of the educational and social changes relating to human resources which have influenced the development of the system. Continued educational and social changes are likely to be a permanent feature of the environment. The historical analysis has also shown up that the different HRM systems denote a shift in the balance of influence between employer and employed. There is a connection here with the literature on the changing face of American industrial relations and the phenomenon of the non-union firm and there is conjecture that a new form of industrial relations may be emerging which combines some of the features of the traditional approach with features of the commitment system. Certainly the historical analysis highlights certain extremes in behaviour and perspective, for example, mutuality/adversarialism, control/commitment, specialisation/flexibility, standardisation/innovation, alienation/identification and so on. These polarised versions of management may indeed mark two extremes with the scientific management school on the one hand and perhaps the human relations school on the other. Too little is known as yet to reach any lasting conclusions. What can be said with some certainty is that some fundamental changes have been taking place in terms of the management of people but it seems too soon to accept that the HRM 'commitment' model is the sweeping new paradigm which some have proclaimed it to be.

From around the early 1980s, it would seem that the concept of strategic human resource management started to develop in parallel with the older established HRM concept. There is overlap between the two concepts in terms of strategic orientation, rationale and philosophy. Is the shift in title justified? It is possible to view it as the next phase in the evolution that seems to have been occurring between personnel management and HRM and it has two distinguishing qualities. Firstly, its explicit aim is to obtain a theoretical understanding of the potential link between the strategic process and the human resource management process. This combination of itself, because it marks a new sphere of conceptual development, gives credence to a claim for separate identity. Secondly, a further aim is to find ways to put this strategic activity into practice. In order to do this it seeks to utilise the best of HRM's functional practices and to put some managerial techniques, especially strategic planning tools, to use in bringing a strategic orientation to HRM activities. This gives it a further claim for separate identity. It could be argued that HRM as epitomised by the Harvard model is more slanted towards management implementation tactics while strategic human resource management incorporates this within the strategic management process but also endeavours to advance HRM functional activities to strategic level and capture a concept that can make this happen.

Returning to the UK context, it is not yet clear what evolution may have taken place in UK organisations. Some empirical research evidence is beginning to emerge. No doubt the picture will become clearer as more accumulates. Apart from theoretical modelling and empirical research, there is also benefit to be derived from both political and historical analyses.

In conclusion, it may be speculated that a fully developed theory of strategic human resource management will incorporate what is known of HRM and that the title of the former designates the distinctive nature of the concept and should, for the present, be retained.

A MODEL OF STRATEGIC HUMAN RESOURCE MANAGEMENT

The literature, reviewed in this chapter and in chapter 1, has been synthesised in order to consider if there is a rationale for a concept of strategic human resource management and to propose a model for the process.

A rationale

The reasons put forward in the literature denoting an evolution from strategic planning to strategic management and the lack of consensus as to the elements in the implementation phase point to a need to develop strategic management's weak, and mainly behavioural elements. This suggests that there is a theoretical gap which might be filled by HRM.

The reasons put forward for detecting an evolution from personnel management to HRM with its distinctive characteristics and signs of the emergence of a concept of strategic human resource management demonstrate the historic weaknesses in the function and subsequent efforts to become more strategic. There is also, in this field, a gap in theoretical development.

It is proposed that the development of strategic human resource management could make a significant contribution towards closing these gaps.

Design of a model of strategic human resource management

The design aim is to find a means to integrate the evolving strategy and HRM concepts. The resultant model is not intended to be prescriptive. By its nature it is experimental and a vehicle for research. In relation to this book it provides a method of thinking through the process of strategic human resource management in order to assist practice in this sphere of activity. The theoretical perspectives underpinning the model are explained below.

1 It will be recalled that an analysis of the meaning of strategy in chapter 1 led to defining the concept as containing: (a) the strategic process, consisting of processes of formulation and implementation directed at positioning the organisation in its environment, securing competitive advantage and deploying resources; (b) leadership, meaning the actions of those concerned with directing the company; and (c) organisation effectiveness, defined as securing success in a specific environmental context. The nature of the relationship between leadership and strategy is an important one but does not form part of the model, except in

so far that there are decision-makers intrinsic to the concept. The significance of leadership is explored in chapter 3 which examines the state of the art in the practice of strategic management. The remainder of the definition of the strategy concept is integrated into the model.

2 The literature has revealed lack of consensus with regard to strategy formation. At issue is that the environment is so dynamic that the future is no longer predictable, and therefore, so the argument goes, it can no longer be planned for. This suggests that there should be reservations about adhering solely to the conventional wisdom which is dominated by the rational planning approach. The case made is that an analytic, rational approach locks an organisation into strategies when what an organisation, operating in a turbulent environment, needs is the capacity to be flexible and innovative. The main alternative is to take an incremental approach which, it is claimed, is rich in creativeness and use of organisational learning. The element of control is high in the rational approach and low in an incremental approach. More recent research has sought to broaden perspectives on strategy and to find ways of classifying the process so that the practising manager can make choices. One view is that the dynamics of organisations suggest a system of bounded instability in which a means must be found to accommodate both control and innovation. Turbulence in the environment must be matched by increasingly sophisticated approaches to strategy. A process, for example, of 'real time' issue management enables an organisation, provided it has the internal flexibility and mentality, to pick up and respond strategically to even very weak environmental signals.

3 Of further significance in developing a model is to take account of the argument offered in the literature to explain the evolution from strategic planning to strategic management which, essentially, makes the point that it is ineffective to view formulation and implementation as completely separate processes. Implementation has been neglected relative to formulation and there is increasing realisation of the importance of the implementation process as being critical to an organisation's success, even its survival.

The concept of capability planning addresses this issue. It handles the interconnection between environmental scanning and assessing the internal capability of the organisation, in relation to strategic options. It also allows for the view that internal capability may lead strategy as well as follow after strategy.

4 It has also been seen that literature on modelling the strategy process has fallen into two broad prescriptive areas. There were configurations which consisted of specific elements which when linked with strategy would enable the organisation to plan and implement strategy. More recently, there have been models of strategic management consisting of broad phases of formulation, implementation and control, the latter either mentioned as a component in its own right or as an integral part of implementation. The implementation phase has been presented as containing elements similar to those in the configurations and is thought to be signs of an evolution towards a refinement of the strategic management models which is still continuing.

A process of rationalising the elements of both the configurations and the implementation phase of the strategic management process has resulted in generic terms of structure, systems and processes which an organisation would configure in terms of its strategic choices. This would form part of the capability planning process referred to above.

5 An analysis of the elements of the control process has indicated emphasis on standards, performance, measures and evaluation.

6 A further point, emphasised repeatedly, is that change is a permanent feature in a turbulent environment. As a consequence, the process of change and its management must be a significant element in a model of strategic human resource management. It is important to adopt an open systems perspective in designing a model in order to accommodate contingencies of adaptation and change.

7 There is emphasis in the literature promoting an HRM strategic orientation for the achievement of fit between the HRM activities such as, selection, appraisal, or rewards and the strategy of the organisation.

It was concluded therefore that strategic human resource management should be explicity linked to a strategic management process. The following components should be present in the combined concepts.

• Formulation and implementation.
• Capability planning. The process spans formulation and implementation thus addressing the issue of dichotomy between the

two. It also incorporates a rationalisation of the various elements in the configuration models and the implementation phase of the strategic management models, to provide a generic framework (structure, systems and processes) for internal capability assessment.

- Organisation change, based on systems and contingency perspectives.
- A system of control linked to organisation effectiveness criteria.
- A specific HRM input into each of the above components.
- The framing of an HRM plan as an integral part of the organisation's strategic plan.
- A process to develop HRM implementation needs in which all HRM activities are supportive of organisation strategy.

It will be seen that the approach taken is to have a rational approach as a macro framework. There is a great deal of knowledge accumulated, in the conventional wisdom, in relation to environmental analysis and the formation of strategy. It would be illogical to cast this aside. It is considered essential, however, that the organisation engage in the strategy process from a position of awareness that there are other options, such as incrementalism, which may have a part to play. An overview of the field of strategy research and a philosophy about how an organisation's own strategy is developed should be considered essential management information. Review of the process in terms of its continued appropriateness should be an ongoing requirement. Figure 0.1 (p. 4) illustrates the overall strategic management dimension of the model. Some explanation is provided.

The figure provides for a rational planning approach with an integrated human resource dimension. Although a functionally structured organisaton has been chosen, the principles in the concept will apply to any form of organisational structure.

A process of environmental scanning provides each functional area with data, in terms of opportunities and threats, for planning purposes. Each draws in specialised data in a process of continuous surveillance. The data are used to evaluate strategic options. This is achieved by engaging in a process of capability analysis, that is, an audit of the internal strengths and weaknesses of the organisation within each functional resource area, to pursue a particular option. The generation of such data from various specialist functions makes it possible to assess the impact between functions which might constrain the choice of a particular option. After weighing up alternative options a choice can be made and this forms the basis for the strategic plan. It is then possible to draw up details of implementation requirements and this forms the basis of individual functional plans, that is, objectives to be reached. These, due to the fact that they are derived after integration at strategic level, represent a consistent and cohesive set of objectives. This therefore is a formal template and a standard method of operating against which organisation decision-makers can judge to what extent the reality facing the organisaton dictates that they utilise a different approach, for example, a gradual emergent strategy process, or permit bounded instability in parts, in which systems and/or processes may be destroyed in a revolutionary manner, to enable the new to emerge.

In figure 0.2 (p. 5) the strategic human resource management dimension of the strategic management process has been extracted in order to explain its functioning.

The environmental factors to be analysed from a human resources perspective are labour, social, education, demographic, legislative, and economic. The internal capability analysis which takes place, in relation to various strategic options, is specific to human resource management and incorporates an analysis of capability in relation to structure and its various related elements within the organisation's systems and processes. When the process of capability assessment has been completed the organisation may move on to select a new strategic direction. The strengths and weaknesses in an organisation's capability are also capable of generating strategic options which the organisation might consider.

The next part of the model deals with implementation. It is proposed that an essential element in the development of implementation plans relate to establishing core effectiveness criteria. Core criteria define the contribution which human resources can make to the achievement of organisation strategy. They are derived from the strategic human resource management plan, an outcome from the organisational planning process. The strategic human resource management plan would contain details of implementaton needs and a statement of the philosophy which would underpin the development of the organisation culture. Incorporated in this would be inputs from the main decision-makers (and other relevant stakeholders). Core effectiveness criteria would be derived from this. Some of those identified in the literature have been, for example, creativity, commitment and involvement. A human resource management mission statement would then be developed. Job descriptions should be available for key positions in the organisation and these will provide an overview of the key tasks and responsibilities specific to the various parts of the organisation. These specific performance criteria should be listed in relation to each position and each area of the organisation. Core effectiveness criteria and specific criteria should be combined to design a structure, systems and processes which support strategy.

The human resource management activities which may be utilised in support of strategy are selection, performance appraisal, training and development, rewards and employee relations. Effectiveness criteria would be used to specify selection to match the organisation's strategic position. Standards of performance would be linked with the criteria and would form the basis of performance appraisal, training and development and rewards. The criteria would also influence the relationship between the employer and employee, and if there is a union, the negotiation process. The use of the criteria in this way would ensure that there is integration between the various activities so that they are mutually supportive of the organisation's strategy rather than being, as has been the case in the past, piecemeal interventions. State of the art knowledge in each of the activity areas would ensure that reliability and validity can be a major consideration in their design.

The model also incorporates the change process and the classification of the environment on a stable/dynamic continuum. In a stable environment, in which the organisation is making slight strategic change, the human resource management strategy might be to control and maintain the human resource management system. In a dynamic environment there would have to be capability to respond to surprise and ill-defined events and change structure, systems and processes with regularity. A process of organisational learning will ensure that the organisation has the capability to maintain or renew itself. It has been seen that there is anticipation that the scale of environmental change is set to heighten and accelerate rather than diminish. It also seems that organisations will increasingly have to accommodate the capacity to deal with both stable and dynamic conditions within the one organisation. The concept of strategic human resource management, however, can facilitate an organisation's performance in any environment.

The final aspect of the strategic human resource management model deals with evaluation of effectiveness. There should be mechanisms in place by which the efficiency and effectiveness of the organisation's structure and its various human resource management systems and processes can be monitored. As strategic human resource management is an interative process such evaluation will be an on-going activity.

CONCLUSION

When the literature on strategy and HRM are synthesised a convincing case can be made for a concept of strategic human resource management. From this synthesis a working model of the concept has been developed and this will likely change with further research into theory and practice. There are certain aspects of the model which, even at this early stage, are clearly in need of development. There is need for the development of frameworks for capability audit in order to bring a focus to the process of capability planning. There is also need for a process which provides for the use of incremental or emergent strategy, where this is needed. It will be seen that chapter 8 on strategic training and development makes reference to the potential use of the learning organisation concept to institutionalise the knowledge, skills and experience derived from the management of the strategy process. Further work, however, is required.

REFERENCES

Ackermann, K.F. (1986) 'A contingency model of HRM strategy: empirical research findings reconsidered', paper presented at European Institute for Advanced Studies in Management Workshop on Strategic Human Resource Management, Brussels, 1986.

Alper, W. W. and Russell, E.M. (1984) 'What policies and practices characterise the most effective human resource departments?' *Personnel Administrator*, 29(1): 120–25.

Anthony, P. and Norton, L.A., (1991) 'Link HR to Corporate Strategy'. *Personnel Journal*, April: 75–86.

Armstrong, M. (1987) 'Human resource management: a case of the Emperor's new clothes', *Personnel Management*, August: 32–5.

Baird, L. and Meshoulam, I. (1988) 'Managing two fits of strategic human resource management', *Academy of Management Review*, 13(1): 116–28.

Baird, L., Meshoulam, I. and DeGive, G. (1983) 'Meshing human resource planning with strategic business planning: a model approach', *Personnel*, September/December: 14–25.

Beer, M., and Spector, B. (1985) 'Corporate transformations in human resource management', in R.E. Walton, and P.R. Lawrence, (eds) *HRM Trends and Challenges*, Boston, USA: Harvard Business School Press.

Beer, M., Spector, B., Lawrence, P.R., Mill, Q.D. and Walton, R.E. (1984) *Managing Human Assets*, New York: The Free Press, Macmillan.

Brewster, C. and Smith, C. (1990) 'Corporate strategy: a no-go area for personnel?' *Personnel Management*, July: 36–40.

Burack, E.H. and Smith, R.D. (1977) *Personnel Management*, New York: West Publishing.

Constable, J. and McCormick, R. (1987) *The making of British Managers*, London: British Institute of Management.

De Santo, J.F. (1983) 'Work force planning and corporate strategy', *Personnel Administration*, October: 33–5, 88.

Devanna, M.A., Fombrun, C.J. and Tichy, N.M. (1981)' Human resource management: a strategic perspective', *Organisation Dynamics*, 9(3): 51–67.

Devanna, M.A., Fombrun, C.J. and Tichy, N.M (1984) ' A framework for strategic human resource management', in C.J., Fombrun, N.M. Tichy, and M.A. Devanna, (eds) *Strategic Human Resource Management*, USA: John Wiley & Sons.

Drucker, P. (1968) *The Practice of Management*, London: Pan.

Drucker, P. (1988) 'The coming of the new organisation', *Harvard Business Review*, January–February: 45–53.

Farnham, D. (1984) *The Corporate Environment*, London: Institute of Personnel Management,

Farnham, D. (1990) *The Corporate Environment*, London: Institute of Personnel Management.

Fisher, C.D., Shoenfeldt, L.F., and Shaw, J.B. (1990) *Human Resource Management*, Boston, USA: Houghton Mifflin.

Foulkes, F.K. and Livernash, E.R. (1982) *Human Resource Management: Texts and Cases*, New Jersey, USA: Prentice Hall.

Fowler, A. (1987) 'When chief executives discover HRM', *Personnel management*, May.

Frohman, M. and Frohman, A. (1984) 'Organisation adaptation: a personnel responsibility', *Personnel Administrator*, January: 45–47, 88.

Garrahan, P., and Stewart, P. (1992) *The Nissan Enigma*, London: Mansell Publishing.

Gehrman, D.B. (1981) 'Objective based human resource planning' *Personnel Journal*, December: 942–6.

Goldsmith, W. and Clutterbuck, D. (1984) *The Winning Streak*, Harmondsworth: Penguin.

Guest, D. (1987) 'Human resource management and industrial relations', *Journal of Management Studies*, 24(5): 503–21.

Guest, D. (1989) 'Personnel and HRM: can you tell the difference?', *Personnel Management*, 21(1): 48–51.

Guest, D. (1991) 'Personnel Management: the end of orthodoxy?' *British Journal of Industrial Relations*, 29(2): 149–75.

Handy, C. (1987) *The Making of Managers*, a report on management education, training and development in the USA, West Germany, France, Japan and the UK, London: National Economic Development Office.

Hendry, C. and Pettigrew, A. (1986) 'The practice of strategic human resource management, *Personnel Review,* 15(5): 3–8.

Hendry, C. and Pettigrew, A. (1990) 'Human resource management: an agenda for the 1990s', *International Journal of Human Resource management,* 1(1): 17–43.

Hunt, J.W. (1984) 'The shifting focus of the personnel function', *Personnel management,* February: 14–18.

Kanter, R.M. (1983) 'Frontiers for strategic human resource management', *Human Resource Management,* 22(1/2): 9–21.

Kanter, R.M. (1989) 'The new managerial work', *Harvard Business Review,* November/December: 85–92.

Kaufman, D.J. (1984) 'Planning strategy, human resources and employment: an integrated approach', *Managerial Planning,* 32(6): 24–29.

Keenoy, T. (1990) 'Human resource management: rhetoric, reality and contradiction', *The International Journal of Human Resource Management,* 1(3): 363–84.

Kidd, C.T. and Oppenheim, L. (1990) 'Using human resource management to enhance competitiveness: lessons from four excellent companies', *Human Resource Management,* 29(2): 145–66.

Klatt, L.A., Murdick, R.G. and Schuster, F.E. (1985) *Human Resource Management,* Columbus, Ohio: Merrill.

Kochan, T.A., Katz, H.C. and McKersie, R.B. (1986) *The Transformation of American Industrial Relations,* New York: Basic Books.

Lawrence, P.R. (1985) 'The history of human resource management in American industry', in R.E. Walton, and J.R. Lawrence, (eds) *HRM: Trends and Challenges,* Boston: Harvard Business School.

Legge, K. (1978) *Power, Innovation and Problem Solving in Personnel Management,* Maidenhead: McGraw-Hill.

Legge, K. (1989) 'Human resource management: a critical analysis', in J. Storey, (ed.) *New Perspectives on Human Resource Management,* London: Routledge.

Lengnick-Hall, C.A. and Lengnick-Hall, M.L. (1988) 'Strategic human resources management: a review of the literature and a proposed typology, *Academy of Management Review,* 13(3): 454–70.

Miller, E.L. and Burack, E.W. (1981) 'A status report on human resource planning from the perspective of human resource planners', *Human Resource Planning,* 4(2): 33–40.

Miller, P. (1989) 'Strategic HRM: What it is and what it isn't', *Personnel Management,* February: 46–52.

Miller, P. (1991) 'Strategic human resource management: an assessment of progress, *Human Resource Management Journal,* 1(4): 33–39.

Miles, R.E. and Snow, C.C. (1984) 'Designing strategic human resources Systems', *Organisational Dynamics,* 13(1): 36–52.

McKersie, R.B. (1987) 'The transformation of American industrial relations: the abridged story', *Journal of Management Studies,* 24(5), September. 434–40 .

McEwan, N., Carmichael, C., Short, D. and Steel, A. (1988) 'Managing organisation change – a strategic approach, *Long Range Planning,* 21(6): 71–8.

Nininger, J.R. (1980) 'Human resources and strategic planning: a vital link', *Optimum*, 11(4): 33–46.

Ondrack, D.A. and Nininger, J.R. (1984) 'Human resource strategies – the corporate perspective', *Business Quarterly*, 49(4): 101–109.

Peters, T.J. and Waterman, R.H. Jr. (1982) *In Search of Excellence*, New York: Harper Row.

Porter, M. (1991) *The Competitive Advantage of Nations*, London: Macmillan Press.

Purcell, J. (1985) 'Is anybody listening to the corporate personnel department?', *Personnel Management*, September: 28–31.

Redwood, A.(1990) 'Human resources management in the 1990s', *Business Horizons*, January/February.

Reinmann, B. (1991) 'Strategic bridging: highlights of the 1990 strategic management society conference', *Planning Review*, 19(1): 39–47.

Rowland, K.M. and Summers, S.L. (1981) 'Human resource planning: a second look', *Personnel Administrator*, 26(12): 73–80.

Schuler, R.S. (1981) *Personnel and Human Resource Management*, St Paul, Minnesota: West.

Schuler, R.S. (1990) 'Repositioning the human resource function: transformation or demise', *The Academy of Management Executive*, 4(3): 49–60.

Schuler, R.S. (1992) 'Strategic human resources management: linking the people with the strategic needs of the business', *Organisatinal Dynamics*, Summer: 18–31.

Schuler, R.S. and McMillan, E.C. (1984) 'Gaining competitive advantage through human resource management practices', *Human Resource Management*, 23(3): 241–255.

Schuler, R.S. and Jackson, S.E. (1987) 'Linking competitive strategies with Human Resource Management practices', *The Academy of Management Executive*, 1(3): 207–19.

Schuler, R.S. and Walker, J.W. (1990) 'Human resources strategy: focusing on issues and actions, *Organisational Dynamics*, 19(1): 5–20.

Sheehan, B. (1976a) 'Personnel management: in search of definition', *Personnel Management*, August: 10–17.

Sheeham, B. (1976b) 'Personnel management: in search of definition?', *Personnel Management*, September: 10–17

Sparrow, P.R. and Pettigrew, A.M. (1988a) 'Contrasting HRM responses in the changing world of computing', *Personnel Management*, February.

Sparrow, P.R. and Pettigrew, A.M. (1988b) 'Strategic human resource management in the UK computer supplier industry, *Journal of Occupational Psychology*, 61: 25–42.

Starkey, K. and McKinlay, A. (1993) *Strategy and the Human Resource*, Oxford: Blackwell.

Storey, J. (1989) 'Introduction: from personnel management ot human resource management' in J. Storey (ed.) *New Perspectives on Human Resource Management*, London and New York: Routledge.

Storey, J. (1992) *Developments in the Management of Human Resources*, Oxford: Blackwell.

Storey, J. (1993) 'The take-up of human resource management by mainstream companies: key lessons from research', *The International Journal of Human Resource Management*, 4(3): September: 529–53.

Storey, J. and Sisson, K. (1990) 'Limits to transformation: human resource management in the British context', *Industrial Relations*, 21(1): 60–66.

Walton, R.E. (1985) 'Towards a strategy of eliciting employee commitment based on policies of mutuality' in R.E. Walton and P.R. Lawrence (eds) *HRM Trends and Challenges*, Boston: Harvard Business School Press.

Watson, J. (1977) *The Personnel Managers: A Study in the Sociology of Work and Employment*, London: Routledge and Kegan Paul.

Part II

The foundations for strategic human resource management

Strategic human resource management requires the planner to be able to able to work with certain concepts. This capability planning stage of the strategic human resource management model utilises knowledge and techniques of strategic management, organisational structure, culture, change management and human resource planning. The planner not only considers new data from the environment, but also utilises on-going feedback data from the organisation's structure, systems and processes in a specifically human resource-orientated input to the strategic decision-making process.

A central element in this process is the articulation of the core effectiveness criteria required to drive the attainment of strategy and inform consideration of new strategic direction.

Chapter 3

Strategic management

INTRODUCTION

An analysis of the meaning of strategy in chapter 1 led to the conclusion that, in a business sense, the concept's constituent elements were (a) the strategic process, consisting of formulation and implementation components, directed at positioning the company, securing competitive advantage and deploying resources, (b) leadership, meaning the actions of those concerned with directing the company and (c) organisation effectiveness, defined as securing success in a specific environmental context.

This analysis is used as a framework in the development of this chapter which has the aim of providing an overview of the state of the art in the practice of strategic management. Two questions flow from the framework and are addressed at the start of the chapter. What does the concept of organisational effectiveness mean and what is the nature of the leadership role in the strategic management process? This is followed, in order to facilitate discussion of the strategic management process, by an overview of some relevant planning tools and techniques. Against this background the dynamics of the strategy formulation and implementation aspects of the framework are examined.

THE CONCEPT OF ORGANISATIONAL EFFECTIVENESS

The distinction between efficiency and effectiveness

In much that is researched and written with regard to the advancement of management theory and its application and, as has been seen when reviewing, in chapter 1, the various configurations and models of strategic management, there is the notion, either implicitly inferred or explicitly stated, that 'organisational effectiveness' will be the outcome. Frequently, too, in discussions of organisational performance confusion is generated when the terms efficiency and effectiveness are used interchangeably. Most people find it easy to recall a distinction made by Drucker (1979) that 'efficiency is concerned with doing things right, effectiveness with doing the right things'. Effectiveness, in his view, is the foundation of success, while efficiency is a minimum condition for survival after success has been achieved. Lowe and Soo (1980) take a systems perspective with efficiency being rated on the ratio of inputs to outputs and effectiveness being judged by the extent to which organisational goals have been achieved. A conclusion which may be drawn from considering the distinction between the terms is that an organisation may be efficient but not effective and vice-versa.

Conceptual dissaray

A further conclusion which may be drawn, on examination of the literature on organisation effectiveness is that while there is no consensus as to its definition, identification of core effectiveness criteria or how best to design research in the area, there is considerable agreement that, conceptually, the field is in disarray (Steers, 1975; Connolly et al., 1980; Strasser et al., 1981 and Cameron, 1986).

In a review of 17 research models, Steers (1975) found little consensus on what constitutes a valid set of effectiveness criteria. Adaptability and flexibility were the only criteria common to just more than 50 per cent of models. Steers concluded that the concept was so complex that more comprehensive research models than presently existed would be required to accommodate it. The domains of relevant criteria, for example, productivity, satisfaction and profitability, would have to be identified. It would be necessary to consider the measurement of variables and their interrelationships. Varying frames of reference would have to be accommodated. Future attempts to measure effectiveness should take account of organisational goals, capacity to use resources successfully towards specific ends, what differential weights to place on evaluation criteria in order to reflect the valences attached to each goal and the constraints that work on the maximisation of each criterion.

The search for core effectiveness criteria

Campbell (1976) identified 30 effectiveness criteria contained in the main models of effectiveness and recommended rationalisation in order to identify core criteria. Quinn and Rohrbaugh (1981) developed this theme and by utilising a process of consulting effectiveness researchers, reduced the list to 16 core criteria which they organised into a three-dimensional representation of effectiveness consisting of focus (person v. organisation orientation), structural preference (stability/control v. flexibility/change) and organisational outcomes (concern for ends of effectiveness v. means towards effectiveness). The three dimensional space graphically represents four effectiveness models: human relations; open systems; rational goal; and internal process. Each model is imbedded in a particular set of competing values and each has a polar opposite model with contrasting emphasis. One criterion of effectiveness, 'output quality', did not emerge in criterion analysis, as being linked with any of the remaining 15 criteria. These writers feel that 'output quality' may be an important element in any criterion or all other criteria and have placed it at the centre point of their four models.

The nature of the concept

Cameron (1980) suggests that two properties of organisational effectiveness have contributed to the confusion and ambiguity surrounding it. Firstly, it is a construct at a high level of abstraction and cannot be directly observed. The boundaries of the concept are unknown and therefore no model of the concept can capture the total meaning. Furthermore effectiveness criteria that are contradictory can exist simultaneously in the same construct space. Secondly, the construct is subjective. As a consequence strategic groups, within an organisation, will define it according to their own values and preferences and a criterion can be eliminated from the construct space only if it is inconsistent with the values and preferences of these groups.

Models of organisation effectiveness

In a meta analysis, Cameron (1981) organised the research on effectiveness into four models: goal attainment (concerned with how well an organisation accomplishes its goals); systems resource (concerned with how successful an organisation is in obtaining needed resources from its environment); internal process (concerned with the extent to which there is absence of internal strain among organisational members); and multiple constituencies (concerned with the extent to which all groups that have some stake in the organisation are, at least minimally, satisfied). Cameron suggests that particular models may be appropriate for particular organisations. Others have taken up research into the multiple constituencies model, for example, Gaertner and Ramnarayan (1983) and Zammuto (1984). Ivancevich and Matteson (1993) reject sole dependence on a goal model in favour of a systems model linked to a multiple constituencies perspective and a time dimension. They perceive an organisation as being one element in a number of elements that act interdependently. Systems theory can accommodate the transformation of resources, the behaviour of individuals and groups, the influence of the environment and the properties of feedback. Over time, the organisation takes, processes and returns resources to the environment. The ultimate effectiveness criterion is survival which requires adaptation. The organisation must have indicators that assess the probability of survival. There may be short-run indicators (such as productivity, turnover, rate of return, employee satisfaction, or absenteeism) of long-run survival. The overarching dimension that cuts across each time dimension is quality.

It can be seen, therefore, that into the 1990s the lack of clarity with regard to the effectiveness concept remains and its efficacy to the business organisation is still, therefore, an issue.

THE LEADERSHIP ROLE

'Leaders are born not made' – a well-worn phrase but one which retained currency for a long time and which would still gain some support. As with organisational effectiveness, a lot of research has been devoted to trying to understand and if possible, 'bottle' leadership. In a business sense the image of the captain of industry leading the organisation to success is a popular one.

Overview of theories

In an overview of theories of leadership, Banner and Blasingame (1988) demonstrate a progression from 'trait' theories to the present time. The 'trait' theory, as typified by the 'leaders are born' view, sought to find universal personality traits that good leaders had to some greater degree than ineffective leaders. The approach ignored the leadership situation, did not specify the relative importance of traits and the findings from research studies are inconsistent with each other. The 'behavioural' theory of leadership concentrates on styles of leadership and this led to prescriptions for an 'ideal' leadership style. However, further research has indicated that no one leadership style is right for all, under all circumstances, and this has encouraged a 'contingency' or 'situational' approach which prescribes that the correct leadership style is contingent on such factors as the leader–subordinate relationship, the leader's characteristics, the followers' characteristics, the organisational culture and organisational environment. An 'attribution' theory of leadership suggests that the complexity of the leadership process cannot be revealed without considering the dynamic interaction between the leader and the follower. According to attribution theory, leadership exists only as perception. Individuals develop their own implicit cause–effect theories to help them understand events in their lives. Leadership therefore depends on an interactional context which includes how others view a leader's performance and its effects and this is influenced by the leadership expectations and preferences of the subordinates.

The 'transformational' leader

More recently a so-called 'new age' or 'transformational' theory of leadership has emerged which is typified by language such as 'empowerment', 'setting the tone', 'defining the corporate purpose', 'aligning the organisation with its purpose', 'vision', 'corporate culture' and so on. This theory typically casts the organisational leader (chief executive) as one having special powers of inspiration.

The 'excellence' association

In a survey of excellent companies, Peters and Waterman (1982) found that a strong leader was associated with almost every company. The companies developed cultures that incorporated the values and practices of these leaders and this helped them to survive. In their view the leader's most important role is to manage the values of the organisation. Leadership was one of the essential characteristics of success which Goldsmith and Clutterbuck (1984) identified in the excellent companies which they investigated in the UK. Leadership was demonstrated through visible top management. The chief executive had a clear vision of where the company was going and communicated that vision down the line.

The components of successful leaders

Bennis (1984) surveyed successful leaders with the objective of determining if they possessed common traits and he identified what he believes are four essential components:

- management of attention – the ability to communicate to others, a 'focus' of 'commitment';
- management of meaning – the ability to make goals apparent to others and align people with them. Communication and alignment work together to make ideas tangible by creating meaning;
- management of trust – the main determinants of which are reliability and constancy. Trust is essential to all organisations and it requires that the leader conveys what he/she stands for;
- management of self, which is the ability to know one's skills and deploy them effectively.

Leadership is so powerful that it gives pace and energy to the workforce and empowers them. Empowerment is demonstrated in four themes: people feel significant; learning and competence matter; people are part of a community; and work is exciting. People are being pulled rather than pushed towards a goal.

Adair (1985) says that the first responsibility of leadership is to achieve the common task, which requires the chief executive to have three important characteristics: the ability to think deeply, communicate and make things happen. Leaders have a sense of direction and they inspire. They are team builders and team leaders. No one is a leader until his/her appointment is ratified in the hearts and minds of subordinates. 'You can call yourself a manager, you can't actually call yourself a leader until that mysterious acceptance happens.'

In the view of Tichy and Devanna (1990) the key to global competitiveness will be the capability of organisations to continuously transform and a 'transformational leader' is one who takes responsibility for revitalising the organisation. Such leaders, 'define the need for change, create new visions, mobilise commitment to those visions, and ultimately transform an organisation'. They have common characteristics. They identify themselves as change agents, are courageous individuals, believe in people, are value driven, are life long learners, have the ability to deal with complexity, ambiguity and uncertainty and they are visionaries.

Transformation theory – the most promising?

Van Setters and Field (1990) in a review of leadership theory identify nine eras of leadership theory culminating in the 'transformational era' which they judge to be the most promising in the history of leadership theory evolution. While admitting that it has not yet been subjected to appropriate scrutiny and empirical testing its superiority lies in the fact that it appears to synthesise aspects of previous theories. They feel that there are many further variables to be added to the leadership concept and that there will, therefore, be need for future development. They say, '[i]t must be realised that leadership effectiveness can be determined not from any one approach alone, but rather through the simultaneous interaction of many types of variables'. They conclude, on the basis of the current state of theory, that a leader must have many new qualities. They must be visionary, risk-takers, adaptable to change, able to delegate, and willing to empower others. The new leader must exemplify the values, goals and culture of the organisation; be highly aware of environmental factors; and place emphasis on innovation. Leaders will be 'effective primarily in their ability to comprehend, visualise, conceptualise, and articulate to their peers and subordinates the opportunities and threats facing the organisation'.

As with organisational effectiveness, the findings of leadership research are inconclusive. This latest 'new age' or 'transformational' trend has emerged as a powerful one and it is intertwined with organisational initiatives such as culture change, which will be more fully discussed in chapter 5. There is a direct link, of course, with the discussion, in chapter 2 of the emergence of human resource management and the evolution towards strategic human resource management. There is little doubt that the leadership role has significance in the process of strategic human resource management because, it would appear, there are powerful human resource management dimensions to the role.

AN OVERVIEW OF PLANNING TOOLS AND TECHNIQUES

The process of strategic planning and more recently, strategic management is facilitated by the use of various tools and techniques. It is beyond the scope of this chapter to do more than highlight the range and purpose of these. For the purpose of discussion the use of financial information is separated from other tools and techniques.

The use of financial information

An analysis of the financial state of an organisation may be gained by using published accounts and accounting ratios. A summary, drawn from Morden (1993) of the main areas of financial appraisal, the purpose to which such data is put and the key ratios used, is provided in table 3.1.

Accounting data and ratio calculations are used as an appraisal guide and to identify issues to be addressed. A financial appraisal of an organisation can reveal the extent of its ability to gain additional funds and will indicate (a) the feasibility of strategic growth options and (b) ability to survive a recession through self-finance. It is necessary to examine data over a period of years in order to reveal trends in terms of growth, stagnation or decline. The data might indicate, for example, that an organisation is ripe for takeover. The ratios can also be utilised in interfirm comparisons.

While much of the above information may be available in external data, some information is normally available only internally. 'Margin of safety' calculations are useful in an internal appraisal of strengths and weaknesses. They are based on 'contribution' accounting in which contribution = (sales revenue − variable cost). The data permits a breakeven analysis to be worked out. In a breakeven analysis for a product, for example, the 'margin of safety' is represented by the level of sales in excess of the breakeven point. Obviously when the excess is high the organisation will be less vulnerable to a decline in sales of the product. The implications are that the company needs to monitor the gap between actual and breakeven sales on a continuing basis and it needs to control or reduce its fixed costs so that the breakeven point is maintained as low as possible.

Also of utility in internal appraisal is the practice of 'zero-based

Table 3.1 Corporate appraisal using financial data

Appraisal areas	Purpose of data	Key ratios
Performance, profitability and asset utilisation	Investigates how well the business is being run	Profit margin Return on capital employed Return on net assets Return on equity Profit per employee Asset turnover Stock turnover Debtor turnover Average collection period Effectiveness of administration
Solvency and liquidity	Investigates if the organisation can pay its way	Current ratio Acid test
Ownership, capital structure and debt management	Investigates if the organisation can meet its obligations in relation to its sources of finance	Gearing ratio Long-term debt ratio
Stock market requirements	Investigates the organisation's acceptability to stock market as assessed by its performance	Earnings per share Market price per share Dividend per share Dividends paid
Cover	Investigates the extent to which the organisation can meet its commitments to shareholders and lenders	Dividend cover Interest cover

Source: Adapted from Morden, 1993.

budgeting'. This approach monitors the activities of the organisation using as its basis the assumption that each activity is being carried out for the first time, that is from zero base. Alternative means of provision are considered for each activity in terms of the benefits to be obtained from them. This form of budgeting uses concepts of opportunity cost and priority setting. It challenges the assumptions of traditional 'incremental' budgeting, which plans ahead using current or immediate past practice, by questioning the right of existing activities to receive a continuing allocation of resources.

'Performance gap analysis' uses appraisal information to evaluate the quality of the organisation's planning by comparing current plans and objectives with what was intended. Gap analysis may also be used to assess competitor strengths and weaknesses and to establish future plans.

Financial strategy options

An organisation can select its financial strategy from a range of strategies such as: obtaining funds for the business at the most appropriate cost; investing funds so as to achieve the required return; satisfying the demands and expectations of the financial stakeholders; managing the risk in (a) obtaining and using funds and (b) servicing the return/capital repayment needs of stakeholders; using skills of financial management to achieve competitive advantage; and preserving the value of assets that represent the capital invested in the organisation. There are also financial implications in an organisation's choice of strategy, for example, the investment appraisal required for proposed business development.

Strategic planning tools and techniques

Planning tools and techniques are strategic decision-making aids which facilitate the translation of strategic thinking into strategic reality. A useful guide to what is available in this sphere has been provided by Webster *et al.* (1991). Based on research evidence obtained from over 100 chief executives and other senior managers, corporate planners, staff specialists and functional managers, they found that most companies only utilise a limited number of techniques most of which are used to build data bases. Following an extensive review of the literature they have identified 30 planning techniques. Using a planning framework of mission statement, environmental/corporate analysis, organisatonal analysis, planning assumptions, objectives and priorities, action plans and control systems, they have produced a 'manager's guide' to help strategic planners examine the merits of the 30 techniques in terms of their utility at each part of the planning framework. Exhibit 3.1 provides an overview and descriptions of these tools and techniques while figure 3.1 demonstrates their utility.

Exhibit 3.1 Brief descriptions of strategic planning tools and techniques

1 Dialectic enquiry

Development, evaluation, and synthesis of conflicting points of view through separate formulation and refinement of each point of view first, by assigned groups using debate format; and second, by bringing the two groups together for presentation and debate between the two points of view – followed by synthesis.

2 Nominal group technique

Development, evaluation, and synthesis of individual points of view through an interactive process in a group setting.

3 Delphi technique

Development, evaluation, and synthesis of individual points of view through the systematic solicitation and collation of judgements on a particular topic through a set of carefully designed sequential questionnaires interspersed with summarised information and feedback of opinions derived from earlier responses.

4 Focus groups

Bringing together recognised experts and qualified individuals to develop, evaluate, and synthesise individual points of view on a particular topic in an organised setting.

5 Driving force

A directional way of thinking in which the 'Driving Force(s)' of business is identified and serves as the guiding parameter for analysis and strategy formulation.

6 Stakeholder analysis

Identification and evaluation of individuals or groups who can affect or be affected by the achievements of the organisation's objectives.

7 Simulation technique

Computer-based technique for simulating future situations and relationships, and then predicting the outcome of various courses of action against each future situation.

8 PIMS analysis

Application of the collection of experiences of a diverse sample of successful and unsuccessful businesses.

9 Market opportunity analysis

Identification of markets and market factors in the economy and industry that will affect the demand for and the marketing of the product or service.

10 Value chain analysis

A diagnostic process for identifying and analysing primary (manufacturing, marketing and sales, service) and support (information systems, research and development) activities that add value to product or service.

11 Benchmarking

Comparative analysis of competitor programmes and strategic position(s) for use as reference point(s) in the formulation of organisational objectives.

12 Situational analysis (SWOT or TOWS)

Systematic development and evaluation of past, present, and future data to identify internal strengths and weaknesses, and external threats and opportunities.

13 Critical success factors/strategic issues analysis

Identification and analysis of a limited number of areas in which high performance will ensure a successful and competitive position.

14 *Product life cycle analysis*

Analysis of market dynamics where a product is viewed according to its position within distinct stages in sales history.

15 *Product/market analysis*

A systematic approach to defining market(s) and market segment(s) along with product(s), product function(s), and technology(ies), both leading to the identification of market niches to serve.

16 *Future studies*

Development of probable future situations and factors based on agreement of a group of 'experts' often from a variety of functional areas within an organisation.

17 *Multiple scenarios*

Smoothly unfolding narratives that describe an assumed future expressed through a sequence of time frames and snapshots.

18 *SPIRE (Systematic Procedure for Identification of Relevant Environments)*

A computer-assisted, matrix-generating tool for forecasting environmental changes that can have a dramatic impact on operations.

19 *Environmental scanning, forecasting, and trend analysis*

Continuous process of monitoring external factors, events, situations, and the projections or forecasts of trends. Usually computer based.

20 *Experience curves*

An organising framework for dynamic analyses of cost and price over an extended period of time for product, company, or industry.

21 Competitive analysis (Porter)

Appraisal of five major competitive factors: potential new entrants; buyers; potential product substitutes; suppliers; and competitors.

22 Portfolio classification analysis

Classification and visual display of the present and prospective positions of businesses and products according to the attractiveness of the market and the ability to compete within that market.

23 Financial models analysis

Utilisation of ratio analyses to understand an organisation's financial situation, and the development of *pro forma* financial statements.

24 Metagame analysis

Thinking through a series of differing viewpoints on a proposed strategy in terms of every competitor and combination of competitive responses to arrive at a strategic direction.

25 Strategic gap analysis

Examination of the difference of current performance levels (current sales) and the projection of desired performance objectives and goals (desired sales level).

26 McKinsey 7-s framework

Process of strategy implementation focusing on strategy, structure, systems, style, shared values, staff, and skills.

27 Operating budgets

Formal statements of policies, plans, and goals designed to assure that actions are taken within specified boundaries, and upon which performance can be measured.

28 Management by objectives (MBO)

A systems approach to the management of an organisation by (1) setting objectives at lower levels of the organisation that are congruent with corporate objectives: (2) monitoring and comparing progress to the objective: and (3) feeding back results to those accountable at all levels.

29 Sustainable growth model

Financial analysis of growth rate in sales required to meet market share objectives, and the degree to which capacity must be expanded to achieve the desired rate of growth.

30 Strategic funds programming

Tool to determine costs, funding, and control mechanisms for implementing strategy.

Source: Adapted from Webster et al., 1991

Worthy of note is the fact that comparatively few of the tools and techniques are categorised as having utility at the implementation phase (AP and CS in table 3.2) of the planning process. This is a reflection of the point made in chapter 1 that strategic implementation has been neglected relative to strategic planning.

Computer modelling

Although the majority of the tools and techniques listed in exhibit 3.1 are not computer dependent, a number are routinely supported by computer modelling. The use of computers for this purpose is projected to grow. An example is given, Rowe et al., (1987), of the program for a 'company capability profile' model. The program is an aid in assessing a company's strengths and weaknesses in dealing with variables in both the internal and external business environments. The program examines four capability categories: managerial, competitive, financial and technical.

Data are input by the planner/s into a series of variables relating to each category. Additional variables can be added. Each variable is displayed on a continuum of 1–9. Number 1 will mean that the company is weak on a particular variable. Five means that it is normal and 9 that it is very strong. The results are displayed

Table 3.2 The range of planning tools and techniques and their utility

Tools and techniques	Planning steps						
	MS	EA	OA	PA	OP	AP	CS
Dialectic enquiry	X	X	X	X			
Nominal group technique	X	X	X	X			
Delphi technique	X	X	X	X			
Focus groups	X	X	X	X			
Driving force	X	X	X	X			
Stakeholder analysis	X	X	X				
Simulation technique		X	X	X	X	X	
PIMS analysis		X	X	X	X	X	
Market opportunity analysis		X		X			
Value chain analysis			X	X			
Benchmarking		X		X			
SWOT		X	X	X			
Critical success factors		X	X	X			
Product life cycle analysis		X	X	X			
Product market analysis		X	X	X			
Futures studies	X	X	X	X			
Multiple scenarios	X	X		X			
SPIRE		X		X			
Environmental scanning, forecasting and trend analysis	X	X		X			
Experience curves				X			
Competitive analysis (Porter)		X		X			
Portfolio analysis		X	X	X			
Financial models analysis			X	X	X		
Metagame analysis		X			X	X	
Strategic gap analysis			X		X	X	
McKinsey 7-S framework					X	X	X
Operating budgets					X	X	X
Management by objectives	X	X	X	X	X	X	X
Sustainable growth model					X	X	
Strategic funds programming					X	X	X

Source: Adapted from Webster *et al.*, 1991

Abbreviations for steps in the strategic planning process:

MS = Mission Statement

EA = Environmental/Competitive Analysis

OA = Organisational Analysis

PA = Planning Assumptions

OP = Objectives and Priorities

AP = Action Plans

CS = Control Systems

graphically on screen for each variable. The variables for the managerial category, for example, are:

- Corporate image, social responsibility
- Use of strategic plans and strategic analysis
- Environmental assessment and forecasting
- Speed of response to changing conditions
- Flexibility of organisational structure
- Management communications and control
- Entrepreneurial orientation
- Ability to attract and retain creative people
- Ability to meet changing technology
- Ability to handle inflation
- Aggressiveness in meeting competition
- Other

Some of the tools and techniques reviewed in this section are more fully considered during the discussion of elements in the strategic management process which follows.

ELEMENTS IN THE STRATEGIC MANAGEMENT PROCESS

A review of literature in chapter 1 has revealed that more recent models of strategic management have, for the most part, contained components of formulation, implementation and control. Table 3.3 illustrates the various elements found in a selection of such models.

As can be seen all cover essentially the same ground, although they are divided as to whether determination of organisation needs constitutes the first step or whether environmental analysis should be first.

To facilitate discussion in this chapter the components of formulation and implementation, incorporating control, are taken as the overarching framework within which to discuss the various elements of the strategic management process.

Formulation

The formulation process consists of elements of mission, objectives, environmental analysis, capability analysis and choice of strategy.

Table 3.3 Elements in the strategic management process as proposed
by various authors

Sharplin (1985)	Bosemen *et al.*, (1986)	Thomas (1988)	Certo and Peter (1991)
Assessment of organisation and environment	Assessment of organisation strengths and weaknesses	Formulation of purpose and mission	Environmental analysis
Determination of mission	Formulation of mission	Analysis of external environment	Establishing organisation direction
Setting specific objectives	Formulation of philosophy and policies	Analysis of organisation	Formulation
Determination of strategy	Determination of objectives	Strategic choice	Implementation
Activation of strategies	Determination of strategy	Implementation	Control
Evaluation	Implementation	Control	
Control	Evaluation		
	Control		

Mission

The mission of an organisation defines how it is distinct from other organisations. It consists of its philosophy and the image it wishes to project. The mission indicates the principle product or markets served and identifies the primary needs the company will try to satisfy (Thomas, 1988). According to Certo and Peter (1991), its mission states the purpose for which, or reason why an organisation exists.

Campbell and Tawadey (1990), in the course of survey and case-study research in over 100 companies throughout the world, which they conducted for the Ashridge Management Centre, analysed 75 mission statements and found that they included statements on the following topics: customers, products or services, location, technology, concern for survival, philosophy, self-concept, concern for public image and concern for employees. Figure 3.1 represents a model of mission which they developed.

Purpose, they say, expresses why the organisation exists. It exists

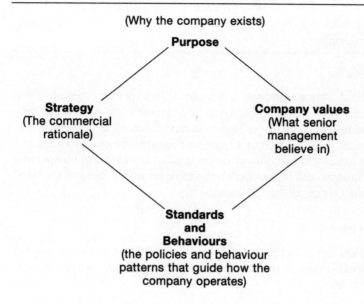

Figure 3.1 The Ashridge mission model
Source: Campbell and Tawadey, 1990

not just for its shareholders but also for an association of other stakeholders: employees, customers, suppliers, etc., and it must define its relationship with each. A mission defined in an inspirational way will help to draw the stakeholders together in support of the organisation's objectives.

Strategy expresses the commercial rationale for the business of an organisation. It helps to link behaviour and decisions to purpose. The rationale must also define the organisation's competitive advantage.

Standards and behaviours express how management and employees should behave and are drawn not only from the strategy but also from the values which it espouses. Campbell and Tawadey underline the significance of organisational values, describing them as the 'emotional logic' which underpin the organisation's mission and which determine both its management style and and ethics. A mission that is strong will have closely integrated purpose, strategy, behaviour standards and values.

An example of a mission statement is provided in exhibit 3.2.

Exhibit 3.2 Ford Motor Company: mission, values and guiding principles

Mission

Ford Motor Company is a world-wide leader in automotive and automotive-related products and services as well as in new industries such as aerospace, communications and financial services. Our mission is to improve continually our products and services to meet our customers needs, allowing us to prosper as a business and to provide a reasonable return for our stockholders, the owners of our business.

Values

How we accomplish our mission is as important as the mission itself. Fundamental to success for the company are these basic values:

People

Our people are the source of our strength. They provide our corporate intelligence and determine our reputation and vitality. Involvement and team work are our core human values.

Products

Our products are the end result of our efforts, and they should be the best in serving customers world-wide. As our products are viewed, so are we viewed.

Profits

Profits are the ultimate measure of how efficiently we provide customers with the best products for their needs. Profits are required to survive and grow.

Guiding principles

Quality comes first

To achieve customer satisfaction, the quality of our products and services must be our number one priority.

Customers are the focus of everything we do

Our work must be done with our customers in mind, providing better products and services than our competition.

Continuous improvement is essential to our success

We must strive for excellence in everything we do: in our products, in their safety and value – and in our services, our human relations, our competitiveness and our profitability.

Employee involvement is our way of life

We are a team. We must treat each other with trust and respect.

Dealers and suppliers are our partners

The company must maintain mutually beneficial relationships with dealers, suppliers, and our business associates.

Integrity is never compromised

The conduct of our company world-wide must be pursued in a manner that is socially responsible and commands respect for its integrity and for its positive contributions to society. Our doors are open to men and women alike without discrimination and without regard to ethnic origin or personal beliefs.

Source: Starkey and McKinlay 1993

Campbell and Tawadey consider that the main advantage from creating a sense of mission is in its power to motivate employees. People will be loyal and committed if they believe in what they are doing and if they trust the organisation. It follows therefore that there should be a link between desired behaviours, organisational values and employee values.

Objectives

There is difference of opinion as to whether objectives and goals are one and the same thing. Richards (1978), in his text on organisational goal structures, considers that 'goals, objectives, purposes, and ends are interchangeable'. Quinn (1988) also uses the terms interchangeably. Ansoff and McDonnell (1990) separate the two with 'objective' appearing to mean a high broader aim and 'goal' meaning the more precise target aimed at, for example, the objective of growth may be achieved through a goal of a specific future annual percentage rate of sales.

The view that the organisation exists only for its shareholders and has one objective, that of profit maximisation, cannot be sustained in reality (Bowman and Asch, 1987). Within the organisation an important influence on the formation of objectives and their attainment is concerned with the distribution of power. There are power coalitions in organisations and the objectives of a group/s may be in conflict with those of the dominant coalition (usually senior management) so that, in reality, decisions are taken which satisfice rather than maximise.

Thomas (1988) defines objectives as targets or intermediate goals needed to translate an organisation's mission statement into specific, concrete, measurable terms and towards which it directs its efforts. Certo and Peter (1991) say they provide the foundation for planning, organising, motivating and controlling. In their view there are eight key areas in which an organisation should set objectives: market standing, innovation, productivity, manager performance and development, worker performance and attitude and social responsibility. High quality objectives, (Morden 1993) should be specific, attainable, flexible and measurable. They should also require a level of effort sufficiently high for employees to be challenged, interested and motivated. As an illustration Sainsbury's company objectives are noted below:

1 To discharge the responsibility as leaders in our trade by acting with complete integrity, by carrying out our work to the highest standards, and by contributing to the public good and the quality of life in the community.
2 To provide unrivalled value to our customers in the quality of the goods we sell, in the competitiveness of our prices and in the range of choice we offer.
3 In our stores, to achieve the highest standards of cleanliness and hygiene, efficiency of operations, convenience and customer service, and thereby create as attractive and friendly a shopping environment as possible.
4 To offer our staff outstanding opportunities in terms of personal career development and in remuneration relative to other com-

Table 3.4 Ranking of corporate objectives: United States and Japan

	United States	Japan
Return on investment	8.1	4.1
Share price increase	3.8	0.1
Market share	2.4	4.8
Improve product portfolio	1.7	2.3
Rationalisation of production and distribution	1.5	2.4
Increase equity ratio	1.3	2.0
Ratio of new products	0.7	3.5
Improve company's image	0.2	0.7
Improve working conditions	0.1	0.3

Source: Abegglen and Stalk, 1985

Note: 291 Japanese companies and 227 US companies ranked factors weighted 10, for first importance, to 1, for least importance.

panies in the same market, always practising a concern for the welfare of every individual.

5 To generate sufficient profit to finance continual improvement and growth of the business whilst providing our shareholders with an excellent return on their investment.

The objectives of organisations are also, apparently, linked to national culture. In a study reported by the Japanese government, the corporate objectives of some 500 major US and Japanese companies were compared (Abegglen and Stalk, 1985). Table 3.4 indicates the differences in organisation priorities between the two countries.

The US organisations ranked return on investment as their principal objective. Share price increase was second and market share third. In contrast, among the Japanese organisations, market share was ranked first, return on investment second and refreshment of the product portfolio third. Share price increase was last among the Japanese objectives. It seems that, for example, in relation to market share that the Japanese company feels that if it is successful in this respect return on investment will follow. The success of companies such as Toyota and Matsushita is quoted.

Environmental analysis

The environment contains many factors which have strategic significance, in terms of representing opportunities and/or threats, to an organisation. An organisation needs to continually scan its environment for strategic issues. New strategic decisions must be informed by understanding of the organisation's current position. Johnson and Scholes (1989) suggest that an organisation should take an analytical approach, consisting of five steps, to assessing its position in its environment:

1 Auditing of environmental influences

Examples of environmental influence are: economic, demographic, socio-cultural, capital markets, technology, labour markets, competitors, government, suppliers, and ecology. Johnson and Scholes suggest that an organisation should audit its environment with three central questions in mind: what general environmental factors are affecting the organisation, which of these are the most important at the present time and which are likely to be the most important in the future? In relation, for example, to the economic factor they suggest that issues of interest are: business cycles, GNP trend, interest rates, money supply, inflation, unemployment, disposable income, energy availability and cost.

2 Understanding the nature of the environment

Strategic decisions are made under conditions of uncertainty and each organisation should plan from a position of having some general understanding of the level of uncertainty in its particular environment. Two measures, complexity and dynamism, combine to establish uncertainty levels. Complexity relates to: the diversity of influences faced by an organisation; the level of knowledge required to deal with environmental influences; and the extent to which there is interconnection between the influences. In a dynamic environment an organisation faces major and frequent change. The nature of its environment will also have bearing on the choice of planning tools and techniques used for analysis, for example, in a simple and stable environment a detailed analysis of past environmental influences may be appropriate while scenario planning, model building and simulation may be more suitable in a dynamic environment.

3 Structural analysis of the competitive environment

Johnson and Scholes use Porter's work to discuss this aspect of environmental analysis. Porter provides a structured approach through which the organisation can obtain a clear understanding of its competitive situation. There are five key forces in the competitive environment: threat of entry; power of supplier; power of buyers; threat of substitutes; and intensity of competitor rivalry. The approach, although designed primarily with business organisations in mind, is of value to most organisations which face strategic problems.

The threat of entry is concerned with barriers which an organisation might face in trying to enter a particular market or industry, etc. or barriers which an organisation might erect to prevent rival entry. Threat of entry includes issues such as: economies of scale (the cost to a manufacturer of producing below optimum levels of scale that are the norm for the industry); capital requirement of entry (the cost of setting up business to operate at the appropriate economy of scale level); access to distribution channels (the possession of extensive, exclusive channels); cost advantages independent of size (mainly to do with 'experience curve' advantages gained by early entrants into the market); legislation or government action (deregulation and privatisation, for example, have left many businesses facing competition for the first time); and differentiation (a barrier set up by an organisation that has managed to provide a product or service that is different from the competition.

The power of buyers and suppliers can be considered together as they have similar effects on the competitive environment. The greater the power of buyers and suppliers the more likely it is that profit margins will be low. Supplier power will be high when there is a concentrated rather than a fragmented source of supply, the costs of switching from one supplier to another are high, there is a chance that the supplier may integrate forwards if the profit margin sought is not forthcoming, and the supplier's customers are of little importance. Buyer power will be high when there is concentration of buyers, especially if the volume purchased is high, there are alternative sources of supply, the component or material cost is a high percentage of their total costs, thus encouraging the buyer to shop around and there is a threat of backward integration by the buyer if satisfactory prices or suppliers cannot be obtained. The problem of developing strategies which will maintain or provide power along the supplier-buyer channel is very important for competitive success.

The threat of substitutes is concerned with the potential range of substitute products which could enter the market. A substitute produce may compete in three ways: as an alternative product; as a depressant on profit margins; and as a rival for discretionary expenditure. Clearly the organisation is concerned with assessing to what extent substitutes may interfere with an organisation's activities and how might such risks be minimised. It is also interested in discerning if its products could find new markets as substitutes for some other product.

The organisation is also interested in assessing the extent and intensity of competitor rivalry that exists in its own industry. Rivalry is based on a number of factors: balance (if the market is shared fairly evenly among competitors there will be rivalry for dominance); slow growth (especially at maturity stage in the life cycle where there is rivalry to become market leader); high fixed costs (competitors will cut prices to increase turnover and this may lead to price wars); differentiation (if there is no differentiation customers are likely to switch between competitors and thus cause rivalry); and high exit barriers (where it is, for example, costly to exit the market, there may be persistence of excess capacity and therefore increased rivalry).

4 Identifying the organisation's competitive position

There are several frameworks of analysis which can help an organisation identify its competitive position. The concept of market life cycle is one such framework. A market for a product/service moves through a cycle of initial development to growth, maturity and decline. Each stage presents different market conditions and can affect competitive behaviour. In a situation, for example, of market growth an organisation would expect to grow through developing its market share while in a situation of market maturity, an organisation might have to grow by taking the market share of competitors. Each strategy requires different competitive behaviours. Information on market growth is therefore important in both formulating and evaluating strategy.

The organisation will also want to know the nature of its competition in terms of identity of its most direct competitors and the basis on which competition is likely to be conducted. Armed with this information an organisation is in a position to assess if a particular strategy is appropriate. A further framework, strategic group analysis, offers the opportunity to map the competitive terrain. The underlying principle is that there are a range of strategic characteristics shared by organisations, for example: product/service diversity; geographic coverage; market segments served; distribution channels; extent of branding; marketing effort; extent of vertical integration; product/service quality; technological leadership; R&D capability; cost position; utilisation of capacity; pricing policy; level of gearing; ownership structure; influence groups; and size.

By associating these characteristics with the organisations in an industry, more finely defined groupings of organisations having similar strategic characteristics can be identified and an organisation, using this analysis, can locate itself as a member of a group or groups. Organisations, it seems, usually compete on the basis of two or three key characteristics, for example, geographic location and size. The analyst is looking to establish which characteristics most differentiate firms or groups of firms from one another and this is used to gain a better understanding of the competitive characteristics of rivals and to assess how easy it would be to move between groups.

A further way to identify an organisation's competitive position is achieved by analysing its market share relative to its competitors. Market share is a measure of market power. To conduct such an analysis the market is broken down into segments and market shares within the segments are examined. The extent to which an organisation has identified and exploited a clear market segment is likely to affect its vulnerability to substitutes, its bargaining power with regard to suppliers and buyers, the threat of entry into the segment and the amount of rivalry encountered. Segmentation of the market must be done from a strategic point of view. The strategic importance of segments could be for several reasons, for example, some segments are more competitive than others, segmentation in a particular way may result in new opportunities for product differentiation, some segments are growing while others are not, and some segments are bigger than others.

5 Identify key opportunities and threats

The organisation uses all the data it has gathered to determine what opportunities and threats face the organisation. Johnson and Scholes warn against taking these as 'absolute', meaning that an opportunity may not be classifiable as such when considered in relation to other variables such as availability of resources, organisation culture and so on. The aim of this step is to develop a strategy that takes advantage of opportunities and avoids the threats. Strategy formation can only take place when the organisation has analysed its capability to deal with its environment.

Capability analysis

Capability can be assessed through an analysis of the organisation's resources. Galbraith and Nathanson (1978) are of the view that an analysis of resource strengths and weaknesses is critical to the strategy formulation process because it helps identify: (a) what types of strategic options are feasible; (b) what the organisation cannot do and (c) particulary in times of environmental uncertainty, the types of resources and skills that the organisation should build for the future.

1 Tangible and intangible resources

Grant (1992) suggests classifiying the main types of organisation resource into two broad categories: tangible (consisting of an organisation's physical and financial assets) and intangible (human skills, technology and reputation). Tangible assests are analysed and evaluated mainly through an organisation's financial records. An assessment is made from the point of view of identifying opportunities for (a) economising on the use of finance, inventories and fixed costs and (b) using existing assets more profitably.

Intangible resources may be divided into human and non-human intangibles. The measurement of human capital is both difficult and complex. See more detailed consideration of the concept in chapter 8 on strategic training and development. The development of an organisation and its ability to respond positively to new opportunities depends on it having knowledge of employee performance in present and past jobs and of their range of skills and abilities. In this respect a human resource information system can be a valuable asset in sustaining an organisation's competitive advantage. Examples of intangible non-human resources are a reputation for quality, customer service/product support and high profile company name and/or brand name. Some of the most consistently profitable organisations are known for having established and safeguarded their core intangible resources.

2 The concept of value chain

A further method of resource analysis is to assess the extent to which value is added at discrete links in the chain of activities which an organisation performs, from the design of a product through to its use by the comsumer. Porter (1985) says that competitive advantage cannot be understood by looking at the organisation as a whole. Each of the activities it performs in designing, producing, marketing, delivering and supporting its product can contribute to its relative cost position and create a basis for differentiation. A cost advantage could stem, for example, from a low-cost physical dis-tribution system or a highly efficient assembly process. Porter suggests the concept of value chain as a tool for analysing sources of competitive advantage. The chain disaggregates an organisation into its strategically relevant activities in order to understand the behaviour of costs and existing and potential sources of differentia-tion. An organisation could gain competitive advantage by perform-ing these activities at less cost or better than its competitors. The value chain is embedded in a larger stream of activities (the value system). Suppliers are upstream of the value system, in relation to the organisation value chain, and they create and deliver the inputs used by the organisation. Additionally, many products pass through the value chains of channels (channel value) on their way to the buyer. Channels perform activities that can affect the buyer as well as the organisation's activities. The product eventually becomes part of its buyer's value chain. An organisation's value chain and the manner in which it performs the activities in its chain reflect its history, strategy, approach to implementing its strategy and the underlying economics of the activities in themselves.

Value is the amount buyers are willing to pay for a good or service and it is measured by total revenue gained by the organisation, calculated on the basis of price and total sales. An organisation is profitable when the value it commands exceeds the costs involved in creating the product. The value chain is illustrated in figure 3.2 below.

Value activities in the value chain use purchased inputs, human resources and technology in the performance of their function. They use and create information and also create financial assets or liabilities. There are two categories of activity: primary (those involved in the physical creation of the product and its sale and transfer to the buyer, including after-sale service), and support

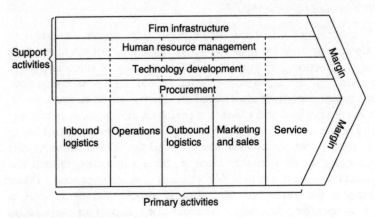

Figure 3.2 The value chain
Source: Porter, 1985

(those which assist the primary activities and each other by providing purchased inputs, technology, human resources and various organisation-wide functions). The dotted lines in figure 3.2 reflect the fact that procurement, technology development and human resource management may be associated with specific primary activities as well as support of the entire chain. Firm infrastructure supports the entire chain and is not associated with specific primary activities.

There are five primary activities identified by Porter: inbound logistics (activities involved in receiving, storing, and disseminating inputs to the products, for example, inventory control); operations (activities concerned with transforming inputs into their final form, for example, machining); outbound logistics (activities associated with collecting, storing and distributing the product to buyers, for example, delivery vehicle operation); marketing and sales (activities associated with providing a means by which buyers can purchase the product and encouraging them to do so, for example, sales force activity) and service (activities which enhance or maintain the value of the product, for example, parts supply).

There are four support activities. Procurement refers to the function of purchasing the inputs for the organisation's value chain. Improving the purchasing process can have a strong effect on the cost and quality of purchased inputs as well as to the activities associated with their use. Technology development is linked with every value activity (know-how, procedures, technology associated with process equipment, etc.) and its activities are aimed at improving the technologies used in any aspect of the value chain.

Human resource management supports both primary and support activities and the whole value chain through the application of its processes for recruitment, hiring, training, developing and rewarding all those involved with the organisation. Human resource management affects competitive advantage through its role in determining the skills and motivation of employees and the costs of recruitment and training. One problem is that the costs associated with human resource management are not well understood and these require development. The firm infrastructure includes activities such as general management, planning, finance, accounting, legal, government affairs and quality management. These activities can be a powerful source of competitive advantage, for example, the contribution to cost advantage made by effective management information systems.

3 Analytical methods in resource analysis

Johnson and Scholes (1989) also see the value chain concept as an important analytical method in resource analysis. Their categorisation of these methods: value chain analysis; comparative analysis and assessing balance, are discussed below.

Value chain analysis consists of: resource audit; measures of resource utilisation and measures of resource control. In the view of Johnson and Scholes, value chain analysis takes the process of resource analysis beyond a simple listing of resources and provides an audit in which resources have been linked with the organisation's strategic purpose. In addition to this audit is also necessary to have data on how resources have been utilised and controlled. The value chain provides the database which, when subjected to further analysis, will enable understanding of the strategic capability of the organisation to be reached. They point out that the concepts of efficiency and effectiveness are useful measures for analysing resource utilisation. Efficiency is concerned with how well resources have been utilised. Effectiveness of resource utilisation can be significantly influenced by the organisation's ability to get all parts of the value chain working in harmony. It is a key managerial task and is concerned with developing and sustaining a culture of attitudes and values amongst those in the value chain so that there is a common understanding of purpose and agreement on which activities are critical to success. An organisation needs also to investigate the extent to which its resources are being properly controlled. It is possible for example to have good quality resources which are being used efficiently but are producing ineffective performance because they are poorly controlled. The whole of the value chain should be investigated for signs of poor control. Examples of resource control areas are: key personnel (individuals or departments may be operating in ways which run counter to the needs of the organisation as a whole); costing (lack of understanding of how good costing can influence the profitability of the company); and quality of materials (ensuring quality at all value chain links such as the components or materials from suppliers).

Comparative analysis consists of historical analysis and comparison with industry norms and experience curve analysis. An historical analysis of how an organisation has deployed its resources in the past provides opportunity to gain knowledge from the past and may reveal trends which may lead to a reassessment of strategy. The analysis can utilise both financial ratios and qualitative data. An organisation can improve the utility of such analysis by considering similar data for its own industry, other industries and those in other countries. Comparative data will enable the organisation to judge its relative competitiveness. One drawback is that the maintenance of such profiles is both difficult and expensive. Experience curve analysis is based on findings from a consultancy organisation, the Boston Consulting Group (BCG) which concluded, from studies of company performance, that there is a direct and consistent relationship between the aggregate growth in volume of production and declining cost of production. The principles underlying the concept are: the level of organisation learning (job performance improves over time and, as experience increases, labour costs should decline at about ten to fifteen per cent each time cumulative experience doubles); specialisation (as the scale of production increases it becomes possible to divide jobs into increasingly specialised units so that doing a small part of a job more often permits a further decline in labour costs); and scale (the capital costs of financing additional capacity reduce as capacity increases). Since cost, considered in this way, is a function of experience then, by extrapolation, it is also a function of market share. Viewed in this way, gaining and retaining market share is a very important source of competitive advantage. Experience curve analysis is a useful qualitative comparison of an organisation's resource situation in relaton to competitors in terms of cost efficiency.

Assessing balance of resources consists of product portfolio analysis, skills analysis and flexibility analysis. Consideration of the extent to which an organisation's resources are balanced as a whole is an additional issue in resource analysis. Portfolio analysis enables an organisaton to judge if its mix of products, services or businesses is balanced across the organisation in terms of security/risk, allocation of resources and resource strengths. The organisation can use the approach to locate each of its products/services/businesses on a matrix which has axes of business growth rate and relative market share, classifying them into rapidly growing/strong market position (stars), high market share/low growth (cash cows), low growth/low market share (dogs), and high growth/low market share (question marks). See figure 3.3. The portfolio analysis approach draws on the concepts of product life cycle and experience curve. A 'star' may be spending in order to gain market share but the effect of the experience curve should mean that costs are reducing over time and ideally at a faster rate than competitors so that it should become self-sustaining. The 'question mark' may be spending to increase market share but the experience gained is not sufficient to reduce

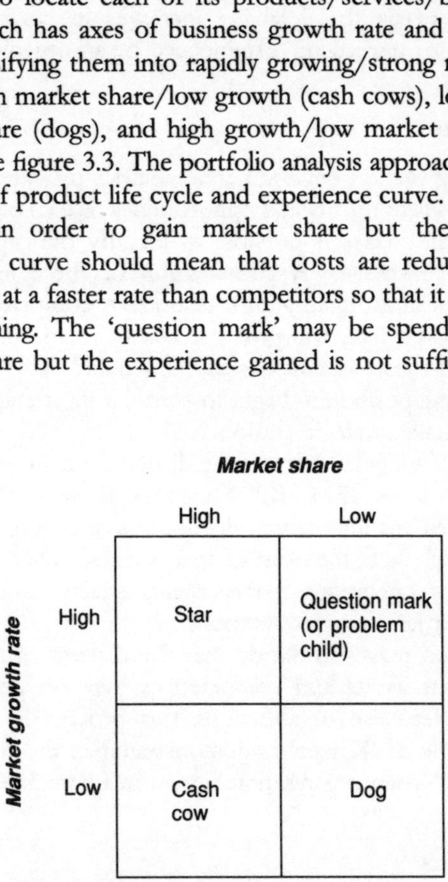

Market share

	High	Low
High	Star	Question mark (or problem child)
Low	Cash cow	Dog

Market growth rate

Figure 3.3 Product portfolio
Source: Johnson and Scholes, 1989

costs quickly enough. Its utility and future are doubtful. The 'cash cow' is in a mature market where conditions are more stable and the need for heavy spending is less. High market share means that experience continues to grow and thus costs can be reduced. It is therefore a source of cash for the organisation. The 'dog' has the worst combination of conditions and may be a cash drain on the organisation.

A skills analysis will enable an organisation to judge if it has the balance of skills needed to run its business effectively. It also needs to know if it has sufficient flexibility and adaptability in all its resources. The needs for flexibility increases in correspondence with the degree of uncertainty experienced by an organisation.

Strategic choice

In the foregoing section environmental analysis provides the basis for considering which threats and opportunities face an organisation. Capability analysis makes it possible to identify the organisation's strengths and weaknesses. A combination of these leads to an understanding of the organisation's distinctive competences,, that is, those strengths which will give the company an edge over its competitors and those weaknesses to be avoided. This places the organisation in the position to begin to consider its strategic options and ultimately make strategic choices.

Morden (1993) suggests that it is the distinctive competences that organisations such as IBM, BP, Mercedes Benz or Sony have developed in their manufacturing, distribution and operations staff and systems which lie at the heart of their success. They have made the processes of operations management, quality assurance and added value their key strategic weapons.

An organisation may also decide that the process of developing and improving its assets and competences may, on principle, be continuous. In Japanese organisations this process is known as 'Kaizen'. The role of 'Kaizen' is demonstrated in the frameworks used within the Nissan organisation shown in figure 3.4 below.

Strategic options

An organisation's options include basic generic strategies, alternative directions for pursuing strategy, and the methods to be adopted to achieve its aims.

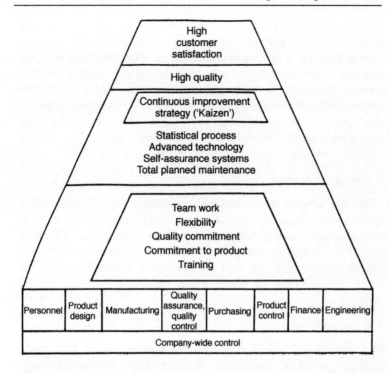

Figure 3.4 The Nissan Triangles
Source: Morden, 1993

1 Generic strategies

Porter (1980) proposes that there are three generic strategies, (cost leadership, differentiation and focus) which can be used singly or in combination to create a   defendable position from which to out-perform competitors. An organisation trying to follow a cost leader-ship strategy will seek economies of scale and pursue learning curve reductions in costs. It will minimise and control costs in all aspects of its value chain activities. Low cost relative to competitors is the main theme of this strategy. A differentiation strategy will involve an organisation in creating something that is perceived throughout industry as being unique. A differentiation strategy does not allow an organisation to ignore costs but they are not a primary aim. In a focused strategy an organisation concentrates on a particular buyer group, segment of the product line or geographic market. The basis of the strategy is the view that an organisation is able to serve its narrow strategic target more effectively or efficiently than competitors who are competing more broadly. In following a focused strategy an organisation can utilise either differentiation, cost leadership or both generic strategies in the service of its particular target. Each generic strategy differs in terms of its requirements for skills, resources, organisation structures and systems, etc.

2 Strategic alternatives

There are various alternatives an organisation may consider when deciding upon future strategy. In considering strategic alternatives an organisation is dealing with the issue of strategic change (Thompson, 1990). Some organisations are entrepreneurial and actively seek change while others wait until circumstances dictate the need. The range of alternatives are noted below:

'Do nothing'

The organisation takes a decision to continue with its existing strategies, whether or not these are successful. The decision might be taken after careful consideration or it may be due to lack of strategic awareness, laziness, complacency, etc.

Internal growth strategies

There are four internal growth strategies:

- **Concentration**   The efforts of the organisation are concentrated on a limited combination of technology–customer–product. The organisation works at doing better what it already does well.
- **Market development**   The organisation markets its present products with some modifications and range increases to customers in related market areas. It may make changes in distribution and advertising in support of the strategy.
- **Product development**   The organisation makes substantial modifications or additions to present products in order to increase their market penetration among existing customer groups.
- **Innovation**   The organisation replaces existing products with new ones and thus enters new product life cycles.

An organisation which has a number of products or business units could be applying one or more of the growth strategies at the same time.

External growth strategies

There are four categories of external growth strategy:

- **Horizontal integration** An organisation acquires or merges with another firm positioned at the same stage in the value chain.
- **Vertical integration** An organisation acquires a company which either supplies raw materials or components or is a customer (perhaps distributor or assembler) of its products/ services.
- **Concentric diversification** An organisation moves away from existing products and markets but the new products/services may relate to these in terms of technology or marketing. The assumption is that the new diversified company will gain in strengths and opportunities while reducing its weaknesses and risks.
- **Conglomerate diversification** Diversification, in this case, is chosen for its investment potential. It is unrelated to existing and new products, services and markets. It is a high risk choice because the new technologies, skills and markets involved are unknown and uncertain.

Disinvestment strategies

There are four main categories of disinvestment:

- **Retrenchment** This is an option when an organisation is experiencing declining profits for reasons such as, economic recession, production inefficiency and competitor innovation. In order to improve efficiency the organisation engages in cost reduction (e.g. redundancies); asset reduction (selling-off anything which is not essential) and revenue generation (from debtor and stock turnover ratios)
- **Turnaround** A turnaround strategy may follow on from re-trenchment which has released resources for re-allocation. In a turnaround strategy activities such as strategic refocusing for a product/service; re-allocation of managerial talent or product/ service modification may be adopted.

- **Divestment** If retrenchment fails or is considered inappropriate, a decision to divest a part of the business may be taken. It is the most likely strategy when an organisation needs to raise money quickly or when a particular product/service or business does not fit well with an organisation's portfolio.
- **Liquidation** The strategy represents disinvestment in its most extreme form, when a company is sold as a going concern either completely or in parts.

3 Strategic means

An organisation needs to combine its choice of a strategic alternative with the means of achieving this. It may decide upon:

- **Organic growth** In this method of achieving strategy the organisation pursues its chosen strategy through its own internal efforts perhaps through reinvestment of profits and/or developing its strengths and capabilities.
- **Acquisition, merger and joint venture** These methods are likely to be used if an organisation is lacking in a particular success factor for a market.
- **Franchising** In this method a company enters into a contract with a number of small businesses. In return for a lump sum investment and on-going royalties a franchisor provides a franchisee with exclusive rights to supply a product or service under the franchisor's name and in a particular area. The deal would usually include know-how, equipment, materials, training, advice and advertising and permits the franchise company to grow rapidly without corresponding capital investment.

Strategic evaluation

Strategy may be evaluated against a number of criteria. Thompson (1990) suggests 'appropriateness, feasibility and desirability' and using slightly different terminolgy Johnson and Scholes (1989) suggest 'suitability, feasibility and acceptability'.

1 Suitability To what extent do the proposed strategies overcome the resource weaknesses and environmental threats identified in the strategic analysis, exploit the organisation's strengths and environmental opportunities, and fit in with its objectives?

2 Feasibility To what extent is the strategy capable of being implemented? The question must be asked in relation to, for example, achievement of performance, achievement of market position, dealing with competitive reactions, and availability of funding, skills and technology.

3 Acceptability To what extent has the strategy the ability to satisfy the expectations of the organisation's stakeholders? This question should be considered, for example, in terms of profitability, level of risk, and effect on capital structure.

Thompson (1990) lists various evaluation techniques which are of use in assessing whether a particular strategic option is appropriate, feasible and desirable.

- Swot analysis
- Planning gap analysis
- Porter's industry analysis and competitive advantage frameworks
- Investment appraisal techniques using discounted cash flows:
  Net present value
  Internal rate of return
  Payback
- Cash flow implications
- Breakeven analysis
- Sensitivity analysis
- Portfolio analysis
- Scenario modelling
- Simulations of future possibilities using PIMS

IMPLEMENTATION AND CONTROL

The state of strategy implementation

Bourgeois and Brodwin (1984) provide an interesting perspective on the historical evolution of the process of strategic implementation which culminates in growing awareness of the fact that it is, increasingly, unrealistic to separate formulation from implementation. Their research also underlines the centrality of the chief executive to the whole process.

Organisations, in their view, have been traditionally divided into 'thinkers' and 'doers'. They identify five process approaches. A 'commander' model is traditional rational–economic in nature. It is characterised by the use of strategic planning under the control of a chief executive who has the sole power to command implementation. This was the first model in the evolution of the planning process. A 'change' model followed as a response to the failure of strategic planning in some organisations. The chief executive makes use of a range of behavioural science techniques to help change take place. A 'collaborative' model attempts to enhance implementation by broadening participation. It extends the decision-making to the top coalition in the organisation. The chief executive acts as coordinator to develop a senior management team who contribute to strategic decision-making. There has to be recognition of a fine balance between the status quo of economic rationality and the increased need to accommodate the viewpoint of the various interests among the top coalition.

The 'cultural' model aims to carry strategy to the lower levels of the organisation as a means of obtaining commitment. The chief executive guides the organisation by communicating and instilling a vision of the mission of the organisation. The tools of the 'cultural' model are the use of symbols, leadership style, communication of shared values, and the use of collaborative teams and quality circles. The 'crescive' model (Latin *crescere*, to grow) is one in which strategy comes up from the bottom of the organisation. The chief executive encourages management at lower levels to develop, champion and implement sound strategies. The chief executive sets broad decision premises and leaves room for innovation. He/she selects from among projects or strategy alternatives that come to his/her attention. Strategic management under the 'crescive' model depends on the chief executive's ability to attain a fine balance between autonomous strategic behaviour at lower levels with maintenance of control at the top. Bourgeiois and Brodwin think that it is essential to develop ability to nurture this sort of entrepreneurship in organisations. It is, they feel, the key to the next generation of strategic management. The five models are not mutually exclusive, but a means of thinking about the range of options open to a chief executive. Contingent factors will be the degree of diversification, the rate of growth and change and the existing culture. The models represent an increasing attention to bringing implementation forward in the strategic management process. The first three models assume implementation after the fact. The number of formulators are few and the remainder of the organisation is somehow manipulated into implementation. In the 'cultural' model the large amount of time invested in consensual decision-making pays off with easier and faster implementation. In the 'crescive' model by the time the strategy has emerged it is also virtually in its implementation. They see a growing acceptance of formulation and implementation as simultaneous rather than separate activities, a trend particularly suited to environments characterised by frequent and/or unpredictable change.

A number of findings in relation to strategy implementation emerged from the review of literature in chapter 1, in relation to the implementation phase of strategic management. Briefly, it has been seen that:

• There has been a false dichotomy between formulation and implementation of strategy.
• Strategy implementation has been neglected relative to strategy formation.
• There are many variables associated with strategy implementation.
• Analysis of these variables has suggested a rationalisation to consist of structure, processes and systems.

It has been concluded that strategy implementation is in need of further theoretical development. Barnett and Wilsted (1988) point to the wide range of structural, systematic and procedural alternatives which confront management when trying to implement strategy. The result is a complex web of 'new strategy, current structure, and leadership style'. Many interacting and important variables offer many different solutions and each situation has several 'right answers'. Management, having based its formulated strategy on the organisation's distinctive competences (the matching of the organisation's strengths with both a market opportunity and with a comparative advantage over its competitors) will endeavour to select implementation alternatives that will support and strengthen these. If for example, an organisation has a distinctive competence in high technology, it will select an organisation structure and control system which encourages innovation and research. Its assessment and reward systems will provide incentives for new developments and its culture will support a climate of research and professionalism. Moreover, the organisation will seek to achieve congruence between these various elements of implementation.

It has been seen in chapter 1, that, as often as not, the control phase in models of strategic management has been integrated with the implementation phase. In terms then of what has been said above and as has been seen at the beginning of the chapter, the state of the art in relation to organisation effectiveness, the control phase is also in need of attention. The purpose of strategic control, according to Sharplin (1985), is to monitor and evaluate progress and to guide or correct the process or change the strategic plan. Boseman, Phatak and Schellenberger (1986) suggest six steps in control: establishment of standards of performance; measurement of performance against performance standards; diagnosis of deviation from standard; initiation of corrective action; feedback from internal and external environments; and continuation of performance monitoring. This area is fraught with problems. Control has traditionally been performed by monitoring past circumstances. This has limited utility when the 'real' time may be different and the future unpredictable. In similar vein, behavioural science demonstrates that standards of performance and criteria for their measurement in relation to human behaviour present difficulties of control which have yet to be overcome.

The way forward

If therefore, as seems apparent, implementation and control have, too frequently, been left to just 'happen', a similar lacuna in personnel management/HRM has left it in need of a strategic role. This realisation has led, in chapter 2, to the development of a model of strategic human resource management. This model, from awareness of the false dichotomy between formulation and implementation integrates the newer concept of strategic management with HRM. A concept of capability planning consisting of structure, systems and processes is utilised both in the formation of strategy and in the design of implementation. The strategic human resource management planner/designer requires a deep understanding of structure, systems and processes.

The reality, however, is that, while knowledge and skills in relation to structure, systems and processes exist, it is fragmented. In order to advance the development of strategic human resource management it will be necessary to bring together the tools and techniques of strategic management with those that are available in HRM and general management. Generic theories of strategy formation such as Miles and Snow (1984) and Porter (1985) offer organisations a way to conceptualise their competitive environment but these require much fuller development from a HRM perspective in terms of obtaining a match with HRM support activities. Similarly, while there has been some effort in the HRM literature to develop the strategic planning techniques, such as the product life cycle, product market portfolio, and experience curve analysis, in terms of HRM activities such as selection, there are others which could be explored. Concepts of organisational development and motivation are already being utilised in organisational interventions such as culture change. However, many interventions such as quality circles, team working, multi-skilling, etc. have been introduced piecemeal. Nutt (1989) recommends organisations to take a contingency approach to implementation interventions. He has identified four categories of implementation tactics: intervention, persuasion, participation, and edict, drawn from 50 cases of strategic planning carried out by organisations. Retrospectively, each tactic was found to have some degree of success and his research has moved on to attempt to identify conditions under which each tactic can be most effective. The intervention tactic is derived from the concept of change agent in which a manager becomes an agent of change by taking over key steps in the strategic management process, regulating and controlling social and political issues. In the participation tactic a manager initiates planning in relation to a specific option and delegates the development of this to a group, carefully selected so that key points of view and information are represented. This tactic has its origins in the view that participation generates commitment. In a persuasion tactic a manager delegates the development of ideas consistent with strategic direction to 'expert' technical staff. The 'expert' persuades the manager of the benefits of the resultant plan. In an edict implementation tactic the use of power rather than process is dominant. Managers use rewards and coercion as well as the more subtle forms of power based on information, expertise, and charisma. Nutt suggests that a contingency approach to choice of tactic be adopted depending on the needs of a situation. He proposes a framework in which a series of questions are posed in a decision tree format which lead the manager to determine a preferred implementation tactic for a given situation.

CONCLUSION

In terms of strategic management therefore, there is, at present, no ultimate blueprint for the process. As the bottom line is survival then an effective process is of critical importance. This means that an organisation must achieve a match with its environment while securing both efficiency and effectiveness internally. As the literature indicates, organisations when involved in strategic management, are dealing in complexity, human perspectives and values. As has also been seen the leadership role appears to have central importance. If a 'transformational' leader is charged with aligning people with an organisation's mission and vision, this can prove difficult when strategic implementation has been neglected and when other important areas such as effectiveness and leadership are not conceptually well developed. The area, it is generally agreed, is in need of development. Greater coherence must be brought to bear on what is currently known so that a genuinely holistic approach to strategic management may be taken. The consequences of the alternative is reflected in the quotation below.

> Many . . . 'best-laid plans' are failing to see the light of day. Plans to innovate fizzle out after a series of task-force meetings; plans to improve quality get no farther than some airy rhetoric and the hiring of a 'quality guru'; . . . in short many of our strategies just aren't happening. Without successful implementation, a strategy is but a fantasy.
>
> Hambrick and Cannella (1989: 278)

REFERENCES

Abegglen, J. C. and Stalk, G. (1985) Kaisha, The Japanese Corporation, New York: Basic Books.

Adair, J. (1985) 'Leadership – be helmsman and navigator, but stay out of the engine room'. *International Management*, June.

Ansoff, I. and McDonnell, E. (1990) *Implanting Strategic Management*, Hemel Hempstead Prentice Hall International.

Banner, K.D. and Blasingame, J.W. (1988) 'Towards a developmental paradigm of leadership' *Leadership and Organisation Development Journal*, 9(4) p: 7–16.

Barnett, J.H. and Wilsted, W.D. (1988) *Strategic Management: Concepts and Cases*. Boston: PWS-KENT.

Bennis, W. (1984) 'The 4 competencies of leadership', *Training and Development Journal*: 5–8.

Boseman, G., Phatak, A. and Schellenberger, R.E. (1986) *Strategic Management: Text and Cases*, New York: John Wiley & Sons.

Bourgeois, L. J. and Brodwin, D.R. (1984) 'Strategic implementation: five approaches to an elusive phenomenon', *Strategic Management Journal*, 5: 241–64.

Bowman, C. and Asch, D, (1987) *Strategic Management*, London: Macmillan Education Ltd.

Cameron, K. (1980) 'Critical questions in assessing organisational effectiveness', *Organisational Dynamics*, 9(2): 66–80.

Cameron, K. (1981) 'Construct space and subjectivity problems in organisation effectiveness', *Public Productivity Review*, 5(2): 105–121.

Cameron, K. (1986) 'A study of organisational effectiveness and its predictors', *Management Science*, 32 (1): 87–107.

Campbell, J.P. (1976) 'Contributions research can make in understanding organisational effectiveness', *Organisational and Administrative Sciences*, 7(1&2): 29–45.

Campbell, A. and Tawadey, K. (1990) *Missions and Business Philosophy: Winning Employee Commitment*, Oxford: Heinemann Professional Publishing.

Certo, S. and Peter, J.P. (1991) *Strategic Management: Concepts and Applications*, Singapore: McGraw-Hill.

Connolly, T., Conlon, E.J. and Deutch, S. J. (1980) 'Organisation effectiveness: a multiple constituency approach', *Academy of Management Review*, 5(2): 211–19.

Drucker, P. (1979) *Management: Tasks, Responsibilities, Practices*, London: Pan.

Gaertner, G.H. and Ramnarayan, S. (1983) 'Organisational effectiveness: an alternative perspective', *Academy of Management Review*, 8(1): 97–107.

Galbraith, J.R. and Nathanson, D.A. (1978) *Strategy Implementation: The Role of Structure and Process*, St. Paul, Minnesota: West Publishing Co.

Goldsmith, W. and Clutterbuck, D. (1984) *The Winning Streak*, Harmondsworth: Penguin Books.

Grant, R.M. (1992) *Contemporary Strategy Analysis: Concepts, Techniques, Applications*, Oxford: Blackwell Business

Hambrick, D.C. and Cannella, A.A. Jr. (1989) 'Strategy implementation as substance and selling', *Academy of Management Executive*, 3(4): 278–85.

Hofer, C.W. and Schendel, D. (1978) *Strategy Formulation: Analytical Concepts*, St Paul, Minnesota: West.

Johnson, G. and Scholes, K. (1989) *Exploring Corporate Strategy: Texts and Cases*, Hemel Hempstead: Prentice Hall International.

Ivancevich, J.M. and Matteson, M.T. (1993) *Organisational Behaviour and Management*, Homewood, IL and Boston, MA: Richard D. Irwin.

Lowe, E.A. and Soo, W.F. (1980)'Organisational effectiveness – a critique and proposal', *Managerial Finance*, 6(1): 63–77.

Miles, R.E. and Snow, C.C. (1984) 'Designing strategic human resources systems', Organisational Dynamics, 13(1): 36–52.

Morden, T. (1993) *Business Strategy and Planning: Text and Cases*, Maidenhead: McGraw-Hill.

Nutt, P.C. (1989) 'Selecting tactics to implement strategic plans', *Strategic Management Journal*, 10: 145–6.

Peters, T.J. and.Waterman, R.H. Jr. (1982) *In Search of Excellence*, New York: Harper Row.

Porter, M.E. (1980) *Competitive Strategy: Techniques for Analysing Industries and Competitors*, New York: The Free Press.

Porter, M.E. (1985) Competitive Advantage: Creating and Sustaining Superior Performance, New York: The Free Press.

Quinn, J.B. (1988) 'Strategies for change' in J.G. Quinn, H. Mintzberg, and R.M. James, (eds) The Strategy Process: Concepts, Contexts and Cases, Englewood Cliffs, NJ: Prentice Hall International.

Quinn, R.E. and Rohrbaugh, R.E. (1981) 'Competing values approach to organisation effectiveness', Public Productivity Review 5(2): 122–40.

Richards, M. (1978) Organisational Goal Structures. St Paul, Minnesota: West.

Rowe, A.J., Mason, R.O., Dickel, K.E. and Westcott, P.A. (1987) Computer Models for Strategic Management. Reading, Mass: Addison-Wesley.

Sharplin, A. (1985) Strategic Management, Singapore: McGraw-Hill.

Starkey, K. and McKinlay, A. (1993) Strategy and the Human Resource: Ford and the search for competitive advantage, Oxford: Blackwell.

Steers, R.M. (1975) 'Problems in the measurement of organisatonal effectiveness'. Administrative Science Quarterly, December, 20: 546–58.

Strasser, S., Eveland, J.D., Cummins, G., Deniston, O.L. and Romani, J.H. (1981) 'Conceptualising the goal and system models of organisational effectiveness – implications for comparative evaluation research', Journal of Management Studies, 18(3): 321–40.

Thomas, J.C. (1988) Strategic Management: Concepts, Practice, and Cases, New York: Harper & Row.

Thompson, J.L. (1990) Strategic Management: Awareness and Change, London: Chapman and Hall.

Tichy, N.M. and Devanna, M.A. (1990) The Transformational Leader, New York: John Wiley & Sons.

Van Setters, D.A. and Field, R.H.G. (1990) 'The evolution of leadership theory', Journal of Organisational Change Management, 3(3): 29–45.

Webster, J.L., Reif, W.E. and Bracker, J.S. (1991) 'The manager's guide to strategic planning tools and techniques'. Planning Review, 17(6): pp: 4–13, 48.

Zammuto, R.F. (1984) 'Comparison of multiple constituency models of organisation effectiveness', Academy of Management Review, 9(4): 606–16.

Chapter 4

Strategic structures

INTRODUCTION

Organisations are collections of people brought together for a purpose. To achieve this purpose successfully, people need to be organised within the best possible structure. Decisions on structure are primary strategic decisions. Structure can make or break an organisation.

Rapid change in their environment has major implications for the structure of organisations. The business news contains frequent references and comment on household name organisations which are having to change their shape and direction. Terms such as 'downsizing', 'de-layering', and 'decentralisation' have entered everyday language. This chapter considers the issues relevant to the design of more successful structures, and the following chapter then examines the related issues of culture and change.

STRUCTURE AND STRATEGY

Until recently conventional wisdom amongst authorities on business strategy has been that decisions on structure should be made following the development of corporate strategy, and not as part and parcel of strategy, hence the phrase 'structure follows strategy'. The purpose of structure has been seen as facilitating the achievement of strategic objectives. It has been assumed that organisations have a relatively free hand in designing their structure, that issues of structure impose few or no constraints on strategy, and that structure is not a primary strategic consideration. This approach has been particularly linked with the name of Alfred Chandler. Following a study of nearly one hundred of America's largest firms over the period 1890 to 1959, including companies such as Du Pont, General Motors, and Standard Oil of New Jersey, he wrote 'A new strategy required a new or at least refashioned structure if the enlarged enterprise was to be operated efficiently . . . unless structure follows strategy, inefficiency results' (Chandler, 1962).

Note Chandler's reference to the 'enlarged' enterprise in this quotation. Organisation growth remained fashionable until the late 1970's. But because of the economic and social pressures already alluded to in earlier chapters which arose in the 1980's, many authorities now consider that 'small is beautiful' and that 'downsizing' should be the order of the day.

The idea that structure should follow strategy dies hard. This approach is still taken intuitively by many chief executives and top managers, who tend to attach primacy to financial and marketing decisions, relegating structure to a secondary role. But in recent years this sequence of strategic decision making has been challenged (Mintzberg, 1990). It is now recognised that most organisations cannot be treated as 'greenfield' sites where management has total freedom to decide what kind of structure it would like. The reality, it is argued, is that there exists only a limited number of options (Johnson and Scholes 1989, Thompson 1990). The history of the enterprise, its culture, and its environment act as major constraints on financial and marketing decisions, and should therefore be considered from the outset. For banks, building societies, local government authorities or manufacturing plants to take sensible strategic financial and marketing decisions that will prove to be successful, structural issues need be considered at the same time.

STRUCTURE AS A PRIMARY CONSIDERATION

Today some authorities go further than this, and see structure as not just a constraint or a vehicle for strategy, but as providing significant competitive advantage. Get your structure right, they argue, and an appropriate strategy will then emerge. In the new era of international competition and rapid change, so this argument runs, productivity, cost-effectiveness, and market penetration can only be achieved by new style organisations. Organisations now require structures which will unleash the full potential of employees, who will as a result make the appropriate financial marketing and production or service decisions. The best known advocate of this approach is Tom

Peters. In his recent book *'Liberation Management'* he answers a question about the importance of management priorities thus:

> 55 per cent for structure, 30 per cent for systems, .15 per cent for people, and nought for top management decision making and strategy setting . . . call in the best consultants and create the best strategies. It will make no difference unless the arteries are unclogged (the 'structure' part), and then radically rewired (the 'systems' part).
>
> (Peters 1992)

Many would not go all the way with Tom Peters. There are grave dangers in advocating a universalistic philosophy or formula that should be applied to all organisations. This repeats the basic mistake of the Scientific Management movement that was so dominant in the first half of this century. But most authorities now agree on the significance of structure.

It is important to remember from the outset that reorganisation sets in train social change and psychological stress, with accompanying feelings of trauma and insecurity. These need to be catered for, if they are not to impact on performance. It is not unusual for example, for those staff who survive a downsizing exercise to feel guilty that they have survived. In addition structural change needs to be seen in the context of the total process of organisation re-design, which involves issues of culture and the successful implementation of change, dealt with in the next chapter.

We now turn to the options available to management when taking strategic decisions on structure, and the relevant considerations to be taken into account.

TYPOLOGY OF ORGANISATION STRUCTURES

Small organisations, such as family run firms, tend to have very simple structures, with the owner as the boss, and employees reporting directly to the owner. 'Not for profit' small organisations such as charities and religious groups also tend to cluster round one charismatic figure, who may be the founder, and as they get bigger, set up committees to manage affairs on a day to day basis. But once organisations start employing scores of people there arises a need for some sort of structure even if they aim to keep formality to a minimum.

Traditional functional structures

As organisations grow and employ more people, so they employ specialists. At this stage it appears sensible to group these specialists together in their own departments, and to link the departments together in some kind of formalised structure reporting to a chief executive. As numbers continue to grow, control appears to be the principal problem, and so rules for processes and procedures are laid down, and greater authority status and power are taken by those at the top. Thus is created the traditional functional structure typified by the organisation charts at one time so popular in manufacturing companies, representing a hierarchy, with directors and senior managers at the top, and shop-floor workers at the bottom.

This type of structure was advocated by the so-called 'Scientific Management' writers in the first half of this century. Associated with famous names such as F W Taylor, the founder of Work Study, they laid down a number of principles of organisation design, some of which are still popular with senior managers today. In a simplified form, these are listed below.

Concepts such as 'line' management are still popular today, and the term 'line manager' is in common use. Whilst 'line manager' is frequently used to describe a direct reporting relationship, in scientific management terminology it referred to the management of so called 'line' departments. These were the departments that generated cash-flow and profits, such as production and sales. Accounting and personnel were seen as 'staff' or supporting departments, providing

---

1 Group employees together by specialism and function within discrete departments.
2 Operate the organisation as a hierarchy, with power at the top, operating through a chain of command.
3 Ensure each employee reports to only one superior.
4 Limit the spans of control of managers and supervisors to not more than eight persons.
5 Describe, and limit the scope of jobs, in written job descriptions.
6 Categorise departments as either 'line' or 'staff' departments. Staff departments provide support to line departments.

Figure 4.1 Scientific management's principles of organisation design

a service to the 'line'. Line departments were considered to be preeminent.

Special versions of functional structures were developed in large bureaucratic organisations, such as the Civil Service and Local government. Here there was even greater emphasis on hierarchy and control, job descriptions, specialisation, and the detailed procedures that came to be called 'red tape'.

Different structures have good and bad points, and may be more or less relevant to particular situations. Functional structures and scientific management provide us with orderly well regulated organisations, where people 'know their place', where there are clear career structures, and where top management possess authority and have an overview of the whole structure. However these structures can become inflexible, promote conflict and poor communications between departments, become out of touch with the needs of customers, over-bureaucratic, and unable to respond to changes in the environment. Seminal research by Burns and Stalker into the British electronics industry in the late 1950s, which makes good reading even today, indicated that this type of structure was appropriate in a stable but not in a dynamic environment (Burns and Stalker, 1966). More recent studies have supported this conclusion (Kanter, 1983).

Divisional structures

As organisations become larger still, employing thousands rather than hundreds, it has made sense to many employers to adopt a divisional structure. These divisions usually reflect the different products and services offered. Thus IBM at one time had different divisions marketing mainframe and desk-top computers, and BT had different divisions based upon overseas markets, domestic consumers, and large business customers. (BT'S new structure is described later in case study 2.) The argument for this is that the different types of business are best served by different groupings of employees, who can focus on a particular set of customers and their needs. An alternative type of divisional structure adopted by some organisations is geographic divisions, whereby for example, the country is divided into regions, and each region operates as a division. A major construction firm like John Laing operates through a number of regional offices.

However the composition of each division is still based on

traditional functional structures, with each division simply replicating the original structure. This requires a headquarters office which coordinates the different divisions, sets them targets, monitors their performance, and provides central services such as purchasing, information technology, and management development programmes. The strengths and weaknesses of traditional structures are replicated at divisional level but with the advantage that this structure moves employees closer to the customer, and with the danger that head office can become too large, bureaucratic, and remote.

Matrix structures

A matrix structure formalises team working by drawing staff from different specialisms, and is therefore radically different from a functional structure. In order to accomplish specific projects, and to overcome problems created by internal politics, poor communications, and the jealousies that frequently come about because staff in functional structures identify first and foremost with their own specialist departments, matrix structures place staff from different specialisms under a project leader. In its most common form, staff are located intermittently in a 'home base', which is their functional departments, but 'loaned' for varying periods to a project group. They are are then accountable to the project group leader for the duration of the project. A matrix structure in a successful chemical engineering design company is shown in figure 4.2.

More complex versions of matrix structures are possible, and are particularly to be found in large international organisations, where staff may report to both functional, geographic, and project heads simultaneously. Research on matrix structures indicates that they can be very effective where specific tasks have to be achieved, project leaders are well trained and have the power and resources to reward and motivate staff, and an appropriate culture of team working has been developed (Davis and Lawrence, 1978, Cooke-Davies 1990). However, conflict may develop between functional heads and project heads, and staff may play one boss off against the other, and as a result, clear accountability may be lost.

Flexible structures

As we have noted, traditional organisation structures tend to be rigid, being based on the need to weld together large numbers of full

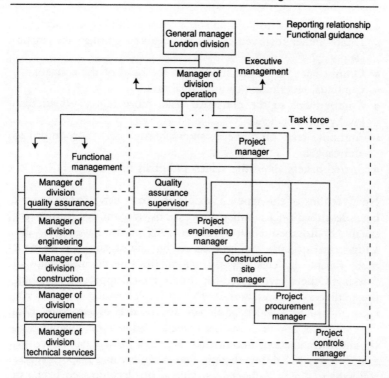

Figure 4.2 A project task force/management matrix in an engineering design organisation

time employees. As the pace of change in the environment has increased – technological, economic, social and political change being the most significant – so ways have been sought to make organisations more flexible. Similarly in military history flexible fighting forces, including 'guerilla' armies such as the *Chindits* fighting behind Japanese lines in the last war and the North Vietnamese fighting the Americans and South Vietnamese in Vietnam, have had the edge over formalised and inflexible armies in situations where the terrain has been difficult, change the order of the day, and surprise in attack essential. The research report by Burns and Stalker already referred to came to the conclusion that 'organic' forms of structure were more appropriate to rapidly changing environments (Burns and Stalker, 1966). Organic structures include the following characteristics:

- A network structure of control, authority, and communication
- Lateral rather than vertical communications through the organisation
- Omniscience no longer imputed to the head of the concern
- Continual redefinition of individual tasks
- Commitment to the concern's tasks more highly valued than loyalty and obedience
- Authority rests on whoever shows himself (*sic*) more informed and capable
- Shared beliefs about the values and goals of concern.

New versions of this type of flexible and responsive structure have been described on a number of occasions over the last thirty years, notably by Rosabeth Kanter (Kanter, 1989). Some have argued that a functional structure can be retained, but the organisation be made more flexible by changing the culture to suit the new ways of working. Others have argued for a more radical approach, scrapping the traditional organisation chart, and implementing a 'free form' type of structure which is almost an absence of structure. One version of this approach has been labelled 'adhocracy', characterised by low formalisation, decentralisation, high horizontal differentiation, low vertical differentiation, and flexibility and responsiveness (Mintzberg, 1983). Adhocracies depend on decentralised teams of professionals for decision making. Fast growing IT firms are frequently put in this category, such as Hewlett-Packard, Applied Data Research and Digital. In these organisations most employees are well educated professionals, and power flows to those considered to possess the necessary expertise, regardless of position or rank. Specialists work together in flexible teams that have few rules, and coordination between teams is by mutual adjustment. Adhocracies stimulate creativeness and cooperation, but because of their deliberate ambiguity there exist many opportunities for conflict, and these can lead to social stress and psychological tension. Employees in these organisations have to be able to cope with a large measure of uncertainty.

A flexible structure which recognises the trend towards employing fewer permanent full time employees and more employees either on short-term contracts or on part-time or on self-employed status, is described by Charles Handy as a 'Shamrock' organisation (Handy 1988). A Shamrock organisation resembles the three leafed plant after which it is named by having three categories of people working for it. The first category is the professional core, the managers, supervisors, technical and professional staff who perpetuate the organisation and hold the organisational knowledge required to do key jobs. These people have permanent contracts and power, and in turn are expected to devote their working lives to the organisation. Secondly there are people on short service contracts, consisting of individual experts, small specialists groups, and subcontractors. And thirdly there are the part-time workers, taken on to cope with peaks and troughs in demand and seasonal pressures. These last two groups are cheaper to employ than long-term core employees, and can be laid off quickly during times of recession. Each of these groups needs to be treated differently and possess different degrees of loyalty to the organisation. The advantages lie in flexibility and reduced labour costs, the disadvantages in lack of commitment by staff to the employer.

A similar concept is the 'flexible firm'. This has been described by the Institute of Manpower Studies as encompassing three types of flexibility – functional, numerical, and financial (Atkinson, 1984). Functional flexibility refers to the capability of employees to switch between different tasks, as with multi-skilled craftsmen or assembly teams, where problems of job-demarcation have been overcome. Numerical flexibility refers to the ability to take on or release staff at short notice, assisted by greater use of subcontractors and short-term contracts. Financial flexibility refers to flexible pay systems based on local conditions, rather than nationally negotiated contracts resulting from collective bargaining. As with Handy's 'Shamrock' organisation a core group of employees is envisaged who provide continuity surrounded by staff on a variety of flexible contracts. The structure is depicted in figure 4.3.

Inverted structures

As indicated earlier, traditional organisation structures represent a triangle with the chief executive located at the apex, and shop-floor workers at the base. The growing realisation that customer care is critical, that quality products and services rest on the effort and commitment of shop-floor workers, that customer relations depend on the behaviour of those staff who interact directly with customers, and that the modern role of the manager is to create conditions in which staff can optimise their performance has led some organisations to invert their structures and to include

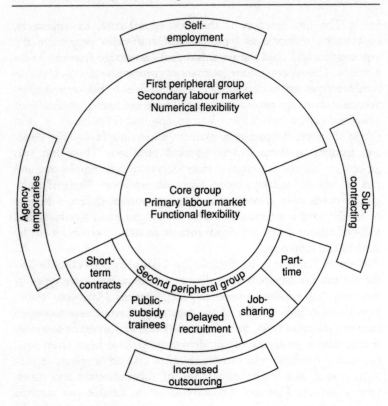

Figure 4.3 The flexible firm
Source: Atkinson, 1984

customers on organisation charts. A good example of this is provided by the Carnaud–Metal Box (CMB) organisation chart devised at the time of the merger between the two companies in the late 1980s. This is depicted in figure 4.4.

There is all too frequently a credibility gap between the official organisation structure depicted on the organisation chart and the reality of what actually happens. But where this approach is genuine it raises interesting questions of power and authority. If there truly is an inversion of the structure, and not just a cosmetic exercise, managers can no longer rely on traditional forms of authority and position power. They are in the situation of having to earn loyalty and trust. Furthermore the organisation now relies on commitment

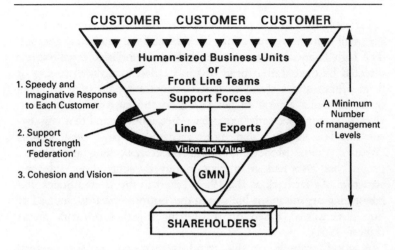

Figure 4.4 CMB's inverted pyramid: a mind-set for all our organisational thinking

to corporate objectives rather than fear of punishment and obedience to the boss to drive things forward. This is a tall order for most organisations, and likely to meet strong resistance. Yet it remains a possible strategy for organisations that have of necessity to become customer focused or perish, and many facets of this approach are to be found in organisations that have fully adopted a TQM culture.

It is instructive to note that CMB encountered severe problems in attempting such a radical approach. Not least of the problems was overcoming the differences between French and British organisational cultures, which in turn reflected differences in national culture. This is a theme we shall return to in the next chapter, because culture is all too frequently overlooked as a critical factor in the design and review of organisations.

'Small is beautiful' – structures based on small units

Size has its advantages and disadvantages. In human resource management terms, size permits sophisticated manpower planning, career planning, large central staff development budgets, job rotation programmes for executives, and the feeling of security for employees that comes from working for a large organisation. This is now changing as big organisations shed staff in 'downsizing' exercises.

Probably the biggest push towards organisation structures based on small units has come about for financial and marketing reasons. The high financial costs of running large monolithic organisations directed by over-staffed head offices has led to savage pruning of head offices and a trend to federal structures consisting of small operating units aiming to get closer to the customer. Moreover, studies of employee satisfaction have frequently found that employees feel less satisfied and more alienated in large organisations (Weaver, 1980). Modern emphasis on teamworking and project groups has also had an impact in our thinking about size and structure. As far back as the 1960s Likert in the United States was advocating organisations built from the 'bottom upwards', instead of 'top downwards', based on the linking together of work teams (Likert, 1961).

A good example of this trend is provided by Tom Peters' advocacy of such structures. He asserts 'Overall size is largely irrelevant for competitive advantage', and then goes on to say

almost all big firms are working overtime to try and act like small firms. Competitive pressures, out-of-whack costs, enlightened application of information technology, the still volatile 'market for corporate control' (that is, the threat of raiders), and new found obstreperousness of outsider board members (demanding executive accountability) have all conspired to induce big firms to try and get into fighting trim: shed misfitting bits of portfolios, create more autonomous subsidiary units, hack away at central staffs and group staffs and division staffs.

(Peters 1992)

Peters argues that two primary forces – globalisation and information technology – mean that speed and flexibility are becoming of paramount importance, and new units will usurp traditional management structures, liberating individuals in the process. An organisation Tom Peters is fond of citing as a successful example of his theories is the company ABB (Asea Brown Boveri), described later in this book in case study 5.

The case for structures based on small units is supported by contemporary marketing and human resource management theory. Both disciplines rest heavily on theories about human behaviour. The available evidence is that people are more likely to be motivated and productive as well as 'close to customers' if they operate in small groups (Steers, 1979). For some types of organisation these are now paramount considerations. But what about institutions such as the Civil Service and Local government, which are traditionally large scale and bureaucratic in structure? And what about 'high-tech' organisations such as Glaxo and Beecham, which rely heavily on applied research, and therefore require large laboratories and development units? In practice many of these organisations are also now attempting to achieve some of the benefits of downsizing by decentralising structures and putting more emphasis on team working, without going as far down the road as companies like Asea Brown Boveri.

However there does exist a danger that a highly decentralised structure based on small groups may eventually lose cohesion and loyalty, encouraging centrifugal forces. This can lead to groups of employees leaving to set up their own independent companies, taking their know-how and contacts with them. Additionally, tight technical control procedures do not fit easily with a structure based on decentralised units. The need to produce items to very tight specifications, using advanced technology, requires an appropriate organisation structure. In companies like Nissan which are based on highly trained work teams, procedures are tightly controlled. The trend in these types of organisation is towards team working, as described in case study 8 on the Rover company.

CENTRALISATION AND DECENTRALISATION

Decentralisation has probably been the most popular trend in structural change within organisations over the last 10 years. As far back as 1984 a survey of British organisations by the Institute of Personnel Management found considerable evidence of a move to decentralisation, partly in response to the pressures imposed by the 1980–81 recession and Thatcherist monetary policies (Cowling and Evans, 1985). The explanations given by British firms for decentralising included the need for decisions to be made nearer to markets or work groups, better communications, greater motivation and enthusiasm amongst staff, better highlighting of the performance of individual managers, and a breaking down of the departmental rivalries and functional barriers found in centralised bureaucracies. It is interesting to note that the one exception to this trend was in a national chain of supermarkets that had opted for greater centralisation, on the grounds that new developments in information technology, including electronic point of sale techniques (EPOS) enabled the centre to make the right purchasing and re-stocking decisions based on up to date and accurate information on what was happening in supermarkets many miles away.

STRUCTURE, POWER AND POLITICS

The issue of centralisation versus decentralisation is not simply one of rational decision making concerning best possible structures. In real life it is also frequently to do with the twin considerations of decision making and power. Top management very often wish to protect their power position, and are therefore reluctant to delegate, clinging to centralised decision making. Under pressure they may concede some of their power by insisting that all decisions are made in accordance with central policy directives and a strategic framework, whilst allowing unit managers a degree of freedom in making operational decisions in pursuit of the defined strategy. But today more organisations are likely to go so far as to encourage units to determine their own strategy as long as financial targets are met and units adhere to company philosophy.

Power is a subtle issue. Power and politics dominate the hidden agendas of most organisations. Nice tidy rational models for making the correct strategic decisions expounded in the classical approaches to strategy, referred to in earlier chapters, are seriously flawed in their neglect of power as a key variable (Whittington, 1993). The central elite in most organisations are understandably keen to retain power and the principles that go with it, and this will influence their views on centralisation or decentralisation of decision making (Pettigrew, 1985). This is one reason why it so frequently takes a crisis of major proportions to force organisations to restructure, and possibly to decentralise. A newly installed chief executive may deliberately develop his or her power base by decentralising the structure, at the same time limiting the power of senior managers to resist innovations and change.

Centralised decision making offers the possible benefits of consistency, uniform coordination, control, and speedy decisions. On the other hand it has the possible disadvantages of an inability to respond flexibly to local conditions, distance from the customer, cumbersome execution, costly central bureaucracy, poor communications and ignorance of the true feelings of employees. Decentralised structures offer possibilities of rapid response to local conditions, closeness to customers, low overhead costs, better inter-personal relations, and greater motivation. The downside may be a repetition of mistakes made in other parts of the organisation, a lack of consistency, the inability to call on the assistance of central resources and expertise, shortened career structures, and frustration caused by complex control structures and policy decisions.

CONSIDERATIONS IN CHOOSING AN APPROPRIATE STRUCTURE

As has already been indicated, there exists no such thing as a perfect structure − only structures that are more or less appropriate to prevailing circumstances. Organisation theorists writing in the 1960s developed the concept of a 'contingency' approach to organisation design (Lawrence and Lorsch, 1967). This approach sees organisation design responding to so called 'key' contingency variables, of which the most obvious include size, technology, social and legal environment, markets, and past history and culture. This view of organisations achieving some kind of appropriate match with their environments has been a persistent theme amongst writers on strategic management until the present time, and is supported by a degree of logic, for an organisation which does not match some critical facet of its environment is likely to have problems in that direction. However thinking has changed on certain of these key contingencies in the last decade (Mintzberg, 1979). Size is a case in point. It used to be assumed that large size necessarily implied a bureaucratic and formal structure, largely on the basis of a prevailing correlation at the time between size and bureaucracy. However, as indicated earlier in this chapter, it has now been demonstrated that large organisations can successfully downsize, de-layer, and decentralise into small operational units, as illustrated later in case study 5.

Technology has been frequently cited as a factor in determining structure, particularly in manufacturing, where mass production has been held to equate with large mechanistic type structures and unit or craft production to equate with small more flexible structures (Woodward, 1965). This has also been largely turned on its head, first by innovative organisations such as Volvo doing away with assembly line manufacture in favour of team working and subsequent adoption of Japanese practices such as just in time (JIT) and related flexible methods. We have also noted how information technology has led to greater centralisation in retail firms.

The social and legal environment continues to be an important consideration. A case in point is the Thatcherite legacy of privatisation, which means for example that local authorities have had to adapt their structures in quite radical fashion to cope with legal requirements for compulsory competitive tendering (CCT). This is illustrated later in case study 6 featuring two local authorities.

Markets have increased their significance for organisation design in recent years as international competition has grown, and customers have demanded a better quality service, hence the quest for organisations that are 'closer to the customer'. As noted, market turbulence creates pressures for decentralisation. In the light of these developments, the application of key contingency variables to organisation design needs to be modified by a consideration of the overall corporate strategy being adopted.

NATIONAL CULTURES AND ORGANISATION STRUCTURE

Until comparatively recently the term 'organisation structure' meant only one thing when applied to major Western organisations – a hierarchical and functionally based structure encompassing many levels of management, based on prescriptive authority and communications. This system, comments Kenichae Ohmae, perpetuated a major weakness in separating thinkers from doers, and information collectors from strategists. Most Japanese organisations lack an organisation chart. 'Honda with a $5 billion turnover, is obviously quite a flexible strategy-oriented company capable of making prompt and far reaching decisions. Yet nobody knows how it is organised, except that it employs project teams very frequently' (Ohmae, 1982).

Thinking on structures in the West has now changed radically. IBM's Anthony Cleaver recently observed that nine out of ten large organisations had removed at least one level of management within the last five years. IBM has cut three of its seven levels. Permanent jobs are a thing of the past. But only a minority of organisations in the West have as yet succeeded in integrating thinkers with doers and information collectors with strategists. This is an essential step on the path to total quality and continuous improvement.

STRATEGIES AND STRUCTURES

Two models of strategic management which have been particularly influential in recent years in influencing thinking on organisation structures are outlined briefly below.

1 The Miles and Snow model

A classic typology of strategy and structure is provided by the Miles and Snow model, which puts forward four strategic types from which top management may choose (Miles and Snow, 1978). These types are 'Defenders', 'Prospectors', 'Analysers' and 'Reactors', illustrated in figure 4.5.

Defenders produce a limited set of products within a well defined segment of the market, and then seek to defend their patch against all-comers. They attempt to do this by competitive pricing and paying attention to efficiency, but ignore new developments and innovation outside their narrow focus. This is a low risk strategy and

Characteristics	Defender	Strategic Types Analyser	Prospector
Environment:	Stable	Moderately changing	Dynamic, growing
Strategy:	Seal off share of market Protect turf Advertise to hold customers	Maintain market but innovate at edges. Locate opportunities for expansion while protecting current position	Find and exploit new market opportunities Scan environment, take risks
Internal characteristics:	Efficient production: Retrench Tight control Centralised, mechanistic	Efficient production, yet flexibility for new lines. Tight control over current activities, looser for new lines	Flexible production Innovation and coordination Expansion Decentralised, organic

Figure 4.5 The Miles and Snow model

Source: Adapted from Raymond E. Miles, Charles C. Snow, Alan D. Meyer, Henry J. Coleman, Jr., (1978) Organizational strategy, structure, and process, *Academy of Management Review* 3: 546–62, with permission.

is associated with conservative beliefs. Their organisation's structures emphasise centralised control, formality, and hierarchy.

Prospectors aim to find and exploit new products and market opportunities, and are therefore constantly scanning their environment and adopt high risk strategies. Since flexibility is crucial in this type of activity their structures are flexible, decentralised, informal, and based on small units.

Analysers attempt to get the best of both worlds, minimising risk, but maximising opportunities for profit. They move into new markets only after careful preparation, in the wake of smaller, more innovative prospector-type organisations. They therefore adopt organisation structures which are both flexible and stable. Parts of the organisation have high levels of standardisation and mechanisation, whereas other parts are flexible and adaptive.

Reactors represent an unsatisfactory strategic type, organisations that respond late and inadequately to changes in their environment. They represent a model to be avoided, not copied.

2 The Porter model

Michael Porter, a contemporary leading authority on strategy, advises that management must choose from one of three strategies: cost

Competitive advantage

		Lower cost	Differentiation
Competitive scope	Broader target	1. Cost leadership	2. Differentiation
	Narrow target	3A. Cost focus	3B. Differentiation focus

Figure 4.6 Three generic strategies
Source: Porter, 1985

leadership, differentiation, and focus (Porter, 1985). These are illustrated in figure 4.6. Which one management chooses must depend on the organisation's strengths and competitors' weaknesses.

A cost leadership strategy rests on efficiency of operations, economies of scale, technological innovation, low employment costs, and access to cheap raw materials. The best structure for achieving this is a centralised formal one. A differentiation strategy emphasises innovative design, quality, service, technological capability and brand image. This demands a flexible structure, which is, informal and decentralised. A focus strategy aims at a cost advantage or a differentiation advantage in a narrow segment of the market, unlike the first two which aim at a broad range of industry segments. The goal is to exploit a narrow segment of the market. In consequence it must choose one of the two types of structure described above, depending on which is more appropriate to its market.

CONCLUSION

In this chapter we have reviewed the options available in the design of organisation structures, their respective advantages and disadvantages, and their strategic implications. Changing a structure almost invariably requires a corresponding change in values and attitudes. In the next chapter we consider the nature of organisational culture and its relationship to strategy.

REFERENCES

Atkinson, J. (1984) Manpower Strategies for Flexible Organisations, *Personnel Management*, August.
Brennan, R. (1993) *British Telecommunications plc: Facing up to the 90's*, Cranfield: Cranfield Case Clearing House.
Burns, T. and Stalker, G. M. (1966) *The Management of Innovation*, Welwyn Garden City: Tavistock Publications Ltd.
Chandler, A. D. (1962) *Strategy and Structure: Chapters in the History of the American Industrial Enterprise*, Cambridge, MA: MIT Press.
Cooke-Davies, T. (1990) 'Return of the Project Managers', *Management Today*, May: 119–20.
Cowling, A. and Evans, A. (1985) 'Organisation planning and the role of the personnel department', *Personnel Review*, 14(4).
Davis, S. and Lawrence, P. (1978) 'Problems of matrix organisations', *Harvard Business Review*, May–June, 56 (3): 131–42.
Handy, C. (1988) *Understanding Voluntary Organisations*, London: Penguin.

Johnson, G. and Scholes, K. (1989) *Exploring Corporate Strategy, Text and Cases*, Hemel Hempstead: Prentice Hall.

Kanter, R. M. (1983) *The Change Masters*, New York: Simon and Schuster.

Kanter, R. M. (1989) *When Giants Learn to Dance*, New York: Irwin.

Lawrence, P. and Lorsch, J. W. (1967) 'Organisation and environment: managing differentiation and integration', *Division of Research*, Boston: Harvard Business School.

Likert, R. (1961) *New Patterns of Management*, New York: McGraw-Hill.

Miles, R. E. and Snow, C. C. (1978) *Organisation Strategy, Structure and Process*, New York: McGraw-Hill.

Miles, R.E., Snow, C.C., Meyer, A.D. and Coleman, H.J. Jr. (1978) 'Organization, strategy, structure and process', *Academy of Manaement Review*, 3: 546–62.

Mintzberg, H. (1979) *The Structuring of Organisations*, Englewood Cliffs, New Jersey: Prentice-Hall: 233.

Mintzberg, H. (1983) *Structures in Fives: Designing Effective Organisations*, Englewodd Cliffs, NJ: Prentice-Hall.

Mintzberg, H. (1990) 'The design school: reconsidering the basic premises of strategic management', *Strategic Management Journal*, 11: 171–95.

Ohmae, K. (1982) *The Art of Japanese Business*, New York: McGraw-Hill.

Peters, T. (1992) *Liberation Management*, London: Macmillan.

Pettigrew, A. (1985) *The Awakening Giant: Continuity and Change in ICI*, Oxford: Blackwell.

Porter, M. E. (1985) *Competitive Advantage: Creating and Sustaining Superior Performance*, New York: Free Press.

Steers, R. M. (1979) 'Work environment and individual behaviour', in Richard M. Steers and Lyman W. Porter (eds) *Motivation and Work Behaviour*, 2nd edn, New York: McGraw-Hill

Thompson, J. L. (1990) *Strategic Management: Awareness and Change*, London: Chapman & Hall.

Weaver, C. N. (1980) 'Job in the United States in the 1970's', *Journal of Applied Psychology*, 65: 364–67.

Whittington, R. (1993) *What is Strategy, and Does it Matter?*, London and New York: Routledge.

Woodward, J. (1965) *Industrial Organisation; Theory and Practice*, Oxford: Oxford University Press.

Chapter 5

Culture, strategy and change

INTRODUCTION

Developing the right strategy for an organisation is hard work. Implementing that strategy successfully can be even harder, and people usually present the biggest problem. Changing people's behaviour requires a change in organisational culture. This is because the manner in which employees behave is profoundly affected by the norms of conduct which are subtly or not so subtly reinforced by the prevailing culture. In the previous chapter reference was made to the links between structure and culture, and the need to integrate structural and cultural change.

Strategic decisions usually commence with consideration of financial, marketing, operational and structural issues, as described in earlier chapters. Successful implementation however requires an integrated approach, in which culture and behaviour are taken into account in the planned management of change. This point has been made succinctly by Colin Carnall in his comment that

> To manage change effectively involves the ability to create a new synthesis of people, resources, ideas, opportunities and demands. The manager needs skills rather like those of an orchestral conductor. Vision is essential and creativity paramount. Yet the capacity to create systematic plans to provide for the logistics of resources, support, training and people is central to any change programme. People must be influenced, departmental boundaries crossed or even 'swallowed up. New ideas must be embraced.
>
> (Carnall, 1986)

This chapter commences with a consideration of the meaning, definition and significance of corporate culture in the context of human resource strategy, and then reviews ways of implementing strategic change.

INCREMENTAL CHANGE

That all organisations are having to change in order to survive in the face of increasingly rapid change in their environments is now taken for granted by most of us. Most of us in turn would probably favour a gradual process of change that does not create too many shocks and surprises. This approach has been dubbed 'logical incrementalism' by Quinn. Formulated as strategy, this consists of a series of small steps, as strategic decision builds upon strategic decision (Quinn, 1980). This incremental approach is seen as logical, because managers are not and cannot be aware of all the influences that might possibly affect the future of the organisation, and major leaps in the dark are deemed to be illogical. Managers are also aware that strategies in the real world consist of compromises and trade-offs between different groups. To cope with these uncertainties and compromises, strategies must be incremental, with each step being carefully tried out, and with the support of powerful groups at each stage.

However, logical incrementalism may not be enough in this day and age. Crucial factors in the environment may change with such rapidity that a corresponding response is called for, necessitating traumatic change in the quest for survival. The process of incremental change may overlook changes in the environment until it is almost too late. IBM was by most standards a well run organisation that was constantly making incremental changes, yet had become too complacent to notice that its domination of the computer market had been undermined by smaller, leaner, but more dynamic suppliers, capitalising on new technology and access to compatible computer languages. Xerox Corporation, ICL and International Harvester are well known examples of successful organisations that had to initiate radical change in order to survive. Facing bankruptcy, International Harvester had to downsize dramatically, restructure financially, and overhaul its corporate culture, in order to re-emerge as Navistar. In the process it succeeded in transforming its culture from being internally focused to being market-orientated.

RADICAL CHANGE

Radical change processes are being taken even further today, with a focus on 'reinvention', and 'reengineering'. Reinvention has been described 'as not changing what is, but creating what is not'. (Goss, Pascall, and Athos, 1993), and reengineering as a 'fundamental rethink and radical redesign of business processes to achieve dramatic improvements in critical contemporary measures of performance, such as cost, quality, service and speed' (Hammer and Champy, 1993). Such radical change clearly carries a high risk of failure, and requires a very incisive and well planned strategy of change, including culture change, if it is to be successful.

However, the risk of not undergoing radical change may be even greater. The need for major change may arise because the incremental change favoured by managers may not be sufficient to meet the threat of competition. Gerry Johnson suggests that it is prevailing culture that so conditions managerial thinking that the threat of competition is not taken sufficiently seriously. He describes this as 'ideational culture, which creates an organisational "paradigm", embracing assumptions about the nature of the organisational environment, the managerial style, the nature of its leaders, and the operational routines seen as important to ensure the success of the organisation'. 'It is this paradigm which, in many organisations, creates a relatively homogeneous approach to the interpretation of the complexity that the organisation faces.' (Johnson, 1992). Prevailing company culture can blind us to the reality of what is happening. Because of this, suggests Richard Whittington, outsiders frequently have to be brought in when a crisis develops in order to achieve a major turnaround. 'Studies of corporate "turnarounds" following periods of organisational decline repeatedly confirm the necessity of hiring new chairmen or chief executives in order to achieve strategic change and recovery.' (Whittington, 1993). We return to the role of outsiders in implementing strategic change and fashioning a new culture later in this chapter.

IN SEARCH OF EXCELLENCE

'Culture' became something of a 'buzz-word' during the 1980s in management circles, when it became fashionable to talk about changing an organisation's culture. The primary cause of the interest in culture was the success of Japanese manufacturers, and the

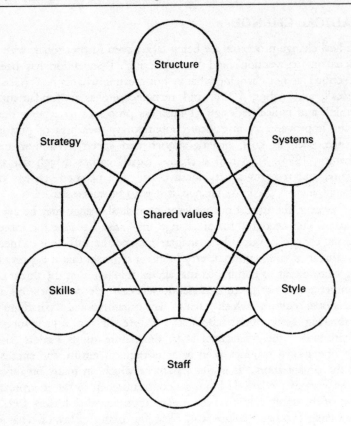

Figure 5.1 McKinsey 7-S framework

assumption that their superiority was in part due to a supportive national and corporate culture. The book which more than any other publication helped to foster this interest in corporate culture was *In Search of Excellence*, written by Tom Peters and Robert Waterman, now a classic of management literature. (Peters and Waterman, 1982). Based on a study of so called 'excellent' American Corporations, Peters and Waterman concluded that the key to excellence lay in achieving a state of shared values amongst all the employees in an organisation. They concluded that Western management had been placing far too much emphasis on the so called 'hard Ss' of strategic decision making, namely issues to do with structure, systems, and strategy itself. Excellent American (and Japanese) firms however placed equal emphasis on the so-called 'soft Ss' of staff, style and skills, with a special emphasis on shared values. This is illustrated in figure 5.1 depicting the well known McKinsey '7-S' framework.

It soon became fashionable, particularly amongst academic critics, to point to the deficiencies in Peters and Waterman's analysis. A number of the American companies portrayed as 'excellent' could no longer be deemed to be excellent a few years later. For example, Walt Disney went through a period of producing unsuccessful films, Caterpillar lost a major share of its market for heavy plant machinery, and Atari, well known for its computer games, suffered severe losses, and the case of IBM has already been referred to. However these failures did not diminish the interest in corporate culture as a key to achieving success.

As well as placing an emphasis on shared values, Peters and Waterman promulgated a number of 'rules of thumb' for achieving excellence, many of which have passed into the vocabulary of managers everywhere. These include:

- A bias for action
- Close to the customer
- Autonomy and entrepreneurship
- Productivity through people
- Hands on, value-driven
- Stick to the knitting
- Simple form, lean staff
- Simultaneous loose-tight properties.

Whilst these can be deemed to be simple 'motherhoods',they do underline certain home truths, for example, that productivity can only come through people. Whether these home truths have been fully understood and applied by top management in the UK is another matter. Only a handful of British companies have yet reached international standards of excellence and quality.

A major criticism of the Peters and Waterman approach is that it fosters a continuation of the 'one best way' of managing philosophy perpetrated by scientific management writers in the first half of this century referred to in the previous chapter (Wilson, 1992). All the evidence from major studies of the connection between ways of organising and management, from Joan Woodward's classic study in the 1950s until the present day, show clearly that what may be the right approach for one organisation may be the wrong approach for another (Woodward, 1965).

CONDITIONS FOR SUCCESS

Writers on organisation as well as managers frequently fail to distinguish between 'necessary' and 'sufficient' conditions when attempting to describe cause and effect, and this is particularly important in the case of strategic change. Strategic human resource management is concerned with defining and implementing the 'necessary' human resource strategies for survival and success, but cannot supply, and cannot be expected to supply, 'sufficient' conditions to achieve these aims. There are too many arm-chair critics of practising managers who fail to understand this basic point.

A 'sufficient' condition means that the prescribed consequence will always follow. This state of affairs can be found in the physical sciences, but rarely if at all, in the social sciences, including the practice of management. 'Necessary' conditions on the other hand are those which are essential to a result being achieved, but of themselves do not guarantee a result. It is for example necessary for the majority of companies in the private sector in Western economies to be market-orientated to survive, but being market-orientated is not of itself a guarantee of survival, that is, it is not a sufficient condition. None the less, no one would sensibly deny the importance of marketing. The same can be said of the importance of achieving a high quality well motivated workforce operating within a mutually supportive culture. Such a culture is not a sufficient condition for the success of the enterprise, but is a necessary condition for companies operating in a competitive environment. All British firms of any size achieving and maintaining a standard of international excellence, for any length of time, demonstrate this fact. Excellence in marketing or financial excellence alone is not enough to maintain a premier position year after year. This is particularly the case where organisations are having to face the challenge of change.

PERSPECTIVES ON CULTURE

Peters and Waterman placed an emphasis on shared values, and this has led some people to define culture in these terms. There exist a large number of definitions of culture, depending on where the emphasis is placed, and some of these are reviewed below. Three approaches can usefully be distinguished which are of particular relevance to organisational change. The first is sociological, the second socio-psychological, and the third, managerial. Each one has implications for developing a strategy of change.

The sociological approach focuses on society and societal norms, and has as its purpose the better understanding of national cultures, and society at large. Organisations are viewed as microcosms of the societies in which they are located. The following statements are typical of traditional sociological writing employing a functional framework:

- 'shared norms, values and beliefs are. . . the culture of society'
- 'shared goals help to integrate the activities of individuals in a social system'
- 'but there must be agreement on means as well as ends'
- 'consensus on means (shared norms) together with consensus on ends (values) channel social actions and help to promote integrated systems of action'.

(Cotgrove, 1978)

The implications of this view of the organisation as a social system are that a change in culture requires a change in norms, values, beliefs, and a high degree of consensus amongst employees.

Industrial sociologists in this country have more recently reminded us that different frames of reference can be used in looking at society, culture and organisations. Which frame of reference we use will strongly influence the manner in which we view the workplace. (This point is taken up again in chapter 10 on strategic employee relations.) These distinguish between 'unitary' 'pluralistic' and 'radical' frames of reference (Fox, 1966). A unitary approach prefers to see social groups with shared norms, a pluralist approach emphasises that in reality society (and organisations) are composed of a plurality of groups with different norms, and a radical approach sees society (and organisations) as essentially split between the power elite and the rest ('us and them').

Management writers like Peters and Waterman not unnaturally adopt a unitarist view. Sociologists suggest that the reason why many attempts to impose a unitarist culture on organisations by top management has failed has been because of a lack of recognition that organisations are essentially pluralist in nature, and that the conflict inherent in this situation has to be resolved (Wilson and Rosenfeld, 1990). While sociologists may provide a good understanding of the way in which societies function, they provide limited assistance to managers in their task of beating the competition, improving quality, making unpleasant but necessary decisions that may involve wholesale redundancies, and managing change.

The socio-psychological approach is more pragmatic, and places an emphasis on group dynamics. A group is typically defined as 'an organised system of two or more individuals who are interrelated so that the system performs some function, has a standard set of role relationships among its members, and has a set of norms that regulate the function of the group and each of its members' (McDavid and Harari 1968). As organisations are perceived as being composed of groups, the keys to culture and successful change are seen to lie through changing group norms. Norms are developed and reinforced through work groups, and attitude can only be successfully changed through group processes. There is indeed a body of well-founded research findings to support the significance of groups in changing attitudes and behaviour (see for example, Bass, 1990, Bettenhausen and Muringham 1991, Feldman 1984).

The attractions of a psycho-sociological approach to culture and change is that it offers a pragmatic way to influence attitudes that appeals to managers, and is based on sound research. It finds expression particularly in the process known as organisation development (OD) which is popular with training managers, examined in more detail later in this chapter. Its drawbacks include a failure to tackle social norms developed outside the place of work (for example the 'us and them' theme prevalent in society) and the cost and time involved in developing every single work group in a large organisation.

The third approach is 'managerial' and is essentially pragmatic. It recognises the importance of culture, but argues that behaviour can be directly changed by management and leadership, and doesn't accept that considerable amounts of time and energy need to be expended on changing underlying values and feelings. It favours the popular definition of culture as 'the way things are done around here', and aims therefore to change the way things are done by changing job descriptions, rewards, methods of supervision, and the like, arguing that any necessary culture change will follow. Implicitly this approach rests on a behaviourist version of psychology, where behaviour is seen to be caused by conditioning, and reinforcement, although this theoretical basis in rarely acknowledged. It is naturally attractive to Western managers who are in a hurry to get things done, but its downside is represented by the large number of Western companies who have tried to change their cultures this way and failed miserably in the process, unable to win the 'hearts and minds' of employees from start to finish.

These three approaches to culture find expression in correspondingly different approaches to changing culture. If strategic culture change is to be successful, those responsible for leading the change must decide which approach is most relevant and useful in their particular situation.

DEFINITIONS OF CORPORATE CULTURE

The simplest and probably best known definition of corporate culture is 'the way we do things around here' (Martin Bower, quoted in Deal and Kennedy 1982). This implies that to change culture, managements simply need to change the way things are done. If only life were so simple! More sophisticated management writers refer to the system of shared meanings that distinguish one organisation from another as well as referring to working practices, such as the degree of emphasis on rules and regulations, the encouragement of individual autonomy, the extent of participation by staff in decision making, delegation of authority, emphasis on customer service, and expectation about commitment to the goals of the organisation.

Ed Schein's definition of culture is representative of the social psychologists view. Culture for him is 'the basic assumptions that a given group has invented, discovered or developed in learning to cope with its problems of external adaptation and internal integration' (Schein, 1985). As described in the previous section, traditional sociology sees culture as 'the shared norms and values of members of a social system' (Cotgrove, 1978). A useful synthesis is provided by the following definition:

> The basic values, ideologies and assumptions which guide and fashion individual and business behaviour. These values are evident in more tangible factors such as stories, ritual, language and jargons, office decoration and layout, and prevailing modes of dress among the staff.
>
> (Wilson and Rosenfeld, 1990)

FACTORY CULTURE

The relevance of culture to work organisations had been highlighted in this country by Elliot Jaques well before it was popularised by

Peters and Waterman. Based on his observations and research in a large engineering factory in North West London in 1951, he commented:

> The culture of the factory is its customary and traditional way of thinking and of doing things, which is shared to a greater or lesser degree by all its members, and which new members must learn, and at least partially accept, in order to be accepted into service in the firm. Culture in this sense covers a wide range of behaviour: the methods of production; job skills and technical knowledge; attitudes towards discipline and punishment; the customs and habits of managerial behaviour; the objectives of the concern; its way of doing business; the methods of payment; the values placed on different types of work; beliefs in democratic living and joint consultation; and the less conscious conventions and taboos. Culture is part of second nature to those who have been with the firm for some time. Ignorance of culture marks out the new-comers, while maladjusted members are recognised as those who reject or are otherwise unable to use the culture of the firm.
>
> (Jaques, 1951)

TYPOLOGIES OF CORPORATE CULTURE

A number of typologies of organisation culture have been described by social scientists which are helpful in planning strategic change. Best known of these is probably Roger Harrison's typology, which has in turn been adapted and presented to a British audience by Charles Handy. Roger Harrison describes four cultures, termed the achievement culture, the support culture, the power culture, and the role culture (Harrison, 1972). An achievement culture is based on self-expression, and emphasises growth, success, and distinction. A support culture is based on a sense of community, and emphasise mutuality, value, service, and integration. A power culture is based on survival, and emphasises strength, decisiveness and determination. A role culture is based on a desire for security, and emphasises order, stability, control, and profit. These are illustrated in figure 5.2.

Another frequently used typology describes 'strong' and 'weak' cultures. In a strong culture, members accept core values and have a high commitment to the common cause, and the opposite is the case with a weak culture. However strong culture will only benefit an organisation if the commitment of employees is aligned with the

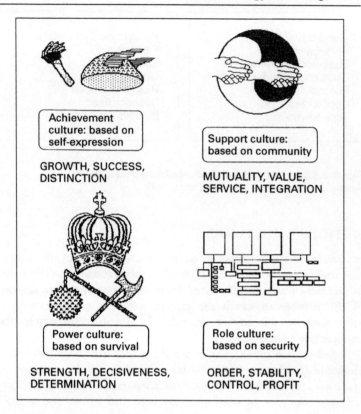

Figure 5.2 Four organisational cultures
Source: Adapted from Harrison, 1972

direction in which the organisation wishes to progress. Changing a strong culture to a different set of work-values is going to be harder than changing a weak culture. None the less, conventional wisdom favours a strong organisational culture, and strategic human resource management programmes frequently aim to build strong cultures (Mowday, Porter and Steers, 1982).

A high proportion of management consultants appear to favour a particular type of culture. Research by Storey and Sisson provides evidence of a contrast between the type of culture found in many contemporary organisations with that recommended by management consultants, to be achieved by strategic change (Storey and Sisson, 1993). This is illustrated in figure 5.3.

Current culture Rule-based Engineering-orientated Customer-avoidance Procedure-focused Centralised Top–down	*Recommended culture* Flexible Market-led Customer service Results-focused Decentralised Bottom–up

Figure 5.3 Old-fashioned and new-fashioned cultures
Source: Adapted from Storey and Sisson, 1993

NATIONAL CULTURES

Human resource strategies in multi-national companies, or companies trading with other nations, need to take account of differences in national culture. Locally based organisations need to take account of the manner in which the culture 'inside' the organisation is influenced by the culture 'outside' the organisation within the surrounding community.

A well known typology of national cultures is provided by Geert Hofstede (Hofstede, 1980). Based on a study of the attitudes of employees of a large multi-national corporation working in forty different countries, he used four criteria to differentiate the national groups. These were, respectively:

- **Power distance** The extent to which society accepts that power in organisations is distributed unequally.
- **Uncertainty avoidance** The extent to which a society feels threatened by ambiguity, and tries to avoid such situations by the use of formality and structure.
- **Individualism/collectivism** The extent to which society prefers a loosely knit social framework or a tight framework with absolute loyalty.
- **Masculinity/femininity** The extent to which values in society are 'masculine' (i.e. assertive, acquisitive and un-caring) or 'feminine' (i.e. caring for others, and for quality of life).

These results scored countries such as the Philipines, Indonesia and Yugoslavia as high on power distance, Austria, Denmark and Israel as low, and the UK as relatively low. Strong uncertainty avoidance was manifested in Portugal, Greece, Belgium and Japan, but not in Denmark, Sweden or Singapore. The UK scored relatively low again on this dimension. Australia, the USA and the UK showed up as individualistic societies, and Pakistan, South America and South East Asia countries as collectivist. Masculine societies included Japan, Italy and Austria, and feminine societies included Scandinavian countries and Yugoslavia, with the UK located in the more masculine group. Not surprisingly, the United States stands out as a highly individualistic and masculine society but low on power distance and uncertainty avoidance.

Other research studies into differences between national cultures have provided broadly similar results (Ronen and Kraut, 1977). A recent international study suggests four broad types of culture, giving rise to four styles of management (Trompenaars, 1993), described graphically as 'the family', 'the Eiffel tower', 'the guided missile', and 'the incubator'. The 'family' model is a power-orientated corporate culture in which the leader is regarded as the caring head of the family who knows best for his subordinates, and is to be found extensively in Japan, France, Italy and India. In the 'Eiffel Tower' model, authority stems from formal roles, and job specifications form a superstructure and a hierarchy, and is typified by large German engineering corporations. A 'guided missile' model is orientated towards tasks and objectives, usually undertaken by teams or project groups, roles are not fixed, and it is based on the view that the organisation should be like a missile homing in on strategic objectives. This framework has been used recently by a number of American, British and Swedish corporations for organisation development purposes. 'Incubator' companies are structured round the fulfilment of the needs and aspirations of individuals, and the management framework exists to free employees so that they can pursue creative activities. This model is typified by California's Silicon Valley.

NATIONAL CULTURE AND MULTI-NATIONAL ENTERPRISES

National cultures are of particular concern to multi-national organisations, and/or organisations aiming to do business in two or more countries. Historically, the simplest example is where an organisation in one country does business with organisations in a foreign country, and possibly sends its own employees to that country ('expatriates') or even takes over a foreign corporation. The history of the British Empire is littered with examples of trade following the flag (and regrettably of many British expatriates and their wives who could not or would not adapt to new cultures). In many cases, expatriates shielded themselves from strange cultures by withdrawing into a ghetto mentality, and setting up exclusive social clubs. However modern corporations can no longer behave in this way, and their strategic human resource planning, including adaptation of employment packages, has to take due account of significant differences in national cultures. Giant American corporations that have in the past attempted to impose their ways of working and structures on foreign subsidiaries have subsequently learned that it pays to plan for a degree of cultural diversity.

The five principal goals and concerns of multi-national enterprises (MNEs) are described by Bartlett and Goshal as global competitiveness, efficiency, local responsiveness, flexibility, and organisational learning (Bartlett and Ghoshal, 1989). Because of intense global competition, MNEs are seeking to identify the methods and processes that are most appropriate (Schuler, Dowling, and De Ceiri, 1993), taking into account local culture, economy, legal systems, religious beliefs, and education. This raises the question of whether it is possible to export modern Western practices of decentralisation and empowerment to more traditional cultures favouring power distance, collectivism, and masculinity. Local managers must develop HR practices that reflect local conditions and culture (Brewster and Tyson, 1991, Mead, 1993).

MNEs must take account of national culture, a key issue in mergers and takeovers. Within the European Community major cultural differences exist which are easily overlooked by those who perceive Europe as having a common cultural heritage. Laurent surveyed managers from 10 Western nations about their human resource management assumptions (Laurent, 1983). He found that French managers typically view organisations as a formal pyramid and hierarchy of power, and that success comes about through 'working the system' by managing these power relationships effectively. British managers hold a less hierarchical view of organisations and achieve success by influencing each other through communications and negotiations. If Laurent's findings are correct, we would expect cultural problems to arise when French and British organisations merge, or when major change programmes are initiated by MNEs in these countries. This has been borne out by studies of mergers between French and British firms. A recent study of top managers in taken-over and merged corporations in these two countries found that national culture imparts a strong influence on the perceived compatibility of French and British organisations involved in mergers (Very, Calori, and Lubatkin, 1993). For example, when a French firm acquires a British firm, the level of competitiveness among organisational members is perceived to increase by the British managers subject to the takeover, consistent with the finding that the French are more competitive amongst themselves than the British. When French firms have been acquired by British companies, French managers perceive a decrease in competitiveness, but also perceive a decrease in emphasis on long term issues. An example is provided by CMB Packaging, the Anglo-French group formed in 1989 through the merger of the old Metal Box company and Carnaud, creating Europe's largest packaging group. (CMB's new structure was shown in the previous chapter.) Unfortunately a clash of cultures at the top level of the newly formed company led to indecision about organisation and strategy. The old British company had operated with a top–down centralised approach, whereas the French favoured a decentralised form of management. The result was a series of crises for the new company before a new form of direction could be established (Munchau, 1991).

The problems likely to arise in cultural integration across European boundaries has been highlighted in an analysis of a Towers Perrin worldwide survey of HRM practices (Towers Perrin 1992) by Paul Sparrow and Jean Hiltrop (Sparrow and Hiltrop, 1994). Taking the key issues of empowerment, promoting diversity and equality, and promoting customer service, this analysis found that the USA, UK, German and French companies gave a high importance to promoting an empowerment culture, in marked contrast to Italy. France and Italy were least concerned about the promotion of diversity and equality, with the USA showing the greatest concern. France was most concerned about promoting customer service, while the USA, Germany and the UK showed similar high levels of concern, and Italy showing least concern.

MODELS OF CHANGE

Human Resource strategies can choose from a number of different models when implementing strategic change. Much of the thinking on change processes has been influenced by Lewin's model for change developed in the 1950s (Lewin, 1962). This well known model is of the socio-psychological type described earlier in this chapter, and is associated with group dynamics and organisation developoment (OD) processes. It takes the sensible line that people are unlikely to change their attitudes and cooperate whilst they feel suspicious of change and set in their ways. Therefore they have to be metaphorically 'unfrozen' before they will consider the arguments for change in a sympathetic manner. Once they have taken on board the new set of attitudes and methods of working, they have to be 're-frozen' into their new state to ensure conformance. Six tactics have been proposed for use by change agents in unfreezing and dealing with resistance to change (Kotter and Schlesinger, 1979).

- **Education and communication** This tactic assumes that the problem lies with a lack of information, or misinformation. Presentations, newsletters and briefings will do the trick. However, this requires pre-existing level of trust and credibility.
- **Participation** If employees are involved in the change process and can have a say in how things are done, they are more likely to cooperate.
- **Facilitation and support** Employee counselling and support by trained staff can help employees to overcome fear, but this is expensive and time consuming.
- **Negotiation** Reward packages and the like can be offered to break down resistance.
- **Manipulation** People can be cynically manipulated, but this is likely to backfire as the truth emerges.
- **Coercion** This does not facilitate unfreezing, but is a method of forcing change that is sometimes used. Threats to those not cooperating of loss of job, pay and status may achieve compliance, but not the degree of cooperation long term required by modern corporations.

A more recent sequence and system put forward by Gerry Johnson and Kevan Scholes seeks to embody the experience of Western organisations in implementing successful change, and embodies much conventional wisdom (Johnson and Scholes, 1993).

- Clear mission and corporate values, which are owned throughout the organisation and relevant to the market.
- A 'loose-tight' system that incorporates analysis, planning and

control, but also encourages organic management, internal competition, a challenging/ questioning approach and experimentation, absence of political elites, flat integrative structures, task forces, project teams, and symbolic communications.

- Support by a visible top management, 'change heroes', an absence of political elites, flat integrative structures, task forces, project teams, and symbolic communication.

Pettigrew and Whipp, based on their study of the way high performing companies manage change, highlight five factors as key to the process (Pettigrew and Whipp 1991)

- **Environmental assessment** Effective strategy creation should emerge from an assessment and processing of information at all levels within the company concerning its environment, that is, the company must operate as an open learning system, not depending on just one specialist function.
- **Leading change** Leadership must be sensitive to, and appropriate to, the context in which change is taking place. The leader has to construct a climate for change while at the same time laying out new directions.
- **Linking strategic and operational change** Intentions need to be implemented and transformed over time, as the effects of operational change become apparent.
- **Human resources as assets and liabilities** HRM relates to 'the total set of knowledge, skills and attitudes that firms need to compete' which has a considerable impact on competitive performance. However this may involve a long term learning approach.
- **Coherence in the management of change** A change strategy must exhibit consistency, consonance, feasibility, and provide for the maintenance of competitive advantage.

Rosabeth Moss Kanter places an emphasis on consensus as the key to successful change and survival, recognising the danger of disruptive internal politics (Kanter, 1992). Life in the 1990s is about response to 'motion in the environment' for all organisations. She recommends eight steps in implementing change.

- Coalition building, assembly backers and supporters
- Articulating a shared vision
- Defining the guidance structure and process
- Ensuring communication, education and training

- Undertaking policy and systems review
- Enabling local participation and innovation
- Ensuring standards, measures and feedback
- Providing symbols, signals and rewards.

A contrast has been drawn in this chapter between the so called incrementalist approach to change and radical change. The latter approach is epitomised by Richard Pascale's 're-invention roller coaster', referred to at the start of this chapter, which he describes as 're-inventing the present for a powerful future' (Goss, Pascale and Athos 1993). This view holds that incremental change is not enough for many companies today, and comments that

> Managers groping about for a more fundamental shift in their organisations' capabilities must realise that change programmes treat symptoms, not underlying conditions. These companies do not need to improve themselves, they need to reinvent themselves. Reinventing is not changing what is, but creating what isn't.

The activities required to achieve this are:

- Assembling a critical mass of key stakeholders, defined as employees 'who really make things happen round here'
- Doing an organisational audit. The first task of these key stakeholders is to reveal and confront the company's true competitive situation, and to uncover the barriers to significant organisational change.
- Creating urgency, discussing the undiscussable. The code of silence that in most corporations conceals the full extent of their competitive weakness must be broken.
- Harnessing contention. This is because 'almost all significant norm-breaking opinions or behaviour in social systems are synonymous with conflict', but participants must learn to disagree without being disagreeable.
- Engineering organisation breakdowns. Organised breakdowns make it possible for individuals and organisations to take a hard look at themselves and confront the work reinvention.

In almost total contrast are Japanese models of change, particularly those incorporated into successful developments in the UK, such as Toshiba, Nissan, Toyota and Komatsu. The last three were 'green-field' site operations, creating new organisations. The first named was a 'brown-field' site, inheriting a large factory in Plymouth (Trevor, 1988). All have been continuously involved with change since inception, and all place great emphasis on Kaizen, or continuous improvement, and benchmarking. Clive Morton describes the Komatsu approach to culture change as creating a cooperative atmosphere (Morton, 1994). Morton describes the process as:

- Constant efforts to improve industrial relations
- Emphasis on training and education of workers
- Developing team leaders among the workers
- Formation of small-group activities such as QC circles
- Support and recognition for workers' Kaizen efforts
- Conscious efforts for making the work place a place where workers can pursue life goals
- Bringing social life into the work place as much as practicable
- Training supervisors so that they can communicate better with workers and can create a more positive personal involvement with workers
- Bringing discipline to the workshop.

(Case study 9 on Komatsu contains a fuller description of this process.)

The successful examples of continuous improvement, with their overtones of logical incrementalism, are a useful reminder that models of radical change are not the only successful paradigm, and that Western preoccupations with traumatic change programmes spearheaded by a handful of top managers might with benefit be the exception rather than the rule.

LEADERSHIP AND CHANGE

As already indicated, a number of models for strategic change underline the importance of good leadership. When staff feel threatened by change, they need confidence in their leadership if their morale is to be maintained. Recent economic history has brought to the fore chief executives who have earned a reputation for successful leadership, usually with a degree of charisma and flair – names such as John Harvey-Jones at ICI, Peter Bonfield at ICL and John Egan at Jaguar come readily to mind. The danger of course is to assume that one man or woman alone can bring about a transformation. Harvey-Jones was quite categorical on this subject.

I do not believe in the myth of the great leader who can suddenly engender in his people a vision and lead them to an entirely new world. I believe that the reality is more traumatic and more demanding, but we all know that there is no substitute for being in a winning team, and are prepared to make quite a lot of sacrifice to ensure that one 'team' does win.

(Harvey-Jones, 1988)

A scientific study of leadership is difficult, not least because leaders have to perform in so many different situations. What soundly based evidence we have from social psychology is based on a measurement of the performance of small groups, operating under different leadership styles. The classic studies of group leadership at Michigan and Ohio State Universities pointed to the significance of a concern for people and a concern for task as two key factors in achieving results, and subsequent evidence has continued to support this (Likert, 1961; Fleishman and Harris, 1962; and Hersey and Blanchard, 1988). The evidence for successful leadership styles in top management positions is harder to establish, but Bernard Bass (Bass, 1985) identified five factors that describe transformational leadership. They are:

- Charisma, the ability to instill a sense of value, respect and pride, and to articulate vision
- Individual attention to followers' needs, and the assignation of projects that help people to grow
- Intellectual stimulation, helping followers to be creative and rethink situations
- Contingent rewards, informing followers on ways to achieve rewards
- Management by exception, not intervening unless goals are not being accomplished in time and on cost.

He adds that in addition to charisma, transformational leaders need assessment skills, communication abilities, and a sensitivity to others. They must be able to articulate their vision, and must be sensitive to the skill deficiencies of followers.

Andrew Pettigrew and Richard Whipp warn against the simplistic expectation of a charismatic and visionary leader leading troops to instant success (Pettigrew and Whipp, 1991). Sensitivity to questions of time and process and the accumulation of more modest preparatory actions is all-important. Based on their research findings, the art of leadership in strategic change, is described as '. . . the ability to shape the process in the long term, rather than direct it through a single episode. Leading change requires action appropriate to its contexts'.

Richard Whittington reminds us that, whilst leadership may be a vital and empowering force in contemporary organisations, it is nevertheless cultural, historical and gender-specific phenomenon (Whittington, 1993). This we should expect from the studies of national cultures examined earlier in this chapter. Anglo Saxon cultures are individualistic, and the English and Americans are particularly fascinated by business leaders. The French do not have an equivalent word to 'leadership' in their language, and the Germans are wary of individual leaders as a result of their political history. We are also prone to define leadership in masculine terms, emphasising the macho and authoritarian qualities, whereas women favour participative methods and forms of empowerment.

POWER, POLITICS AND CHANGE

The successful implementation of strategic change requires both power and political skill. The significance of coalitions and alliance building has already been touched on, but when the forces resisting change in most organisations are considered, the challenge of overcoming these forces can be immense. It is hardly surprising that major change is frequently spearheaded by a newly appointed chief executive. A chief executive is usually appointed because he or she is deemed to possess the vision and skills to point the organisation in the right direction, but the power base is greatly enhanced if there exists a genuine sense of crisis which creates obedience and a sense of unity (Cowling and Evans, 1985).

Social psychologists have analysed the bases of power in organisations. French and Raven's list is frequently quoted: legitimate power (based on position in a hierarchy), control of rewards, ability to punish and coerce, expertise, and charisma (French and Raven, 1959). Research into strategic change frequently shows all these power bases coming into action. Johnson and Scholes add to this list the important power base of control of strategic resources (Johnson and Scholes, 1993). What is currently deemed to be strategic depends on the environment affecting the organisation. They put forward a useful three stage model of change in which power, politics, and the control of resources change with each stage:

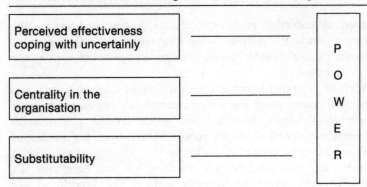

Figure 5.4 A contingency model of power

- Building the power base, requiring control of resources, alliance building, and emphasising legitimate authority.
- Overcoming resistance, requiring tactical withdrawal of resources, breaking down elites, rewarding change agents, and fostering a degree of conflict and confusion.
- Achieving compliance, requiring the giving of resources to new groups, removing resisters, creating heroes, and creating reassurance.

Contingency theories of power provide a good illustration of why certain groups or individuals acquire or maintain power, and therefore have relevance to strategic change. In the Hickson and Hinings model the key factors are centrality to the nature of the business, substitutability, and perceived effectiveness in coping with uncertainty. These are illustrated in figure 5.4, adapted from Hickson, Hinings, Lee, and Pennings, 1971.

The power of the individual or group implementing strategic change, according to this model, will be contingent on whether they are perceived by the stakeholders (employers, shareholders, key customers and suppliers) as being effective in coping with what is a highly uncertain situation, maintaining their centrality to the purposes of the organisation, and ensuring that they cannot be substituted. A serious erosion in any one of these categories will lead to an undermining of their power base, and their position in charge of the change process.

CONCLUSION

It is impossible to separate the study of power in organisations from the study of politics. Driving through strategic change requires political skills of a high order. Political power in organisations is not formally authorised, widely accepted, or officially certified (Mintzberg and Quinn, 1993). Mintzberg describes 13 types of political game within organisations, including insurgency, sponsorship, coalition-building, line versus staff, and whistle blowing (Mintzberg, 1983), all of which can be seen taking place during change programmes.

A contemporary illustration is provided by the National Health Service, where medical groups who feel threatened are creating insurgency, senior managers are seeking sponsorship to buttress their positions, coalition building between professional groups is continuously taking place, line management are frequently having problems with specialist medical staff, and whistle blowing to the press and television is going on continuously. In consequence, chief executives of large NHS Trusts require political skills of a high order if they are to achieve change at the same time as delivering a quality service. The wonder is that a large number succeed, a fact which also points to the importance of the values that underlie much of the work in the health services.

REFERENCES

Bartlett, C. and Ghoshal, S. (1989) *Managing Across Borders*, Boston: Hutchison.

Bass, B. M. (1985) *Leadership and Performance Beyond Expectations*, New York: Free Press.

Bass, B. M. (1990) *Handbook of Leadership*, New York: The Free Press.

Bettenhausen, K.L. and Muringham, J.K. (1991) 'The development and stability of norms in groups', *Administrative Science Quarterly*, 20–35.

Brewster, C. and Tyson, S. (1991) (eds) *International Comparisons in Human Resource Management*, London: Pitman.

Carnall, C.A. (1986) 'Managing strategic change: An integrated approach, *Journal of Long Range Planning* 19(6): 105–15.

Cotgrove, S. (1978) *The Science of Society* (3rd edn), London: George Allen and Unwin: 21.

Cowling, A. and Evans, A. (1985) 'Organisation planning and the role of the personnel department', *Personnel Review* 14(4).

Deal, T. E. and Kennedy, A. (1982) *Corporate Culture, the Rites and Rituals of Corporate Life*, Reading, MA: Addison-Wesley.

Elliot, Jacques (1951) *The Changing Culture of a Factory*, London: Tavistock.

Feldman, D.C. (1984) 'The development and enforcement of group norms', *Academy of Management Review*, January: 47–53.

Fleishman, E. A. and Harris, E. F. (1962) 'Patterns of leadership behaviour related to employee grievances and turnover', *Personnel Psychology*, 15: 43–56.

Fox, A. (1966) *Research Paper Number 3, Royal Commission on Trade Unions and Employers' Association*, London: HMSO.

French, R.P. and Raven, B. (1959) 'The bases of social power' in D. Cartwright (ed.) *Studies in Social Power*, Ann Arbor, Mich.: Institute for Social Research.

Goss, T. Pascale, R. and Athos, A. (1993) 'The reinvention of the roller coaster: risking the present for a powerful future', *Harvard Business Review*, Nov–Dec.

Hammer, M. and Champy, J. (1993) *'Reengineering the Corporation: a Manifesto for Business Revolution'*, London: Nicholas Brealey Publishing.

Handy, Charles (1976) *Understanding Organisations*, Middlesex: Penguin.

Harrison Roger (1972) 'How to describe your organisation', *Harvard Business Review*, Sept–Oct.

Harvey-Jones, J. (1988) *Making it Happen*, Glasgow: William Collins.

Hersey, P. and Blanchard, K. (1988), *Management of Organisational Behaviour*, (5th edn), Englewood-Cliffs, NJ: Prentice Hall.

Hickson, D., Hinings, C., Lee, C., Schreck, R. and Perrings, J. (1971) 'A strategic contingencies theory of intraorganisational power', *Administrative Science Quarterly*, 16.

Hofstede, G. (1980) 'Motivation, leadership and organisation: do American theories apply abroad?', *Organisational Dynamics*, Summer: 42–63.

Jaques, E. (1951) *The Changing Culture of a Factory*, London: Tavistock.

Johnson, G. (1992) 'Managing strategic change – strategy, culture and action', *Long Range Planning* 25 (1): 28.

Johnson, G. and Scholes, K. (1993) *Exploring Corporate Strategy*, (2nd edn), London: Prentice Hall.

Kanter, R. M., Stein, B. A. and Jick, T. D. (1992), *The Challenge of Organisational Change*, New York: The Free Press.

Kotter, J.P. and Schlesinger, L.A. (1979) 'Choosing strategies for change', *Harvard Business Review*, March–April: 106–14.

Lewin, K. (1951) *Field Theory and Social Science*, New York: Harper.

Laurent, A. (1983) 'The cultural diversity of Westerm conceptions of management', *International Studies of Management and Organisations*, 13(1–2): 75–96.

Likert, R. (1961) *New Patterns of Management*, New York: McGraw-Hill

McDavid, J.W. and Harari, M. (1968) *Social Psychology: Individuals, Groups, Society*, New York: Harper and Row.

Mead, R. (1993) *International Management Cross-Cultural Dimensions*, Oxford: Blackwell.

Mintzberg, H. (1983) *Power in and Around Organisations*, Englewood-Cliffs NJ: Prentice Hall.

Mintzberg, H. and Quinn, J. B. (1973) *The Strategic Process*, (2nd edn) New Jersey: Prentice Hall International

Morton, Clive (1994) *Becoming World Class*, London: Macmillan.

Mowday, R. T., Porter, L. W. and Steers, R. M. (1982) *Employee-Organisation Linkages: The Psychology of Commitment, Absenteeism and Turnover*, New York: Academic Press.

Munchau, W. (1991) 'Clashes of culture laced with French dressing', *The Times*, 11 September.

Peters, T.J. and Waterman, R.H. (1982) *In Search of Excellence*, New York: Harper and Row.

Pettigrew, A. and Whipp, R. (1991) *Managing Change for Competitive Success*, ESRC/Blackwell: Oxford.

Quinn, J.B. (1980) *Strategies for Change: Logical Incrementalism*, Homewood, Ill.: Richard D Irwing.

Ronen, S. and Kraut, A. (1977) 'Similarities among countries based on employee work values and attitudes', *Columbia Journal of World Business*, Summer p: 89–96.

Schein, E. (1985) *Organisational Culture and Leadership*, San Francisco: Jossey Bass: 25.

Schuler, R.S., Dowling, P.J. and de Cieri, H. (1993) 'An integrative framework of strategic international human resource management, *International Journal of Human Resource Management*, 5(4): 717–64.

Sparrow, P. and Hiltrop, J. M. (1994) *European Human Resource Management in Transition*, Hemel Hempstead: Prentice Hall International (UK).

Storey, J. and Sisson, K. (1993) *Managing Human Resources and Industrial Relations*, Buckingham: Open University Press.

Towers, Perrin. (1992) *Priorities for Gaining Competitive Advantage: A Worldwide Human Resources Study*, London: Towers Perrin.

Trevor, Malcolm. (1988) *Toshiba's New British Company*, London: Policy Studies Institute.

Trompenaars (1993) *Riding the Waves of Culture*, London: Nicholas Brealey.

Very, P., Calori, R. and Lubatkin, M. (1993) 'An investigation of national and organisational cultural influences in recent European mergers', *Advances in Strategic Management*, 9: 323–46.

Whittington, R. (1993) *What is Strategy, and Does it Matter?* London: Routledge.

Wilson, D.C. (1992) *A Strategy of Change*, London: Routledge.

Wilson, D. C. and Rosenfeld, R. H. (1990) *Managing Organisations*, London: McGraw-Hill.

Woodward, J. (1965) *Industrial Organisation, Theory and Practice*, London: Oxford University Press.

Chapter 6

Human resource planning and human resource strategy

INTRODUCTION

Those responsible for developing a strategy for human resources require up to date information and soundly based forecasts concerning staff and labour markets. Strategies also need to be translated into plans and implemented through procedures. This is where human resource planning can help. Human resource planning has its roots in the manpower planning frameworks developed in the 1970s by personnel and operations management specialists attempting to apply quantitative models and measurements to the employment function. This development was assisted by the introduction of computerised personnel information systems (CPIS) and boosted by the reappearance of skill shortages in the 1980s. Manpower planning allowed staff in personnel departments to demonstrate that they were as sophisticated as their colleagues in marketing and finance when it came to making business plans.

MANPOWER PLANNING

Manpower planning assumed a relatively stable economic and social environment and organisation structure based on bureaucratic principles (Smith and Bartholomew, 1988). These assumptions no longer hold because of the pace of change in the last decade, and the trend to flatter and more flexible organisations described earlier in chapter 4. The term 'manpower' has also fallen out of favour and human resource planning has replaced manpower planning. Contemporary human resource planning is more flexible and responsive to change than manpower planning. Nevertheless, planning still has to take place. Recruitment, training and performance management still needs to be coherent across an organisation and work towards a common set of objectives. Otherwise the organisation comes to resemble a Balkan state, with each department and faction fighting for itself in a culture of continuous crisis management.

HUMAN RESOURCE PLANNING

There is still some debate on the extent to which manpower planning has successfully transformed into human resource planning (HRP). John Bramham argues that

> In HRP the manager is concerned with motivating people – a process in which costs, numbers, control and systems interact and play a part. In manpower planning the manager is concerned with the numerical elements of forecasting, supply-demand matching and control, in which people are a part. There are therefore important areas of overlap and interconnection but there is a fundamental difference in underlying approach.
>
> (Bramham, 1994)

In essence, this resolves itself into a debate on 'hard' and 'soft' approaches to employment, 'quantity' versus 'quality' and 'measurement' versus 'leadership'.

The most recent survey of human resource planning practices in this country was not very encouraging (Cowling and Walters, 1988). While over 60 per cent of the 245 respondents stated that they were systematically identifying future training, retraining, and development needs, and 50 per cent or more were analysing labour costs and productivity and assessing the need for structural change, less than 50 per cent were regularly reviewing the labour market and the external business environment, forecasting the impact of business plans on employee relations and culture, analysing the current manpower stock, estimating the impact of labour turnover, forecasting medium term staffing requirements, and the future availability of staff from within the organisation. Even fewer were assessing the effectiveness of pay and benefit packages and revising HRP practices to meet changing business circumstances. In general, the private sector emerged as being more proactive than the public sector, but altogether the results pointed to an absence of proactive planning in over half the personnel departments surveyed.

MANPOWER MODELS

Planning the intake of labour, and attempting to measure productivity and output, has exercised the minds of managers since the building of the pyramids, and before. However, it was not until the 1970s that mathematical modelling was brought to bear upon the problem, aided by the development of new stochastic techniques that could take account of dynamic processes.

Manpower models traditionally started from the premise that a balance needs to be achieved between the supply and demand for manpower. It was assumed that the demand for manpower could be derived from corporate plans for production (or services). The supply of manpower was derived from two sources of supply – internal and external. The internal supply was represented by the current stock of employees, and the external supply represented by potential employees in the labour market. Reconciliation of supply and demand then formed the basis for particular plans relating to functional areas such as recruitment and training. This process is illustrated in figure 6.1.

Another important function of this modelling process has been an examination of the internal flows of manpower between different levels within the organisation, and between departments. This has been seen as essential to forecasting promotion rates and providing useful information for career planning. The basic assumption in this modelling process has been that the organisation is bureaucratically structured, with a hierarchy of grades, and a career structure based on regular intakes of school and college leavers. Thus the organisation can be depicted as 'pulling' employees through to higher grades

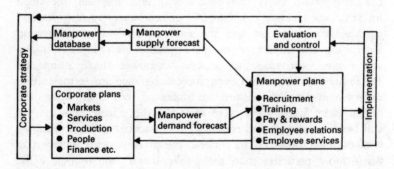

Figure 6.1   Manpower planning, information and control model

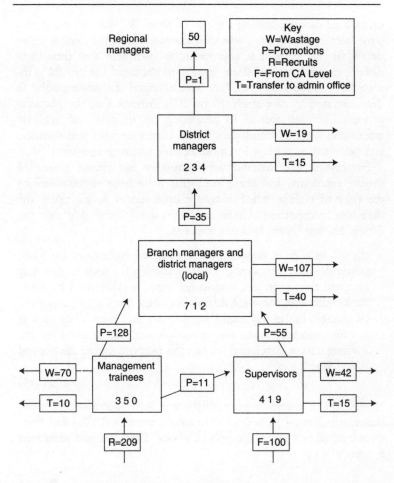

Figure 6.2   Manpower model of a building society

in replacement of those leaving through retirement or (more rarely)
quitting the organisation. This process is depicted in figure 6.2,
based on a manpower model in a large building society.

It may be objected that today few organisations continue as
bureaucratic and hierarchical structures, and that frequent restructuring makes irrelevant any need to forecast and plan internal manpower movements several years ahead. Furthermore, it might be
argued that the trend to smaller decentralised business units makes

centralised career planning a waste of time. We shall return to this issue later in this chapter, when we examine career planning in more detail. At this stage it is appropriate to comment that these new developments have not done away with the need for careful planning for human resources, but have changed the assumptions as demonstrated in case study 10 on ICL. Attention in the planning process has now turned to producing up to date and accurate information about employees, their competencies, performance, and potential, as a basis for more flexible planning scenarios.

Forecasting the demand for manpower has always presented thorny problems, and these problems have been accentuated by the pace of change which makes it even harder to anticipate the skills and competencies likely to be required some way into the future, leading David Bell to comment

> the advance most needed is in generalised techniques for manpower demand forecasting. The foundations for such models may be there already in the work-study based models used by some banks, although these are difficult to adapt quickly to fundamental changes in the way banks' services are delivered. They may lie in older models, based on regression analysis, or even on the learning curves developed for just this purpose during the Second World War.
>
> (Bell, 1994)

Modelling the internal supply of labour requires accurate and up to date computerised personnel information systems (CPIS) and forecasts internal and external supply of labour. These are now examined in turn.

CPIS

Accurate and up to date information about employees is essential for manpower planning and for decision making by both line managers and human resource/personnel management departments. This information can only be supplied by good CPISs. Most medium to large organisations now possess these. But most organisations only use them for routine operational tasks such as record-keeping, word-processing, and absence-control. Less than a third use them for resource planning (Kinnie and Arthurs, 1993).

Practical applications of CPIS will be illustrated later in this chapter in the context of labour supply forecasting. There is however some disagreement amongst leading authorities on the role of information systems in strategic decision making. Colin Richards-Carpenter argues that 'The potential value of computerised personnel systems has hardly been explored: standard models for recruitment, training, job evaluation etc. exist, but the job of managing people using the power of technology has not been addressed' (Richards-Carpenter, 1994). Yet some leading personnel directors pour cold water on the idea that CPIS assist directly in strategic decision making. They argue that strategic decision making attempts to answer different questions than those posed in the manpower planning process. For Peter Wickens, strategic decision making is about answering the questions 'Where do we want to be in five years time?' and 'How do we get from where we are today to where we wish to be?' (Wickens, 1992). In his organisation, Nissan Motor Manufacturing (UK), 'computerised information helps us to be the type of company we wish to be. The availability of sophisticated material supply planning systems allow us to be a JIT manufacturer'. Andrew Mayo says that the experience of ICL is that in a de-layered and decentralised organisation

> IT systems provide flexible manpower modelling capabilities, looking at a company's needs in terms of core staff and contractual employees required. In the area of career management and people development they aid the coding of skills profiles of employees, in disseminating information on appraisal, development and selection, and in planning international movements of employees.

> (Mayo, 1992a)

FORECASTING THE INTERNAL SUPPLY

Quantitative approaches to the internal supply of human resources has concentrated on predicting the attrition likely to take place to the stock of employees in forthcoming years on account of socio-economic pressures and the existing demographic structure. The focus of interest has been on wastage, absenteeism, and age profiles.

Even today most recruitment consists of refilling vacancies created by staff leaving their employment, whether voluntarily or involuntarily. Predicting labour wastage both assists planning, and provides an incentive to improve retention rates. A typical survival curve is depicted in figure 6.3. The evidence is that the propensity to quit employment is highest during the early stages of employment,

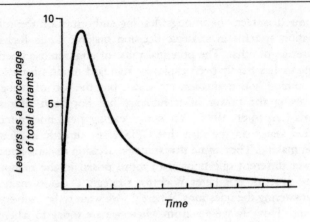

Figure 6.3   A survival curve

and after employees have settled down they are less and less likely to leave voluntarily as time passes. This settling down period varies from organisation to organisation, and from category of employee to category of employee. Therefore organisations need to do their own homework, using personnel records to contruct their own survival curves.

Survival curves show up as length of service profiles, and these can easily be constructed from data held on CPIS. An example of an actual length of service profile for a major UK police force is illustrated in figure 6.4. Note how the number of police officers likely to retire over the next 10 years shows up very clearly in this example, providing a useful input in plans for recruitment and training. This profile takes on added significance if the strategy is to civilianise a significant proportion of these police posts, and to follow the Sheehy report's recommendations that the police force should adapt a flexible and flatter organisation structure.

Labour turnover is influenced by pressures both within and outside the organisation, and historical patterns may vary in response. The variables which planners have to take account of in predicting turnover are illustrated in figure 6.5.

Echoing the comment by Peter Wickens quoted in the previous section, measuring, understanding and controlling labour wastage is not itself a strategic issue. It can however be a key issue in implementing HR strategy. Not only does measurement help in forecasting, and therefore makes planning possible, but measurement also provides

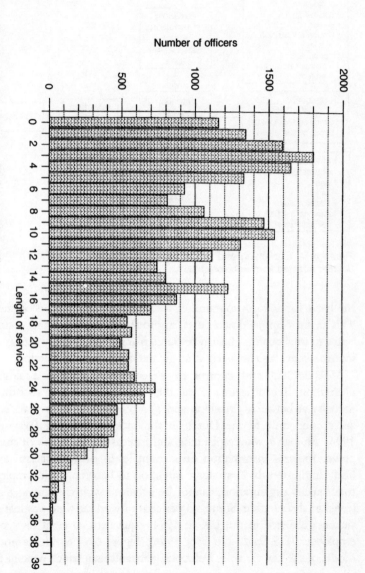

Figure 6.4 A length of service profile for a major police force

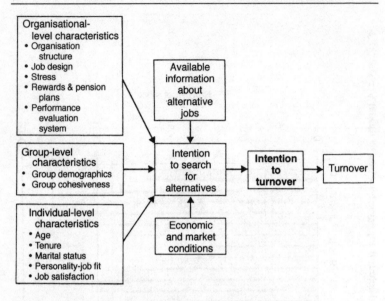

Figure 6.5   Explaining and predicting turnover
Source: Adapted from Robbins, 1986

the basis for action programmes to improve the retention of staff. This in turn brings down costs, improves productivity, and contributes to total quality. Human resource planning in this way acts as an intermediate stage between strategic intent and practical action.

Measurement and control of absenteeism provides a similar illustration. Recent estimates put the cost of absenteeism to British industry at between £9 billion and £13 billion, and British workers are second only to the Dutch in the 'sick-note' league (Watkins, 1994). Human resource planning and forecasting the stock of man-power requires information on current levels of absenteeism and likely future trends. A strategic intention to become, for example a total quality organisation, cannot be achieved with continuing high levels of absenteeism. Some 3.5 per cent of working time was lost to sickness absence in the UK in 1994, equivalent to eight days per employee (IDS Study No 556, 1994). Figure 6.6 provides a good model of the key variables influencing absenteeism which need to be taken into account in human resource planning.

Age profiles provide the third quantitative input into internal supply side forecasts. Plotting the age structure of a work force

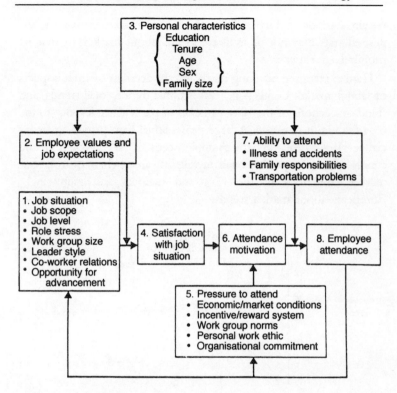

Figure 6.6 Explaining and predicting attendance
Source: Steers and Rhodes, 1978

throws into quick relief whether, for example, a large proportion of employees are coming up to retirement age, or whether the cadre of key executives is young and likely to be jostling each other for promotion in the near future. Once again a CPIS can provide this information quickly and easily.

FORECASTING THE EXTERNAL SUPPLY

The earlier chapter on strategic selection drew attention to the importance of labour market trends and the changing nature of the work force. Human resource planning revolves around the classic question faced by all planners – 'Do we make, or do we buy?'. In this context this translates into whether it is better to retrain staff or to buy in from the labour market. However, the desired staff may not be available in the labour market, or may be prohibitively expensive.

Human resource planning needs to take account of three aspects of labour market trends – general national trends, local trends, and trends in sections of the labour market of particular relevance to the organisation in question. A large professional firm providing financial services in the City for example needs to take account of the supply of trained professionals in relevant areas, changes in labour market conditions in the City, and national and increasingly, European labour market trends.

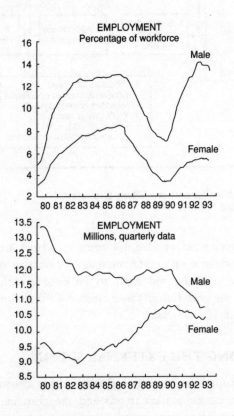

Figure 6.7 Employment and unemployment levels for men and women in the UK
Source: Department of Employment

The national scene in this, as in many European Countries, is affected by demography, the trend to part-time working, and unemployment. The decline in the number of school and college leavers entering the labour market during the late 1980s and early 1990s is generally well known. What is probably less well known is the steady decrease in full-time employment, in spite of the economy's emergence from recession, and the correspondingly steady increase in part-time employment. Male job seekers have been particularly badly hit by the decline in full-time employment opportunities. As recently as early 1990 there were more than 11 million men in full-time employment in the UK. Four years later this had dropped to 9.6 million men, and in consequence, unemployment levels for men are considerably higher than women. This situation is illustrated in figure 6.7.

It is estimated that in the next few years about 1.9 million new jobs will be created in value-added service occupations, at a time when 1.2 million blue-collar jobs will go (Rajan, 1992). The trend is for employers to retain a small core work force complemented by a temporary periphery staff with limited prospects. Recruiters are likely to find a surplus of unemployed workers on the labour market who are either unskilled, or with obsolete skills, but a shortage of candidates with the new skills required by technological advance, and a better educated flow of young people entering the labour market who are more demanding in what they seek.

An example of a local labour market is provided by the City of London. The last three years has seen major rationalisation programmes by City companies, leading to the loss of 50,000 jobs. They now need to create about 20,000 new jobs by 1998 in order to retain their competitive edge in world financial markets (Rajan, 1994). There will be an increased demand for knowledge workers, and a further decline in clerical positions. In consequence, human resource planning by City based institutions will need to take into account an increase in competition for new knowledge workers, such as fund managers, professional dealers, analysts, accountants and lawyers, alongside a likely increase in labour turnover amongst these grades.

A good example of positive response to a local labour market situation in the town of Peterborough is provided by Stephen Connock. Working with the local authority in Peterborough where his company Pearl Assurance had relocated, he was able to estimate the number of people coming onto the labour market up to the year 2000, and set it against the probable demand caused by expansion of commercial activity in the area. This produced an estimated short fall in skills that were particularly important for his company, such as computer staff, and financial professionals. This information formed the basis for revised recruitment and training plans (Connock, 1991).

CAREER PLANNING

Career planning might seem to be an anachronism in this day and age. Careers in just the one organisation lasting for thirty years or more are largely a thing of the past, and the pace of change in organisations today makes prediction about career paths increasingly difficult. Yet if organisations are to succeed they need to retain, motivate, and develop their best employees, and this entails a degree of career planning.

In a sense, career planning is a microcosm of human resource planning, with an emphasis on supply and demand and the development of plans to ensure a continuous stream of capable individuals willing and able to lead the organisation forward into the next decade. This is brought out in figure 6.8. Career planning is linked with succession planning, the process by which large organisations have traditionally ensured that at least one potential successor has been nominated for each and every middle and senior manager.

Matching people and posts				
Position	**Person specification**			**Personal profile**
Short-term specific	Relevant knowledge skills attitudes experience	< - - - - - - Career plan < - - - - - - < - - - - - -		Current knowledge skills attitudes experience
Short-term generic				
Long-term specific				Current perception of potential
Long-term generic				

Figure 6.8 Matching people and posts: the ICL approach
Source: Mayo, 1992a

These plans were frequently bureaucratic by nature, and assumed a relatively stable organisation structure. Other past weaknesses include an elitist approach that neglected significant areas of the work force, and a narrow focus on the cadre of graduate recruits to management trainee positions.

Current trends are in the direction of fusing career planning and succession planning processes in an attempt to create a better balance between the career aspirations of individuals and the needs of the organisation. A recent working definition of succession and career management describes this as

> processes and actions aimed at ensuring a suitable supply of successors – for current senior or key jobs and future roles arising from business strategy – so that the careers of individuals can be planned and managed to optimise the needs of the organisation and the aspirations of individuals.
>
> (Wallum, 1993)

Career planning should be tailored to the nature and needs of an organisation. The needs of large well established multi-national organisations are quite different from those of young and rapidly growing companies, or those which have diversified into a number of market places. Diversified companies such as BAT operate in many markets, each with different needs and forces, and may use what Goold and Campbell term a 'strategic planning model', whereas others, like Hanson and BTR, operate a 'financial control business' (Goold and Campbell, 1987). Each requires a different approach to career planning (Gratton and Syrett, 1990).

The processes of succession management identified in the IPM's Handbook of Performance Management, are:

- Analysis of the demand for managers by level, function and skill
- Audit of existing executives and projection of likely future supply from internal and external sources
- Planning individual career paths based on objective estimates of future needs and drawing on reliable performance appraisals and assessment of potential
- Career counselling undertaken in the realistic understanding of the future needs of the firm, as well as those of the individual
- Accelerated promotion schemes, with development targeted against the future needs of the business

- Performance related training and development to prepare individuals for future roles as well as their current responsibilities
- Planned strategic recruitment not only to fill short term needs but also to provide people for development to meet future needs.

(Neale, 1991)

Andrew Mayo defines career management more broadly as 'making sure the organisation will have the right people with the right skills at the right time' (Mayo, 1992b). (See case study 10 on human resource planning at ICL.) Research into succession planning by the Institute of Manpower Studies has revealed a trend to greater openness by organisations.

> Effective organisations [this study noted] use all the modern techniques available to them to establish what skills, personal qualities and knowledge their senior managers will require. Improved assessment of individuals against these criteria and a more open discussion of the results makes identifying senior managers less arbitrary.
>
> (Hirsh, 1990)

This study goes on to warn against the dangers of traditional fast-track schemes, based on the flawed assumption that candidates are willing pawns in a game outside their control. The solution recommended is a more open programme that makes better use of advice and career workshops to help candidates think about their career options more carefully.

Career planning is also having to take into account the managerial aspirations of women, and the trend today amongst both male and female graduates to take mid-career breaks. Professionally qualified women are starting families later, and planning either to maintain their careers, or return to them at a later date.

Alternatives to promotion are also emerging in de-layered organisations, where the chances of promotion have become much reduced. Research reported by Peter Herriot shows the recent impact of de-layering on career structures in financial management organisations. 'What managers have to realise' he says, 'is that with fewer rungs on the career ladder, structural plateaux are now inevitable for most people' (Herriot, 1994). There are however alternatives to promotion that will ensure career development, and the stigma must be taken away from reaching a plateaux. Organisations should stop assuming they know what managers want, and start asking. Frequently the answer lies in increased responsibility, variety, innovation, and the linking of rewards to performance as an alternative to promotion.

CONCLUSIONS

Human resource planning fulfils an important role in supplying information for strategic decision making, as well as translating these decisions into plans and procedures. Employers need to ensure that human resource stocks match forecast demand, a careful eye is kept on the careers of talented individuals, and trends in the labour market are carefully monitored. This provides an intelligent framework for the processes of selection, training, motivation and consultation described in the next section of this book.

REFERENCES

Bell, D.J. (1994) 'New demands on manpower planning', *Personnel Management Plus*, Feb: 7.

Bramham, J. (1994) *Human Resource Planning* (2nd edn), London: Institute of Personnel Management.

Connock, S. (1991) *H R Vision: Managing a Quality Workforce*, London: Institute of Personnel Management.

Cowling, A. and Walters, M. (1988) 'Manpower planning – where are we today?' *Personnel Review* 19(3).

Goold, M. and Campbell, A. (1987) *Strategies and Style: The Role of the Centre in Managing Diversified Companies*, Oxford: Basil Blackwell.

Gratton, L. and Syrett, M. (1990) 'Heirs apparent: succession strategies for the future', *Personnel Management*, January.

Herriot, P. (1994) 'Rewards on the level', *The Times*, 20 January.

Hirsh, W. (1990) 'Success planning: current and future issues', *IMS Report 184*, Brighton: Institute of Manpower Studies.

IDS Study No 556 (1994) 'Absence and sick pay policies', *Incomes Data Services Ltd*, June.

Kinnie, N. and Arthurs, A. (1993) 'Will personnel people ever learn to love the computers?', *Personnel Management*, June.

Mayo, A. (1992a) 'A framework for career management', *Personnel Management*, February.

Mayo, A. (1992b) 'The day of the super-system is past', *Personnel Plus*, July.

Neale, F. (1991) *Handbook of Performance Management*, London: Institute of Personnel Management.

Rajan, A. (1992) '1990's: Where Will the New Jobs Be?', *Institute of Careers Guidance Special Report*.

Rajan, A. (1994) 'Winning people', special report, Tunbridge: Create.

Richards-Carpenter, C. (1994) 'Why the CPIS is a disappointment', *Personnel Management*, May.

Robbins, S.R. (1986) *Organisational Behaviour*, Englewood Cliffs, N.J.: Prentice-Hall International: 493.

Smith, A.R. and Bartholomew, D.J. (1988) 'Manpower planning in the United Kingdom: an historical review', *Journal of Operational Research Society*, 39: 235–48.

Steers, R.M. and Rhodes, S.R. (1978) 'Major influences on employee attendance: a process model', *Journal of Applied Psychology*, August: 393.

Wallum, P. (1993) 'A broader view of succession planning', *Personnel Management*, September.

Watkins, J. (1994) 'Sick excuses for swanning around', *Personnel Management*, April.

Wickens, P. (1992) 'The importance of computerised information in strategic personnel decision making', paper presented to Computers in Personnel Annual Conference, London: Institute of Personnel Management.

Part III

Strategic human resource integration

In part III the human resource activities of selection, performance assessment, training and development and employee relations are integrated together in the interests of a common purpose. This purpose is to drive the organisation's current strategy through a particular configuration of structure, processes and systems and to also generate data for new strategy analysis and potential change.

At this stage, capability planning is being translated into a blend of implementation and potential renewal. Central to this part of the strategic human resource management model is the utilisation of core and specific effectiveness criteria as an identifiable thread running through the staffing of the organisation, the management of performance and the achievement of an appropriate employment climate. In other words, the criteria for selection will be utilised in performance assessment, provide the rationale for a reward system, be the focus for training and development and find expression in employee/management relations.

The philosophy that blends these activities together is to be found in the concept of learning. Management will consciously unite individual learning and organisational learning in a process of organisational transformation and renewal.

Chapter 7

Strategic selection

INTRODUCTION

Although a convincing argument can be made for the advantages accruing from selecting human resources to match the strategic needs of the organisation, a dilemma is straightaway encountered in any attempt to apply this idea. There is very little information available on how to go about such a process. In fact, as has been seen in chapter 2 only the most basic of connections have been made between the concept of human resource management and the more advanced (both theoretically and applied) concept of strategic management. In the case of selection the situation is further weakened by its particular state of theory and practice in that it can be demonstrated that there are serious flaws in the human capacity to select.

The chapter commences with a definition of selection. It is presented as a process through which decisions are taken regarding entry and induction and subsequent movements, such as promotion and transfer within the organisation. The environmental context for the organisation is seen to contain issues of significance to selectors. An overview of strategic selection in action suggests that, as a practice, it could not be described as advanced. There has been only limited theoretical development of appropriate tools and techniques with which to make the strategic link. It will be seen that, in terms of securing an effective process, the ability to select is of equal importance as the ability to select strategically and also, that the state of the art of the former raises some specific issues with which human resource specialists and other managers must be conversant.

DEFINING STRATEGIC SELECTION

In a framework entitled 'The human resource cycle', Devanna *et al.* (1984) refer to four generic functions (selection, appraisal, rewards and development) that are performed by human resource managers in all organisations and which are an intrinsic part of a broader strategic management framework. In this latter framework, which has already been discussed in chapter 2, organisation mission and strategy, organisation structure and human resource management are linked together within a context of economic, political and cultural forces in the environment. In defining the 'generic function' of selection, Devanna *et al.* include 'all activities related to the internal movement of people across positions as well as to hiring'. Others however, refer to 'staffing' as covering much the same ground, for example, (Miller, 1984; Butler *et al.*, 1991). In Butler *et al.*'s view the staffing function covers those tasks associated with, 'acquiring and allocating employees within an organisaton'. It includes recruitment and selection, orientation and socialisation, and employee movement within the organisation.

The essential point to make, it seems, is that the key activity is that of selection. An organisation will go through a 'selection' process in order to recruit into the organisation, induct new entrants (which may be a further phase of initial selection through the use of probation), and choose those for promotion, transfer and sometimes severance from the organisation. It is difficult to look at the process in isolation from the other activities such as appraisal. However, such somewhat artificial distinction is necessary in order to understand the state of theory and practice within each of these activities. The significance of this being that ineffective practice of any of the activities, for example, biased selection interviewing, will undermine any benefits gained from linking the process with organisation strategy. The selection concept is therefore defined in this text as including all movement of human resources into, within and from the organisation. However, the term staffing will be used in instances where such reference is made in the literature. Unless otherwise indicated such usage of the term staffing can be assumed to carry the same meaning as selection.

The premise underlying the concept of strategic selection is that selection issues should form part of strategic thinking within an organisation at both formulation and implementation stages. Butler *et al.* in a review of research linking strategy and selection, concluded that the link between intended strategies and staffing was 'unexplored' and under-researched. An organisation, for example, considering an intended strategy of diversification should consider staffing levels, skill inventories in the firm and ability of existing employees to learn new business areas. If the firm moves into unfamiliar areas then management must consider the trade-off between recruiting employees for the new business areas as opposed to retraining current employees who are perhaps more committed and undoubtedly more knowledgeable about the organisation. When it comes to 'unintended strategy', research is 'almost non-existent'. A heavily labour-intensive manufacturing organisation, for example, might be unable to acquire workers with needed skills at a price the organisation is able to pay. As a result, management may decide to pursue other manufacturing areas or perhaps automate. Unintended strategy can therefore emerge as a result of staffing related issues, in this case the general availability of labour.

THE ENVIRONMENTAL CONTEXT OF STRATEGIC SELECTION

When reviewing the strategic management process in chapters 1 and 3 it was seen that one of its essential components is environmental scanning in order to identify threats and opportunities of consequence to the organisation. Scanning undertaken with human resource opportunities and threats in mind is found to reveal many strategic issues which have a bearing on organisation selection.

Labour market

A number of significant changes in the labour market have implications for recruitment and selection, both in what an organisation looks for and the methods used. These changes form the environmental context for the selection process (Williams, 1991). Drawing on Elliott (1991) the main changes in the labour force are summarised below:

1 Work force participation

It seems that the total population over school leaving age, who are economically active has changed little in the UK over the last century. The participation rate of those aged 20 and over was 61.3

per cent in 1890 and in 1981 it was 61 per cent. This stability, however, in the overall participation rate hides a number of substantial changes. The participation rate for males has been declining, in particular among the young and the old. Young people have stayed longer at school and more have gone on to higher education. Older workers have retired earlier. For males aged 25–44 there has been practically no change in economic activity over the 90 years since 1890. In contrast there has been a marked rise in female participation rates at all ages. In the UK fewer than 1 in 10 married women were in the labour force in 1921 but by 1981, it is estimated that 1 in every 2 was economically active. The participation rate of married women has risen faster than women in general, the reason being that the majority work part-time. Part-time work has facilitated the return to work of married women after childbearing. Placed in a wider context it is found that, as measured in 1984, the activity rate for women in the USA, Japan, Germany and the UK was 51.9 per cent, 48.9 per cent, 39 per cent and 45.9 per cent respectively.

The pattern for female labour force participation traditionally displayed a bimodal pattern with peaks around the early twenties and again in the late thirties, reflecting the pattern of behaviour of married women who comprise the biggest part of the workforce. The pattern reflected the timing of childbearing and rearing with activities being concentrated in the early twenties. In recent years however, there are signs that family size has fallen. There are also signs that women are posponing the age at which they get married and the proportion of never married among 25–29 year olds is higher. Having married, there is also a trend towards an increase in the number of years before women start a family. These developments have the effect of permitting women to build a career and invest in the acquisition of skills. It is also easier for women to raise a family without interrupting their careers, due to maternity leave, changing attitude towards women at work and facilities for the support of working mothers. It would appear therefore that while women's labour force participation continues at a lower level than males, it is beginning to demonstrate a similar pattern over the life cycle.

Earlier retirements account for some reduced workforce participation. In 1930–1 around half of all men aged 65 and over were still in the labour force. By 1980–1 this had reduced to approximately one in 10. In 1930–1, one in 12 females aged 65 and over was working, by 1980 this had reduced to one in 25.

Similarly, young people staying longer in education have contributed to changes in participation rates. In 1981 65 per cent of males and 56 per cent of females under 20 were economically active as compared to 85 per cent and 71 per cent respectively in 1931.

When taken together the reduction in life time labour force participation rates, and the gradual reduction in hours per week and weeks per year means that the total number of hours worked per life time has fallen substantially.

2 Demography

The main determinants of a country's population are the rates of birth and death and the level of migration. The UK has recently experienced, and it is projected to continue, a reduction in birth rates during the late 1970s. The fertility rate has been falling steadily over the last few decades. The proportion of women marrying has fallen since the early 1950s. Further, the average ages at which women married and had their first child was increasing while the average number of births per marriage had fallen due to the availability of contraception. The birth rate fell from around 18 per 1000 of the population in the mid 1960s to less than 12 in the mid-1970s at which level it stabilised. Death rates are projected to be much more stable over this period. It is therefore variations in the birth rate that are the principle determinants of the projected changes in the size of the population of working age in the UK during the 1990s.

With regard to migration, the UK is one of the few developed countries which is a net exporter of people. Projections of labour force participation up to 1995 suggest that the activity rate among males of 65–69 will decline further from the 13.4 per cent rate of 1984 to 8.7 per cent in 1995. This will result in an overall decline in male participation from 74.3 per cent in 1984 to 73.3 per cent in 1995. In contrast the rate among females will rise from the 48.4 per cent rate of 1984 to 53 per cent in 1995. This will give a projected increase, in the size of the population of working age, of about 3 million, a growth rate of 11 per cent over the period from 1975 to 1995.

3 Unemployment

An analysis of unemployment for the period 1979–91, Kessler and Bayliss (1992) highlights the pattern of movements in this aspect of the labour market. The deep recession of 1971–81 brought about a large increase in unemployment. It doubled between June 1979 and June 1981 from 1.14 to 2.3 million. It continued to rise to over 3 million reaching its peak in 1986. There was a steady reduction in enemployment to nearly 1.5 million by the end of 1989. There were further small reductions in the early part of 1990 but it resumed its upward movement in the latter part of the year and by early 1991 it had again exceeded 2 million and most estimates were that it would increase to between 2.5 and 3 million before it would begin to fall. Projections for the 1990s are that it will continue to be high.

4 Legal constraints

Over recent decades there has been a spate of legislation which defines and protects the rights of employees. In terms of selection this deals with equality of opportunity between men and women and freedom from unfair discrimination on the basis of race, colour, nationality or ethnic origin (the Sex Discrimination Act 1975 and The Race Relations Act 1976). Increasingly, organisations have come 'under pressure to demonstrate their ability to select'. '[D]ecisions about hiring, firing, promoting or providing benefits to employees must be objective and job related' (Fisher et al., 1990). Mistakenly many people assume that discrimination implies some form of illegal act, but in fact, to discriminate means simply, 'to make a clear distinction; distinguish; differentiate'.

The selection process, in particular, directly discriminates between people in order to offer the reward of a job to one and not to others. 'Facts rather than prejudice and relevant facts rather than irrelevant facts are important criteria in determining what type of discrimination is acceptable' (Torrington and Hall, 1991). He points out, however, that the law expects more than this, it expects employers to exercise social responsibility in the decisions they take. He cites the model Equal Opportunity Policy produced by the Equal Opportunities Commission. Care should be taken that recruitment information has an equal chance of reaching both sexes and does not indicate a preference for one group of applicants. Care must be taken that job requirements are justifiable and that interviews are conducted on an objective basis. There must also be an intention not to discriminate unfairly in promotion. The same principles apply when seeking to ensure racial equality.

The implication of this legislation is that employers must be able to demonstrate through their policies and practices that they are not in breach of these laws. An added pressure is that, since the passing of the Industrial Relations Act 1971, employees are protected from unfair dismissal. This reduced the flexibility to be gained by expanding and contracting the workforce in response to business requirements which many employers took for granted up until then.

Impact of environmental context

Several points can be made about the impact of the environmental context on organisations. Firstly, as has been seen in chapters 1 to 3, organisations face a trend towards high and increasing environmental turbulence within what is now a global marketplace. Fast and adaptive responses are required. However, it has also been seen that, in terms of utilisation of labour, there has been a reduction in flexibility coupled with accountability for and scrutiny of selection activities brought about by legislative changes. A projected continuing high level of unemployment and increasing economic activity among women constitutes an over-supply of labour. While this may reduce recruitment problems it also challenges the selection process. With less young people in the labour force, due to trends in education and demography, and less experienced older people, due to reduction in the overall working life time, employers are faced with having to find substitutes for the traditional patterns of employment. Furthermore, higher education levels result not only in more qualification but also changed attitudes towards work. Employers therefore need, perhaps, to rethink their recruitment strategies.

One strategic response from employers has been to utilise a concept of 'core' and 'periphery' workforce composition. As Williams (1991) puts it, 'the watchword for the 1980s and for the foreseeable future, has become "flexibility"', with employers drawing a distinction between two categories of employee. The 'core' staff are key staff on whom the organisation depends for its future. They are likely to be employed in relatively 'permanent' contracts and will be eligible for career development opportunities both upwards and lateral. These staff are expected to be functionally flexible, taking on training and retraining. The use of rigorous methods of selection, for example, psychological tests and simulations, is considered to be justified because of the 'long-term' nature of this category.

The 'periphery' is a larger category with two broad groups of employees. The first group is employed on a relatively permanent basis like those in the 'core'. They are in low skilled jobs where there is often a high turnover. This turnover gives the organisation the flexibility it needs to manage employment levels. Selection instruments may be less rigorous and there is no need to assess for promotion. The second group are those working to various contractual arrangements with the amount of time worked being the key factor. Patterns such as part-time, job-sharing, short-term and fixed-term contracts, subcontracting, temporary staff and various consultancy arrangements fall into this latter category.

In the light of the above discussion it must be clear that, in relation to selection activity, an organisation's environmental context contains strategic information and poses strategic challenges. It, in fact, sets an agenda which contains three imperatives: a) being socially responsibile in the selection of human resources to enter, move through and exit from the organisation, b) ensuring that the actual selection process itself is both effective and valid, and c) continually integrating selection into the strategic aims of the organisation.

An example is taken of the Nissan organisation in part IV to demonstrate a strategic approach to selection.

THE STATE OF PRACTICE OF STRATEGIC SELECTION

There are many articles which describe what organisations 'should' do to accomplish strategic human resource management, but few which describe 'how' to do this (Kydd and Oppenheim, 1990). This deficiency also applies in the realms of strategic selection. There is a paucity of cases which demonstrate strategic selection in action.

Research evidence of a selection/strategy link

1 Kydd and Oppenheim

Four large US organisations were studied with the objective of determining how they linked their strategic direction to the planning of their human resources (Kydd and Oppenheim, 1990). The findings offer a number of insights including how these organisations utilised the selection process. Only successful organisations (leaders in their industry, growing at a steady rate and profitable within industry standards) were chosen. The organisations also had to be excellent in terms of human resource management practice as judged by the opinions of experts in the field. All of the organisatons, although highly successful, each faced a different set of environmental conditions and each utilised a different competitive strategy.

In terms of selection, the researchers considered the issue of how the organisations positioned themselves to compete for good managers. It was found that across companies different definitions of the labour market emerged. In every case it was found that the labour market definition paralleled the perceived market for the firm's products or services. Two financial service firms, for example, one based in a major money centre and the other located in a regional centre for financial activity, were distinctly different. The first-mentioned competed nationally for managers and also with companies outside of its industry, even though most of its operations were located within one region. The second-mentioned competed for staff primarily with other banks in its region.

In the organisations studied it was found that the educational or training requirements that further define the labour pool for each organisation were those that were necessary to keep the company on the leading edge of the competition. In a leisure product company, for example, which had a stable and predictable environment in terms of known products, known competitors and widely acknowledged factors for success, marketing was seen as being the key to success and careers were made or lost on share points. The organisation stressed selection of the best and brightest from the MBA labour market believing that it needed, 'razzle-dazzle people to sell a razzle-dazzel product'. On the other hand, a group of technological businesses in which technical excellence is the key to remaining competitive, emphasised long-term innovation and quality. The organisation required highly and specifically trained employees of which there was a limited pool. It therefore recruited specifically for people with technical skills and commitment to their work area which, it was thought, would enhance role performance over time.

The researchers concluded that human resource managers must cope with the special human resource needs of their organisations and that these are often determined by the environment within which it operates and the strategic directives established to deal with the environment. In their view special needs bring forth special solutions. One technological organisation, for example, needed to respond to an environment characterised by highly specialised skills, relatively expensive human resources, and a highly cyclical business pattern. It competed with other large organisations for government contracts. A successful bidder would need to increase its technical staff, while an unsuccessful bidder might need to cut back. The organisation responded to this environment by maintaining what it termed an 'open door' policy. Employees who left the company were welcome to reapply and indeed were actively encouraged to do so.

The researchers hypothesise that two dimensions (the level of environmental turbulence that an organisation must face and the extent to which its key competitive thrust is to be an innovator) will determine the approach which will be taken to human resource management issues. The level of turbulence will limit the organisation's ability to plan. High turbulence organisations would be more concerned with 'means', that is, high turbulence precludes evaluation solely on the 'end' result because of difficulty with prediction. Such organisations therefore must select managers on the basis of their ability to respond quickly and appropriately to dynamic conditions, rather than on the basis of meeting static, predefined goals. Organisations which rely on an innovation strategy need to have a broad and long-term focus. Managers who will fill positions in such an organisation must have an awareness of contextual factors surrounding the specific position to be able to perform the duties of the position. In other words, to be open to innovative ideas it is necessary to be aware of environmental events as well as organisational and specific job factors. The individual must, therefore, monitor a wide set of variables, the job is less focused and performance will be linked to the long-term contribution to the organisation's innovation strategy. Furthermore, the researchers concluded that turbulence and innovation are interdependent. High turbulence frequently leads to high innovation and, in such cases, the researchers discerned that selection for promotion was usually made from within. However, this was also discerned in organisations having low turbulence but where innovation was the main driving force. In the latter case the organisation could plan for future skill needs and train specifically for these needs. As innovative managers need to work in a secure environment, innovative organisations tended to have a job security policy. There was, therefore, an appropriate pool of candidates for selection for promotion to higher levels.

It can be seen, therefore, that in these companies, the concern for strategic selection led them to define their specific labour markets and identify what it takes, in terms of educational and training requirements, to maintain a leading edge within the wider context of their competitive environment.

2 Sparrow and Pettigrew

A study of ten companies in the UK computer industry (Sparrow and Pettigrew, 1988), illustrates the use of strategic selection as one of a number of human resource management responses to radical strategic change within the context of dynamic environmental forces. On a worldwide basis to 1985 the companies surveyed had, collectively, revenues from data processing in excess of $71 billion and employed over one million people. At the time of the research in 1986 these suppliers were faced with a business market that was slowing down in terms of revenue growth but accelerating in terms of technological change, and a competitive restructuring was taking place as a result of many business and environmental changes.

The industry was dominated by IBM which, since 1979, has been engaged in a price war aimed at weeding out many potential competitors. Falling profit margins on hardware led to falls in the stock price of many data processing companies, making them ripe for takeover. The suppliers responded with strategic partnerships. For several years an increasing proportion of suppliers' revenues came from the non-hardware part of the business, that is, support consultancy, training, supplies, software applications and maintenance. Such services require high quality and skilled people. In 1985, due to the weakness of sterling and the fact that most UK suppliers had to 'purchase' their computers from US multi-national parent companies for dollars even though the computers are made in the UK, suppliers found that revenues from the services part of the business, which were costed and charged locally, produced a much higher proportion of profits than the hardware part.

Thus, in response to a more competitive and consumer orientated marketplace, the suppliers conceived of offering a 'total solution', 'total service' or 'full service product' to customers which involved provision of compatible hardware, software applications geared to particular markets or sectors, communications facilities, pre-sales · consultancy, post-sales support, and flexible maintenance. Quality of service became the key to survival for these suppliers.

In order to offer this quality service they have to acquire and develop people with new skills. During the course of interviews with ten personnel directors and executives and three industry experts it emerged that there has been identification of a need for more general 'process' skills as opposed to technical skills. The managers are looking for general attributes in people that indicate ability to cope with change, such as leadership, entrepreneurship, project management, tolerance of uncertainty, management skills and communication ability.

Recruitment is currently the most important human resource management activity. More than half of the suppliers experience major difficulties because of skill shortages in the above areas. Only 12 per cent of recruitments look for academic qualifications and three out of every four of those appointed are experienced people. People are sought for their experience, paid to perform, and there is little emphasis on career planning. As a result there is little loyalty to employers as evidenced by a high attrition rate. Many suppliers are beginning to question the strategy of reliance on high pay as competition for staff is pushing the salary bill out of proportion. The researchers suggest that these companies are going to have to look at other aspects of human resource management in addition to recruitment and salary rewards, such as culture creation, people development, productivity, etc. in order to achieve a closer match with strategy.

A concept of 'total service' then emerged out of a strategy geared to the formation of 'strategic partnerships'. The employee 'process' skills identified as being required to deliver this concept led to the formation of specific selection strategies for the acquisition and development of human resources.

3. Hendry, Pettigrew and Sparrow

Hendry, Pettigrew and Sparrow (1988) reviewing their case study research, in a number of industrial sectors, found a clear message emerging, and it was that those organisations that have made developments in their human resource management process have done so under competitive pressure. Interestingly, they also found evidence that a complex set of business environment changes have resulted in generic strategic responses. They identify seven, often interdependent, responses that have driven and dictated developments in human resource management. These are competitive restructuring, decentralisation, internationalisation, acquisition and mergers, 'total quality' processes, technological change, and new concepts of service management. Such changes created needs among the firms for new operating structures and systems and new skills, knowledge and capability from staff at many organisational levels. The researchers also found that a considerable degree of internal organisation and cultural changes were actually occurring. These included change in top leadership, culture change, and major redundancy programmes. These external and internal changes were managed by responses in a range of human resource management areas of activity, one of which was skill supply. The strategic significance of this area of activity to the organisations surveyed is indicated by Hendry *et al.*:

> The acquisition of new skills has become the underlying imperative, both in the conditions of growth affecting many of these firms now, and in the situations of change affecting those that had been through a trough and were beginning to strike out in new directions.

Most of the firms had experienced a shift in skill requirements. There were, however, supply problems. Tight labour markets had created a need to find new supply sources and regional differences in pay levels (and cost of living) had limited mobility. Sudden labour cutbacks during recession had led to missing cohorts of new recruits which caused development gaps. Such cutbacks were sometimes followed by an equally sudden need to increase the labour force. There was a wide spectrum of behaviour among organisations in terms of strategy towards skill supply. Most organisations did not take a consistent approach. Shrinkage during recession was for many a means towards survival. However, internationalisation, technical changes and moves into new business areas have forced many organisations to develop explicit human resource management strategies and a major tool has been the manipulation of recruitment criteria.

Some organisations raised recruitment standards in order to develop a more flexible skills base. Others relaxed them in order to broaden the net and increase the volume of recruits. The introduction of 'new blood' was an essential feature of cultural change processes, moves into new business areas and development of new products, etc.

Alongside recruitment, other human resource management mechanisms were important in creating and retaining new skills. These included reduction of attrition, use of part-time labour, use of flexible working time patterns, and work restructuring to produce flexibility.

USES OF TOOLS AND TECHNIQUES IN STRATEGIC SELECTION

There has been some speculation as to how strategic planning tools and techniques might be applied to developing the theory and practice of strategic human resource management, and for the purposes of this chapter, to the strategic selection process. Such tools and techniques as exist are, in the main, linked to the theory and practice of the rational approach to the strategic process. Such speculation therefore must be viewed in the light of conclusions reached in chapter 1 as to the status of the main approaches to planning. Setting that aside for the present however, it has also to be said that work to apply tools and techniques to strategic selection is in its infancy.

Use of product life cycle

One approach has been to make use of the concept of the product life cycle which consists of phases of introduction of product, growth, maturity and sales decline. The implications for staffing levels at successive phases of the life cycle range from expansion during the growth phase to contraction during the decline of the product. Management styles which match the cycle range from entrepreneurial during product introduction to administrative during maturity and decline. Sets of characteristics are ascribed to each style. These are used as the basis of strategic selection (Kelleher and Cotter, 1982).

Baird, Meshoulam and DeGive (1983) also recommend the product life cycle. They say that the development phase requires innovators and entrepreneurs. Maturity requires aggressive managers who will hold down costs and expand market share and, decline calls for managers who understand what is involved in liquidation

Miller, P. (1991) has some reservations about the feasibility of

Table 7.1 Matching managers to strategy

The objective of the business	The main business activities	The Chief Executive should be/have
Growth	1. Pursuit of increased *market share* 2. Earnings generation *subordinate* to building dominant position 3. Focus on *longer term* results 4. Emphasis on *technical innovation* and market development	A. *Young*, ambitious, aggressive B. Strong development and growth potential C. High tolerance for *risk taking* D. Highly *competitive* by nature
Earnings	1. Pursuit of *maximum earnings* 2. Balanced focus on *short range/long range* 3. Emphasis on complex analysis and clearly articulated *plans* 4. Emphasis on increased *productivity*, cost improvements, strategic pricing	A. *Tolerates* risk, doesn't seek it B. Comfortable with variety and flexibility C. *Careful* but not conservative D. *Trade-off* artist, short/long, risk/reward
Cash flow	1. Pursuit of maximum positive *cash flow* 2. Sell off market share to *maximise* profitability 3. Intensive *pruning* of less profitable product/market segments 4 Intensive *short range* emphasis/minimise 'futures' activities	A. *Seasoned* and experienced B. Places high premium on profitability *efficiency* C. High tolerance less profitable for stability, no change for sake of it D. *Not* a dreamer, turned on by results *now*

Source: Miller, P., 1991

using strategic planning tools and techniques and he raises some interesting points with respect to this. He refers to his research (Miller and Norburn, 1981) in which they use a life cycle model to map out the characteristics of the manager who was most likely to implement successfully the strategies to be found at the differing stages of the life cycle. See table 7.1.

Miller thinks that the managerial characteristics that match particular strategic situations are not difficult to identify. He feels that such schema have not been introduced into widespread practice, mainly for four reasons. First, the product cycle 'map' and other representation of the strategic situation are recognised as simplistic. Second, selection techniques fall short of being able to identify such characteristics. Third, the model does not take account of corporate culture. The problem of implementing strategic change has been identified, by some, as the problem of organisation culture. The question is whether the selection process should seek matches to the organisation's current culture or the culture it aspires to. Finally, there is the overall complexity of the task of managing a system which matches managers to strategy, particularly when the organisation is made up of many strategic situations.

Use of portfolio mix

Baird, Meshoulam and DeGive (1983) recommend use of the concept of portfolio mix. This concerns the relationship among an organisation's business units. Products at different stages in their life cycle are played off against one another to support an overall corporate strategy. The money generated in a mature business where expenses are low and market share already established may be used to develop a new business or improve the market position of one that already exists. Resources are transferred from one business unit to another as they are needed. Organisations also have a portfolio mix of human resources because people have varying areas and degrees of competences and interests. People, as is the case with other resources can be transferred from one unit to another where they are most needed. Talented managers from a unit that is being sold may be moved to an established or growing business.

Use of competitive strategies

Schuler and Jackson (1987) focus on Porter's (1980, 1985) framework of competitive strategies: innovation, quality enhancement and

1. Highly repetitive, predictable behaviour	. . . .	Highly creative, innovative behaviour
2. Very short-term focus	. . . .	Very long-term behaviour
3. Highly cooperative, interdependent behaviour	. . . .	Highly independent, autonomous behaviour
4. Very low concern for quality	. . . .	Very high concern for quality
5. Very low concern for quantity	. . . .	Very high concern for quantity
6. Very low risk taking	. . . .	Very high risk taking
7. Very high concern for process	. . . .	Very high concern for results
8. High preference to avoid responsibility	. . . .	High preference to assume responsibility
9. Very inflexible to change	. . . .	Very flexible to change
10. Very comfortable with stability	. . . .	Very tolerant of ambiguity and unpredictability
11. Narrow skill application	. . . .	Broad skill application
12. Low job (firm) involvement	. . . .	High job (firm) involvement

Figure 7.1 Employee role behaviours for competitive strategies
Source: Schuler and Jackson, 1987

cost reduction and consider what employee role behaviours would be needed to pursue each, in addition to the specific skills, knowledge and abilities required to perform a particular task. Following extensive reviews of the literature, they have developed proposed role behaviours. These are illustrated in figure 7.1. There are twelve dimensions along which employees' role behaviours can vary.

The dimensions shown are those for which there are likely to be major differences across competitive strategies. These role behaviours are then considered in terms of what their implications would be for each of the human resource management practices of planning, staffing, appraising, compensating, and training and development. Each practice is arranged in a typology with a menu of choices being suggested in relation to each area of practice. Each choice is presented on a continuum. The staffing choices are illustrated in figure 7.2.

One of the choices for recruitment is concerned with where to

Internal sources	. . . .	External sources
Narrow paths	. . . .	Broad paths
Single ladder	. . . .	Multiple ladders
Explicit criteria	. . . .	Implicit criteria
Limited socialisation	. . . .	Extensive socialisation
Closed procedures	. . . .	Open procedures

Figure 7.2 Human resource management practice menu – staffing choices
Source: Adapted from Schuler and Jackson, 1987.

recruit. An organisation may rely on the internal labour market and other levels in the organisation, or it may rely on the external labour market exclusively. This choice has important policy implications. Recruiting exclusively from internal sources essentially means a policy of promotion from within. With regard to career paths the choice is whether to establish broad or narrow paths. The broader the path, the greater the opportunity to acquire skills relevant to many functional areas and gain exposure and visibility within the firm. The time frame for broad skill acquisition is longer and promotion may thus be slower. The organisation needs also to decide in favour of one ladder or several promotion ladders. An important part of this relates to the nature of the criteria used in deciding who to promote. These may vary from very explicit to very implicit. The more explicit the criteria, the less adaptable is the system to exceptions and changing circumstances. The more implicit the criteria, the greater the flexibility to move employees around to develop them more broadly. When an employee has been hired or promoted, he or she then has to be socialised. When socialisation is minimal, there will be few informal rules or procedures to immerse employees in the culture and practices of the organisation. The result is likely to be a more restricted psychological attachment and commitment by the employee to the firm, and perhaps less predictable behaviour from the employee. A final choice concerns the degree of openness in staffing procedures. The more open the procedures, the more likely there is to be job posting for internal recruitment and self-nomination for promotion. An open procedure allows employees to select themselves into jobs and is a critical aspect of attaining successful job-person fit. The more secret the procedures, the less employee involvement there will be but the selection decision can be taken more quickly.

The key aspect is that different selection choices will stimulate and reinforce different role behaviours. As these role behaviours have already been deduced from the organisation's choice of competitive strategy, then theoretically, the final outcome should be strategic selection.

Another piece of research, Govindarajan (1989) has taken Porter's (1980) competitive strategies of differentiation (creating and offering a product that is perceived, industry-wide, as unique) and low-cost (emphasis on the need to be 'the' low-cost producer in the industry) and sought a link between choice of strategy, managerial characteristics and organisation performance. The research foci were the strategic business unit (SBU) and the characteristics of the role of general manager.

The position taken in the research, drawn from reviews of literature, was that high performance will be derived when there is congruence between strategy and managerial characteristics. Different strategies require different tasks, behaviours, knowledge, skills and values for effective performance. Individual general managers, as a result of differences in their biographical background and personality orientations, differ in their behaviours, knowledge, skills and values. Managers might be able to change their styles but lack the flexibility to function effectively in all types of strategic contexts. As a consequence of these factors superior performance can best be achieved by selecting managers whose skills, knowledge, and behaviours are congruent with the requirements of particular strategies.

The study examines a portfolio of managerial characteristics including a mix of both biographical background and personality orientations: (i) functional background; (ii) industry familiarity: (iii) locus of control and (iv) problem-solving style. See exhibit 7.1 which explains the use of these orientations.

Exhibit 7.1 Strategy and managerial characteristics

The usefulness of 'functional' background is based on the view that each competitive strategy will benefit if the functional background of the general manager matches the strategy, for example, a differentiation strategy will likely require someone with particularly strong marketing and R&D skills while a low-cost producer is likely to benefit from strong manufacturing and finance/accounting skills. 'Industry familiarity', is probably most useful in a differentiation strategy where the aim is to be unique in the industry. A strong external orientation, in terms perhaps of knowing what product the customer wants and what they think about the product, is an advantage. In a low cost strategy, the manager will focus much more on the internal efficiency of the organisation.

'Locus of control' refers to the degree to which an individual perceives success and failure as being contingent upon personal initiative. At one end of an internal-external continuum are 'highly internal' individuals who perceive effort to be largely instrumental in attaining success. 'Highly external' individuals ascribe little or no value to initiative, since it is unrelated to ability and effort. Different information-processing capabilities are associated with each type with 'internals' being more proactive in the acquisition and utilisation of information. 'Internals' are thought to be more suited to differentiation strategies as there is need to make unique and varied responses to the market which would be accomplished through a variety of programmes and would require a general manager to have a high information processing capacity. The 'internals' more active search for, and more efficient processing of, task-relevant information is in keeping with their belief in the controlling value of their own behaviour as the significant determinant of task outcomes. A counter explanation is made in relation to requirements of a low-cost strategy which will be more suited to an 'external'.

'Problem solving' refers to the processes through which individuals organise information from the environment and evaluate it. There are four psychological functions underpinning the process: sensing, intuition, thinking, and feeling. The research organises these in two dimensions. The sensing–intuition functions are paired opposites on an information-gathering continuum and the thinking–feeling functions on an information-evaluation continuum. The characteristics of each function are described. The sensing types are most comfortable when attending to details and would be described as realistic, practical, and good at remembering and working with a large number of facts. They prefer structured problems with standard solutions, have patience for routine details, rarely have inspiration, seldom make factual errors, and are good at precise work. Intuitive types focus on meanings and relationships between items, and concentrate on the hypothetical possibilities of a situation rather than on facts and details. They allow their unconscious to generate and add on perspectives, possibilities, and other associations to the data they collect. Intuitives therefore tend to be imaginative and inspired and become good at developing new ideas. They perceive problems as a whole and dislike routine and repetitive work. New, unstructured problems serve to inspire intuitive types. The research proposes that low-cost strategies require sensing types while differentiation strategies require intuitive types.

Thinking types process information in an analytical, logical fashion. Decisions are made on the basis of cause and effect. They place a high emphasis on logic and systematic inquiry and usually ignore the wishes of others when making decisions. They tend to be impersonal, rarely show emotion and are uncomfortable dealing with other people's feelings. Feeling types tend to be very aware of how their decisions might effect other people and their feelings. Personal factors, rather than logic, serve as the basis for problem solving. Feeling types focus on human interactions and the emotions and feeling of the individuals involved. In contrast to thinking types, they gain satisfaction through social, interpersonal contacts. It is suggested in the research that the greater a general manager's reliance on peers and superiors for successful performance, the greater would be the need for the general manager to be a feeling type. A low-cost SBU is more likely to share resources with other SBUs than a differentiating SBU. The low-cost SBU general manager would rely on peers and superiors for successful performance and would need to engage in effective coordination and joint problem solving. Thus, it is thought that a feeling type would be a more beneficial match for a low-cost SBU.

Source: Govindarajaz, 1989

Data was collected from general managers of 121 SBUs which included functional background, industry familiarity, and they were administered a questionnaire on problem-solving style. Various hypotheses based on the above descriptions were tested using the following form: 'the positive impact of Xi (managerial characteristic variable) on Y (effectiveness) will be stronger when Xii (competitive strategy variable) is high (or low) as compared to when Xii is low (or high).' The findings were: (1) greater R&D experience and greater internal locus of control on the part of the SBU general manager contribute to effectiveness in the case of differentiating SBUs and hamper it for low-cost SBUs; (2) general managers who have manufacturing experience and who are feeling types contribute to performance in the case of low-cost SBUs, but hamper performance for differentiating SBUs; (3) experience in general management and industry familiarity are beneficial in a universalistic sense and (4) experience in finance/accounting has a negative effect on performance.

The research recommended two practical applications, derived from the findings, to the employer: (1) during the strategy implementation phase companies should attune the choice of the general manager to the strategy being implemented; (2) during the strategy formulation phase the findings of this study could be used to project future management need. This may, under certain circumstances, lead to a reconsideration of the strategies chosen, especially where the intended strategic direction is overambitious in the light of present management capabilities and recruitment limitations.

It may be said that this research, which attempts to link the business life cycle, portfolio mix and generic competitive strategies with selection, provides valuable insights into the strategic selection process but there is need of considerable refinement through empirical research before these tools and techniques could be used with confidence.

THE SELECTION PROCESS

The ultimate effectiveness of strategically selecting will be undermined if the selection system that is being linked with strategy is of poor quality. It is essential that all human resource systems and processes that are brought to bear on the strategic process reflect what is state of the art in human resource theory and practice. With this in mind it is important to reflect on the central principles relating to selection.

Selection principles

Human resource selection is a process of measurement, decision making and evaluation. The goal of a selection system is to select individuals who will perform well on the job. It must be fair. If it is to be fair it must be as accurate as possible and therefore must use reliable and valid measures of job applicant characteristics. The system must also include a way to combine information about applicants in a rational way so as to produce correct decisions. A good system should add to the overall effectiveness of the organisation (Fisher, Schoenfeldt and Shaw, 1990).

In this definition it can be discerned that implicit in selection is the aim of 'predicting' that an individual will perform satisfactorily in a specific job situation and that the prediction should be fair. The key principles in the process are the concepts of 'reliability' and 'validity'. In exhibits 7.2 and 7.3 below these important concepts are explained. The principles of reliability and validity are essential to discussion not only of the selection process, but also, as will be seen later, to discussion of performance assessment, reward management and training. Attention to the concepts at the present point will serve to lay the ground work for examination of the remaining human resource functions later in the text.

Exhibit 7.2 Reliability

Reliability refers to the extent to which a test (the term test, measure or instrument may apply to any form of measurement that takes place in the selection process) is consistent whenever a measure is taken of an individual. There may be some error in measurement. Systematic error or bias occurs when a test is inaccurate by a consistent amount. Random error affects a test by causing the score to be sometimes higher and sometimes lower than the true score, in an unpredictable way. Systematic error affects measurements in a consistent, predictable fashion while random error is inconsistent or variable in its effect. A test score is consistent (and therefore reliable) if random error is low. There are minimal fluctuations in observed scores. It can be consistent even if systematic error is present. Ideally, the human resource management specialist wants tests that have neither systematic nor random error.

There are three common methods of assessing reliability: test–retest, parallel forms and internal consistency. In each of these, the correlation coefficient is used as the index of reliability. A correlation of about 0.80 or higher is considered good reliability. The test–retest method examines the consistency of a test over time. The correlation is computed between the time 1 score and the time 2 score. This correlation is called the coefficient of stability. The parallel forms method of assessing reliability is appropriate when two versions of the same test are used. The correlation is computed between scores for form A and form B of the test. The correlation is called the coefficient of equivalence. Another variation is to give form A to a sample group followed by form B at a later date to the same sample. The correlation between scores for form A, time 1 and form B, time 2 is called the coefficient of stability and equivalence.

Human resources can be viewed as parallel forms of a test. If a job applicant is interviewed by 2 different interviewers and rated separately by each on several dimensions, the interviews can be viewed as parallel forms of the same interview test. The correlation between two evaluations is referred to as inter-rater reliability.

The third method of assessing reliability is 'internal consistency'. It is similar to the parallel forms method except that individual items on a test, rather than the whole test, are assessed for their 'equivalence' to one another. This type of reliability helps to assess whether all the items on a test are measuring the same trait or ability, that is whether the test's content is internally consistent. A coefficient is computed that represents the average correlation of each item on the test with each other item. This is called coefficient alpha. Coefficient alpha will be high (0.80 or above) if most of the items on the test measure the same thing. Each method of assessing reliability provides different information about the types of error that may affect a particular test. To cover all possible sources of error the use of multiple methods may be necessary. Reliability serves as the foundation upon which the validity of a test can be established. If a test cannot measure people consistently, it cannot be valid.

Source: Fischer, Schoenfeldt and Shaw, 1990

Exhibit 7.3 Validity

A measuring instrument is valid if it does what it is intended to do. In the selection process, measuring instruments are intended to:

- Exhibit a predictive relationship with an important variable such as job performance.
- Represent a specific job performance domain, that is, include a representative sampling of the types of work employees have to do in the performance of their jobs.

- Measure a specific psychological, personality or ability characteristic of an individual.

The above represent three types of validity: criterion-related
validity, content validity, and construct validity.

In conducting a criterion-related study the job is first analysed.
Tests are chosen which seem likely to predict job performance.
One method of determining criterion-related validity is through
'concurrent validation'. This is achieved by a) selecting a sample
of current employees, b) giving each the proposed selection test
and simultaneously collecting information on the criterion variable, and c) correlating test scores and criterion scores. Another
method of assessing criterion-related validity is through 'predictive validation'. The procedure uses job applicants who are tested
and then hired. The test scores are not used to decide who to
select because the test has not yet been proven valid. Performance is measured at time 2. A correlation is then made between
time 1 test scores and time 2 performance scores.

Content validity deals with whether or not a test is representative of the type of work employees have to do in the performance
of their jobs. A content validation strategy can be used only when
applicants are expected to already possess skills or knowledge that
is directly used in performing the job. There needs to be a one to
one correspondence between test content and job content.
Content validation begins with job analysis. Test items are
written to correspond to the skills and knowledge needed to
perform critical job tasks. The content validity is then verified
by a panel of experts to rate the items on the test as to whether or
not each represents essential items of the performance domain.
The ratings yield a content validity ratio for each item. It is then
possible to compare the content validity of one test to another
and to delete poor items. Averaging the content validity ratio of
all items yields a content validity index for the whole test. This
can be used to compare several proposed tests to each other in
order to identify the test that most closely corresponds to the
performance domain of a given job.

Construct validity deals with two issues: a) what the test
measures and b) how well the test measures it. It is important
to attempt to measure abstract characteristics that are not readily
observable, for example, creativity, intelligence, and various personality traits. No single study is sufficient to prove construct

validity because there is no perfect criterion variable against which to validate the test. The researcher must use several different techniques to show that the test appears to behave the way a test of the construct should behave. For example, in a study of a new test for anxiety, the researcher would give the test together with existing tests of anxiety to an 'anxious' individual and obtain a strong correlation, while there should be weak correlation with tests, say of intelligence. The test would then be given to students doing final examinations and a group of people on relaxation drugs. There should be a difference between the two groups. Construct validity is essential in tests for personnel selection. However, even if proven that construct validity exists. There must be proof that the characteristic measured is useful in predicting job performance. This usually means doing a criterion related validity study using the test.

Source: Fischer, Schoenfeldt and Shaw, 1990

In the next section it will be seen how these principles are applied in relation to current theory and practice in selection.

Current theory and practice in relation to selection instruments

It is vital that the human resource management specialist has up-to-date knowledge of current theory and practice in relation to the various selection instruments in order to be able to evaluate their theoretical standing, appropriateness to the organisation and, if utilised, their effectiveness.

As has been seen, reliability is the foundation for establishing validity. To achieve reliability the human resource management specialist or manager must use selection instruments that are as error free as possible. Tests (meaning all selection instruments) must be robust enough not to be contaminated by the test user. Test items must be internally consistent. It may be necessary to use multiple measures, such as is the case with assessment centres, in order to improve reliability. Validity requires that the criteria that are chosen to link variables of the individual with variables of job performance or success truly represent the content of the job and that the measures used achieve their purpose. Clearly there is a great dependence here on excellent job analysis and description.

Job analysis

There are a range of approaches to job analysis (see, for example Fisher *et al.*, 1990; Gatewood and Field, 1987). Some recent research, Schneider and Konz (1989) is based on the questioning of a 'frequently overlooked assumption that underlies the use of job analysis . . . which implies that the job in question is static,' when there is so much evidence to indicate that the environment for business is rapidly changing and, as a consequence, jobs are unlikely to remain static for any period of time. They suggest that strategic job analysis is needed, which they define as 'specification of the tasks to be performed and the knowledge, skills, and abilities required for effective performance for a job as it is predicted to exist in the future'. To do this they have devised workshops attended by experts, for example, job holders, supervisors, managers, human resource staff, strategic planners and job analysts. Participants could also include experts in a relevant technical field, economists, demographers, and so on, depending on the particular job.

To incorporate strategic issues into a 'present' job analysis they gather information about the kinds of issues in the job, the company, and/or the environment that may affect the job in the future. The issues emerge from a process of brainstorming with the experts involved. The issues are listed and rated to begin to define the target job for the future. The ratings cover: the importance and time spend on each task or cluster of tasks; the importance of the knowledge, skills and abilities required; the difficulty in learning these and when they will be learned. The ratings are correlated with those obtained from a traditional job analysis of the job as it currently stands. Thus, the present job is redefined in the light of the changes the workshop participants identify. The researchers intend to conduct a validity study to follow up the findings from the workshops to assess to what extent the ratings made by the experts turn out to be accurate predictions. Job analysis suffers from research neglect and, for this reason, research such as that outlined above, is to be welcomed.

Typical selection instruments

Most organisations use more than one selection instrument to gather information about applicants for entry to and promotion or transfer within the organisation. These instruments may be used sequentially as a series of hurdles with candidates being eliminated by failure at any stage.

A typical sequence of instruments is:

- application blank
- interview/s
- test/s
- medical examination
- references.

The purpose in using these instruments is to predict job performance and to use the assessments to make selection judgements. Figure 7.3 gives a list of some of the instruments available to the selection process. It would appear that very little has changed over the last 20 years. Measures have been refined and improved but there has been nothing really novel except perhaps situational interviews and work on accomplishment records (Robertson and Smith, 1989).

1. Interviews

   - Unstructured
   - Situational
   - Behaviour description

2. Tests (Analytical or signs)

   - Cognitive ability
   - Perceptual
   - Personality
   - Interests

3. Tests (Analagous or sample)

   - Work sample
   - Situational (intrays, role plays, simulations)
   - Trainability

4. Computer assisted tests
5. Repertory grids
6. Biodata and accomplishment record
7. Future autobiography
8. References
9. Graphology
10. Astrology
11. Self-assessment
12. Supervisor's/Peer assessment

Figure 7.3 List of predictive instruments
Source: Robertson and Smith, 1989

It is important for the human resource specialist to have such knowledge of the reliability and validity of these predictors as may be be available. It is, for example, interesting to note that despite having a very low validity coefficient (Ulrich and Trumbo, 1965; Arvey and Campion, 1982; and Cook, 1993) the interview is the most popular selection instrument (Lewis, 1984; Robertson and Makin, 1986).

Use of interview

Research has indicated that the use of the interview for selection is of dubious value. Its main flaws, arise out of human subjectivity, in that there is a tendency to stereotype people into groups and associate certain characteristics with such groups. Both negative and positive stereotyping would create the opportunities for inequality in the interview situation. Similarly, bias for or against other individuals for a variety of reasons has the same potential effect. Research, which has focused on the decision-making process within the interview, may be summarised as follows. The content of interviews varies greatly with interviewers asking different questions of different applicants. Most interviewers tend to make their selection decision early in the interview and thereafter look for information to support this first impression. Untrained interviewers are more likely to be influenced by negative information about the candidate. Interviewers, assessing the same candidate, have reached widely differing conclusions. A poor interview environment reduces the amount and level of information received. The form of questioning used can have unfairly discriminating results. The interviewer is unduly influenced by non-verbal signals. Positive non-verbal signals, such as good eye contact are erroneously associated with traits that suggest, for example, that the candidate is a 'responsible' individual, can show 'initiative', or is 'dependable'.

With such a poor track record, the interview has attracted a lot of advice as to how to overcome these subjectivity problems and improve its reliability and validity:

1 It is recommended that the process could be improved through the use of:

   • A structured and standardised approach.
   • A foundation of full job analysis and job description.
   • Applicants interviewed by more than one interviewer.

2 Interview decisions could be improved through the use of:

- Carefully framed and situational questions.
- Improved listening.
- Time control over sections of the interview and delay of decisions to the end.
- Assessment of each candidate immediately after the interview.
- Avoidance of stereotyping/bias.
- Awareness of the influence of non-verbal signals.

Use of tests

The same principles of reliability and validity apply to the use of psychometric testing. One of the main dangers in the use of tests is the possibility that they will, either through their form or content (or both), measure something which is present to a greater extent in an advantaged, rather than in a deprived part of the population. In view of this it has frequently been suggested that tests should be banned. As Drenth (1991) says, 'this rigorous step is not unlike the ancient practice of slaying the bearer of bad tidings'. He argues that it is incorrect to accuse the test as such of being discriminatory. It is in the interpretation or the use of the test data that discrimination can occur. The suggestion is that if a test has a satisfactory validity coefficient as a predictor of job performance then other means should be found to remedy the possible adverse effects on minority or other disadvantaged sections of the population. Arnold *et al.* (1991) say that while the status of personality tests as predictors of performance has been low for two decades, there are signs that tests may be about to take their rightful place as an important determinant of behaviour at work because personality constructs can provide useful predictions of performance.

Overview of validity coefficients of predictors

In a review of literature, Robertson and Smith (1989) found that, of the criteria used to evaluate predictors, overriding importance is usually attached to validity (normally predictive validity). Drawing on this literature they demonstrate validity coefficients for various selection methods. This is illustrated in figure 7.4.

Work sample tests and ability composite (general mental ability and psychomotor ability) tests produce the best validity coefficients. Supervisor/peer assessments, assessment centres, biodata and general mental ability are the best remaining methods. References,

Selection method	Approx. sample size	Range of mean validity coefficient
Work sample	3,000+	0.38–0.54
Ability composite	30,000+	0.53
Assessment centre	15,000+	0.41–0.43
Supervisor/peer evaluation	8,000+	0.43
General mental ability	30,000+	0.25–0.45
Biodata	5,000+	0.24–0.38
References	5,000+	0.17–0.26
Interviews	2,500+	0.14–0.23
Personality assessment	20,000+	0.15
Interest	1,500+	0.10
Self-assessment	500+	0.15
Handwriting	small	0.00

Figure 7.4 Approximate total sample sizes and mean validity coefficients for selection methods
Source: Robertson and Smith, 1989

interviews, personality assessments, interest inventories and self-assessment provide very low, but positive validity coefficients. More recent evidence from meta-analytic studies on the validity of interviews suggests that different types of interview may have different validities. The evidence does not provide any support for the use of handwriting as a predictor of work performance. The authors note that for several methods (e.g. references) only very limited information is available.

Use of assessment centres

It is for these issues relating to achieving reliability and validity that some selectors have been turning increasingly to the use of assessment centres. The principle being that the criteria relating to performance are each measured through several different instruments. The concept helps to overcome some of the flaws of the selection process. Some of the instruments will be directly work related, for example, a work sample or simulation. The overal assessment for each candidate is made by a team of assessors. They are most frequently used for selection for promotion, when they are combined with career counselling and planning. One important drawback in using the assessment centre approach is that they are expensive to operate.

Woodruffe (1990) notes that the use of assessment centres in the United States is widespread and in the United Kingdom it has grown rapidly in the 1980s. Feltham (1991) says that the assessment centre is now commonly believed to be one of the most valid approaches to selection and identification of long-term potential. While it is reasonable to expect assessment centres which have been professionally designed and operated to result in good quality decisions, a note of caution is sounded against making the mistakes of quite a number of organisations that have paid insufficient attention to such things as job analysis, exercise design and assessor training. He suggests that such organisations will have assessment centres which have negligible validity.

Reflection on the problems inherent in these human resource management predictors should, without doubt, serve to re-emphasise just how essential it is to bring as effective a selection process as possible to any proposed linkage with the organisation's strategic process.

STRATEGIC SELECTION CRITERIA

It has been seen in chapter 2 that a central element in the model of strategic human resource management, upon which the book is based, relates to the development of criteria for the implementation of strategy. The process of identifying these criteria brings to attention two issues in relation to criterion development. It is useful, first, to have some concept of what such criteria might specify and second, to also have some understanding of current developments in this sphere.

Effectiveness criteria in a turbulent environment

Kanter (1983), for example, provides a view as to the criteria organisations operating in the current business environment might require. She suggests that organisations will need flexibility to deal with rapid environmental change. Employees will be required to be adaptive, innovative, enterprising, tolerant of ambiguity, able to assume responsibility, collaborative and good team workers.

McEwen *et al.* (1988) also suggest that in a turbulent business environment achieving competitive success and thus effectiveness requires an organisation to have employees who have flexibility, a sense of involvement in the affairs and future of the organisation,

and capacity to adapt to change. They summarise these characteristics as 'competence, commitment and capacity to change'. They
define commitment, for example, as 'readiness (on the part of
employees) to pursue objectives through the individual job in cooperation with others'. The remainder of their definition of commitment deals with how commitment is developed, but, in fact, offers
insights into what they perceive to be the characteristics needed in
those who manage within the organisation.

• Commitment is gained through effective leadership which pro-
  vides guiding values and delegates authority.
• Commitment comes when people feel involved and valued.
• Commitment is fostered by two-way communication so everyone
  knows what is happening and how it will affect them.
• Commitment is created and reinforced by trust and openness.

Exhibit 7.4 illustrates the employee characteristics, in terms of
effectiveness behaviours and qualities, which chief executives, in
21 Northern Ireland organisations, employing 500 and upwards,
considered were making a significant contribution towards the
achievement of organisation strategy.

Exhibit 7.4 Employee behaviours and qualities which chief
executives identify as contributing most towards the achievement of organisation strategy

Behaviours	*Qualities*
Cooperativeness	Commitment
Effective leadership	Capability
Customer orientation	Innovative thinking
Quality awareness	Understanding of
Takes responsibility	company objectives
Technical skill	Vigour
Personal involvement	Positive attitude
Good communication	Enthusiasm
High productivity	Stamina
Responsive to company	Application
Acceptance of overtime	
Work hard	

Source: Lundy, 1990

Developments in criterion development

Arnold *et al.* (1991) note the difficulty inherent in moving from job analysis to specification, in human terms, of what is required for successful performance. As has been seen the process is not entirely objective and inferences have to be made. When attempt is made to link the core effectiveness criteria emanating from strategy to job specific criteria the difficulty is increased. With this in mind, it would seem that the human resource management specialist and manager require as much help as possible in this process of identifying criteria and standards of performance.

However, in recent years, it has been an area of research which has actually declined. This is due to a combination of factors, for example, in the wake of the passage of the Civil Rights Act in America, plaintiffs' experts became expert reviewers of research, eager to point out the ambiguities and shortcomings in validity studies. The result was that many organisations discouraged their human resource staff from publishing validity studies. Also many organisations simply stopped using tests and other standard predictors. A certain renewal of attention focused on criterion development as the use of assessment centres began to grow in the 1980s. However, in the UK, the greatest surge of activity has been in the aftermath of the institution of the National Council for Vocational Qualifications (Jessup, 1991) and the Management Charter Initiative (MCI, 1987). These were outcomes from government-led initiatives to increase the UK's competitiveness in international markets by improving its education and training performance.

The managerial competences produced by MCI have not been without criticism, for example, (Woodruffe, 1991; IRS, 1991 Baker, 1991). In relation to the work of managers MCI have produced sets of competence which are further broken down into elements of competence with related performance criteria. Range statements have also been produced which are intended to provide guidance on the contexts or situation where the competences may be performed. The competences were derived from a systematic job analysis approach known as functional analysis. The result has been a set of 'generic' competences. Baker suggests that systematic analysis harks back to scientific management which has the premise that there is 'one best way' to perform a job. There is also an assumption that jobs are static and not dynamic, ever-changing roles. Baker points out that many companies, for example, Kodak, Cadbury

Schweppes, and BP have rejected the idea of a single generic list of competences and have argued that only competences which are derived from the organisational context can be appropriate. Many companies have gone on to design their own 'organisation specific' sets of competences which take account of their specific organisation needs within a changing environment. Baker says that there has to be 'serious doubts about any approach that sets managerial competences in stone.'

Another problem he discerns with the MCI competences is that they represent what is termed a 'threshold' approach, that is, the job holder is either competent or not. In contrast a 'differentiation' approach will mark out an effective performance from a superior effective performance. He says the MCI interpretation of competence with its allusion of 'adequacy' seems dated in a world which demands excellence and outstanding performance. He also suggests that the emphasis on outputs, which is inherent in the approach, and which focuses on what a manager is able to do, understates the thinking process, and the personal inputs, for example, attitudes, personal qualities, or value positions which the individual contributes. He thinks the rigid narrow approach of MCI could run into the same difficulties which the earlier 'objectives' movement encountered. The 'soft' attributes may be difficult to operationalise but this should not mean they get ignored. He cites company specific schemes as including, for example, sensitivity, creativity, innovation, adaptativeness, boundary management, intuitiveness, assertiveness and self-development. Miller, L. (1991) on the other hand, puts up an argument for MCI, and in particular rejecting the claims that MCI expects to impose its generic approach on organisations. The case is made that the MCI can provide the 'core' managerial competences while organisations are free to take account of organisation specific competences they may need. It is pointed out that the MCI is funding projects to enable organisations to do this.

It will be seen that, although the discussion in relation to MCI, is concerned with management competences, there are lessons here, relating to criterion development, which apply to all jobs. The critics of MCI also lend support to the research, reported earlier in the chapter, which criticised traditional approaches to job analysis as not being suited to the study of jobs in a dynamic changing environment. The research proposed an approach to counter this weakness.

It is difficult both to define criteria and find instruments appropriate for their measurement. It is important, therefore, that the human resource specialists and managers concerned with criterion development be aware of the pitfalls and develop a system that is as valid as possible and which takes account of the strategic needs of the organisation. Account should be taken of competences developed by MCI and those of other industry lead bodies where appropriate. However, the competences used by organisations should always be organisation specific in terms of strategic needs. The development of core effectiveness criteria within the model of strategic human resource management meets this requirement.

CONCLUSION

If organisation selection is informed by the organisation's environment, linked to strategy, socially responsible, valid, periodically evaluated and maintained by knowledge of leading theory and pracitice, then such selection is, indeed, strategic selection. The same statement can be applied to each of the other HR activities which support strategic human resource management.

REFERENCES

Arnold, J., Robertson, I.T. and Cooper, C.C. (1991) *Work Psychology: Human Behaviour in the Workplace*, London: Longman.

Arvey, R.D. and Campion, J.E. (1982) 'The employment interview: a summary and review of recent research', *Personnel Psychology*, 35: 281–322.

Baird, L., Meshoulam, I. and DeGive, G. (1983) 'Meshing human resource planning with strategic business planning: a model approach', *Personnel*, September–October: 14–25.

Baker, B.R. (1991) 'MCI management competences and APL', *Journal of European Industrial Training*, 15(9): 17–26.

Butler, J.E., Ferris, G.R. and Napier, N.K. (1991) *Strategy and Human Resources Management*, Cincinnati, Ohio: South West Publishing Co.

Cook, M. (1993) *Personnel Selection and Productivity*, Chichester: John Wiley & Sons.

Devanna, M.A., Fombrun, C.J. and Tichy, N.M. (1984) 'A framework for strategic human resource management' in C.J. Fombrun, N.M. Tichy and M.A. Devanna (eds) *Strategic Human Resource Management*, New York: John Wiley & Sons: 33–56.

Drenth, P.J.D. (1991) 'Psychological testing and discrimination' in P. Herriott, (ed.) *Assessment and Selection in Organisations*, Chichester: John Wiley & Sons: 71–80.

Elliott, R.F. (1991) *Labour Economics: A Comparative Text*, Maidenhead: McGraw-Hill.

Feltham, R.T. (1991) 'Assessment Centres' in P. Herriott (ed.) *Assessment and Selection in Organisations*, Chichester: John Wiley & Sons.

Fisher, C.D. Schoenfeldt, L.F. and Shaw, J.B. (1990) *Human Resource Management*, Boston: Houghton Mifflin.

Garrahan, P. and Stewart, P. (1991) 'Work organisations in transition: the human resource management implications of the "Nissan Way" ', *Human Resource Management Journal*, 2(2): 46–62.

Gatewood, R.D. and Field, H.S. (1987) *Human Resource Selection*, New York: The Dryden Press.

Gessup, G. (1991) *Outcomes: NVQs and the Emerging Model of Education and Training*, London: The Falmer Press.

Govindarajan, V. (1989) 'Implementing competitive strategies at the business unit level: implications of matching managers to strategies', *Strategic Management Journal*, 10: 252–69.

Hendry, C., Pettigrew, A. and Sparrow, P. (1988) 'Changing patterns of human resource management', *Personnel Management*, November: 37–41.

Kanter, R.M. (1983) 'Frontiers for strategic and human resource planning and management', *Human Resource Management*, 22(1/2): 9–21.

Kelleher, E.J. and Cotter, K.L. (1982) 'An integrative model for human resource planning and strategic planning', *Human Resource Planning*, 5(1): 15–27.

Kessler, S. and Bayliss, F. (1992) *Contemporary British Industrial Relations*, Hong Kong: Macmillan.

Kydd, C.T. and Oppenheim, L. (1990) 'Using human resource management to enhance competitiveness: lessons from four excellent companies', *Human Resource Management*, Summer, 29(2): 145–66.

Landy, F.J. and Rastegary, H. (1989) 'Criteria for selection' in M. Smith and I.T. Robertson (eds) *Advances in Selection and Assessment*, Chichester: John Wiley & Son: 47–66.

Lewis, C. (1984) 'What's new in selection', *Personnel Management*, January: 14–16.

Lundy, O. (1990) *Strategic Human Resource Management*, Ph.D thesis, (unpublished), Belfast, The Queen's University.

McEwen, N., Carmichael, C., Short, D. and Steel, A. (1988) 'Managing organisational change – a strategic approach', *Long Range Planning*, 21(6): 71–8.

MCI (1987) *The Management Charter – A code of practice*, London: Management Charter Initiative March.

Miller, E. (1984) 'Strategic staffing', in C. Fombrun, N.M. Tichy and M.A. Devanna (eds) *Strategic Human Resource Management*, New York: John Wiley & Sons: 57–68.

Miller, L. (1991) 'Managerial competences', *Industrial and Commercial Training*, 23(6): 11–15.

Miller, P. (1991) 'Strategic human resource management: an assessment of progress', *Human Resource Management Journal*, 1(4): 23–39.

Miller, P. and Norburn, C. (1981) 'Strategy and executive reward: the mismatch in the strategic process', *Journal of General Management*, 6(4): 17–27.

Porter, M. (1980) *Competitive Strategy: Techniques for Analyzing Industries and Competitors*, New York: The Free Press, Macmillan.

Porter, M. (1985) *Competitive Advantage: Creating and Sustaining Superior Performance*, New York: The Free Press, Macmillan.

Robertson, I.T. and Makin, P.J. (1986) 'Management selection in Britain: a survey and a critique', *Journal of Occupational Psychology*, 59: 45–57.

Robertson, I.T. and Smith, M. (1989) 'Personnel selection methods' in M. Smith and I.T. Robertson (eds) *Advances in Selection and Assessment*, Chichester: John Wiley & Son: 89–112.

Schuler, R.S. and Jackson, S.E. (1987) 'Linking competitive strategies with human resource practices', *The Academy of Management Executive*, 1(3): 207–19.

Schneider, B. and Konz, A.M. (1989) 'Strategic job analysis', *Human Resource Management*, 28(1): 51–63.

Sparrow, P.R. and Pettigrew, A.M. (1988) 'Strategic human resource management in the UK computer supplier industry' *Journal of Occupational Psychology*, 61: 25–42.

Torrington, D. and Hall, L. (1991) *Personnel Management: A New Approach*, Hemel Hempstead: Prentice Hall International.

Ulrich, L. and Trumbo, D. (1965) 'The selection interview since 1949', *Psychological Bulletin*, 63: 100–16.

Williams, R.S. (1991) 'Patterns of employment and the job market', in P. Herriott (ed.) *Assessment and Selection in Organisations*, Chichester: John Wiley & Sons: 13–24.

Woodruffe, C. (1990) 'Assessment centres', London: Institute of Personnel Management.

Woodruffe, C. (1991) 'Competent by any other name', *Personnel Management*, September: 30–3.

Chapter 8

Strategic training and development

INTRODUCTION

Strategic training and development has a central part to play in bringing about the alignment of an organisation's human resource capability with its strategies. This chapter considers the scope of training and development and attempts to define the area within a single concept. The economic and political dimensions of this area of strategic human resource management are also considered. An examination of the state of its theoretical base leads on to discussion of the emerging strategic dimension and assessment of the contribution to be made, to the attainment of organisation strategy, by the concept of organisational learning. The chapter concludes by considering the interface between strategic training and development and performance appraisal.

DEFINITIONS

Dictionary definitions provide a starting point for defining four basic concepts relevant to this chapter.

Train:	Bring to desired standard of performance or behaviour by instruction and practice.
Develop:	Make or become bigger or fuller or more elaborate or systematic; bring or come to active or visible state or to maturity.
Educate:	Train or instruct intellectually, morally, and socially.
Learn:	Gain knowledge of, or skill in, by study, experience or being taught; be informed (of); find out (that, how, etc.).

There is some confusion in the application of these terms to a business setting. Farnham (1984) in a review of the UK education and training system highlights the distinction which traditionally tends to be drawn between the two. Education is associated with having a purely academic orientation, that is, consisting mainly of acquisition of knowledge, with attainment being evaluated by written examination. Education is subsequently used by employers as a screening device for entry into various parts of the labour market. Training has tended to be viewed as having a lower status than education. It is regarded as being skills centred and a means of preparing individuals for jobs, work roles or professions.

Fisher, Schoenfeldt and Shaw (1990) define training as 'a planned effort by the organisation to facilitate the learning of job-related knowledge and skills by employees'. Development, on the other hand is 'a process of enhancing an individual's present and future effectiveness' (Fombrun, Tichy and Devanna, 1984). Harrison (1989) says:

[D]evelopment is the all-important primary process, through which individual and organisational growth can through time achieve their fullest potential. Education is a major contributor to that developmental process, because it directly and continuously affects the formation not only of knowledge and abilities, but of character and of culture, aspirations and achievements. Training is the shorter-term, systematic process through which an individual is helped to master defined tasks or areas of skill and knowledge to predetermined standards.

There is as yet no all-embracing concept that brings together the processes of education, learning, training and development. However, it must be clear that they are inextricably linked.

They share many common principles, for example, learning theories, assessment and evaluation, and design of programmes. Equally clearly there is need for synthesis.

Drawing on the above, therefore, it may be said that each individual matures over a lifetime and that development is the process which can enable each to reach a personal full potential. Development is therefore, for the most part, long-term in focus. Education contributes to each individual's development by facilitating the attainment of mental powers, character and socialisation, as well as specific knowledge and skills. Training is a more short-term aid in the process of education which helps individuals to master defined tasks or areas of skill and knowledge to predetermined standards.

In business terms, therefore, development is the primary concept and 'strategic' human resource development (HRD) would change and develop the individual and organisation processes, systems and structures in line with the organisation's present improvement needs and future strategies. The concept of effectiveness must be included because development is not strategic, even though its programmes are based on organisational strategy, unless development interventions are subsequently shown to be effective. Finally, effectiveness can be sustained by what may be termed 'organisational learning' a process by which the organisation consciously plans its development and learns from its experiences.

It is inevitable that the literature will contain the conceptual ambiguities referred to; however, the analysis provided above should be used to inform the material introduced in the remainder of this chapter. Strategic HRD within an overarching framework of organisation learning represents the approach which would be utilised in the model of strategic human resource management.

THE POLITICAL AND ECONOMIC CONTEXT

Economic policy

The education, training and development of the population of working age in the UK are political issues because of their relationship to levels of unemployment, national productivity and industry competitiveness (Begg, Fisher and Dörnbusch, 1984). A government's economic policy is an important factor of consideration when an organisation is scanning its environment in the course of strategy formation. The national infrastructure for education and training forms a significant part of the economic environment and, as will be seen, both were elevated on the national agenda during the 1980s, a trend which seems set to continue.

The popularity or otherwise of a government's policy choices in these areas go some way to determining whether it will remain in power. In order to understand the nature and potential impact of such policy choices it is necessary to be aware of the main elements in macroeconomic theory.

Macroeconomic perspectives

Among economists there are two competing macroeconomic view-points. 'Positive' economics uses historical data to make judgements about how the economy works while 'normative' economics relates to value judgements about what is desirable. There are three main areas of disagreement which can affect policy decisions. First, there is the rate of market clearance (a market clears and is in equilibrium when the quantity sellers wish to supply equals the quantity pur-chasers wish to demand). Second, there is expectations' formation (acceptance that beliefs about the future are an important determi-nant of behaviour today), and these are formed mainly through three different approaches. An 'exogenous' approach analyses the beha-viour of the economy by treating expectations as exogenous or given. Expectations represent one of the inputs to the analysis. The analysis can indicate the consequences of a change in expecta-tions but does not investigate the cause of the change and it is unrelated to other parts of the analysis. At best this produces an incomplete account of how the economy works and at worst may neglect some inevitable feedbacks from variables being analysed to the expectations that were inputs in the first place. An increase, for example, in expected future profits might lead to an organisation increasing its investment spending.

An 'extrapolative' approach provides a way to make expectations endogenous or decided by what is occurring elsewhere in the analysis. It is assumed that people forecast profits by extrapolating from past inflations to develop future inflation expectations. The economists who favour this approach suggest that this seems to correspond to what people do in real life.

If the money supply is expanding and inflation accelerating, extrapolation from past inflation will consistently underforecast future inflation. The view of the 'rational' approach is that people will not follow a practice which continually makes the same mistake (that is, underforecasting). The approach makes the assumption that people will, on average, guesstimate the future correctly. They will not use forecasting rules that systematically give results that are too high or too low. As a result expectations that are systematically in error will be detected and put right. The rational expectation view is that people will make good use of information available today and will not make forecasts that are knowably incorrect.

Third, there are expectations about whether particular policies will have 'short-run' benefits, but 'long-run' costs or vice versa. A government's Policy Options are illustrated in exhibit 8.1.

Exhibit 8.1 A government's policy options

Aggregate demand The demand for domestic output. The sum of consumer spending, investment spending by firms, government spending on goods and services, and net exports.

Demand management Policies to stabilise aggregate demand close to its full-employment level. The government tries to influence aggregate demand either directly, by changing the government component of aggregate demand, or indirectly. Indirect policies include changes in taxation, which affect private expenditure, and monetary policy. Changes in the money supply and the interest rate affect domestic spending but also influence net exports via their effect on the exchange rate.

Potential output The level of output that firms wish to supply when there is full employment. It depends both on the level of full employment and on the capital stock with which labour combines to produce output.

Full employment The level of employment when the labour market is in equilibrium. At the equilibrium real wage, the only people unemployed are the people who do not wish to work at this real wage but are nevertheless part of the labour force.

Supply-side policies Policies aimed at increasing potential output. These include policies such as investment grants, aimed at increasing the capital stock, and tax cuts or retraining grants, aimed at increasing the effective supply of labour at each real wage rate. Reducing inflation is also a kind of supply-side policy if high inflation leads to real economic costs.

Source: Begg *et al.*, 1984

In practice the above areas of decision making are closely connected, for example, the more quickly it is believed that markets clear, the less scope there will be for demand management in the short run and the greater will be the importance attached to supply-side policy aimed at increasing potential output over the long run.

There are four major schools of contemporary macroeconomic thought and their interpretation of the three criteria set out above is demonstrated in table 8.1.

Macroeconomic philosophy in action can be seen by reference to policy choices during the Thatcher administration. When Margaret Thatcher assumed office in 1979, her view was that her predecessors had intervened too much and conceded too much to labour (Judge and Dickson, 1991). This, it was thought, had resulted in a bureaucratic state which supervised a large, unproductive public sector which required massive debt to fund its services. This structure had been promoted and supported by an aggressive labour movement motivated by self-interest. The private sector was overburdened, lacking in efficiency and enterprise and its international reputation was severely diminished. In Thatcher's economic strategy the aim of international competitiveness for the UK was

Table 8.1 Competing views analysed according to the schools of macroeconomic thought

	New classical	Gradualist monetarist	Eclectic Keynesian	Extreme Keynesian
Market clearing	Very fast	Quite fast	Quite slow	Very slow
Expectations	Rational – adjust quickly	Adjust more slowly	Could be fast or slow to adjust	Adjust slowly
Long run/ short run	Not much difference since fast adjustment	Long run more important	Don't neglect short run	Short run very important
Full employment	Always close	Never too far away	Could be far away	Could stay far away
Policy conclusion	Demand management useless; supply side vital	Supply side more important, but avoid wild swings in demand	Demand management important too	Demand management is what counts

Source: Begg *et al.*, 1984

paramount. As will be seen its policies on education and training were to be central to its efforts to achieve this aim.

Between 1979 and 1990, the Conservative government, during 11 years in office, set about transforming the face of British macro-economic policy (Healey, 1993a; 1993b). At first widely referred to as 'monetarism', the term 'new classical' macroeconomics is now generally used to refer to the theoretical framework that has under-pinned Conservative policy in this period. In philosophy it departed radically from the postwar consensus between the two major political parties, through which, since 1945, successive governments had sought to maintain aggregate demand at a level sufficient to achieve full employment. The Conservatives were elected on a programme that rejected the use of supply-side policies to promote high levels of output and employment, which it said, would lead to ever-increasing inflation. Instead it proposed that fiscal and mone-tary policies should be used to re-establish price stability, regardless of the short-run costs in terms of falling output and high employ-ment. The only way to achieve the high rate of economic growth and low rates of unemployment which had characterised the 1950s and 1960s was to sweep away state interventionism and introduce privatisation, deregulation and liberalisation.

Eventually, however, as Healey points out the Conservatives had to abandon the policy goal of full employment thus allowing demand management policies to be used to achieve price stability. Despite this, inflation remained endemic in the economy, and Healey suggests that this failure occurred because both the design and execution of policy were deficient. Real markets are not perfect and prices are not flexible. As a consequence the government faced a negative trade-off between unemployment and inflation and unemployment stayed high long after inflation had adjusted to the slow-down in the rate of growth of aggregate demand. Moreover, there was a weakness in the way that aggregate demand was controlled through reliance on monetary rather than fiscal policy which led to an explosion of credit which raised interest rates. This disadvantaged the manufacturing and the construction industries which relied on borrowing and whose vitality is so important to the UK's long-term supply-side performance.

Healey is adamant that the economic benefits that many claim have been derived from Thatcherism have been illusionary and that, once the distortions injected into the statistical data by a deep recession in 1979–82 and the unchecked boom between 1982–9 are taken out, that Britain's underlying performance is either little changed or actually worse than before and the social costs in terms of greater social and regional inequalities have proved unacceptably high, as witnessed by the fact that the government had to do a 'U' turn towards demand policy in the face of rapidly rising unemployment.

No attempt is made here to judge the efficacy or otherwise of respective government policies. The point being made is that organisations taking strategic decisions may find them, depending on circumstances, to be a threat or an opportunity. It will be seen, in the following analysis of the historical development of national training and educational policy, that growing awareness of a mismatch between provision in these areas and the needs of business, which, it is claimed, is at the roots of Britain's failure to be competitive, has led to sweeping changes in both these spheres of policy.

Historic background to education and training policy

Underinvestment in training

There is, in UK business, a history of chronic under-investment in the training of employees (Handy, 1987; Keep, 1989; Storey and Sisson, 1993). The state, traditionally, although intervening at times through legislation, had largely left responsibility for the function in the hands of employers, until, it will be seen, the 1980s when it became, through the medium of the Manpower Services Commission (MSC), a major source of funds for training provision (Kenney and Reid, 1990). The majority of UK employers tend to have an attitude of indifference towards training, in general regarding legislative attempts at its reform as unwarranted interference in the operation of their businesses. The reasons put forward for employers' attitudes are: a) they, historically, regard training as mainly associated with the craft apprenticeship because it is skilled work while non-craft work is not and they question the wisdom of training non-craft employees, taking the view that it is up to employees to learn a job without formal assistance or be replaced; b) as it is very difficult to evaluate training and as employers, for the most part, have no experience of doing this, there is no economic case to be made for the contribution of training to the organisation; c) increasingly mobile workers and decline in the tradition of life-long service with one company, suggests that training undertaken by an employer would mainly benefit other employers and therefore it does not make sense to train; and d) with training being of low priority to employers, its status is further eroded when, in times of recession, one of the first spending cuts has tended to be in this sphere.

The era of the ITBs

In the 1960s a view emerged that the prevailing approach to training had failed to produce an adequate supply of skilled workers. In anticipation of entry into the European Economic Community (EEC) with its provision for free movement of persons, services, capital and national recognition of qualifications and amid indications that UK training compared unfavourably with that in Germany and France, the government, in a bid to avert potential problems, decided to legislate for training. The Industrial Training Act in 1964 established the Industrial Training Boards (ITBs) the central feature of which was their power to raise a training levy from all organisations and pay a grant to those whose training satisfied the ITB's requirements.

However, by the end of the 1960s there was considerable concern about the achievements of the ITBs. Issues raised in a government discussion paper were that the system did not address the question of the unemployed which had increased to a level such as to be posing both social and political problems for government, there were problems with evaluating the effectiveness of training or obtaining reliable statistics for organisations, and there was a belief that the training activities of the boards should be coordinated and manpower planning implemented. The Employment and Training Act passed in 1973, established the Manpower Services Commission. The Act made provision for career services and temporary work for the unemployed. The bureaucracy of the training boards was alleviated by, for example, the removal of the need to impose a training levy.

In spite of such efforts, skills shortages and industry's under-investment in training remained problems. Confederation of British Industry (CBI) surveys between 1960 and 1978 indicated that even in times of unemployment, about 25 per cent of industrial manu-facturers reported skills shortages which affected their output. In some industries skills shortage, at between 50 per cent and 58 per cent, was particulary high. Although it was concluded that other factors contributed to the problem, such as promotion and pay policies, the cyclical nature of the British economy, and the fact that labour was not a readily disposable commodity, lack of investment in training was seen as a major deterrent in providing the quantity and quality of training required by the UK.

During the 1970s there had been two downturns in the economy in 1972 and 1975 and the onset of the worst depression which the country had experienced since the 1930s. The labour market was characterised by rapidly growing unemployment and business emphasised more than ever the need to only engage in activities which could be shown to improve the 'bottom line'. Employers cut expenditure on training and sought release from what was increasingly perceived as ITB bureaucracy. It was being argued that the strategy of stimulating industry-based training through the ITB system had largely failed. A radical shift in attitude of employers towards training was required. The MSC came in for criticism for not having sufficiently consulted with industry and for not taking firmer control of the Training Boards. The MSC undertook a review of the working of the 1973 Act and the findings, 'Outlook on training' produced in 1980 was to form the basis of its national training strategy for the 1980s. It recommended that, in future, the aims of public policy towards training should be to: ensure that training contributed towards the profitable exploitation of new technology, increased productivity, and faster economic growth; extend vocational training for young people; increase opportunities for adults to enter skilled occupations, or update or improve their skills through retraining; introduce efficient training methods more widely; and ensure that appropriate standards were set and attained.

A new training initiative

The Employment and Training Act of 1981 abolished 16 of the ITBs. A government white paper in 1981, 'A new training initiative (NTI): a programme for action' took up the MSC plans for the 1980s. It had three objectives (Critten, 1993), each of which led to key initiatives in the remainder of the decade. These were to: enable young people to acquire agreed standards of skill appropriate to the jobs available; enable young people under 18, not in full-time education to benefit from planned work experience, in combination with work related training and education, and enable adults to increase and update their skills and knowledge during their working lives. These led to the establishment of: a Youth Training Scheme (YTS) in 1983; the Open College (to provide open access to training and reskilling to adults) in 1987 and, also in 1987, the National Council for Vocational Qualifications (NCVQ) to provide a national vocational qualification framework for all occupations in England, Wales and Northern Ireland. Reference to exhibit 8.2 demonstrates that considerable advances have been made in developing this framework.

Exhibit 8.2 NVQ

An NVQ is defined as 'A statement of competence clearly relevant to work and intended to facilitate entry into, or progression in, employment and further learning, issued to an individual by a recognized awarding body' (Jessup, 1991). An NVQ certificate is a statement of competence of what an individual has achieved and it should incorporate specified standards in: (a) the ability to perform a range of work related activities, and (b) the underpinning skills, knowledge and understanding required for performance in employment. It can be seen that, in the statement, performance is the leading concept, while skills, knowledge and understanding are the underpinning requirements of such performance.

An NVQ statement will set out the title of the area of competence. The area of competence is broken down into units of competence. Each unit contains the elements of competence with their associated performance criteria. The statements of competence are developed by industry lead bodies who have responsibility for maintaining and improving national standards of performance in the sector(s) of employment where the competence is practised. The units of competence are designed so that they may be offered for separate assessment and recording as credits within a national credit accumulation and transfer system.

There will be five levels of competence in total. The higher the level of a qualification the more of the following characteristics it is likely to have:

- breadth and range of competence
- complexity and difficulty of competence
- requirement for special skills

- ability to undertake specialised activity
- ability to transfer competences from one context or work environment to another
- ability to innovate and cope with non-routine activities
- ability to plan and organise work
- ability to supervise others.

Level definitions are provided below:

Level 1 Competence in the performance of work activities which are in the main routine and predictable or provide a broad foundation, primarily as a basis for progression.

Level 2 Competence in a broader and more demanding range of work activities involving greater individual responsibility.

Level 3 Competence in skilled areas that involve performance of a broad range of work activities, including many that are complex and non-routine. In some areas, supervisory competence may be a requirement at this level.

Level 4 Competence in the performance of complex, technical, specialised and professional work activities, including those involving design, planning and problem solving, with a significant degree of personal accountability. In many areas competence in supervision and management will be a requirement at this level.

Level 5 Competence in all professional areas above that of level 4. (Still to be defined.)

The focus in NVQ is on assessing competence through outcomes achieved. It lends itself to continuous assessment rather than end-of-course examinations. Performance must be demonstrated and assessed under conditions as close as possibile to those under which it would normally be practiced.

Source: Jessup, 1991

Additionally, the NTI contained ideas about human capital, (see exhibit 8.4) and the need for a training revolution. (Ainley and Corney, 1990). There would be a permanent training policy for all young people, including a modernised apprenticeship scheme which would replace the skill specific craft training of the ITBs with flexible multi-skilled workers. A bridge would be created between school and work to break down the existing division between academic education and practical training. School leavers would be offered a foundation course combining theory and practice and would not be expected to remain in the one occupation for life.

Exhibit 8.3 The concept of human capital

The idea that education and training is an investment in individuals which is analogous to investment in machinery originated with Adam Smith in 1776. Smith proposed that differences between the wages of individuals with different levels of education and training, reflected differences in the returns necessary to defray the costs of acquiring these skills. In keeping with other forms of investment, increasing the stock of human capital requires outlays now for returns some time in the future. The return to capital would need to be higher than the return to physical capital to warrant such investment.

However, there are important differences between investing in physical capital as opposed to human capital. While a firm may own the services of a machine this dimension is missing from human capital. When investing in human capital firms have fewer guarantees than they do with machines. This constitutes an important reason why firms may be reluctant to bear all the costs of investing in human capital.

The concept of human capital became more fully developed in the 1960s since when it has dominated the economics of education and has had a powerful influence on the analysis of labour markets, wage determination, and other branches of economics.

Investment in human capital remains a controversial issue. Research which has attempted to measure the rate of return to investment in education has been criticised by those who argue that education does not increase the productive capacity of workers but acts as a filter. This enables employers to identify individuals with higher innate ability or personal characteristics which make them more productive, such as attitudes towards authority, punctuality, or motivation, which employers value and which are therefore rewarded by means of higher earnings. It is now being increasingly recognised that education affects attitudes, motivation, and other personal characteristics as well as providing knowledge and skills. More research is needed.

Sources: Elliott, 1991; Woodhall, 1991

With this training strategy the government hoped to promote the development of the concept of the enterprise culture and to promote entrepreneurial initiative. The second Conservative term of office brought the concepts of Thatcherism to their height. The State's commitment to full employment was abandoned. The government/trades union conflict came to a head in a year-long confrontation with the miners' union. The government took a series of initiatives aimed at curbing trade union power, developing new technology, and increasing training provision, all within the ambit of a free enterprise system. Despite the various training efforts, however, when the economy began to expand in 1986, it was immediately clear that there were skills gaps between the UK and its main competitors.

The reform of training

Around this time, two landmark reports highlighted serious problems in management training and fuelled the case for both educational and training reform. Handy (1987) pointed to disparity in amounts spent on training between Japan, West Germany, and USA which spend 3 per cent of their turnover in contrast to the UK's figure of 0.5 per cent. The report showed that West Germany's population contained two thirds with vocational qualifications while Britain had one third. In Britain there was little attention given to human resource planning information while in Germany, Japan and USA this was regarded as being highly important to the success of their training system. Constable and McCormick (1987) in a report commissioned by the government, in collaboration with BIM and CBI, found that British managers lack the development, education and training opportunities of their competitors. The great majority of the 2.75 million managers in the UK have no prior formal management education and training. UK managers receive an average of one day's formal training per year. The majority receive no formal training. The concluding recommendations were that management development should be seen as a continuous career-long process. There should be collaboration between employers, government, individual managers, professional institutes and academic institutions. Management development should be an integral part of the company's strategic plans. A new certification programme in business administration should be developed.

The 1987 Employment Act introduced substantial changes in the training infrastructure. A new Training Commission replaced the MSC. The Conservative third election manifesto had argued for a new manpower authority specifically responsible for training and nothing else, (Ainley and Corney, 1990). The abolition of the tripartite MSC demonstrated Thatcher's determination to break all links with Britain's corporatist past and to put those who benefited most from training, and those who would ultimately have to pay the greater part of its costs, in control. The Training Commission's creation marked a watershed in British training history because training and unemployment were no longer linked together. The government proposed the introduction of employment training. However, when the TUC announced its intention to boycott this, as many saw it, controversial programme, the government abolished the Training Commission and set up, through the employment Act of 1988, a Training Agency reporting to the Department of Employment.

The new Training Agency had a number of main tasks (Kenney and Reid, 1990), among them to encourage employers to develop the skills of their employees and to help the education system become more relevant to working life.

A government White Paper issued in 1988, 'Employment for the 1990s' set up a Task Force composed of industry, TUC, education, the voluntary sector and local authorities to assist the Secretary of State to develop new local training arrangements. To this end Training and Enterprise Councils (TECs) were set up with the aim of forging a better match between training programmes and industries' skills needs. Two-thirds of the Board members of each TEC are chief executives, or the equivalent, from private-sector business. The remainder are from education, local authorities and the unions. Training Agency staff are seconded to each Council.

The reform of education

The 1944 Education Act laid the foundations for the UK's present day education system, but, as Patton (1994) points out, it was a product of its time. It was more concerned with expansion of numbers than with curriculum content. It had little role in promoting standards and levels of achievement within the system. A growing unease about the system emerged in the 1960s and 1970s. As Patton says, it was producer-driven and seen by some as unresponsive to parents, employers and the wider public. Between 1988 and 1994 a series of Acts were passed which reflected the thrust of Thatcherite policy, the central aim of which was to bring market forces to bear on the educational system. The Education Reform Act (1988) introduced a range of measures including: a common curriculum with associated attainment targets and assessment arrangements; more information about the performance of schools; and greater autonomy for schools and Further Education colleges in managing their budgets in line with their educational priorities. The National Curriculum shares many features with the NVQ model, Jessup (1991). It marks a radical shift in school education, for those aged five to 16 years in that it specifies outcomes linked to statements of attainments. Two major White Papers, issued in 1991, (Page, 1991; CNAA, 1991) which set out how the government proposed to shape vocational education, training and higher education into the twenty-first century, provide a good indication of the government's policies for further and higher education. The White Paper, 'Education and training for the twenty-first century' proposed, among other things: a modern system of qualification, widely recognised and used; a comprehensive framework of National Vocational Qualifications (NVQs) for the whole working population; equal esteem for academic and vocational qualifications; and the introduction of diplomas, recording achievement in academic and vocational qualifications or combinations of both. Employers would have greater influence in education. This would be achieved through the development of close working relationships between employers and schools and colleges.

A further White Paper, 'Higher education: a new framework' referred to the government's vision for higher education. This consisted of: targets for increased participation of all 18–19 year olds; a high quality system that benefits individuals, the economy and society; a system that promotes the advancement of learning and high levels of scholarship taking account of industry and commerce and the European context; flexible patterns of teaching and learning; flexibility to plan research and teaching; a unified structure of higher education; a diversity of institutions with distinctive individual missions, and equality of status and standards between academic and vocational awards. The proposed changes to secure expansion, flexibility, diversity and quality were:

- abolition of the distinction between universities and polytechnics within a single framework for higher education;
- the creation of Higher Education funding Councils to distribute public funds for both teaching and research in universities, polytechnics and colleges of further education;
- the extension of degree awarding powers to institutions such as polytechnics and the winding up of the Council for National Academic Awards;
- the extension of the title of university to polytechnics wishing to use it;
- the development by institutions of their own quality control arrangements on a UK-wide basis, with the funding councils establishing quality assessment units to advise on overall standards across institutions so that quality judgements can inform the distribution of public funding.

The infrastructure for the changes proposed in the White Papers, has since largely been legislated for.

The drive for competitiveness

A White Paper, 'Helping business to win', (1994) provides the latest expression of government views in these matters. The paper considers the pressures facing organisations and stresses the importance of a skilled workforce in the drive for competitiveness. The UK faces a world of increasing change, global competition, growing consumer power. 'A world in which our wealth is more and more dependent on the knowledge, skills and motivation of our people.' These conditions represent both opportunities and challenge. It will be necessary to improve economic performance, raise productivity and adapt skills, patterns of work and products to new circumstances.

Competitiveness is the key. In a business organisation this means having the ability to produce the right goods and services in terms of quality and price at the right time. It means meeting customer's needs more efficiently and more effectively than other firms. For a nation (according to the Organisation for Economic Cooperation and Development) this means 'the degree to which it can, under free and fair market conditions, produce goods and services which meet the best of international markets, while simultaneously maintaining and expanding the real incomes of its people over the long-term'. Competitiveness will be achieved by securing:

- a stable macroeconomy based on low inflation and sound public finances;
- a more competitive European Community;
- improvements in education and training;
- flexible labour markets with promotion of good industrial relations and employee involvement;
- commitment to continuous innovation, including achieving improved performance through successful management.

As an important part of the process towards achieving these aims the government has set national targets for education and training qualifications, and lifetime learning (education beyond the normal school attendance age). There will also be a drive to encourage the improvement of management performance.

Strategic importance of education and training

This review of the political and economic context of education and training, very clearly indicates their strategic importance. It can be seen that the Conservative government used a radical macroeconomic approach in an attempt to cure the UK's flagging competitiveness. From the standpoint of education and training it has sought to sweep away state intervention and move training and education provision closer to privatisation. This entailed an effort to bring an end to the dichotomy between education and training and create a greater receptiveness to industry's needs. It also involved action to curb union power.

Such changes require a major cultural shift in which industry's traditional view of training as a cost to be avoided would have to become one in which it was viewed as an investment. The government's skake-out of the system has been intended to produce greater labour flexibility and higher levels of skills linked to a national system of qualification. It is, as yet, too early to judge the effects.

TRAINING – THE THEORETICAL BASE

One likely reason for the under-investment culture referred to above is the fact that, traditionally, training programmes have tended to be unrelated to the real needs of the business. As such they are prime targets for reduction or even elimination in bad times, (Kane, 1986; Casner-Lotto, 1988; Greig, 1988; Butler *et al.*, 1991; Miller, 1991; Nordhaug, 1991). It is proposed here that a contributory factor in this situation lies with weaknesses in the development of the activity's theoretical base. This becomes apparent when the training process is examined.

The training process

The training process is generally represented in the literature as having distinct stages or phases (Douglas *et al.*, 1985; Klatt *et al.*, 1985; Fisher *et al.*, 1990; Wexley and Latham, 1991):

- identification of training needs and setting training objectives;
- identifying and selecting training and development methods and techniques;
- developing a training and development programme;
- implementing the programme;
- evaluating the programme.

A typical model (Fisher *et al.*, 1990) is illustrated in figure 8.1.

In these and other such models training is presented as an analytical and integrated system. While needs and organisation

Assessment phase
Assess training needs through organisational, task and individual analyses

Identify training objectives	*Training phase* Select training methods and apply learning principles	
Develop criteria	Conduct training	
		Evaluation phase Measure and compare training outcomes against criteria

Figure 8.1 The training process
Source: Adapted from Fisher *et al.*, 1990

strategy may be alluded to there is generally no overt discussion of strategy. Later in the chapter consideration is given as to whether there are signs in the literature that a strategic orientation is being brought to bear on the process.

Even if the process were explicitly linked with strategy, the impact of strategic training and development could be lessened by potential problems in its theoretical base. Two theoretical areas underpin the design of the training process: theories of learning, and the evaluation of the success of training interventions. These two areas have not been applied as effectively as they might be to the training process.

In the heyday of the ITBs impressive progress was made in the field of systematic (usually operative) training with the application of learning theory to the design of programmes being held as a central tenet. However, use of the systematic approach did not occur, to the same extent, for jobs which were less characterised by perceptual-motor skills. The application of evaluation theory has tended to be short-term in focus, that is, outcomes of training have been insufficiently linked to job performance.

Training has also, potentially, the same weaknesses inherent in it as activities such as selection, performance assessment, or job evaluation, in which there are performance criteria to be defined and measured. Historically, such activities and techniques have demonstrated deficiencies in both validity and reliability. These weaknesses affect the design and evaluation of training programmes. The processes of learning and learning evaluation are briefly reviewed below.

Theories of learning

Learning can be defined as:

> knowledge obtained by study and/or experience; the art of acquiring knowledge, skills, competencies, attitudes, and ideals that are retained and used; a change of behaviour through experience.
>
> (Gilley and Eggland, 1989)

There is no universal agreement among researchers as to how learning occurs. Four broad theoretical perspectives are referred to below:

1 Behaviourist theory equates the human being with a machine, that is, an input is introduced (stimulus), which is controlled (how the input is processed – known as operant conditioning) and a predetermined output (response) is the result. According to this explanation of learning, its purpose is to produce prescribed behaviours. Positive and/or negative reinforcement are the means used to induce learning.

2 Cognitive theory equates the human being with the brain, in that the one thing that separates human beings from other living things is their capacity to think critically and solve problems. The theory maintains that the purpose of learning is to lead the brain to engage in critical thinking and problem solving.

3 Gestalt theory is also cognitive but involves the whole personality. The whole (the gestalt) is more than the sum of the parts. According to this theory personal needs arise and are satisfied in a pattern of gestalt formations and destructions. A gestalt begins to form when the individual experiences a physical and/or psychological need in relation to the environment. This moves the individual away from equilibrium in the direction of action to satisfy the need. Satisfaction of the need brings about closure and destruction of the gestalt. The individual then experiences equilibrium until another or other gestalt/s form. The learner, therefore, according to gestalt theory, when confronted by a learning problem, experiences tension and disequilibrium until this is resolved. The learner constantly strives to move back to equilibrium.

4 Humanistic theory maintains that all people are unique and possess individual potential. It also maintains that all people have the natural capacity to learn. Therefore the purpose of learning is to encourage each individual to develop to his or her full potential.

Principles of learning

Fisher *et al.* (1990) says there are two preconditions for learning – readiness and motivation. A trainee ready for learning will possess such skills and knowledge as are necessary to learn new material, and see a need for the new learning and how it will be of benefit. There are ways to increase trainee motivation. The organisation could, if appropriate, give the trainee some say in the choice of training programme. It seems also that if trainees can set specific goals for themselves then they perform better than if they have no goals or vague goals. The trainee is likely to have increased motivation if he/she believes that success will be linked with effort. The trainer can help by: 'persuasion' – telling the individual that he or she can do it; 'modelling' – pointing out others like the trainee who have been successful; and 'enactive mastery' – causing the trainee to achieve success in the early part of the programme. There are also important learning principles to consider when designing a training programme:

1 Conditions of training and practice

The programme design must take account of whether the skill will be taught and practised as one whole unit or divided into parts. In general, the more complex a job, the more effective it will be to break it into parts. Most systematic learning programmes, in which the skill is being learned in parts will enable this to be done progressively. The trainee will, by the end of training, be required to integrate, and perform satisfactorily, all parts of the job. A decision also has to be made, in the design of a programme, as to whether practice should be massed or distributed. It seems that massed practice is best where a job is simple. However, where a job is complex, then it is best to distribute practice. Overlearning (practising far beyond the point of mastery) is useful for critical tasks that are performed infrequently and/or under stress and/or where the first reaction must be correct. Overlearning is important for a number of reasons: it increases retention over time; it makes the behaviour more automatic; it increases the quality of performance under stress; and it helps trainees transfer what they have learned to the job setting. Generally speaking, learning which involves the learner is superior to passive learning.

2 Individual differences

Individuals frequently have different goals which may influence the motivation to learn. Individual differences in aptitude and ability will affect the speed of learning and capacity to cope with task difficulty. Successful past learning will increase confidence and the likelihood of accomplishing new learning.

3 Feedback

Feedback, or knowledge of results, is critical to both learning and motivation. Deprived of feedback, a trainee may learn a skill incorrectly. Feedback enables incorrect behaviour to be eliminated and because it reinforces correct behaviour it acts as an incentive because the individual experiences success. It is therefore a powerful source of motivation. Feedback should be linked to programme goals. The sooner negative feedback is provided the more likely it will be seen as relevant. Feedback is particularly valuable where the trainee has been taught how to evaluate his/her own performance.

4 Transfer of learning

To benefit from off-the-job training it is essential to maximise the transfer of learning to the job setting. The ways in which it is possible to do this are listed below:

- Maximise the similarity between the training and the job situations.
- Provide as much experience as possible with the task being taught.
- Provide for a variety of examples when teaching concepts or skills.
- Identify or label important features of the task.
- Make sure that general principles are understood before expecting much transfer.
- Make sure that the training behaviours and ideas are rewarded in the job situation.
- Design the training content so that the trainees can see its applicability.

Evaluation of learning

The most important aspects of training evaluation concern the criteria chosen for evaluation and the design of the evaluation process.

1 Choice of criteria

The effectiveness of a training programme can be evaluated in terms of reaction, learning, behavioural, and/or results criteria (Fisher *et al.*, 1990; Wexley and Latham, 1991; both citing Kirkpatrick, 1987).

(a) Reaction Reaction measures the immediate response to a training programme in terms of its content, delivery, methods, setting, etc. There are limitations to this form of evaluation, although it is probably the one most commonly used. Favourable reactions, for example, to a training programme does not mean that learning has occurred or that the individual has changed in any respect. It frequently takes much longer than 'immediately after the event' for the effects of new learning to become apparent. Reaction evaluation often reflects 'post training event euphoria' rather than objectivity. The most benefit can be derived from it when the criteria to be used have been linked with the aims of the training programme during its design phase. Immediate reaction can be improved by linking it with a follow-up reaction evaluation conducted some months after the event, although it is important to note that memory distortion can occur at this later point.

(b) Learning Learning criteria assess the knowledge and skills acquired by the trainee. Most jobs can be described by the knowledge required on three levels: knowing a range of facts, recalling lists, and stating rules; knowing a range of procedures; and recognising the key features in a particular situation. Tests of various sorts may be used to measure learning. It is essential that such tests are linked to the objectives of the programme.

(c) Behaviour A training programme may effectively impart knowledge and skills but there may be a significant gap between these and demonstrating them on the job, that is, transfer of learning may be minimal. Evaluation measures of how a trainee performs in the job environment are therefore very important.

(d) Results A results-based evaluation considers to what extent cost related outcomes have been affected by the training. Do such cost-related benefits outweigh the costs of developing and implementing the training? Outcomes may, for example, be increases in quality, productivity, attendance, etc.

2 Evaluation design

Evaluation of training has lacked credibility largely because the design, confined to measures taken after the event, has been inappropriate. Two designs fall into this category. In 'case study' design, measures of trainee effectiveness are taken after training has occurred using reaction, learning, behaviour, and/or results criteria. The main problem with this design is that no prior measures of the trainee's condition before training exist. In pretest–posttest design this deficiency is remedied. However, the value of this approach is also limited because no provision is made to take account of the many variables which could affect performance in addition to training interventions.

Evaluation design can be improved by adding a control group to the pretest–posttest approach with the group to be trained and the control group being chosen on a random basis which permits the use of statistical techniques to correct for imbalance between groups. Any changes in equipment, work conditions, management, etc. are constant for each group while the only difference is that one group receives training. Thus any improvement in learning, behaviour, and/or result can be attributed to training.

There are more sophisticated approaches in which more control groups are used and which cover the various permutations possible with the pretest–training–posttest design. Another approach is the 'within group' design which has developed because of the difficulty in obtaining control groups in the organisation setting. One such example is called the 'multiple-baseline' design in which instead of having more than one group, comparisons are made between individuals within a group. The design has two elements: (a) concurrent baselines (data taken repeatedly over a period of time across either multiple behaviours or groups of people), and (b) staggered interventions (the training is first introduced with one behaviour or group of people). When the desired change in performance occurs or after some predetermined number of interventions, the training is then introduced with a second behaviour or group of people. This process continues until training has been introduced with all behaviours or groups. To evaluate training, comparisons are made between the baseline data and post-intervention phases to assess whether the effects of training are replicated at different times. If performance improves at the post-intervention phases over each behaviour or group, then it can be concluded that the training was responsible for the changes taking place.

The state of practice

This review has highlighted problems with the current state of practice in relation to the training process. Broadly speaking, it is found that there is need for:

- A strategic orientation;
- A more rigorous application of the learning concept within the organisation.

These issues are considered in the remainder of the chapter.

STRATEGIC ORIENTATION

It seems that despite extensive literature advocating the use of training in support of strategic implementation, organisations are making few efforts in that direction (Catalanello and Redding 1989).

The impact of environmental forces

The literature typically identifies environmental forces which stress the strategic importance of training. Casner-Lotto (1988), for example, highlights five forces to which leading edge organisations are having to respond.

- Increased global and domestic competition is creating need for competitive strategies.
- Rapid changes in technology cause changes in operations, products, processes, job design, work flow and skill requirements.
- Widespread mergers, acquisitions and divestitures realign organisation structures and functions but not, automatically, the ability of the workforce to work within these new designs. There is a requirement for long-term training plans linked to strategy.
- A better-education workforce which values self-development, personal growth and participation at work is creating major training needs.
- Occupational obsolescene caused by a shift from manufacturing to service industries and the impact of research and new technology are creating new occupations and destroying others. Flexible training policies are required to prevent increased turnover and lower productivity.

It will be noticed that these environmental factors are reminiscent of those identified in chapter 2 in relation to the emergence of strategic human resource management. Literature on training represents a distinct branch in HRM literature and it is interesting to see this convergence in support of a strategic link. It is also, of course, environmental forces which have led the UK government to bring about far-reaching changes in the country's education and training system.

Linking training to generic strategy

Carnevale *et al.* (1990) have linked generic strategy with training. They draw on the work of Pearce and Robinson who identified 12 'grand' strategies linked to 4 'overarching' strategies which organisations use to be competitive. Carnevale *et al.* retain the 'overarching' strategies which they rename 'umbrella strategies' and they expand the 'grand strategies' which they refer to as areas of 'strategic emphasis' (see table 8.2).

Using this framework they explore the training and development implications of each 'umbrella' strategy and its subsets. An example is provided below of the implications of an internal growth strategy with strategic emphasis on innovation.

An organisaton following an internal growth strategy actively fosters innovation, expands markets, develops new related products

Table 8.2 Umbrella strategies and their strategic emphasis

Umbrella strategy	Strategic emphasis
Concentration	Market share
	Operating costs
	Market niche
Internal growth	Market development
	Product development
	Innovation
	Joint venture
External growth	Horizontal integration
	Vertigal integration
	Concentric diversification
Disinvestment	Retrenchment/ turnaround
	divestiture
	Liquidation

Source: Adapted from Carnevale *et al.*, 1990

or joins with another organisation to strengthen its competitive position. The overarching strategy is to channel resources towards building on existing strengths. There are two approaches to innovation: (a) incremental, consisting of new variations on existing products and/or extending and amplifying the life cycle of existing products, and (b) radical, consisting of a major breakthrough that represents a new standard in products or practice and/or a new product life cycle that make other similar products obsolete. There can also be innovations in organisation, marketing, sales, distribution, etc. Innovation is characterised by wide-ranging exploration of the product or the market, sensitivity to markets and flexibility of response. Rapid innovation requires simultaneous development of design, production, marketing and the modification or even abandonment of practices.

In terms of training and development, good communications are essential, bureaucracy is a barrier and risktaking has to be rewarded. Project teams are required to manage new ventures, headed by an entrepreneurial leader. Training is required in creative thinking, analytical skills and team working within a climate which encourages employee ideas, is motivating, and supportive of risk-takers.

Adopting an investment in people philosophy

An approach to linking strategy and training is being fostered by the UK government's 'Investors in People' programme which commenced in 1991. To become recognised as an 'investor in people' an organisation must demonstrate four features (Skills and Enterprize Network, 1994). These are:

- Commitment to develop all employees in order to achieve business objectives and with each organisation having a written business plan setting out goals and targets as to how development needs will be assessed and met;
- Regular planning and review;
- Action;
- Evaluation of effectiveness.

Twenty-four indicators of standards are attached to these criteria all of which an employer has to satisfy if they are to be officially recognised. On recognition the organisation is allowed to use the official logo of 'Investors in People' on company reports, advertising, correspondence, PR, etc.

International Distillers and Vintners UK (IDV UK) was one of the first companies to attain the standard (Finn, 1994). IDV UK is the national marketing company for International Distillers and Vintners, the drinks sector of the GrandMet Group. The company's personnel planning and development manager, says that the company has benefited from 'Investors in People' because it helps to concentrate development activity on meeting business targets and objectives. The company decided to apply for recognition because the standards described under the scheme are benchmarks for good human resources practice. As the personnel planning and development manager says, 'Planning, appraisal and evaluation have to become part of the company culture'.

Strategic Management Development

There is increasing recognition that management is growing in sophistication and is more demanding of both individuals and organisations. Strategic management has become a necessity for survival. The organisation needs to be strategically led and people driven, that is, people both formulate and implement strategy (Buckley and Kemp, 1987). In their view,

> Management development is strategic in that it is vitally important as a means to ensure the nature and mix of management competences for the organisation to secure its current competitive position . . . and to develop management competences to enable the organisation to maintain or shift its competitive position in the future.

> (Buckley and Kemp, 1987: 158)

The strategic importance of management development to the organisation increases as its environment becomes more dynamic. See the example taken of THORN EMI Home Electronics in exhibit 8.4.

Exhibit 8.4 THORN EMI Home Electronics: the context for management development

Home Electronics is one of four sectors through which the THORN EMI business portfolio is organised and strategically managed. The sector was set up in 1984 and consists of eight strategic business units (SBUs). Its business interests are located mainly in the United Kingdom and also in fifteen other countries worldwide. Home Electronics is involved in the manufacture, rental and retail of screen-based consumer electronics as well as home entertainment products. It employs around twenty seven thousand employees and has approximately two and a half thousand high street outlets in the United Kingdom alone. Its businesses operate in increasingly competitive, rapidly changing markets. There is a great deal of customer contact, and customer interfaces include shops, customers' homes, and business to business.

The key success factors for Home Electronics, within this environment, are quality business ideas, their effective implementation and competences of management, including the ways in which managers think and behave towards consumers and each other. The quality of management and the strategies adopted for their development are crucially important to survival and continued growth. People are viewed as a major business asset of considerable strategic importance.

Source: Adapted from Buckley and Kemp, 1987

Buckley and Kemp consider the forms which management development may take at different levels in the organisation.

1 Corporate level At this level strategic management defines the values and mission of the organisation. It determines the product or service market segments it will enter. It is also concerned with the management of synergies among SBUs. The management development strategy will concentrate on developing managers for the future of the organisation. It will also seek to ensure that existing and future management development strategy supports the organisation's values and mission. Board members at corporate level will specify the behaviours required of individuals and the culture within which they will work.

2 Business unit level Management at this level is involved with identifying and maximising performance and profitability. This may be in relation to particular lines of a business or amongst companies in a conglomerate organisation. Management development at this level will be linked to current requirements or those for the near future.

Techniques, such as the Boston Matrix, may be utilised to develop managerial competences in relation to the life cycle stage of the each SBU. The strategy is to develop and match 'growers' with wildcats, 'defenders' with stars, 'harvesters' with cash-cows and 'undertakers' with dogs. Other approaches attempt to match global personality traits, such as tolerance of ambiguity and entrepreneurism or functional background of the manager to the life cycle. The underlying view is that it is possible to systematically develop managers with specific personalities, experience and skills and place them appropriately in the organisation so that they may carry out a particular business strategy.

3 The functional level Management development strategy at this level is concerned with skills and behaviours that are important to the organisation and development aims are directed towards closing the gap between existing management competences and those required by the organisation. Management development initiatives focus on the identification of individual training needs as well as the content and process of individual and group events which are intended to fulfil these needs. Typical programmes are, for example, self-awareness, problem solving, communication, leadership style, etc. at the level of the individual and delegating, team-building, conflict management, etc. at the interpersonal and/or group level.

The challenge, in strategic management development is to remain focused on long and medium-term strategic objectives at corporate and SBU level while being flexible enough to respond to short-term competitive pressures at the functional level.

There is some suggestion, emerging from research by the Ashridge Management Research Group and sponsored by the Foundation for Management Education, that organisations are moving from a 'fragmented' approach to management development in which such activities are seen as peripheral to a 'focused' approach in which development is intrinsic to the organisation (Osbaldeston and Barham, 1992). In the focused approach development is:

- A continuous learning process
- Essential for business survival
- A competitive weapon
- Linked to organisational strategy and individual goals
- On-the-job plus specialist courses

- Self-selected
- Usually non-directive, novel methods
- Line manager's responsibility
- Tolerant

The focused approach develops managers by motivating them through challenge and acceptance of responsibility. The approach also fosters an environment that is supportive of risk-taking and permits mistakes as part of the learning process. 'The learning organisation developed by the focused approach addresses the needs for holistic management development and fosters the flexibility that will be needed to keep pace with change in an increasingly competitive environment.'

Osbaldeston and Barham stress that the focused approach is not typical of management development in most organisations but it is one to which a growing number of organisations would aspire. A survey of European companies, which Ashridge commissioned, revealed the following urgent priorities of companies in developing managers in order to improve overall performance.

Managing on-going organisational change	43%
Increasing the speed and effectiveness of decision-making processes	41%
Introducing quality management principles and practices	38%
Developing the capability at all levels to take an integrative (not specialist) approach	33%
Managing effectively in different cultures	27%
Incorporating ethical issues in management	27%
Working effectively in teams on major projects	24%
Integrating information technology into management practice	19%

THE LEARNING CONCEPT

Perhaps the most promising application of the learning concept to both individual and organisational learning is to be found in the idea of a learning organisation and interest, as evidenced in the literature, appears to be on the increase (for example Attwood and Beer, 1988; Drennan, 1992; Critten, 1993; Cocheu, 1993; Hawkins, 1994).

Its rationale

As with the rationale commonly given for linking human resources with strategy, the need for a learning organisation is seen to arise from environmental conditions which create the need for new forms of organisation in terms of flexibility and capacity to respond to change and with the underlying thinking that people are the only sustainable source of competitive advantage within a complex environment. (West, 1994).

Definition

A suggested definition is that the learning organisation, 'broadly encompasses the concept that successful adaptation to change and uncertainty is most likely to occur when sufficient and appropriate learning takes place throughout the organisation all the time'. Drawing on a definition by Burgoyne, 'a learning organisation continuously transforms itself in a process reciprocally linked to the development of all its members'. West says that 'transformation' is the key focus which differentiates the approach from the organisational development movement of the 1960s and 1970s. The act of transformation appears to emphasise the process by which an organisation develops as opposed to being changed by outside intervention. She detects an evolution from organisation development to organisation learning with much knowledge about individual training to be carried forward from the past history of organisation development and the question now to be answered is how an organisation might accomplish 'continual transformaton'.

Underlying assumptions

West suggests that the assumptions underlying a learning organisaton are that:

- learning is of value;
- while learning happens all the time, the quantity and quality of learning can be increased if it is done deliberately rather than by being left to chance;
- learning is a continuous process with no beginning and no end;
- shared learning with other people is easiest to sustain.

Distinctive characteristics

Critten (1993) highlights the features which, in his view, distinguish the learning organisation from other organisations. The learning organisation:

- has a climate in which individual members are encouraged to learn and to develop their full potential;
- extends this learning culture to include customers, suppliers and other significant stakeholders, whenever possible;
- makes human resource development strategy central to business policy;
- has a continuous process of organisation transformation in which learning and working are synonymous.

Hawkins (1994) says that the field of management and organisational learning is in its infancy and warns against the danger that it might be taken as yet one more panacea. 'In some companies last year's answer is discarded as a failure as the latest bright solution is brought in as this year's fashion.' He recounts the recent comment of one manager: 'Our organisation is suffering from death by a thousand initiatives.' In fact the theoretical perceptions underpinning the learning organisation concept have been developing over a period of twenty years. Some of the major contributions are summarised in table 8.3.

Hawkins feels there is need to move from language that describes learning as something acquired, given to people or introduced into organisations and find metaphors that 'see learning as a flow process that needs to be released and unblocked, within individuals, teams and organisations, and between organisations and their environments'.

A learning organisation, therefore, has certain underpinning assumptions and features that distinguish it from other organisations but what does a learning organisation learn and do?

What does a learning organisation learn and do?

Insights in this respect are gained from a group of 50 United States HRD professionals and frontline managers who met in study groups to draw together ideas and perspectives about learning organisations. The participants included senior trainers, HRD managers, line managers, and internal and external OD

Table 8.3 Review of research on learning processes

Author	Date	Focus
Bateson	1973	Levels of learning.
Argyris and Schon	1974	Building on Bateson's work and introduction of concept of 'double-loop' learning.
Revans	1982	Action learning (reflection on learning/ problem-centred).
Kolb	1984	The learning cycle (continual learning through reflection on experience).
Garratt	1987, 1990	Application of double-loop learning to the policy and operational cycles of learning within organisations.
Honey, Mumford	1989a,1989b	Tools to identify learning styles, remove blocks to learning and create learning opportunities.
Fritz	1989,1991,1993	Challenged the emphasis on learning being problem-centred. Problem-solving promotes return to status quo. This acts against the creation of something new.
Senge	1990	Five building blocks for creating a learning organisation
Pedler *et al.*	1991	Eleven key characteristics of a learning company as a means of looking at company-wide learning processes
		Currently working on a model of organisational learning which will link double-loop learning with earlier learning cycles of Kolb, Mumford, Honey, Revans

Source: Extracted from Hawkins, 1994

consultants. They represented private industry, universities, and government agencies, including: Apple Computers, Amdahl, ASTD, Cable & Wireless Communications, General Electric, George Washington University, Hewlett-Packard, Levi-Strauss, Martin Marietta, Marriott Corporation, Pacific Gas & Electric, U.S. Defense Information Systems Agency, U.S. Office of Personnel Management and Westinghouse (Calvert *et al.*, 1994).

The consensus of the group was that learning organisations learn to:

- Use learning to reach their goals
- Help people value the effects of their learning on the organisation
- Avoid repeating mistakes
- Share information in ways that prompt appropriate action
- Link individual performance with organisational performance
- Tie rewards to key measures of performance
- Take in a lot of environmental information at all times
- Create structures and procedures that support the learning process
- Foster ongoing and orderly dialogues
- Make it safe for people to share openly and take risks.

In terms of what a learning organisation does, the findings were that it:

- Learns collaboratively, openly, and across boundaries
- Values 'how' it learns as well as 'what' it learns
- Invests in staying ahead of the learning curve in its industry
- Gains a competitive edge by learning faster and smarter than competitors
- Turns data into useful knowledge quickly and at the right time and place
- Enables every employee to feel that every experience provides an opportunity to learn something potentially useful, even if only to leverage future learning
- Exhibits little fear and defensiveness; rewards and learns from what goes wrong and right
- Takes risks but avoids jeopardising basic security of the organisation
- Invests in experimental and seemingly tangential learning
- Supports people and teams who want to pursue action-learning projects

• Depoliticises learning by not penalising individuals or groups for sharing information and conclusions.

Knowledge creation is the business

Nonaka (1991) equates the learning organisation with organisation success. 'Successful companies are those that consistently create new knowledge, deseminate it widely through the organisation and quickly embody it in new technologies and products.' In his view the only business of the knowledge creating company, as exemplified in highly successful Japanese organisations such as Honda, Canon, Matsushita, NEC, Sharp and Kao, is continuous innovation. The creation of new knowledge is not just concerned with processing objective information but with being able to tap into the subjective insights, intuitions and hunches of individual employees and making these available to the organisation. In this perspective, the organisation is not a machine but 'a living organism' with a collective identity and purpose. It is the 'organisational equivalent of self-knowledge – a shared understanding of what the company stands for, where it is going, what kind of world it wants to live in, and, most important, how to make that world a reality'. Re-creation of the world according to a particular vision is what innovation is about.

Learning according to the above pattern corresponds with a classification of organisation learning into three levels (McKergow, 1994). The 'doing' level covers all of the operations of the organisation. First level learning or, 'single loop' learning as defined by Argyris and Schon, relates to learning which seeks to improve the 'doing' level. Second level learning or 'double loop' learning would tap in to the tacit knowledge held by the individuals, as described by Nonaka above, and look for ways to change the rules which govern the activity at both the other two levels. An organisation without second loop learning is not a learning organisation.

A complex adaptive system

The contrast, noted earlier, between the organisation as machine or organic entity and the increasing espousal of the latter concept is perhaps a reaction to the inadequacies in the scientific management 'control' model as an approach to managing in the current business environment (Freedman, 1992). Drawing on chaos theory, which is gaining support among scientists, he proposes that the nineteenth century emphasis on predictability and control have given way to a late twentieth century appreciation of the power of randomness and chance. See chapter 1 for a more detailed discussion of this theory. Out of research into chaos theory has come the concept of 'complex adaptive systems'. Such a system is self-managed, consisting of a network of agents that act independently without central control. They are capable of engaging in cooperative behaviour and can form 'communities' that cooperate in producing higher order behaviours that no single agent could accompany on its own. Self-organising systems are learning systems which learn through feedback from the environment. Learning is imbedded in their structure. The system operates through flexible specialisation of groups of agents which rapidly regroup and change according to environmental changes. In such a learning organisation it is the work of all to understand the processes driving human behaviour and change them.

Creating a learning organisation

Moving on from gaining some understanding of the theoretical perspectives imbedded in the concept of the learning organisation, it is appropriate to ask how to go about creating a learning organisation. Garvin (1993) suggests that such an organisation is skilled at five activities: systematic problem solving; experimentation with new approaches; learning from their own experience and past history; learning from the experience and best practice of others; and transferring knowledge quickly and efficiently throughout the organisation. These activities are briefly considered below.

1 Systematic problem solving

This activity draws heavily on the philosophy and methods of the quality movement. Its basic ideas include reliance, when diagnosing problems, on the scientific method (hypothesis generation) rather than guesswork; insistence on data rather than assumptions as a background for decision making; and use of simple statistical tools to organise data and draw inferences.

2 Experimentation

This activity looks beyond internal problem solving but uses the scientific method to search for and test new knowledge. It has two main forms: ongoing programmes and one-off demonstration projects.

(a) Ongoing programmes   These usually involve a continuing series of small experiments which have the aim of producing incremental gains in knowledge. They are the basis of most continuous improvement programmes and are particularly directed at shop-floor working. Ongoing programmes are dedicated to ensuring a flow of new ideas, even if these are imported from outside.

(b) Demonstration projects   These involve systemwide changes in a particular unit, site, etc. often aimed at developing new organisational capabilities. As such projects represent a clear break from the past they are usually designed from scratch. Demonstration projects have distinctive characteristics. They tend to embody principles and approaches which the organisation hopes to introduce later on a larger scale and they involve considerable 'learning by doing'. They are usually developed by strong multifunctional teams reporting directly to senior management. They tend to have only limited impact on the rest of the organisation unless they are accompanied by strategies for transferring learning.

All forms of experimentation seek to move from superficial knowledge to deep understanding. Put simply, it is the distinction between knowing how things are done and knowing why they occur. Knowing how is rooted in norms of behaviour, standards of practice, and settings of equipment. Knowing why captures underlying cause-and-effect relationships and accommodates exceptions, adaptations, and unforseen events.

3 Learning from past experience

In this activity organisations review their successes and failures, assess them systematically and record the lessons in a form which is open and assessible to employees. Fundamental to the approach is a perspective that enables companies to recognise the value of productive failure as contrasted with unproductive success. Productive failure leads to insight, understanding and an addition to the organisation's knowledge. Unproductive success occurs when something goes well and nobody knows how or why.

4 Learning from others

This activity recognises that not all learning comes from reflection and self-analysis. Powerful new perspectives and insights are to be gained by looking beyond an organisation's immediate environment. An enlightened organisation will know that other organisations even in different businesses from its own can be a source of ideas and creativity. This activity, known as 'benchmarking', bring best industry practice to the fore for the purposes of analysis, adoption and implementation. Almost anything can be benchmarked. Another source of external perspective is customers. They can provide up-to-date product information, competitive comparisons, insights into changing preferences and feedback about services.

External sources must find a receptive internal environment. Management must be open to criticism or bad news. Learning organisations cultivate the art of open, attentive listening.

5 Transferring knowledge

In this activity knowledge must spread speedily and efficiently throughout the organisation. Ideas have greater impact when they are disseminated rather than held in a few hands. There are a variety of means of doing this: reports; site visits; tours; programmes of job rotation; education and training; and secondment of experts. Education and training are powerful tools for the transfer of knowledge, however, for most effectiveness, they must be linked to implementation. Trainers must provide opportunities for practice on the job. Exhibit 8.5 below provides some examples of learning organisations in action in a US context.

Exhibit 8.5 Learning organisations in action in America

Systematic problem solving

Xerox launched its 'Leadership through quality initiative' in 1983. All employees have been trained in small-group activities and problem-solving techniques. Today a six-step process is used for almost all decisions: identify and select problem; analyse problem; generate potential solutions; select and plan the solution; implement the solution; and evaluate the solution. Employees are provided with tools in four areas: generating ideas and collecting information; reaching consensus; analysing and displaying data: and planning actions. Practice in the use of these tools is provided in a training programme lasting several days. Training is presented to family groups of the same department or unit and the tools are applied to real problems facing the group. The result is the development of a common vocabulary and a consistent, organisation-wide approach to problem solving. Once trained, employees are expected to use the techniques at all meetings and all topics are valid for inclusion.

Experimentation

Chaparral Steel sends its first-line supervisors on sabbaticals around the world, where they visit academic and industry leaders, develop an understanding of new work practices and technologies, bring back what they have learned and apply it within the organisation. Chaparral attributes a large part of its success, in becoming one of the five lowest cost steel plants in the world, to these initiatives.

Learning from past experience

Boeing, in the wake of difficulties with the 737 and 747 plane programmes, established a process to learn from past experience to ensure that its problems with these aircraft were not repeated. The organisation set up a high-level employee group called 'Project Homework' to compare the development processes of the 737 and 747 with those of the 707 and 727, the latter two being among their most profitable planes. The group were to develop a set of 'lessons' that could be used in future projects. Hundreds of recommendations were produced. Several members of the team were then transferred to the 757 and 767 start-ups and subsequently, guided by experience, the organisation produced the most successful, error-free launches in Boeing's history.

Learning from others

At Motorola, members of the Operating and Policy Committee, including the CEO, meet personally and on a regular basis with customers. Digital Equipment has developed an interactive process called 'contextual inquiry' that is used by software engineers to observe users of new technologies as they go about their work. Milliken has established 'first delivery teams' that accompany the first shipment of all products. Team members follow the product through the production process to see how it is used and they then develop ideas for further improvement.

Transferring knowledge

PPG opened a new float-glass plant in Chelhalis, Washington in 1986, employing radically new technology and innovations in HRM, the latter being developed by the plant manager and his staff. All workers were organised into small, self-managed teams with responsibility for work assignments, scheduling, problem solving and improvement, and peer review. After a number of years the plant manager was promoted to director of human resources for the whole group. Drawing on his experiences he developed a training programme for first-level supervisors which had the aim of teaching behaviours needed to manage employees in a participative, self-managing setting.

Source: Adapted from Garvin, 1993

It takes time to build a learning organisation. The first step is to cultivate an environment that is conducive to learning. Time has to be made for reflection and analysis, thinking out strategic plans, studying customer needs, assessing current work systems and developing new products. This cannot take place in a rushed and pressurised environment. Employees have to be given time for these activities and they need skills in brainstorming, problem solving and, evaluating experiments. A second step is to open up boundaries and stimulate the exchange of ideas through conferences, meetings and project teams across the organisation and with customers and suppliers. A third step is to create learning forums designed around particular learning goals, such as strategic reviews. Each area reviewed fosters learning by requiring employees to work with new knowledge and consider its implications.

Competence curriculum v. learning organisation

While there is seemingly much support for the concept of the learning organisation, some concern is expressed that their growth

may be endangered by the take-up by organisations of the MCI
approach to managerial competences. See exhibit 8.6 for a summary
of the MCI approach.

Exhibit 8.6 The management charter initiative

One of the earliest developments arising from the Constable and
McCormick and Handy reports was the management charter
initiative (MCI), launched by a group of chief executives from
the UK's top organisations, and having the aim of promoting high
standards of modern management practice and business skills
amongst all organisations in both private and public sectors. A
code of practice was drafted with which organisations joining the
initiative were expected to conform. Among its principles are:

- to improve leadership and management skills;
- to encourage and support managers in continuously developing management skills and leadership qualities in themselves
  and in those with whom they work;
- to provide a framework for self development within the
  context of organisation goals which is understood by those
  concerned and in which they play an active part;
- to ensure that the development of managerial expertise is a
  continuous process and will be integrated with the work flow
  of the organisation.

MCI is under the management of a national forum for
management education and development and represents the
CBI, BIM and leading UK organisations. It has established a
new framework for management and supervisory awards based
upon demonstrated ability to manage. There are four managerial
levels: supervisory, certificate, diploma and masters, and competences in relation to each level are in the process of being
specified. The development of MCI competences is outlined
below.

Competences, (MCI, 1990) consist of key roles with each role
having units of competence. Each unit is made up of elements of
competence. Performance criteria are set against each element.
Range indicators relating to each of these describe the areas of
application in which the manager must provide evidence of
competence. In addition, there is a separate set of competences
relating to the kind of personal competences each manager needs

in order to be effective (Critten, 1993). These are summarised below:

Planning

- Showing concern for excellence
- Setting and prioritising objectives
- Monitoring and responding to situations

Managing others

- Showing sensitivity to the needs of others
- Relating to others
- Obtaining the commitment of others
- Presenting oneself positively to others

Managing oneself

- Showing self confidence and personal drive
- Managing personal emotions and stress
- Managing personal learning and development

Using intellect

- Collecting and analysing information
- Identifying and applying concepts
- Taking decisions

Sources: MCI, 1987, 1990; Critten, 1993

Macfarlane and Lomas (1994) very much doubt that the MCI approach to management education is appropriate to the needs of the learning organisation. Its concept of managerial competence has a number of characteristics which would appear to place it in conflict with the aims of organisations which 'search constantly to improve their understanding of structure, the nature of work and its possibilities, [and] . . . encourage the development of all members of the organisation, seeking continuously to transform them in response to dynamic market conditions'. The competence approach is based on absolutes in that the individual is either competent or not. As a consequence it fails to acknowledge that learning is an incremental process. Also there is no allowance for the assessment of relative standards and indeed the learner will quickly realise that there is no need to do more than the mimimum required for competence. 'Managers want to gain recognition but they will resent a system which rewards all, irrespective of individual effort and achievement.' A curriculum which defines the universal (the idea that competences are generic) is stifling. Such a curriculum promotes conformity rather than critical learning. It assigns a passive role to the learner and thus there are no challenges to the status quo. The provision of a 'relevant' curriculum inhibits intellectual curiosity. It preordains learning objectives, which is undemocratic and, because only observable outcomes are seen as valid measures of performance, it will lean towards a quantifiable behaviourist approach and the easily definable. Important qualitative outcomes may be neglected. Table 8.4 illustrates the different orientations between the competence curriculum and a learning organisation.

Macfarlane and Lomas suggest that the MCI model is based on a control philosophy rather than empowerment, equates behaviourism with education, and represents a marginalisation of organisation development as a body of knowledge in favour of a systematic training model of management.

USING PERFORMANCE APPRAISAL IN STRATEGIC TRAINING AND DEVELOPMENT

The assessment of employee performance interfaces with training and development and with the organisation's employee reward system. The latter relationship is dealt with in chapter 9. A performance appraisal system is a source of data on which training and development decisions in relation to improvements to current performance and plans for future development can be based.

Table 8.4 A mirror of disharmony

Competence curriculum	Learning organisation
Addresses current practice	Addresses future practice
Bounded knowledge	Unbounded knowledge
Promotes conformity	Promotes debate
Inward focus	Outward focus
Discourages reflection	Encourages reflection
Control	Empowerment

Source: Macfarlane and Lomas, 1994

Performance appraisal represents an important and potentially· effective tool within a process of strategic human resource management.

Use of performance appraisal

A survey of UK employers in 1986, carried out for the Institute of Personnel Management, indicated that 82 per cent operate some form of performance appraisal scheme (Bramham, 1994). An American study of Fortune's 500 largest industrial organisations found it in use in 78 per cent of these organisations (Klatt *et al.*, 1985). Comparisons of the uses of appraisal within the two cultures demonstrates considerable divergence. See table 8.5.

The American system introduces motivation, counselling, organisational planning, planning for training and development and merit related bonuses, applications which do not appear among the uses named by the UK organisations. All of the applications named could be accommodated within the model of HRM which has been developing over a number of years in America in response to a changing environmental context in which human resources are seen to have strategic significance. Performance appraisal used in this scenario has a strategic orientation. In the UK, the organisations

Table 8.5 Comparison of uses of appraisal in UK and US organisations

UK	%	USA	%
To review past performance	98	Counselling the ratee	88
To assess training and development needs	97	Planning training or development for ratee	85
To help improve current performance	97	Motivating the ratee to achieve higher performance	85
To set performance objectives	81	Considering the ratee for promotion	84
To assist career planning decisions	75	Merit increases or bonuses	75
To assess future potential/ promotability	71	Considering the retention or discharge of ratee	58
To assess increases to new levels in salary	40	Improving company planning	56

Sources: Bramham, 1994; Klatt, Murdick and Schuster, 1985.

surveyed are using performance appraisal to review the past, improve current performance and set performance objectives. It is also used to assess training and development needs and to make decisions about future potential, promotability and career planning. Less than half the organisations link performance appraisal with salary. Clearly its use is more focused on training. Given the poor record of training achievement existing in the UK it seems reasonable to wonder what use is being made of the training needs data gathered through appraisal. Absence of any mention of the use of performance appraisal data in planning bears out that a link between strategy and training and development is not well developed.

Dunphy and Hackman (1988) suggest that the use of performance appraisal is on the increase in both private and public-sector organisations in response to the changing environment of contemporary organisations. There is pressure for greater accountability with managers being asked to justify expenditure on wages and salaries in terms of value added per employee. A further pressure is the complexity and speed of environmental change. With managers having to focus more on the environment, their role has changed from supervisor of every job to that of coordinator who delegates both authority and responsibility. Performance appraisal provides a link to (a) clarify responsibilities and ensure effective performance and (b) identify and develop employee potential in the interest of ensuring a future mix of skills that are appropriate to changing technologies and markets. A third pressure comes from employees themselves. They are more highly educated than in the past and have higher expectations. They are demanding equality of opportunity and their demands are backed by legislation.

Link between performance appraisal and strategic training and development

Anderson (1993) makes the case for a strategic orientation in performance appraisal when he says, 'All organisations must face up to the challenge of how to evaluate, utilise and develop the skills and abilities of their employees to ensure that individuals gain as much satisfaction as possible from their jobs while making effective contributions.'

Dunphy and Hackman (1988) provide some insights into how performance appraisal may serve strategic training and development. Performance appraisal can be used to audit the current workforce and then create a human resource profile that fits the strategic plan. One way to profile the workforce is to classify it on two dimensions of current and potential performance. The resultant human resource profile will consist of: 'high performance, 'high potential, stars'; 'high performance, low potential, workhorses'; high potential, low performance, problem employees'; 'low performance, low potential, deadwood'. The assumption made is that most organisations would wish to turn problem employees into stars, keep the workhorses motivated, utilise their stars to their fullest potential and remove the deadwood from the organisation. Performance appraisal can also be used to develop a flexible workforce. One method of doing this is through multi-skilling. Organisations are moving away from an approach to work organisation based on specialisation and rigidly demarcated jobs to one in which employees perform a range of skills required to complete a whole project or service activity. The performance appraisal system can be structured to support the approach by providing objective measures of skill attainment. It can also be used to identify and develop the skills of employees with potential.

In summary, therefore, it is central to the design of a performance appraisal system to identify and specifiy the criteria by which to measure current and potential performance. This aspect of performance appraisal has a very poor record in terms of reliability and validity (Fisher *et al.*, 1990). Problems in this respect need to be eradicated as do problems with subjectivity which may be introduced into a performance appraisal system by the evaluator. If performance appraisal is to serve strategic training and development then its credibility as a technique must not be in doubt. This is an issue which requires to be addressed with some urgency.

CONCLUSION

In defining terms relevant to this chapter, it has been seen that development incorporates the meanings of training and education in a concept of HR development. It has also been noted that organisational learning provides the overarching concept which can accommodate strategic HR development.

A case for strategic training and development is made on several grounds. First, it has been seen that training and education are political issues because of their relationship with an organisation's competitiveness and growing recognition of the strategic significance of human resources. Second, literature has demonstrated that there is a mismatch between national training and education provision and the needs of industry and that there is underinvestment in training by industry. In public sector terms there is difficulty with demonstrating value for money. The government has been trying to develop an investment in people culture.

Examination of the current state of organisational training demonstrates (a) lack of strategic application and (b) a theoretical base that has yet to be fully put to the service of the organisation. It is found that learning theory and principles were mostly applied to systematic operative training which, while being efficient for the training of particular skills, is tied to a management control model of learning. There is some concern also that the MCI competence model represents application of the systems model at managerial level.

It is suggested that the control model is inappropriate to the needs of flexible, changing organisations. Learning theory is, at present, finding its most 'conscious' expression in the concept of the learning organisation which seems to accommodate the cognitive, gestalt and humanism theories of learning. It is possible that there is room also for the behaviourist theory, on which the systematic approach is said to be based. It may be that the systematic approach represents single loop learning while the learning organisation is second loop learning but can incorporate single loop within it. The learning organisation also utilises the principles of learning in terms of: motivation, individual differences, feedback, distributed (incremental) learning and active experimentation.

It is possible that the learning organisation represents the present state of evolution in organisation development. Further work is needed in an effort to understand the issues involved in such evolution.

A major weakness in relation to strategic training and development lies with inadequacies in ability to evaluate. Progress in this field is closely tied to the state of development in linking training and development with strategy. Evaluation has no basis in effectiveness if criteria being evaluated are not tied to the strategy of the organisation. As has been seen ability to identify, define and set standards in relation to criteria for training and development is weakened by problems of attaining reliability and validity. These weaknesses all converge.

In general, however, it may be said that the state of development in relation to linking training and development with strategy is showing considerable signs of development, particularly in relation to: developing links with generic strategy; approaches to management development and the learning organisation. While much research is needed there is also optimism that strategic training and development has a significant role to play within the concept of strategic human resource management.

REFERENCES:

Ainley, P. and Corney, M. (1990) *Training for the Future: Rise and Fall of the Manpower Services Commission*, London: Cassell Education.

Anderson, G.C. (1993) 'From performance appraisal to performance management', *Training and Development (UK)* 11(10): 10,12,14.

Argyris, C. and Schon, D. (1974) *Theory in Practice*, San Francisco, CA: Jossey-Bass.

Arnold, J., Robertson, I.T. and Cooper, C.L. (1991) *Work Psychology: Understanding Human Behaviour in the Workplace*, London: Pitman.

Attwood, M. and Beer, N. (1988) 'Developing a learning organisation – reflections on a personal and organisatonal workshop in a district health authority', *Management Education and Development*, 19(3): 201–14.

Bateson, G. (1973) *Steps to an Ecology of Mind*, London: Palladin.

Begg, D., Fischer, S. and Dornbusch, R. (1984) *Economics*, Maidenhead: McGraw Hill.

Bramham, J. (1994) *Human Resource Planning*, London: Institute of Training and Development.

Buckley, J. and Kemp, N. (1987) 'The strategic role of management development', *Management Education and Development*, 18(3): 157–74.

Butler, J.E., Ferris, G.R. and Napier, N.K. (1991) *Strategy and Human Resource Management*, Cincinnati, Ohio: South Western Publishing Co.

Calvert, G., Mobley, S. and Marshall, L. (1994) 'Grasping the learning organisation', *Training and Development*, June: 38,40–3.

Carnevale, A.P., Gainer, L.J. and Villet, J. (1990) *Training in America: The Organisation and Strategic Role of Training*, San Francisco, CA: Jossey-Bass.

Casner-Lotto, J. (1988) *Successful Training Strategies*, San Francisco: Jossey-Bass.

Catalanello, R. and Redding, J. (1989) 'Three strategic training roles', *Training and Development Journal*, 43(12): 51–4.

Clark, N. (1991) *Managing Personal Learning and Change*, Maidenhead: McGraw-Hill.

CNAA (1991) 'The White Papers' Council for National Academic Awards, Issue 11, Autumn: 1–2.

Cocheu, T. (1993) *Making Quality Happen*, San Francisco: Jossey-Bass.

Constable, E.J. and McCormick R. (1987) 'The making of British managers'. A report for the BIM and CBI into management training, education and development. Rushden, Northants: BIM.

Critten, P. (1993) *Investing in People: Towards Corporate Capability*, Oxford: Butterworth Heinemann.

Douglas, J., Klein, S. and Hunt, D. (1985) *The Strategic Managing of Human Resources*, New York: John Wiley.

Drennan, D. (1992) *Transforming Company Culture*, Maidenhead: McGraw-Hill.

Dunphy, D.C. and Hackman, B.K. (1988) 'Performance appraisal as a strategic intervention', *Human Resource Management Australia*, 26(2): 23–34.

Economic, Research and Evaluation Division (ed.) (1994) 'Investors in people', *Labour Market Quarterly Report*, Moorfoot, Sheffield: Employment Department.

Elliott, R.F. (1991) *Labour Economics: A Comparative Text*, Maidenhead: McGraw-Hill.

Farnham, D. (1984) *Personnel Management in Context*, London: Institute of Personnel Management.

Finn, R. (1994) 'Investors in people: counting the dividends' *Personnel Management*, 26(5): 30–1.

Fisher, C.D., Schoenfeldt, L.F. and Shaw, J.B. (1990) *Human Resource Management*, Boston: Houghton Mifflin.

Fombrun, C., Tichy, N.M. and Devanna, M.A. (eds) (1984) *Strategic Human Resource Management*, New York: John Wiley.

Freedman, D.H. (1992) 'Is management still a science?' *Harvard Business Review*, 70(6), November–December: 26–38.

Fritz, R. (1989) *The Path of Least Resistance*, New York: Fawcett-Columbine.

Fritz, R. (1991) *Creating*, New York: Fawcett-Columbine.

Fritz, R. (1993) *Corporate Tides* (unpublished MS).

Garratt, B. (1987) *The Learning Organisation*, London: Fontant/Collins.

Garratt, B. (1990) *Creating the Learning Organisation*, London: Institute of Directors.

Garvin, D.A. (1993) 'Building a learning organisation', *Harvard Business Review*, 71(4): 78–91.

Gilley, J.W. and Eggland, S.A. (1989) *Principles of Human Resource Development*, Reading, Mass: Addison-Wesley.

Greig, F.W. (1988) 'National strategies and structures: the international perspective', *Training and Development*, January: 16–18, 20, 22, 24–5.

Handy, C. (1987) 'The making of managers. A report on management education, training and development in the USA, West Germany, France, Japan and the UK', London: National Economic Development Office.

Harrison, R. (1989) *Training and Development*, London: Institute of Personnel Management.

Hawkins, P. (1994) 'Organisational learning: taking stock and facing the challenge', *Management Learning*, 25(1): 71–82.

Healey, N.M. (1993a) 'From Keynesian demand management to Thatcherism' in N.M. Healey, (ed.) *Britain's Economic Miracle: Myth or Reality*, London: Routledge: 1–40.

Healey, N.M. (1993b) 'The Conservative government's fight against inflation: ten years without cheers', in N.M. Healey, (ed.) *Britain's Economic Miracle: Myth or Reality*, London: Routledge: 127–49.

HMSO (1994) 'Competitiveness: helping business to win' HMSO. White Paper, London: HMSO.

Honey, P. and Mumford, A. (1989a) *Using Your Learning Styles*, published and distributed by Peter Honey, Maidenhead, Berks, UK.

Honey, P. and Mumford, A. (1989b) *The Manual of Learning Opportunities*, published and distributed by Peter Honey, Maidenhead, Berks., UK.

Jessup, G. (1991) *Outcomes: NVQs and the Emerging Model of Education and Training*, London: Falmer Press.

Judge, D. and Dickson, T. (1991) 'The British state, governments and manufacturing decline' in E. Esland, (ed.) *Education, Training and Employment*, vol. 1. Wokingham: Addison-Wesley.

Kane, R.L. (1986) 'A strategic look at training and development', *Human Resource Management Australia*, August: 42–52.

Keep, E. (1989) 'A training scandal' in K. Sisson, (ed.) *Personnel Management in Britain*, Oxford: Basil Blackwell: 177–202.

Kenney, J. and Reid, M. (1990) *Training Interventions*, London: IPM.

Kirkpatrick, D.L. (1987) 'Evaluation of training, in R.L. Craig (ed.) *Training and Development Handbook: A Guide to Human Resource Development*, New York: McGraw-Hill.

Klatt, L.A., Murdick, R.G. and Schuster, F.E. (1985) *Human Resource Management*, Columbus, Ohio: Charles E. Merrill.

Kolb, D.A. (1984) *Experiential Learning*, New York: Prentice-Hall.

Macfarlane, B. and Lomas, L. (1994) 'Competence-based management education and the needs of the learning organisation', *Education and Training*, 36(1): 29–32.

Management Charter Initiative (1987) *The Management Charter – A Code of Practice*, London: MCI.

Management Charter Initiative (1990) *Occupational Standards for Managers*, London: MCI.

McKergow, M. (1994) 'What's systemic thinking got to do with anything': organisational learning – a framework for managers' *Organisation and People*, 1(1): 16–20.

Miller, P. (1991) 'A strategic look at management development', *Personnel Management*, August: 45–7.

Nonaka, I. (1991) 'The knowledge-creating company', *Harvard Business Review*, November–December: 96–104.

Nordhaug, P. (1991) 'Human resource provision and transformation: the role of training and development', *Human Resource Management Journal*, 1(2): 17–26.

Osbaldeston, M. and Barham, K. (1992) 'Using management development for competitive advantage', *Long Range Planning*, 25(6): 18–24.

Page, T. (1991) 'What the White Papers say', *Trainer's Briefing Collection*, Issue 3, September: London: Kogan Page: 1–4.

Parker, D. (1993) 'Privatisation ten years on: a critical analysis', in N.M. Healey, (ed.) *Britain's Economic Miracle: Myth or Reality*, London: Routledge: 174–94.

Patton, J., Rt. Hon (1994) 'Education since 1944', paper to *Times Educational Supplement* and University of London Institute of Education Conference, May, London: Department of Education.

Pedler, M., Burgoyne, J. and Boydell, T. (1991) *The Learning Company*, Maidenhead: McGraw-Hill.

Revans, R. (1982) *The Origins and Growth of Action Learning*, Bromley, Kent and Lund, Sweden: Chartwell-Bratt.

Senge, P. (1990) *The Fifth Discipline: The Art and Practice of the Learning Organisation*, New York: Doubleday.

Skills & Enterprise Network (1994) 'How do employers benefit from becoming Investors in People?' Issue 9/94:PO Box 12, Lenton, Nottingham, UK.

Storey, J. and Sisson, K. (1993) *Managing Human Resources and Industrial Relations*, Buckingham: Open University Press.

West, P. (1994) 'The concept of the learning organisaton', *Journal of European Industrial Training*, 18(1): 15–21.

Wexley, K.N. and Latham, G.P. (1991) *Developing and Training Human Resources in Organisations*, New York: Harper and Collins.

'What the White Papers say'. . . Trainer's briefing collection (Education and Training for the 21st century) issue 3, September 1991, London: Kogan Page.

Woodhall, M. (1991) 'Human capital concepts' in G. Esland (ed.) *Education, Training and Employment*, vol. 2. Buckingham: The Open University: 27–34.

Chapter 9

The strategic management of motivation and rewards

INTRODUCTION

It is curious that so little attention has been paid until recently to motivation and reward management in books and articles on strategic management. In part, this is symptomatic of the lack of attention to human resources amongst writers on strategic management already noted in this book, in part it is because the behaviour of employees is frequently taken for granted by planners brought up on a diet of econometric models. A concern for motivation has been left to occupational psychologists, whose findings have been deemed interesting but irrelevant to bottom line results. It is also curious that Japanese writers on strategy, working in a country where attention to human resources is a top priority, also appear to overlook these issues (see, for example, Ohmae, 1982). This may be because in national cultures typified by Japan the loyalty, obedience and motivation of employees can be taken for granted in a manner not possible in the West.

Motivation and rewards now feature increasingly on the agendas of European executives and top managers (Evans and Lorange, 1989). Two dimensions of reward management have created this concern. The first is cost. In an era when organisations have had to reduce their headcount dramatically, reducing the wages bill has been a priority, although this has frequently been addressed in a reactive rather than strategic manner. The second has been the realisation that competitive advantage and customer service can only be achieved if employees are strongly motivated to pursue organisational goals.

REWARD MANAGEMENT AND STRATEGY

Contemporary wisdom is that reward management should be considered after strategy has been decided, in much the same way as organisation structure. An example of this view is provided by Michael Armstrong and Helen Murlis who say that 'reward management is the process of developing and implementing strategies, policies and systems which help the organisation to achieve its objectives by obtaining and keeping the people it needs, and by increasing their motivation and commitment.' They go on to say 'reward management strategies and policies are driven by corporate and human resource management strategies '(Armstrong and Murlis, 1994). Gerry Johnson and Kevan Scholes comment that 'reward systems are an important means of achieving compliance with planned strategic change' (Johnson and Scholes, 1989). John Thompson states that 'it is important to emphasise that, in assessing and designing an appropriate structure, the process aspects must incorporate the need for measuring and rewarding performance' (Thompson 1990).

There are however dangers in treating motivation and reward management as secondary considerations, to be tackled after the primary considerations of financial targets, markets, and operational processes. These dangers are similar to those described in chapter 4, when the tendency to decide structure after strategy was examined. Taken in isolation, decisions on strategy and structure may undermine motivation and reward programmes. As emphasised in the opening chapters of this book, strategic management today is concerned with an increasingly turbulent environment, and must focus from the outset on coping with change and with how to achieve successful implementation.

DEFINITIONS OF MOTIVATION AND REWARD MANAGEMENT

The term 'reward management' is of recent origin, but preferable to more traditional British terms such as 'pay', 'wages', 'salaries', 'remuneration', or 'compensation'. 'Compensation' is an American term, and implies that work is such an unpleasant experience that employees have to be 'compensated' for turning up. 'Wages' and 'salaries' hark back to unfortunate class distinctions in this country between manual workers and office workers. These terms also carry a connotation that money is what an organisation offers to employees in return for their contribution. People in fact seek a whole range of benefits from their employment, of which money is only one, even if it is the primary consideration. The term 'reward management' indicates that these benefits can be 'managed', and are not simply items to be left to the calculation of the wages clerk, the operation of piecework systems, or the consequences of collective bargaining with trade unions.

The range of rewards normally include both direct pay and indirect benefits (holiday pay, pensions, etc.). These are 'extrinsic' rewards, being tangible expressions of the employer's side of the contract with employees in return for their contributions of time effort and skill. But organisational rewards also include 'intrinsic' rewards such as status, recognition, companionship, security, career development, feeling of self-worth, and sense of achievement and purpose. Extrinsic rewards can be measured directly by accountants as costs, and therefore tend to be given a higher priority by management. They have also been the primary focus of industrial relations and collective bargaining, and have therefore been given high priority by trade unions. Employees themselves however frequently attach high priority to intrinsic rewards, and these can have a major bearing on the satisfaction, motivation and productivity of employees.

MOTIVATION

All employees are motivated. This psychological fact is frequently overlooked by managers, who talk about the need to motivate their employees. To psychologists 'motivation is a psychological concept related to the strength and direction of human behaviour' (Robertson, Smith and Cooper, 1992). What management needs to do is to align the motivation of employees with the needs of the organisation. This may on occasion require modification to the goals of the organisation and methods of working, in addition to attempts to influence the motivation of employees. Managing motivation is the process of recognising and providing for the needs of employees in such a manner that high levels of performance are achieved. In its workplace setting, it means providing for those needs which individuals bring with them to their place of work.

Decisions and actions based on a valid model of human behaviour are much more likely to achieve success than if based on incorrect assumptions. Management theories in the first half of this century were based on incomplete, inadequate, or just plain wrong concepts of human motivation (Schein, 1980). A notable example of failure to understand this process was the piece-working methods in use in the British car industry in the 1960s and 1970s, which contributed to the poor industrial relations, low productivity, poor quality of work and subsequent demise of well known car manufacturers.

Plans to motivate employees will not be successful unless they are part of a comprehensive, integrated, and thoroughly up to date scheme of work planning. If the objective is to be competitive and to deliver high quality products and customer service, it is essential to achieve high levels of motivation aligned to company goals and team working. A happier example from the car industry is provided by Nissan. High quality and productivity at their Sunderland factory is achieved by carefully selected and well motivated individuals and teams using appropriate methods using the most modern equipment. This is integrated into a modern 'lean production' system (Womack, Jones and Roos, 1990). As Peter Wickens, personnel director of Nissan, commented, '. . . it is extremely important to recognise that long-term high quality demands not only motivation of the workforce, but also control of the process' (Wickens, 1993). Motivating the workforce, like other important management initiatives, is a necessary (but not sufficient) condition to achieve high levels of productivity and effectiveness.

A theory of motivation relevant to strategic reward management is 'expectancy' theory, (sometimes given the longer title of 'expectancy-valence' theory). Emphasis on the word 'expectancy' indicates that considerable emphasis is placed on the expectations of employees. Expectancy theory predicts that outcomes which have high expectations of being realised and which are highly valued will result in individuals putting considerable effort into their work. It recognises that different people have different types of needs and goals, and that their behaviour will be influenced by the degree to which they perceive that they will be able to satisfy their needs and achieve their goals (Steers and Porter, 1979). The model in figure 9.1. illustrates its logic.

This model reminds us that high performance by individuals or teams will only come about if they are clear about their tasks and have a positive attitude towards them ('role perception'), and furthermore, that they possess the necessary aptitudes, abilities

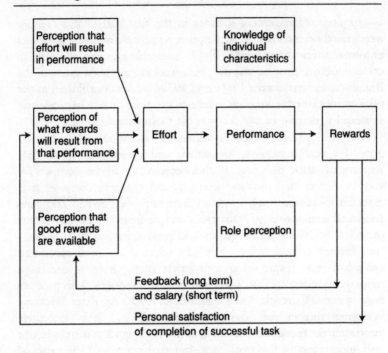

Figure 9.1 Expectancy theory of motivation

and competencies. Effort will then be exerted which will achieve a high level of performance if they perceive:

(a) that their efforts will result in high performance;
(b) that high performance will lead to rewards;
(c) that the rewards available are rewards which they desire.

The final stage is positive feedback, the actual receipt of these desirable rewards (both extrinsic and intrinsic).

A moment's reflection on the large number of organisations where a majority of employees have little confidence that increased effort on their part will lead to increased rewards convinces of the relevance of this theory. The emphasis on perception also reminds us that it is the perception of the employees that counts, and not the perception of management who all too frequently are out of touch with the true feelings of their workforce. Employees need to be convinced before they exert maximum effort.

The strategic implications of expectancy theory then lie in the need to take into account the expectations and perceptions of employees when drawing up plans, and in this sense are akin to the need for strategic planners to take culture into account, as described in chapter 4. Both culture and employee expectations take a considerable amount of time to change, and it cannot be assumed that strategy can be first determined and expectations and perceptions subsequently treated to a 'quickfix' to ensure compliance. In the longer term strategy may aim to change employees' expectations over a period of several years by a process of culture change, but in the short term they have to be treated as a constraint. Expectancy theory can subsequently be used as a basis for shaping more detailed reward policies and practices, as described in subsequent parts of this chapter.

Another modern theory of motivation with significance for reward strategy is 'goal-setting' (Locke, 1968). There is a considerable body of evidence to show that if appropriate goals are set for individuals and groups, and in a manner which is acceptable to those concerned, higher levels of motivation and performance are likely to be achieved. Appropriate goals have been found to direct attention and action, mobilise effort, increase task persistence, and motivate the search for appropriate performance strategies. Difficult goals only lead to higher performance when an individual is committed to them. Commitment to goals can be considerably increased if employees participate in the goal setting process (Locke and Latham 1990, Cooper *et al.*, 1992). Provision of performance feedback is a necessary condition for goals to have their full effect (Locke and Latham, 1990).

The strategic implications of goal setting are brought out clearly in the process of performance management, examined in more detail later. At this point it is useful to note that strategic decisions are frequently expressed in terms of goals and targets. Provided these are then translated into goals and targets at every level in the organisation, and that employees are involved in the process of setting targets (a point usually conveniently overlooked), they have a greater chance of motivating employees and of being successful.

A summary of the characteristics of the work environment most likely to increase levels of motivation based on available research evidence includes the following points (adapted from Robertson, Smith and Cooper 1992):

- Employees have a realistic understanding of the links between effort and performance
- Employees have the competence and confidence to translate effort into performance
- Control systems are only introduced when necessary
- Performance requirements are expressed as hard and specific but attainable goals
- Employees participate in setting these goals
- Employees receive regular and understandable feedback on performance
- Rewards are seen as fair
- Rewards are tailored to individual requirements and preferences
- Jobs are designed to give variety, autonomy, and feedback.

These characteristics provide a useful checklist as we turn to an examination of the options available to those responsible for developing an appropriate reward strategy for an organisation.

THE OBJECTIVES OF A REWARD STRATEGY

Armstrong and Murlis suggest that reward management strategies must (Armstrong and Murlis, 1994)

- Be congruent with and support corporate values and beliefs
- Emanate from business strategy and goals
- Be linked to organisation performance
- Drive and support desired behaviour at all levels
- Fit desired management styles
- Provide the competitive edge needed to attract and retain the level of skills the organisation needs
- Be anchored to the realities of the labour market.

The first of these, referring to corporate values and beliefs, underlines the significance of corporate culture as setting the context for reward management strategies. This is further brought out in the following list drawn up by British personnel director Gareth Trevor, who comments that

In considering strategic compensation planning for a high performance environment we must first determine some of the characteristics of such an environment. I suggest these include:

- Superior achievement by employees

- Better than average skills and capabilities in the workforce
- Commitment to the objectives of the company and to personal objectives
- 'Job space' – a belief that any employee can expand the limits of his job through personal contribution
- 'Can do' attitude – no question of 'we tried that before and it doesn't work'
- A value system which recognises personal and team achievement – both publicly and personally
- An environment which promotes an appetite for change and innovation
- An environment which promotes effective teamwork
- Culture of intense curiosity about the performance of the organisation in every aspect compared with its competitors – external calibration of performance is a way of life
- An environment that takes a consistent approach to non-performance.

In brief all these relate to a Company's culture, and this plays a major role in determining and creating a high performance environment.

(Trevor, 1990)

The need to link reward strategy to performance has been a persistent theme in recent years amongst leading authorities on corporate renewal. Rosabeth Moss Kanter, in a special issue of *Personnel Journal* devoted to 'The Quiet Revolution in Pay Practices' commented that

Traditionally, pay has largely reflected input, not output, factors ... status was the real basis – the standing of the job in the hierarchy of organisational relations. This arrangement is no longer viable or supportable ... From merit raises to giving people a piece of the entrepreneurial action, the new options for determining pay drive towards finding ways to value, and then pay for, contribution.

(Kanter, 1987)

This so called 'quiet revolution' shifting the emphasis from status to contribution in reward strategy is creating the kind of reaction all revolutions produce, and many employees do not feel comfortable with the radical change it has introduced. This is not surprising.

After working for maybe twenty years in a bureaucratic organisation employing a hierarchical graded pay structure, where annual increases are guaranteed and few links between performance and pay exist, it can be quite traumatic for employees to be faced with working in a downsized de-layered organisation where performance determines one's pay and annual increase – if any!

Edward Lawler, the American authority on motivation and pay systems, comments

> it is important to once again stress that the design process needs to start with the organisation's business strategy, as translated into pay system objectives. Without establishing strategic objectives in areas such as the kind of behaviours to be motivated, the kind of people to be attracted and retained, and the kind of structure which an organisation wants to operate with, it is impossible to design a reward system that adds value to the organisation.
>
> (Lawler 1990)

The choices arising from a review of reward strategies have been brought out by Randall Schuler (Schuler, 1987).

Low base salaries	–	High base salaries
Internal equity	–	External equity
Few perks	–	Many perks
Standard fixed package	–	Flexible package
No incentives	–	Many incentives
Short-term incentives	–	Long-term incentives
No employment security	–	High employment security
Hierarchical	–	Egalitarian

Making the correct choices are part and parcel of strategic human resource planning.

JOB EVALUATION

Job evaluation attempts to create a rational pay structure based on the content of jobs, that is, based on job descriptions, and has been the mainstay of many large company schemes in recent decades. It is usually associated with hierarchical grading structures, and bases its appeal to workers on the traditional concept of the 'rate for the job' and to management on providing a tidy and seemingly rational system. A survey by the Institute of Personnel Management found that the principal reason put forward for introducing job evaluation was in order to achieve 'fair pay' (Spencer, 1990). This survey also found less emphasis on traditional collective uses revolving round formalised industrial relations and group pressures; much more emphasis on the explanation of relativities across different categories of job, and determination of reward on an individual basis.

Today a growing number of organisations are critical of traditional job evaluation schemes, principally because they are seen as bureaucratic and hindrances to change. Typical comments include (Murlis and Fitt, 1991):

- Job definition supports a rigid hierarchical organisation and concepts of status, which suppress employee motivation and creativity.
- Placing the heaviest emphasis on job requirements discounts the importance of other compensatable factors – particularly individual capability and performance.
- A small flexible team of multi-skilled people in a flatter organisation structure makes better economic sense than a large number of single-skilled people.
- The future of many industries and private and public sector services lies in the knowledge of their workers, and pay systems need to reflect this.

Reward management needs to be kept under constant review. Where strategic human resource plans indicate a need for more flexible policies to match rapid change in the environment, job evaluation schemes will have to be modified accordingly (usually by simplification), or abandoned altogether. Where the prevailing culture of the organisation still places a heavy emphasis on internal equity, as in much of the public sector, change will have to be more gradual. Even where formal job evaluation schemes have been abolished, it still has to be recognised, as Peter Wickens has commented, that 'inter-job comparisons are made constantly on an informal basis' (Wickens, 1987).

PERFORMANCE MANAGEMENT

An earlier text on human resource strategy claims that there exist just four 'generic' HRM functions. (Forbrun, Tichy and Devanna, 1984) These are selection, appraisal, reward, and development. The appraisal system is stated to be the 'cornerstone of an effective human resource system.' Other writers see appraisal as 'vital in any system that attempts to link the performance of the organisation with the performance of people' (Miller, 1992). Thompson states that

> the attention of general managers might be focused on either strategic or financial performance targets or a mix of the two, depending on the control systems which prevail. Their rewards should be related to the expectations that the overall strategic leader has for performance in their divisions and business units.
>
> (Thompson, 1990)

Appraisal systems have enjoyed a chequered history during this century, shunned by some organisations, adopted enthusiastically by others, and tolerated by some as a necessary administrative procedure that lacks any real significance. Appraisal systems can only claim however to possess strategic significance where they are seen to create a meaningful link between the efforts of employees and the overall objectives of the organisation. Traditional appraisal systems failed to do this because they were limited to one or more of the following three objectives:

- As a control device, to assist managers and supervisors in controlling the output of employees, penalising those who were considered not to be pulling their weight;
- As a basis for training, encouraging managers to send subordinates on relevant training programmes; and
- As a basis for merit pay, providing managers with a procedure for giving usually quite small sums of money to subordinates whom they deemed to be better than the rest.

Not unnaturally many of these types of scheme have proved to be less than satisfactory, disliked by both managers and employees. (Cowling and Mailer, 1990).

The two most significant developments in appraisal schemes occurred in the 1970s, with the recognition that it was inappropriate to ask line managers to appraise the personality traits of their subordinates and the adoption of a 'management by objectives' philosophy in many organisations. These two developments rightly swung the focus of appraisal schemes on to a reinforcement of the links between individual performance and departmental performance. A further significant development was the recognition that subordinates should play an active role in the appraisal process in order to achieve a degree of commitment to the achievement of targets. The necessity for this had been pointed out many years before by Peter Drucker in the chapter on 'Management by objectives and self-control' in his classic book *The Practice of Management* (Drucker, 1961), but it was a decade later before the mounting evidence of research on motivation and appraisal schemes persuaded organisations to treat appraisal as a two way process, rather than just a top–down process (Fletcher and Williams, 1976).

Performance management can be seen as a logical progression in the history of the development of appraisal systems, and is a relatively recently developed method of managing. Whilst a number of different versions are currently in use, fully fledged versions possess a number of common characteristics. These include (Bevan and Thompson, 1991):

- The organisation has a shared vision of its objectives, or a mission statement, which it communicates to all its employees.
- The organisation sets individual performance management targets which are related both to operating unit and wider organisational objectives.
- It conducts a regular, formal review of progress towards these targets.
- It uses the review process to identify training development and reward outcomes.
- It evaluates the effectiveness of the whole process and its contribution to overall organisational performance to allow changes and improvements to be made.

To this list might usefully be added (IDS study 518, 1992)

- Career counselling.

An example of performance management in practice which illustrates the link between individual targets and corporate objectives and strategy is provided in figure 9.2.

The available evidence indicates that only a minority of organisations have as yet embarked on full scale performance management. In a survey sponsored by the Institute of Personnel Management (IPM), just under 20 per cent of responding companies claimed to operate a formal performance management system. This study also found a significant divergence between companies who emphasised the link to financial rewards for individuals as against those who stressed the link to training and development. In this respect

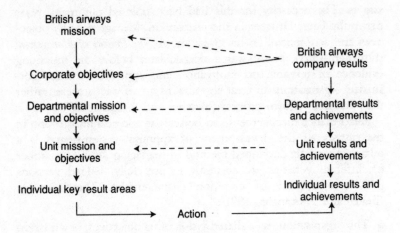

Figure 9.2 Performance management: the annual results cycle

performance management reflects a long standing division of opinion amongst companies operating traditional appraisal systems on the relative merits of an emphasis on rewards or development (Long, 1986). This split is based on the widely held view that a focus on rewards can divert attention from the equally or more important consideration of improving future performance by developing those competencies shown to be necessary by the performance review.

A follow-up study by the IPM (Fletcher and Williams, 1992) found major weaknesses in the manner in which performance management was being conducted in this country. Four crucial issues were highlighted. First there was frequently little indication of a real sense of ownership of performance management among line managers, and therefore, second, no depth of commitment. Too many managers perceived it as a top–down process with no feedback loop operating. Third, there was a widespread perception that performance management was 'owned' by the HR department. And fourth, a lack of thought and imagination had been shown in tackling the issue of rewards. Merit pay was being applied in a blanket fashion to employees of differing organisational levels, ages, functions, career stages, and industries, and hence was not motivating many employees. External constraints in many cases prevented targets being reached, and the merit payments themselves were frequently too small in proportion to gross salary to act as a real incentive. One exception to this pattern was a manufacturing firm that operated rewards in a flexible fashion, related to the differing needs and motivation patterns of its employees. Its message to managers was 'know your staff and know what rewards they value'. It operated a mixture of financial rewards, but in addition provided an indicative list of nearly 40 non-financial rewards its managers could use. This represents a practical application of the expectancy theory of motivation outlined earlier in this chapter.

PERFORMANCE RELATED PAY (PRP)

Strategic decisions at board level frequently encompass performance related pay (PRP), particularly performance related pay for directors and senior managers! PRP is frequently seen as the way to motivate directors and senior managers to achieve targets incorporated into strategic plans. Such considerations are less frequently extended to the rest of the workforce, although more organisations now adopt a PRP philosophy that extends to the shop floor or office desk. PRP has in recent years been adopted in public as well as private-sector organisations, including local government, the Civil Service, and the NHS. However it remains a highly contentious subject, with wide divisions of opinion as to its efficacy amongst practitioners, consultants and researchers.

Today PRP is a term normally used to describe a specialised form of pay system linked to merit and appraisal. Versions of PRP have however appeared in many different forms and guises over the past century. Traditional piecework and payment by results (PBR) schemes for manual workers, commission schemes for sales representatives, annual bonuses, and merit pay schemes can all be included under the PRP umbrella. One might even consider promotion as a form of PRP. Until a decade ago most of the debate on this topic focused on PBR schemes for manual workers. This was because it was taken for granted that white collar workers and managerial grades should be locked into bureaucratic grading structures that took little account of performance, and also because much publicised industrial relations strikes and disputes drew attention to manual worker PBR schemes. But more recently the interest has shifted to the question of how to introduce a PRP element into the pay of office workers, technologists and managers in order to enhance their productivity and change their attitudes.

The primary argument for PRP schemes is of course that the opportunity to earn extra money should motivate individuals to work harder. But there exists a second fundamental argument, which is rarely articulated, but is implicit in many schemes. This is fairness, or 'equity'. 'It is only fair', as this argument runs, 'that employees who work harder and more productively should earn more than those who do not'. This argument can lead to strong emotions amongst employees, and affect their output and cooperation. There is a well known working class slogan 'equal pay for equal work', which can be interpreted either as an argument for relating pay to the amount of 'work' put into a job (that is, PRP) or as an egalitarian slogan demanding that all workers doing the same job should be paid the same (i.e. 'the rate for the job'). And herein lies the nub of the problem of PRP. How can one design and operate a scheme that simultaneously pays the better performers a higher wage, and is accepted as fair by the majority of employees? At the heart of this lies the difficulty of measuring effort or performance in a manner seen to be objective and fair, and which furthermore links pay to effort and performance, howsoever measured, in a manner also seen to be objective and fair.

PAYMENT BY RESULTS

In the early 1980s nearly three quarters of the British working population was on so called 'time rates' or job evaluated pay structures operating on the basis of qualification or security (Bowey *et al.*, 1982). Payment by results (PBR) schemes none the less continued to be popular for manual workers, with the CBI reporting (1985) that two-thirds of firms still used such schemes, and the New Earnings Survey figures for April 1990 showed that 37 per cent of male and 28 per cent of female workers received incentive payments. Piecework has largely been superseded by work-measured incentive schemes. Whilst a recent IPM/NEDO study (Cannell and Long, 1991) also showed traditional PBR schemes to be in decline, it showed no decline in the overall popularity of attempts to link pay to performance. Some of the reasons for the decline in popularity of traditional schemes include the problem caused by fluctuating earnings through no fault of the employee, work study values that are difficult for the employee to understand, distrust of the fairness of such schemes leading to conflict on the shop floor, and the impact of such schemes on skill and quality. The pressure such schemes generate to maximise output can lead to a neglect of quality and a decline in skill. The recent trend to total quality has placed more emphasis on team working and delegating responsibility to employees to use their initiative in a manner not fostered by traditional PBR schemes.

In consequence leading industrial companies are introducing team or cellular working with group bonuses or even flat-rate pay, and in this respect are ahead of public sector employers (Cannell and Long, 1991 and Pickard, 1993). Profitsharing is also on the increase. And as Peter Wickens, personnel director at Nissan, commented, new technology is blurring the differences between white-collar and blue-collar jobs (Wickens, 1987). Robotics, computer controlled machine tools and line-paced operations combine with team working, flexibility and the emphasis on quality to minimise the need for payment systems which enable the employee to directly influence output.

The trend to single status organisations and the harmonisation of conditions of service for blue- and white-collar workers has coincided with the decline in the significance of traditional PBR schemes, but has stimulated interest in PRP schemes encompassing all categories of employee (Kinnie and Lowe, 1990). Recent research by Kessler and Purcell concluded

> It is clear that, at the strategic level, a range of objectives underlie the introduction of performance related pay. Some of these objectives can be viewed as variations on traditional themes of how to recruit, retain and motivate. The others, however, can be placed within a broader organisational context and relate to fundamental issues concerning organisational culture, the structure of the employment relationship, the role of line managers, and financial controls.
>
> (Kessler and Purcell, 1992)

IMPROVING PERFORMANCE RELATED PAY

The single most important objective of performance related pay, according to Brading and Wright, is to improve performance by converting the paybill 'from an indiscriminate machine to a more finely tuned mechanism, sensitive and responsive to a company's and employees' needs (Brading and Wright, 1990). It does this by:

- focusing effort where the organisation wants it;
- supporting a performance-orientated culture;

- emphasising individual performance or team work as appropriate; ·
- strengthening the performance planning process;
- rewarding the right people;
- motivating all the people.

A practical example of this is provided by Anglian Water (Forsyth, 1991). Following redefinition of their corporate objectives, the development of new strategies and sweeping changes to their structure and organisation, a regional personnel manager was quoted as saying

> In our case the most tangible change has been the introduction of performance-related pay structures. In order to bring in a performance culture we had to introduce more training in appraisals, and we put a lot of work into developing a training package on assessment – objectives had to be more precisely defined.

The precise definition of objectives is critical to both performance management and performance related pay, and can in certain cases by very difficult to achieve. The beauty of traditional blue-collar piecework schemes was that one could actually count the 'pieces' being produced, but with many tasks today this is just not possible. 'Performance cannot be measured solely by quantified targets. There are important qualitative elements which require a degree of judgement to assess' (Fowler, 1988). Hay Management Consultants describe performance measures as:

- General or narrative descriptions of performance, which are inherently subjective
- Evaluation schemes, which express subjective judgements on a rating scale
- Time limits, such as target dates for completion of a task
- Ratios, such as the number of errors per employee
- Direct counts – quantified measures which are wholly objective

LINKING PAY TO PERFORMANCE

In addition to deciding on appropriate measures of performance, consideration must be given to the size of the rewards available, and the manner in which they are related to performance. Many organisations, especially in the public sector, have set very low limits on PRP, frequently in the order of 7 per cent or less of basic pay, with a presumed median payment in the order of half of this amount. It is scarcely surprising when such schemes fail to motivate and have a significant impact on productivity. Schemes in the private sector frequently provide the opportunity to earn 30 per cent or more on top of basic pay (Armstrong and Murlis, 1994).

The manner in which the extra pay is linked to performance is normally through some form of appraisal or performance review, usually but not necessarily on an annual basis. Many companies have abolished cost of living increases in order to give performance pay a sharper impact. This means that employees who receive no performance pay or merit increase in effect take a cut in salary, the size of the cut depending on the rate of inflation in the economy. Conventional wisdom is for organisations to draw up a matrix of pay increase to performance management. Thus an 'excellent' performance may lead to a 12 per cent pay rise, an 'effective' performance to 7 per cent, and an 'adequate' performance to 3 per cent, or may be even a zero increase.

PROBLEMS WITH PERFORMANCE RELATED PAY

Unfortunately much of the current evidence points to a considerable degree of dissatisfaction with PRP, and little evidence that it leads to higher levels of productivity. It is important to remember when considering the results of recent research into PRP that it is difficult to establish a causal relationship between the introduction of PRP and higher productivity, and that PRP frequently disturbs working practices and changes expectations in a manner disturbing to employees used to traditional pay systems. However, the pace of economic change is forcing employers to move in the direction of PRP schemes, whether they like it or not. It is therefore unfortunate that insufficient care and attention is being paid to the planning and communication of many new schemes, and to the training of staff. 'There is evidence that many companies did not think through the introduction of individual performance related pay, IPRP, in a coherent manner' states Marc Thompson in a review of PRP in this country (Thompson, 1993). This study found that many employees objected to having the size of their pay packets determined by what they saw as poor line managers and comments further 'The survey evidence shows that performance pay has failed to motivate employees and may have done more to demoralise staff'.

A practical example of the manner in which PRP can go wrong is reported by Sheffield City Council (Knowles, 1993). 'We put in the scheme too quickly with the wrong motivation, without the ground work, and we have ended up buying ourselves out of a payment scheme that wasn't right for Sheffield.' Research by Geary into links between appraisal and reward found similar problems in three organisations, but also found evidence of some successful aspects (Geary, 1993). Employees valued the increase in pay, and the opportunity it provided to discuss one's work and promotion prospects with a supervisor. Managerial attempts to regain control over recalcitrant employees were facilitated. New payment structures helped to translate flexible working into practice. He concludes 'my research provides clear evidence that the effectiveness of management's reward strategy was dependent, firstly, on the reliability and the validity of the measurements underpinning the appraisal and job evaluation schemes, and secondly, on the values and attitudes of workers'.

To overcome these problems Armstrong and Murlis advise:

- Match the culture
- Link PRP to the performance management process
- Ensure individuals are clear about the targets and standards of performance required
- Employees should be able to track their own performance against these targets and standards
- Employees should be able to influence performance
- Employees should be clear about the rewards
- Rewards should be meaningful enough to make the efforts required worthwhile.

(Murlis and Armstrong, 1994)

Note the similarity between this list and the list put forward earlier in this chapter on creating a motivating environment based on the work of Robertson Smith and Cooper.

FURTHER STRATEGIC CONSIDERATIONS IN REWARD MANAGEMENT

The earlier reference in this chapter to the list of critical choices facing human resource directors drawn up by Schuler (Schuler, 1987) reminds us of a number of other strategic considerations on reward management. Frequently cited is the issue of market posi-

tion. A policy decision needs to be taken on whether the organisation will pay above, at the median, or below the rates of pay offered
in the labour market by competitors. This will need to reflect the
organisation's economic position, need to be competitive, and
desired reputation as an employer. Industrial relations considerations, outlined in chapter 10, will also need to be taken into account.

Indirect benefits such as holidays, pension schemes, and sick pay
benefits, represent a considerable cost, usually in the order of 30 per
cent of direct pay roll costs in the UK. It is sensible strategy to
review these from time to time and to check on their cost effectiveness. But it is in the area of non financial rewards that most
attention needs to be given once the performance management
system has been decided upon. As discussed earlier, research
evidence on motivation reminds us that employees desire intrinsic
as well as extrinsic satisfaction from work. The satisfaction of
intrinsic needs, such as feeling a sense of achievement, being given
recognition, and being provided with a challenging job, all have a
major influence on effort and productivity. Developing an appropriate organisation culture also influences motivation. A corporate
culture of positive work norms, shared values, and a leadership
style that commands loyalty and respect will do much for motivation and productivity. The aim should be a balance between
extrinsic and intrinsic rewards when designing and implementing
a reward strategy.

REFERENCES

Armstrong, M. and Murlis, H. (1994) *Reward Management*, (2nd ed), London:
Kogan Page (in association with the Institute of Personnel Management).
Bevan, S. and Thompson, M. (1991) 'Performance management at the
crossroads', *Personnel Management*, November: 36–9.
Bowey, A.M., Thorpe, R., Mitchell, F., Nichols, F., Gosnold, D., Lawson, S.
and Hellier, P. (1982) 'Effects of incentive payment systems in the
United Kingdom 1977–80', Research Paper no. 36, London: Depart-
ment of Employment.
Brading, E. and Wright, V. (1990) 'Performance-related pay', Personnel
Management Factsheets No. 30, *Personnel Publications*, London: IPM.
Cannell, M. and Long, P. (1991) 'What's changed about incentive pay?',
Personnel Management, October: 58–63.
Carrell, M. and Wood, S. (1991) 'Incentive Pay', London: Institute of
Personnel Management
Cooper, M. D. *et al.*, (1992) 'Assigned or participatively set goals: do they

make a difference?', paper presented at the British Psychological Society, Occupational Psychology Conference, Liverpool, January.

Cowling, A. G. and Mailer, C. (1990) *Managing Human Resources*, (2nd ed), London: Edward Arnold.

Drucker, P. (1961) *The Practice of Management*, London: William Heinemann.

Evans, P. and Lorange, P. (1989) 'The two logics behind human resource management', in P. Evans, Y. Doz and A. Laurent (eds) *Human Resource Management International Firms*, Basingstoke: Macmillian.

Fletcher, C. and Williams, R. (1976) 'The influence of performance feedback in appraisal interviews', *Journal of Occupational Psychology*, 49: 75–83.

Fletcher, C. and Williams, E. (1992) 'The route to performance management', *Personnel Management*, October p: 42–7.

Forbrun, C. J., Tichy, N. M. and Devanna, M. A. (eds) (1984) *Strategic Human Resource Management*, New York: Wiley.

Forsyth, M. (1991) 'Relating pay rises to performance', *The Times*, 11 July.

Fowler, A. (1988) 'New directions in performance pay', *Personnel Management*, November: 30–4.

Geary, J. F. (1993) 'Pay, Control and Commitment: Linking appraisal and reward', *Human Resource Management Journal*, 2(4).

IDS Study (1992) Performance management – 'Incomes Data Services Ltd', Study 518, November.

Johnson, G. and Scholes, K. (1989) *Exploring Corporate Strategy*, Hemel Hempstead: Prentice Hall International (UK).

Kanter, R. (1987) 'From status to contribution: some organisational implications of the changing basis for pay', *Personnel*, January: 12–37.

Kessler, I. and Purcell, J. (1992) 'Performance related pay: objectives and applications', *Human Resource Management Journal*, 2 (3), Spring: 16–33.

Kinnie, N. and Lowe, D. (1990) 'Performance-related pay on the shop-floor', *Personnel Management*, November: 45–9.

Knowles, R. (1993) 'Why Sheffield abandoned its PRP scheme', *Personnel Management*, October: 12.

Laster, T. (1991) 'A Structure for Europe', *Management Today*, January: 76–8.

Latham, G.P. and Yukl, G.A. (1975) 'A review of the research on the applications of goal setting in organisations', *Academy of Management Journal*, December: 824–45.

Lawler, E. E. (1990) *Strategic Pay*, San Francisco: Jossey-Bass Publishers.,

Locke, E. A. (1968) 'Towards a theory of task motivation and incentives' *Organisational Behaviour and Human Performance*, 3: 157–89.

Locke, E. A. and Latham, G. P. (1990) *A Theory of goal setting and task performance*, London: Prentice Hall.

Long, P. (1986) 'Performance reviews', IPM Digest No. 249, April, London: Institute of Personnel Management.

Miller, P. (1992) 'Strategic human resource management: an assessment of progress', *Human Resource Management Journal*, 1(4): 23–39.

Murlis, H. (1991) 'Making sense of salary surveys', *Human Resources*, Summer: 6–9.

Murlis, H. and Fitt, D. (1991), 'Job evaluation in a changing world', *Personnel Management*, May.

Ohmae, K.O. (1982) *The Mind of the Strategist: The Art of Japanese Business*, New York: McGraw Hill.

Pickard, J. (1993) 'How incentives can drive teamworking'. *Personnel Management*, September: 26–30.

Robertson, J. Smith, M. and Cooper, D. (1992) *Motivation: Strategies, Theory and Practice* (2nd edn), London: Englewood Cliffs, NJ: Institute of Personnel Management.

Schein, H. (1980) *Organisational Psychology* (3rd edn), Englewood Cliffs, NJ: Prentice Hall.

Schuler, R. (1987) 'Matching effective HR practices with competitive strategy', *Personnel*, September: 18–27.

Sheard, A. (1992) 'Learning to improve performance', *Personnel Management*, September: 40–5.

Spencer, S. (1990) 'Developing job evaluation', *Personnel Management*, January.

Steers, R. and Porter, L.W. (eds) (1979) *Motivation and Work Behaviour*, (2nd edn) New York: McGraw Hill.

Thompson, J.L. (1990) *Strategic Management*, London: Chapman and Hall.

Thompson, M. (1993) 'Pay and performance', IMS Report No. 218, Sussex: Institute of Manpower Studies.

Trevor, G. (1990) 'Strategic compensation planning', papers presented at the Institute of Personnel Management Conference, Harrogate, October.

Whitehill, A.M. (1991) *Japanese Management: Tradition and Transition*, London and New York: Routledge.

Wickens, P. (1987) *The Road to Nissan*, London: Macmillan.

Wickens, P. (1993) 'Steering the middle road to car production' *Personnel Management*, June: 34–8.

Womack, J., Jones, D. and Roos, D. (1990) *The Machine that Changed the World*, New York: Rawson Assoc.

Chapter 10

Strategic employee relations

Philip James

INTRODUCTION

An important theme underlying this book is that the people employed by organisations exert a crucial influence over their performance and success. A further theme that has been reiterated throughout is the need to develop human resource strategies which as far as possible accord with both the needs of employing organisations and the attitudes and aspirations of those working in them. This chapter sets out to provide a more detailed examination of this last issue.

The chapter commences with a discussion of the different patterns of employment relationships that can exist within organisations and their significance for the development and implementation of human resource strategies and policies. It then goes on to further explore this significance through an examination of two issues: the use of employee participation and the handling of conflict at work.

PATTERNS OF EMPLOYMENT RELATIONSHIPS

Much of the academic debate about the nature of management–worker relations, at least in Britain, draws on the work of Alan Fox. In a series of publications dating back to the mid-1960s Fox has analysed the nature of the employment relationships which subsist within organisations in terms of the 'frames of reference' held by managers and their subordinates – a frame of reference being defined as the set of values and beliefs that people hold about the nature of employing organisations. In essence Fox argues that such frames of reference have important implications for the nature and outcomes of relationships at work, and that consequently they should be taken into account when organisations are planning how they intend to manage them.

Three frames of reference have been distinguished by Fox (1973). The unitary, which assumes a fundamental commonality of interest between employers and workers; the pluralist, which takes as its starting point that the objectives and interests of managers and those they manage frequently diverge, at least in the short-term, and therefore carries the implication that mechanisms need to exist to establish some sort of operational equilibrium between them; and the radical, which is based on the view that the employment relationship, as a microcosm of those existing in the wider society, is characterised by gross inequalities of power and wealth and as a result marked by low trust exchanges. Fox (1974) goes on to illustrate the importance of these differing viewpoints by outlining six different sets of ideological relationships that can exist in organisations:

- management and employees share a unitary perspective;
- management holds a unitary perspective, while employees hold a pluralist one;
- management and employees share a pluralist perspective;
- employees hold a pluralist perspective, while that of management varies between the unitary and pluralist – partly in response to the balance of power that subsists between the two sides;
- management predominately holds a pluralist orientation, while employees hold a unitary one;
- employees hold a radical perspective, and management a unitary or pluralist one.

These different types of ideological relationship are argued by Fox to exert an important influence over the patterns of management–employee relations that develop within organisations. For example, he argues that the first will result in a high level of unchallenged managerial prerogative, while the last will lead to situations where the workforce refuses to recognise the legitimacy of management authority and hence continually seeks to challenge them – labelled the 'traditional' and 'continuous challenge' patterns of management–worker relations respectively. The four remaining patterns of relationship distinguished – entitled the 'classic conflict', 'sophisticated modern', 'standard modern' and 'sophisticated paternalist', are seen to encompass varying degrees of management–worker accommodation and conflict within these two extremes.

It must be stressed, however, that Fox is not arguing that employment relationships are solely a reflection of the ideological positions of managers and employees. Rather their precise behaviourial implications are seen to be determined by the interaction between them and the broader organisational environment in which they are acted out. A more recent attempt to distinguish broad patterns of workplace relationships, that of Edwards, serves to further highlight the crucial importance of this point.

Edwards (1986) argues that the key source of variation in the extent to which workers challenge management authority in the workplace lies in the way in which 'social relations are created at the point of production'. He goes on to locate these variations in terms of three different types of worker orientation: the extent to which workers have a militant or acquiescent orientation to the employer; the degree to which an individual or collective orientation exists; and the extent to which a collective orientation has been translated into a collective organisation. Variations in these orientations are then utilised to identify four very different patterns of workplace relations.

At one extreme is the situation where militancy, and a collective outlook and organisation is lacking and hence there is very little opposition to management. At the other is the opposite one, where all three features are present and management authority is subjected to widespread challenge. The two patterns situated between these extremes are held to be characterised by individual militancy but an absence of collectivism, and by a militant and collective orientation which is not supported by any form of collective organisation.

Edwards stresses that his use of the term orientation does not refer to attitudes or beliefs but an 'approach' which influences behaviour. In other words the concept is rather broader than that of a frame of reference. Two other key and inter-related, points about his analysis must also be noted. First, he acknowledges that patterns of relationships falling between those distinguished are possible and that the latter may themselves encompass very different types of management–worker relations. Thus it is noted that the first non-militant pattern may be associated with management approaches varying considerably in sophistication and formalisation – a point which echoes that made by Purcell in relation to managerial strategies informed by a unitarist philosophy (Purcell, 1987). Second, that worker orientations and the way in which these are acted out are themselves influenced by a wide variety of influences, both internal and external to the organisation, for example, the nature of the technology and work organisation in use, labour and product market conditions, the ethnic and gender breakdown of the workforce, the extent and nature of trade union organisation, and the style of management adopted (also see Edwards and Scullion, 1982; and Edwards and Whitson, 1993).

The work of Fox and Edwards therefore usefully highlights the fact that relationships between workers and managers can vary substantially and also illustrates some of the main ways in which they can differ. Taken together their work, although containing marked differences in approach, also draws attention to the crucial way in which worker beliefs, attitudes and orientations can exert an important influence over the nature of these relations. In doing so it also draws attention to the need for employers to take them into account when devising and implementing HRM strategies and policies. The following discussions of employee participation and work-related conflict serve to further emphasise the importance of this point.

EMPLOYEE PARTICIPATION

Employee participation is the subject of a vast literature. Unfortunately, no universal agreement exists as to what the term means (Loveridge, 1980; Ramsey, 1991). Consequently, depending on the viewpoint of a particular author, the concept can be taken to include such diverse practices as profit sharing, team briefing, employee share ownership, job enrichment, autonomous work groups, problem solving groups, joint consultation, works councils, collective bargaining, and worker directors (these practices are examined later in the chapter).

Whether all of these practices can be meaningfully encompassed under one heading is a moot point. For example, the processes they involve vary considerably, including as they do the communication of information to employees, the provision of discretion to work groups concerning how they carry out their tasks, consulting employee representatives and joint decision making through collective bargaining machinery. Their objectives can also exhibit marked differences (Marchington et al., 1992) Thus they can include the engendering of greater understanding among employees about business developments and needs, the more effective tapping of worker capabilities and expertise, the provision of incentives and rewards, the creation of greater job satisfaction, and the avoidance of conflict.

What is clear is that employers have a vast array of 'participative' techniques available from which to choose. In exercising this choice, as has been reiterated throughout the book, a useful starting point when introducing or reviewing existing practices is to consider what are the purposes to be achieved and following on from this, what, in the prevailing context, is likely to achieve them. The importance of adopting such a systematic approach can be illustrated with reference to decisions concerning the recognition of unions and the determination of the level at which collective bargaining should take place, the development of team working, and the use of team briefings.

COLLECTIVE BARGAINING

For collective bargaining to occur trade unions need to be recognised. In Britain there are, at least at present, no statutory obligations on employers concerning the recognition of unions for bargaining purposes. It is therefore an issue which is ultimately determined by management.

Many managers are loathe to recognise trade unions for a number of reasons. For example, it is commonly believed that the establishment of collective bargaining would result in a disproportionate amount of management time being tied up with consulting and negotiating with unions; engender 'them and us' attitudes on the part of workers; limit the ability of organisations to pay individual workers what is merited in terms of their performance and labour market position; cause pay to rise to unsustainable levels; and create inflexibility to change, particularly in relation to working practices.

On the other hand, as already noted, the pluralist analysis of employee relations draws attention to the potential value of collective bargaining as a means of ensuring an appropriate degree of equilibrium between the interests of employers and their staff – an argument that again highlights the importance of ideological or cultural considerations and also draws attention to the need to take into account the ability of disgruntled workers to disrupt or impair operational efficiency. In addition, and more pragmatically, union recognition can provide administrative advantages in terms of the regulation of the employment relationship, notably in terms of adjusting pay levels. A proactive approach to the issue can also provide a means of establishing patterns of recognition which suit the operational needs of an organisation – something that may not be possible if recognition is established after prolonged and uncontrolled attempts at union organisation.

Weighing up these advantages and disadvantages is far from easy, particularly given that the research evidence available on how unions affect pay and productivity is the subject of considerable debate (Nolan, 1992). Two important points about this evaluation process must, however, be stressed. First, care must be taken to ensure that it is essentially 'objective' rather than being merely a reflection of the personal preferences and prejudices of particular managers. Otherwise union recognition may be resisted to the point where it is actually dysfunctional, not to say irrational (Fox, 1966). Second, that it takes into account both short- and long-term considerations. The decision of the Nissan Motor Company to conclude a single union deal with the Amalgamated Union prior to the commencement of its operations provides a good illustration of the importance of this last point (Wickens, 1987). Thus in this case a crucial influence on the decision to concede recognition from the outset was the Personnel Director's concern that as a large employer in the motor industry the company was bound to be the subject of union organising attempts. These might successfully be resisted, but if they were not then the company ran the risk of ending up with a multi-union situation.

If it is decided that recognition should be given, a whole host of supplementary issues have to be resolved, such as which groups of workers are to be covered, which unions are to be recognised, what subjects are to be negotiable, how are disagreements to be resolved (see below), what facilities are to be given to union representatives, and at what level within the organisation is bargaining over pay to take place. Once again these decisions need to be informed by short- and long-term business and cultural considerations.

Within individual organisations pay bargaining can take place at a number of levels: the central or headquarters level; the division/business unit level; or the establishment level. Each of these levels have potential advantages and disadvantages (Palmer, 1990). For example, centralised bargaining can make labour costs more predictable, enable a common approach to be adopted to union recognition and ensure that negotiations are carried out by skilled and experienced negotiators. They can also, by enabling the establishment of common terms and conditions, facilitate the transfer of

staff between different parts of an organisation, ensure consistency·
between workplaces, thereby avoiding jealousies and rivalries
between staff at different locations, and more generally support
the creation of coherent internal labour markets (Walsh, 1993).
On the other hand central negotiations can be very time-consuming
and lead to delays in resolving disputes. They also tend to mean that
pay rates have to be set at a level sufficient to recruit in the most
expensive labour market in which employers operate. In addition, it
can be rather more difficult in such negotiations to take account of
differences in the performance of different workplaces and the types
of work they carry out, and to engage in detailed discussions of ways
of improving efficiency. A further potential problem is that when
negotiations break down, any resultant disputes are likely to affect
the whole organisation rather than one part of it.

The relative significance of these advantages and disadvantages
cannot be weighed up in the abstract. Rather they need to be
informed by a whole host of financial, operational and 'people'
considerations, such as prevailing management structures, product
and labour market conditions, and existing industrial relations
structures and relationships (Purcell, 1989). Otherwise bargaining
arrangements which are inappropriate to the operational needs of
the organisation may be developed.

Thus bargaining arrangements may be decentralised in a situation
where local managers do not have the competence to conduct
negotiations and/or sufficient financial authority to ensure that
they are perceived as 'meaningful' by both themselves and their
union counterparts. Alternatively, they may work for a short time,
but, against a background of falling unemployment and/or buoyant
demand, subsequently allow unions to create a 'wage spiral' through
the use of coercive comparisons between pay levels and settlements
at different locations (Brown and Walsh, 1991).

It is of course true that decisions can be reversed if they are either
wrong or inappropriate to changed circumstances. However, such
reversals can involve considerable administrative costs and can
themselves generate considerable resentment on the part of those
adversely affected. For example, local managers and trade union
representatives may resent the downgrading of their roles as a
result of moves to centralise collective bargaining. More generally,
rapid reversal can in the case of collective bargaining undermine the
trust of union representatives – an important point given the
importance of such trust to the establishment of cooperative,

problem-solving management–union relationships (Walton and McKersie, 1992).

TEAM WORKING

Over the last fifteen years many organisations, in response to increasing and rapidly changing competitive pressures, have reviewed existing working practices. A common outcome has been the decision to increase efficiency by removing tiers of supervision and passing more responsibility to work groups for such matters as quality and the internal distribution of tasks (Brewster and Connock, 1986; Marchington, 1994). Frequently this type of change has been accompanied by moves to create greater interchangeability between work group members by breaking down previous job demarcations. The prime motive force behind these changes vary. In some cases they are primarily seen as a means of cutting labour and increasing the work load of those who remain. In others they have also been informed by a desire to give people more challenging and fulfilling work.

Research conducted on the utilisation of such team working has highlighted a number of problems concerning their use (Marchington, 1994). Inadequate training of staff in their new responsibilities is one. Another is the failure to change prevailing attitudes and behaviour with the result that the team working ethos is only partially taken on board and working practices continue, on the part of both supervisory and subordinates, to contain many of the previously existing patterns (Buchanan and Preston, 1992). For example, supervisory personnel often resist the switch from a 'command' to 'facilitation' role entailed in team working because of its perceived threat to their status and concerns about their ability to cope.

Staff resistance to changes of this type can, as already noted, often reflect inadequacies in training and explanation. However, it is also frequently a reflection of the more general way in which they were designed and implemented.

Psychological research has identified a number of routes through which attitudinal change on the part of workers can be achieved (Kelly and Kelly, 1991): through increasing contact between superiors and subordinates; the creation of superordinate goals – an important objective presumably underlying the present popularity of mission statements; and encouraging changes in behaviour which subsequently prompt employees to reappraise their attitudes and seek to bring them into line with the relevant behaviour. However, each of these routes to attitude change have been found to be dependent on one or more conditions being present: first, employees having some say in the setting up of participative schemes and whether they participate in them; second, whether workers trust management with regard to what they say and their ability to take the appropriate supporting actions; third, the extent to which there is equality of status and outcomes in the operation of such arrangements. Finally, the provision of necessary institutional support, for example in terms of training, time and other resources.

Team working can therefore lead to both improved relationships and organisational performance. It can on the other hand lead to the latter and not the former. This last situation is inevitably a more delicate flower than the latter since it is ultimately dependent on continued management reinforcement and enforcement: that is a negation of what team working is frequently intended to achieve. Unfortunately, the research evidence suggests that this is likely to be the case unless the necessary linkages are established between the introduction of team working and broader aspects of the cultural and organisational environment in which arrangements of this type are to work.

TEAM BRIEFING

Team briefing provides a method by which top management can cascade information through the organisation. Under it each tier of management holds meetings of around half an hour's duration with small groups of between four and twenty subordinates. The information provided at these meetings typically consists of 70 per cent local news of immediate relevance to the employees concerned, with the remainder comprising more general information about developments in the organisation as a whole. During the meetings employees are given the opportunity to ask questions and make comments on the information provided.

The Industrial Society, one of the main advocates of team briefing, argues that it can reinforce the role of supervisors and managers as leaders of work groups; increase worker commitment; reduce misunderstandings; help the acceptance of change; and improve the upward communication of ideas and views. Whether these outcomes are obtained is, however, far from a foregone conclusion. Thus the success of the technique is dependent on a number of factors.

Some of these relate to the presence of the design features mentioned above. Others relate to supervisors and managers possessing the necessary communication and inter-personal skills; the provision of comprehensible and relevant information; the availability of adequate time to hold meetings; and the holding of meetings on a regular basis.

More generally, research on the impact of communication schemes, such as team briefings, has highlighted how the attitudes of managers and workers can exert an important influence over their operation. Those responsible for running briefing sessions, for example, may not see them as of any value and hence as a waste of time, or perceive the dialogue involved in them as undermining their authority or power – the 'information is power syndrome' (Richbell, 1979; Townley, 1994). Similarly, trade unions and their members can also have reservations about such communication schemes.

Where trade unions exist, team briefing may be viewed with suspicion, if not outright hostility, if it is seen as a means of by-passing existing management–union channels of communication and as part of a strategy to create a divide between union representatives and their members (Strauss, 1992). Employees may also exhibit little enthusiasm and support for schemes if they feel that information disclosed is too restrictive or distrust its accuracy or the motives underlying its disclosure (Knights and Collinson, 1987). For example, that it is simply being disclosed in order to persuade staff to accept certain unattractive changes.

The design and operation of team briefing schemes once again therefore highlights the point that the operation of participative techniques cannot be divorced from the broader employment relationships in which they are implemented. They are in other words far from panaceas that can be used to reform what are seen by workers as being inherently unsatisfactory.

CONFLICT AT WORK

People are employed by organisations to provide a given type and level of performance. Sometimes organisational expectations are fulfilled, while on other occasions they are not. Sub-optimal performance comes in various forms. For example, employees may carry out work that is inadequate in terms of quantity or quality; time-keeping and attendance may be poor; and management instructions, rules and proposed changes may be ignored or resisted – perhaps by means of collective action such as strikes, work to rules, and over-time bans. Some such behaviour may occur through no fault of the employees concerned, for example where inadequate work is a reflection of inadequate training or the consequence of poor selection decisions. In other cases a degree of deliberate intent may be present – although the identification, as in the case of absence – may be difficult to determine (Rhodes and Steers, 1981).

Employee interests and expectations are informed by notions of fairness and justice (Hyman and Brough, 1975; Armstrong et al., 1981). Such notions are in part brought to the workplace by employees (Goldthorpe et al., 1968) – hence the increasing emphasis organisations place on selecting staff who have the 'right outlook'. They are also in part shaped by the organisation itself, through for example information provided at the time of appointment, the opinions and behaviour of colleagues, workplace traditions or customs, the types of activities carried out and management structures, philosophies and actions. Management therefore is confronted with something of an ironic situation. Thus it is intimately involved in the generation of employee interests and expectations and yet can find itself frustrated by them at the same time.

Faced with an unsatisfactory response on the part of employees two types of broad response are possible – the use of 'penal sanctions', such as dismissal, or the employment of more persuasive means of bringing behaviour into line with that required. The penal, or what has been referred the 'punishment-centred', approach to discipline is one that is inevitably appealing to many managers (Ashdown and Baker, 1973). It does, however, run the risk of itself creating further problems. The morale and motivation of staff can be adversely affected, and labour lost which may be in short supply and in which a considerable amount of investment has been made. More generally, employee perceptions of injustice and unfairness may be accentuated – particularly if the action itself is seen as arbitrary and inconsistent.

In other words management faces a dilemma – notions of fairness and justice may result in employees failing to deliver required levels of performance and management steps to remedy this situation may serve to compound existing feelings of injustice and unfairness.

Three main strategies can be adopted to avoid or minimise the potentially adverse consequences that can flow from this dilemma. Employers can seek to influence prevailing notions of fairness and justice in a way which is more compatible with the needs of the organisation; organisational rules and procedures can be brought into line with them; and procedures can be adopted to ensure that where actions are required to remedy sub-optimal performance, these are taken in a way which itself is seen to be both fair and just (Clark, 1993). As the following discussions of the design and use of disciplinary, grievance and disciplinary procedures demonstrates, the effective use of all of these approaches requires that they be utilised in a strategic and systematic way.

DISCIPLINARY PROCEDURES

Several analysts have argued that employers' approaches to discipline have varied historically (Ashdown and Baker, 1973; Henry, 1982). The general argument is that over the post-war period employers have sought to move from a punishment-centred approach to discipline to a 'corrective' one. That is one which embodies approaches to discipline handling which seek, through counselling and warnings, to 'reform' employee behaviour before the imposition of penal sanctions – be they fines, demotions or dismissals – is considered. More recently and controversially, it has also been suggested that the present period is marked by a further shift of employer strategies towards the creation of workforce self-discipline through the use of the types of techniques encompassed by Storey's conceptualisation of 'soft' HRM (Walton, 1985; and Storey, 1992).

In practice disciplinary regimes will generally frequently encompass elements of each of these strategies, the balance between them varying between organisations and from one time period to another within them. Sometimes the balance struck between these elements will be the most appropriate in the circumstances. However, this may not always be the case. Thus there is some evidence that over the past decade or so organisations have been pursuing what can be described as a 'twin track' policy encompassing attempts to secure greater employee commitment, and hence self-discipline, and the more rigorous enforcement of work rules and standards (Edwards, 1994). It takes no great insight to see that such an approach can potentially be counter-productive, with the latter policy serving to undermine the effectiveness of the former – not least because, in terms of the foregoing discussion, the former may serve to raise expectations about management behaviour which the latter contradicts.

To a greater or lesser extent all organisations are effectively required by law, as a result of the legislative framework relating to unfair dismissal, to have disciplinary procedures which embody a corrective orientation to the handling of disciplinary matters (James and Lewis, 1992). The ACAS Code of Practice on Disciplinary Rules and Procedures, for example, states that, except in cases of gross misconduct, no employee should be dismissed for a first offence (ACAS, 1977). More generally, the ACAS code is noteworthy because it encompasses elements of the three strategies outlined above concerning how employers can seek to develop a greater congruence between workplace performance standards and the inclinations of employees. Thus it recommends that procedures be agreed with trade unions, where they exist, and that unions also be given the opportunity to comment on or negotiate over disciplinary rules – an approach which can be seen simultaneously to recognise the need to secure employee acceptance of disciplinary rules and procedures, either by adjusting them to more reflect employee view or to convince staff of their legitimacy. It also contains a series of recommendations concerning the content of disciplinary procedures which are essentially concerned with ensuring that disciplinary procedures are handled in accordance with the 'rules of natural justice' – for example, it states that issues should be dealt with speedily, employees should have a right to state their case and be accompanied by a union representative or colleague; and that a right of appeal should be provided.

The formulation of disciplinary procedures in line with the ACAS code requires that careful consideration be given to such issues, which managers/supervisors are to be given the authority to take particular types of disciplinary action, how much emphasis is to be placed on counselling prior to the commencement of formal proceedings, to whom are appeals to be made, and whether unions are to play any direct role in the making of actual disciplinary decisions, a rare but sometimes utilised approach (Henry, 1982). These decisions moreover need to be taken in the light of existing more general management structures and systems. For example, if a devolved management style is employed, careful thought needs to be given as to whether it is appropriate to involve senior management from headquarters in the handling of disciplinary cases.

Finally, it is important to recognise that the preparation of disciplinary procedures is not merely a paper exercise. They must also be implemented effectively. Thus an industrial tribunal will, other than in exceptional circumstances, find a dismissal to be unfair if it was not carried out in accordance with the laid down procedure. It is also likely to reach the same conclusion if it is shown that a decision to dismiss was inconsistent with the actions that had taken in previous cases (James and Lewis, 1992). Consequently, as with other human resource policies, appropriate steps must be taken to ensure that the procedure is both adequately communicated to all staff and that those involved in handling disciplinary matters have received training in their operation and do in practice follow them.

It must, however, be stressed that the mere presence of formal rules and procedures, even if adequately communicated, will not of itself guarantee that they are complied with. The fact remains that if they do not reflect a substantial degree of acceptance on the part of both managers and employees, then attempts are likely to be made to circumvent them where this is considered possible and desirable, for example, because they are considered too inflexible (Evans *et al.*, 1985). To put the matter another way, it is no good consulting and negotiating over rules and procedures in order to gain acceptance of them unless management at the end of the day is willing to take into account the views expressed through these processes. Otherwise the outcomes of them may well still be accorded limited legitimacy. Indeed the ineffective use of such processes may, by raising expectations, serve to make the situation worse rather than better.

GRIEVANCE AND DISPUTES PROCEDURES

The vast majority of workplaces with 25 or more employees have formal procedures for handling grievances and disputes (Millward *et al.*, 1992). The intention of such is to provide a mechanism through which issues can be resolved in the least damaging way. In this sense their use can therefore be seen to reflect the 'corrective' ethos underlying, at least in theory, disciplinary procedures. Inevitably the structure of grievance and disputes procedures vary considerably. Once again, however, the crucial point in designing them is that they accord with the cultural and structural environment within which they are to operate. It must also be recognised, as with disciplinary procedures, that the effectiveness with which they work will be very much influenced by the inter-personal skills of those using them, the relationships that exist between the two parties, and the extent to which their outcomes are considered 'fair' by the parties affected by them (Marsh and McCarthy, 1968; Thomson and Murray, 1976). The relevance of these factors can be highlighted through a consideration of one issue the provision made for third party intervention.

The number of stages involved in grievance and disputes vary considerably, partly as a result of factors like the size of the organisation, the number of tiers of management present, the nature of the associated collective bargaining machinery. The number of stages involved is clearly an important issue, since too many stages may lead to delay and a build up of frustrations, and too few may mean that the views of appropriate parties have not been brought to bear on an issue.

The final stages of disputes procedures can take place at one of three main levels – national, where the organisation is party to a national, industry-wide disputes procedure; the individual workplace level; or some corporate level above that of the workplace. Whichever of these levels is applicable, procedures may provide for the involvement of a third party if the issue concerned remains unresolved.

Third party intervention can take one of three main forms: conciliation, mediation and arbitration. Conciliation and mediation are closely related (Singh, 1986). Both involve the use of a third party to provide assistance when internal discussions have reached an impasse. Equally, both leave the internal parties with ultimate responsibility for resolving issues themselves. The essential difference between them is that a mediator is able to put forward recommendations that are designed to resolve the matters concerned, while conciliators in effect act as facilitators. By way of contrast, arbitration usually involves the third party, making a morally binding award to resolve the issue.

Any form of third party intervention, by definition, brings an outsider into the internal affairs of an organisation. For this reason many employers and union officials are hesitant about placing too much reliance on it. This is particularly true of arbitration, where managerial decision making is effectively usurped by the third party appointed. Against this potential loss of domestic authority, has to be set the potential benefits of being able to draw on an outside source of advice and expertise which can view an issue in a more dispassionate manner and perhaps help avoid the degeneration of the issue into a damaging management–union dispute.

In general, as already indicated, employers and unions frequently have similar views about the use and role of third party intervention. Views, however, are likely to be more divergent with regard to the question of how such intervention is to be 'triggered'. Once again there are three options here: first, joint reference by the parties to a grievance or dispute; second, unilateral reference by one of the parties; third, 'automatic' reference, whereby a failure to agree automatically triggers the referring of an issue to a third party. To confuse the matter even further, where more than one form of intervention is provided for in procedures, it may be decided to use different triggering mechanisms for the different forms.

The joint reference route is the one most commonly used, for the obvious reason that it removes the possibility of either side losing control of an issue. However, unilateral reference does provide a potential means of prolonging discussions or resolving an issue in situations where one party feels that the other is being unduly intransigent – in other words it can act as a form of safety valve where one side feels that the other side is acting in an unreasonable manner. In addition the unilateral approach can enable one side to trigger third party intervention in situations where the other side is unable to do so for internal political reasons, for example, senior management opposition.

The third type of triggering mechanism, that of 'automaticity', has in the past few years attracted considerable attention as a result of its association with so-called 'no-strike' deals that have been concluded in a number of companies, most notably Japanese transplants (Lewis, 1990). Under these agreements an unresolved issue is automatically referred to arbitration, a requirement that when combined with the obligation to follow procedures, has the effect of precluding the calling of constitutional industrial action. Most also have another distinguishing characteristic, namely that they provide for the use of pendulum arbitration – a process whereby an arbitrator has to find for one side or the other and is therefore unable, as with 'conventional' arbitration, to select a compromise award (Wood, 1985).

The issue of whether to adopt a no-strike approach again serves to illustrate how HRM strategies and policies need to take into account the practical realities of the organisation in which they apply. Thus such agreements clearly offer a potential means of avoiding or minimising the possibility of industrial action. They do though confront the problem of management authority being supplanted by that of the arbitrator already mentioned. Moreover, although any procedure will possess a degree of moral authority – bearing in mind that most procedures in Britain are not legally binding – the degree of this may be insufficient to ensure that they are complied with. As a result there is no guarantee, coming back to Fox's analysis at the start of the chapter, that unions and their members will necessarily see it as being in their interests to follow the procedure (Hyman, 1978). For example, the procedure may be considered too time consuming or to be likely to generate results that favour management. If such circumstances are a distinct possibility, then there consequently seems little point in confusing the situation by including a procedural element that is likely to be ignored or at best secure grudging acceptance.

Once again therefore the issues surrounding the use of third party intervention in grievance and disputes procedures highlight the point that has been stressed throughout this chapter. This is that the implementation of HRM strategies and policies is likely to be problematic if they are essentially seen as something 'done' to people, be those people managers, supervisors or ordinary employees, regardless of their own views and expectations and their ability to pursue them.

CONCLUSION

This chapter has sought to demonstrate that the implementation of HRM strategies and policies can be crucially affected by the values, beliefs, attitudes, behaviour and power of those to whom they apply. It has further sought to stress the importance of meaningfully taking such factors into account in their development. The importance of both of these points cannot be stressed enough.

Human resource management is concerned with the 'people' dimension of organisations. Unfortunately, research findings suggest, somewhat ironically, that the development of strategy in the area often pays insufficient attention to how they will be perceived by staff. In other words, all too often human resource strategies are effectively conceived as something which is 'done to people'. Studies, for example, have shown that personnel and industrial relations considerations often weigh relatively lightly in decision making concerning such issues as capital investment, budget setting, acquisitions and takeovers and the introduction of new technology (Marginson et al., 1988).

This lack of concern with the people to whom human resource strategies apply is mirrored in much of the theoretical literature relating to strategy development. The type of 'best practice' model implicitly underlying the conceptual framework developed by Beer *et al.* (1984) is a case in point since such models in effect make universal assumptions about how employees will react to particular human resource strategies. A similar downgrading of the importance of workforce attitudes, expectations, objectives and behaviour is apparent in those conceptual models concerned with establishing a 'fit' between human resource policies on the one hand, and product market conditions or characteristics on the other (for example, Schuler and Jackson, 1987; and Baird and Meshoulam, 1988).

This is not to deny that a particular type of human resource strategy can, given the right conditions, 'deliver'. Nor is it to say that product market factors are not important considerations which should inform strategy development. Rather the point is that in much of the theoretical literature insufficient attention is paid to the way in which strategy implementation is crucially influenced by the reactions of those employed in organisations.

Herein lies the crucial point. This is that if such reactions do exert an important influence over the process of strategy implementation, how are those responsible for strategy formulation to know what they are likely to be? The answer seems relatively simple, namely that mechanisms needs to be put in place to allow employees an effective input into the decision-making process, at the strategic as well as task levels. Otherwise strategies may well be put in place that are based on faulty assumptions about how they will be received by those affected by them (case study 12 on Ford Motor Company refers).

The importance of 'empowering' employees at levels above the task has been highlighted in research conducted in US companies seeking to transform their management–worker relations as a means of enhancing efficiency and competitiveness. Thus such studies have led Kochan and Dyer (1992) to make the following observation:

> 'Strategic' human resource management models of the 1980s were too limited . . . because they depended so heavily on the values, strategies and support of top executives. . . . While we see [these] as necessary conditions, we do not see them as sufficient to support the transformational process. A model capable of achieving sustained and transformational change will, therefore,

need to incorporate more active roles of other stakeholders in the employment relationship, including government, employees and union representatives as well as line managers.

(Quoted in Storey and Sisson, 1993)

The material in this chapter has hopefully served to further highlight the importance of this last argument. Ultimately its central message is therefore that the formulation of HRM strategies should not be conceived as an isolated technical activity since their effective implementation is dependent on the positive support of staff at all levels within the organisation. A failure to heed this message will consequently often mean that much time will be spent on formulating strategies which at best produce sub-optimal improvements in organisational performance.

REFERENCES

Advisory, Conciliation and Arbitration Service (1977) *Code of Practice on Disciplinary Rules and Procedures*, London: ACAS.

Armstrong, P., Goodman, J.F.B. and Hyman, J.D. (1981) *Ideology and Shopfloor Relations*, London: Croom Helm.

Ashdown, R.T. and Baker, K.H. (1973) 'In working order: a study of industrial discipline', *Department of Employment Manpower Papers 6*, London: HMSO.

Baird, L. and Meshoulan, I. (1988) 'Managing two fits of strategic human resource management', *Academy of Management Review*, 13(1), 116–28.

Beer, M., Spector, B., Lawrence P.R. *et al.* (1984) *Managing Human Assets*, New York: The Free Press.

Brewster, C. and Connock, S. (1986) *Industrial Relations: Cost-Effective Sstrategies*, London: Hutchinson.

Brown, W. and Walsh, J. (1991) 'Pay determination in Britain in the 1990s: the anatomy of decentralisation', Oxford Review of Economic Policy, 7(1).

Buchanan, D. and Preston, D. (1992) 'Life in a cell: supervision and teamwork in a "manufacturing systems engineering" environment', *Human Resource Management Journal*, 3(4), 55–76.

Clark, J. (1993) 'Procedures and consistency versus flexibility and commitment: a comment on Storey', *Human Resource Management Journal*, 4(1), 79–81.

Edwards, P. (1986) *Conflict at Work: A Materialist Analysis of Workplace Industrial Relations*, Oxford: Blackwell.

Edwards, P. (1994) 'Discipline and the creation of order' in K. Sisson (ed), *Personnel Management*, 562–92, Oxford: Blackwell.

Edwards, P. and Scullion, H. (1982) *The Social Organisation of Industrial Conflict: Control and Resistance in the Workplace*, Oxford: Blackwell.

Edwards, P. and Whitson, C. (1993) *Attending to Work: The Management of Attendance and Shopfloor Order*, Oxford: Blackwell.

Evans, S., Goodman, J.F.B. and Hargreaves, L. (1985) 'Unfair dismissal law and employment practices in the 1980s', *Department of Employment Research Paper 53*, London: HMSO.

Fox, A. (1966) *Industrial Sociology and Industrial Relations*, London: HMSO.

Fox, A. (1973) 'Industrial relations: a social critique of the pluralist ideology', in J. Child (ed.), *Man and Organisation*, London: Allen and Unwin.

Fox, A. (1974) *Beyond Contract: Work, Power and Trust Relations*, London: Faber and Faber.

Goldthorpe, J.H. (1968) *The Affluent Worker: Industrial Attitudes and Behaviour*, Cambridge: CUP.

Gouldner, A. (1954) *Wildcat Strike*, New York: Harper.

Henry, S. (1982) *Private Justice: Towards Integrated Theorising in the Sociology of Law*, London: Routledge.

Hyman, R. and Brough, I. (1975) *Social Values and Industrial Relations: a Study of Fairness and Equality*, Oxford: Blackwell.

Hyman, R. (1978) 'Pluralism, procedural consensus and industrial relations', *British Journal of Industrial Relations*, 16, 16–40.

James, P. and Lewis, D. (1992) *Discipline*, London: IPM.

Kelly, J. and Kelly, C. (1991) 'Them and us: social psychology and the "New Industrial Relations"', *British Journal of Industrial Relations*, 29(1), 25–48.

Knights, D. and Collinson, D. (1987) 'Disciplining the shop floor: a comparison of disciplinary effects of managerial psychology and financial accounting', *Accounting, Organisations and Society*, 12(5), 457–77.

Kochan, T. and Dyer, L. (1992) 'Managing transformational change: the role of human resource professionals', paper for the Conference of the International Industrial Relations Association, Sydney.

Lewis, R. (1990) 'Strike-free deals and pendulum arbitration', *British Journal of Industrial Relations*, 28, 32–56.

Loveridge, R. (1980) 'What is participation? A review of the literature and some methodological problems', *British Journal of Industrial Relations*, 18(3), 297–317.

Marchington, M., Goodman, J., Wilkinson, A. and Ackers, P. (1992) 'New developments in employee involvement', *Employment Department Research Paper 2*, London: Employment Department.

Marchington, M. (1994) *Team Work*, Oxford: Blackwell.

Marginson, P., Edwards, P.K., Martin, R. *et al.* (1988) *Beyond the Workplace: Managing Industrial Relations in Multi-Establishment Enterprises*, Oxford: Blackwell.

Marsh, A. and McCarthy, W.E.J. (1968) 'Disputes procedures in British industry', *Royal Commission Research Paper No. 2*, Part 2, London: HMSO.

Millward, N., Stevens, M., Smart, D. and Hawes, W.R. (1992) *Workplace Industrial Relations in Transition: the ED/ESRC/PSI/ACAS Surveys*, Aldershot: Gower.

Nolan, P. (1992) 'Trade Unions and productivity: issues, evidence and prospects', *Employee Relations*, 14(6), 3–19.

Palmer, S. (1990) *Determining Pay: a Guide to Issues*, London: IPM.

Purcell, J. (1987) 'Mapping management styles in employee relations', *Journal of Management Studies*, 24(5), 534–48.

Purcell, J. (1989) 'How to manage decentralised bargaining', *Personnel Management*, May: 53–5.

Ramsey, H. (1991) 'Reinventing the wheel? A review of the development and performance of employee involvement', *Human Resource Management*, 1(2): 1–18.

Rhodes, S. and Steers, R. (1981) 'A systematic approach to diagnosing employee absenteeism', *Employee Relations*, 3(2), 17–22.

Richbell, S. (1979) 'Participative design and organisational sub-groups', *Industrial Relations Journal*, 10(1), 40–50.

Schuler, R.S. and Jackson, S. (1987) 'Linking competitive strategies with human resource management practices', *Academy of Management Executive*, 1(3), 209–13.

Singh, R. (1986) 'Mediation and industrial disputes in Britain', *Industrial Relations Journal*, 17(1), 24–31.

Storey, J. (1992) *Developments in the Management of Human Resources*, Oxford: Blackwell.

Storey, J. and Sisson, K. (1993) *Managing Human Resources and Industrial Relations*, Buckingham: Open University Press.

Strauss, G. (1992) 'Workers' participation in management', in J. Hartley and G. Stephenson (eds), *Employment Relations*, Oxford: Blackwell, 291–313.

Thomson, A.W.J. and Murray, V.V. (1976) *Grievance Procedures*, Farnborough: Saxon House.

Townley, B. (1994) 'Communicating with employees' in K. Sisson (ed.), *Personnel Management*, 595–633.

Walsh, J. (1993) 'Internalisation v. decentralisation: an analysis of recent developments in pay bargaining', *British Journal of Industrial Relations*, 31(3), 409–32.

Walton, R. (1985) 'From control to commitment in the workplace', *Harvard Business Review*, 53: March to April, 77–84.

Walton, R. and McKersie, R. (1992) *A Behavioural Theory of Labour Negotiations*, New York: McGraw-Hill.

Wickens, P. (1987) *The Road to Nissan: Flexibility, Quality, Teamwork*, London: Macmillan.

Wood, Sir John (1985) 'Last Offer Arbitration', *Industrial Relations Journal*, 23: 416–24.

Part IV

Aspects of strategic human resource management in action

INTRODUCTION

Part IV contains case studies of organisations which have implemented strategic human resource management policies in the UK in recent years. Most of these are household name organisations with which readers will be familiar. Two are in the public sector, two have been privatised from the public to the private sector, and the remainder have always been in the private sector. Three of the companies are based in the UK, three are based in other European countries, one is American and one is Japanese owned.

All the case study organisations demonstrate that strategic human resource management can be implemented with a fair measure of success provided there is the will, the necessary investment of resources, and a whole-hearted commitment to change-management based on the policies described in part II.

None of the case studies describe failure. The text of this book has made it clear that in many cases – too many cases – strategic human resource management initiatives have failed. This high rate of failure, estimated to be in the order of 70 per cent of cases, is shared with related strategic management initiatives such as MBO (management by objectives), TQM (total quality management), and BPR (business process reengineering). These failures largely come about through lack of application of the principles expounded in this book. But quite apart from the reluctance of organisations to parade their failures in public, making case studies of failure hard to come by, the intention of part IV of this book is to provide examples of best practice which will interest and challenge readers, and encourage emulation.

The case studies are also designed to illustrate the practical application of theories and research findings presented in the main text of the book. Each case study has particular relevance to at least one of the chapters in parts II and III of this book. However a narrow alignment of cases and chapters is not desirable, because strategic human resource management is essentially holistic in nature, with changes in one part of the organisation carrying implications for changes in other parts.

The first eight case studies are linked with part II of the book, with case studies 1 to 7 containing a particular emphasis on structure, culture and change, whilst case study 8 emphasises human resource planning. The remaining case studies link with part III, illustrating the applied areas of selection, development, rewards and employee relations.

The general reader may prefer either to read a chapter at a time in parts II and III and then turn to the corresponding case, or to complete the reading of one or both these parts before tackling the case studies armed with a theoretical overview. Because this book has also been written to be used as a class text for advanced students of management, questions for discussion are provided with each case. There are sufficient cases to form the basis of class discussion over a standard college semester.

Restructuring at British Telecommunications plc (BT)

BT is Britain's biggest company, and was privatised in 1984, following its creation as a nationalised enterprise separate from the Post Office in 1981. In 1990 BT employed 230,000 staff at around 8000 locations in the UK, as well as staff at overseas locations. A review of strategy in 1990 convinced the board of the need for a major restructuring exercise.

For many years BT had been structured in a way which reflected the historical dominance of the business of telephone services to UK customers, but this structure had difficulty in focusing on specific customer needs. Fast changing technology and a globalisation of the business also demanded change.

From April 1991 BT was reorganised into seven major units providing a basis for building flatter organisations within each division. Historically the organisation had relied heavily on general managers who coordinated the work of functional managers, but now required a more targeted approach and a development of team working across functions. Termed 'Project Sovereign', this initiative comprised a comprehensive package of structural and cultural change. A completely new organisation was devised which placed the customer, quite explicitly, at the apex, as shown in figure CS1.1.

Three marketing and sales divisions form the interface between the business and the customer – Business Communications for the business customer, Personal Communications for the domestic customer, and Special Businesses for a range of specialised services such as maritime radio and radioconferencing. The customer facing divisions are supported by Products and Services Management who are responsible for interpreting customer requirements specified by the marketing units and transforming them into practical products and services. Worldwide Networks is the division responsible for

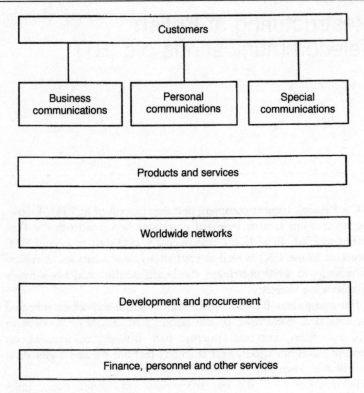

Figure CS1.1   Putting customers first: BT organisation from April 1991
Source: BT Annual Review, 1991

managing the existing networks and for developing technical solutions to satisfy evolving customer needs.

This restructuring represents an implementation of BT's new mission statement and the set of values adopted by the board. The mission statement was set out as follows:

- To provide world-class telecommunications and information products and services
- To develop and exploit our networks at home and overseas so that we can:
  - meet the requirements of our customers;
  - sustain growth in the earnings of the group on behalf of our shareholders;

- make a fitting contribution to the community in which we conduct our business.

And the values were put thus:

- We put our customers first
- We are professional
- We respect each other
- We work as one team
- We are committed to continuous improvement.

The challenge for management has been to achieve a culture where these values are taken onboard by employees at all levels. Senior management have attempted to 'cascade' these values down through the organisation, reinforcing the change process by an emphasis on project management, team-building, a new grading structure, and a major investment in training. All staff were expected to have participated in relevant training programmes by the end of 1993. The philosophy driving this process has been, in the words of the Director of Personnel Policy, 'To turn bureaucrats into managers, and managers into leaders'.

The stated mission of the personnel function in this process has been to enable line management to achieve business goals and fulfil people values by ensuring:

- The most effective use of people (recruit, educate, train, develop, place and retain)
- The company fulfils its people responsibilities, to recognise and reward them, and to treat them as individuals with respect, fairness and individuality.

All has not been plain sailing, as might be expected. An employee attitude survey in late 1991 showed 44 per cent of employees fearing for their jobs, only 54 per cent believing that customers were benefiting from the changes, and only 22 per cent believing that senior management communicated effectively.

Results in the market place however have shown a consistent improvement in the quality of service. More faults are cleared up within two working days, fewer calls fail, and 95 per cent of public payphones are serviceable at any one time. The workforce has been slimmed down. BT did plan to reduce its core workforce of 170,000 down to 100,000 during the 1990s, but has recently had a change of heart on this target, acknowledging the negative impact it has had on staff morale. In consequence the rate of downsizing has recently been appreciably slowed down. BT believes that its radical efficiency drive since Project Sovereign was launched has made it the world's fastest-improving telecoms company. In absolute terms for quality and efficiency it is now put by industry experts in the top 25 per cent of telecoms groups. Profits before tax in the half year to 30 September 1994 were £1.49 on an increased turnover of £6.85 bn.

(Source acknowledgements:
Article by Andrew Lorenz in the *Sunday Times* 'BT Efficiency drive without 40,000 jobs' 9 May 1993; Case study by Ross Brennan 'British Telecommunications plc; Facing up to the 90s', Cranfield Case Clearing House 1992; and presentation by BT Director of Personnel Policy, IPM Annual Conference, October 1992.)

QUESTIONS FOR DISCUSSION

1. To what extent do the theories of organisation design set out in chapter 4 have relevance to the BT Case?

2. The personnel function was described as having a 'missionary' role at BT. Is this an appropriate role in the circumstances described?

3. Do BT's values and mission statements create a sound foundation for the future? Can the desired culture be achieved in time to support strategic business objectives?

Case study 2

Restructuring at Carrington Plant, Shell Chemicals UK (SCUK)

The Carrington plant sited near Manchester was a major manufacturing facility of Shell Chemicals UK in 1985 when it was faced with an urgent need to restructure. In 1985 it had a turnover of about £200m, based on sales of 400,000 tons of petrochemicals, with a workforce of 1150. A strategic review of the business in the light of market conditions came to the conclusion that, in order to survive, the plant had to reduce its fixed costs and its manpower to below 500 employees. Conventional 'pruning' would only reduce manpower to about 700, and therefore major structural change was required, and with it, an appropriate change in culture. The simple question Carrington management had to ask themselves was 'How would we run the site if we were starting out all over again?'

The old organisation had a six layer structure. This was 'flattened' to four layers with the aim of improving communications and allowing each job a bigger scope. People were to be fully responsible for their jobs and the way they performed them. This change is illustrated in figure CS2.1.

The site changed from a functional structure to one based on four performance accountable plant centres, each operated and maintained by six teams of multi-skilled technicians. While on shift these technicians were to run the process operations and attend to minor maintenance as necessary. While on day working these same technicians were to be mainly concerned with plant maintenance. The key role of coordinating each team was to be carried out by a shift manager, who stays with his team throughout the shift cycle. The plant teams were to be supported by service groups supplying essential technical and administrative backup. These structural changes were accompanied by a change programme designed to

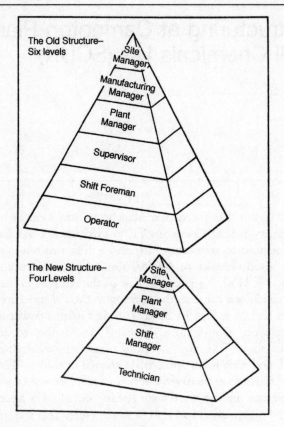

The Old Structure–
Six levels
Site Manager
Manufacturing Manager
Plant Manager
Supervisor
Shift Foreman
Operator

The New Structure–
Four Levels
Site Manager
Plant Manager
Shift Manager
Technician

Figure CS 2.1 The change to a flatter structure

change the culture in an appropriate manner, based on consultation, good communications, retraining and 'ownership' by all managers. The change in culture is illustrated in figure CS2.2.

Site manpower was successfully reduced to target level of below 500 by the end of 1986. Of the 500 odd staff laid off by that date, some 76 per cent were helped to find alternative work outside Carrington by a redeployment unit specially set up for this purpose. The plant was subsequently able to meet its new profitability targets.

(*Source acknowledgement*:

Article by Ian Thornley, (1988) 'Creating a productive culture at Shell Chemicals', *Long Range Planning*, 21(3): 34–9, 1988.)

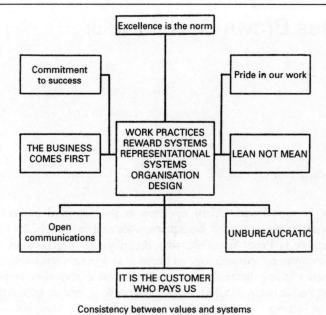

Figure CS 2.2 The new Carrington vision

QUESTIONS FOR DISCUSSION

1. The Carrington Plant restructuring took place at a time of up-turn in the national economy. Would it have been so successful during a period of economic recession?

2. To what extent could this model of restructuring be applied in white-collar industries?

3. How would human resource policies and practices have had to be adjusted in order to facilitate the changes in structure and culture described in this case?

Case study 3

Asea Brown Boveri (ABB)

Asea Brown Boveri (ABB) operates in the electrical power and equipment industry, with headquarters located in Zurich. Its Chief Executive is Percy Barnevik, who describes his organisation as a 'multi-domestic' corporation, and runs it as a matrix structure, with countries as one dimension, and business areas as the other, employing approximately 215,000 people. Barnevik is critical of complex formal business structures which he considers to be slow, inflexible, and bureaucratic:

> Such organisations create barriers between themselves and their customers, take initiative away from those who need to exercise it, and attract and promote the kind of people who operate well in that kind of environment. We wanted to build an organisation with the opposite characteristics.
>
> (quoted in Ghoshal and Bartlett, 1995)

The emphasis in the ABB structure is on decentralisation, response to customer demands, minimal bureaucracy, and individual initiative. The business is organised into approximately 65 business areas, 1300 independently incorporated companies, and 5000 profit centres. Profit centres in turn are constituted out of high performance multi-function teams, usually employing about 10 people each. Each profit centre has its own profit and loss account and balance sheet, owns assets, and serves customers directly. There are just three layers of management, consisting of an executive committee at the centre (13 people), senior executives (250 people), and profit centre managers (5000 people). Business area staff are kept to a minimum and are expected to be responsive to profit centres. Central headquarters employs only 100 professional and 50 clerical staff.

Typical of its approach to slashing central bureaucracy has been the manner in which headquarters staff in the companies it merged with or has taken over have been slashed. ASEA of Sweden in 1980 employed a central staff of 2000, which was subsequently reduced to 200. Stromberg of Finland employed 880 headquarters staff in 1982, which was reduced to 25.

ABB today is a global business, although it denies that it is a global business in the conventional sense of the term. 'We are not a global business. We are a collection of local businesses with intense global coordination', comments Sune Karlsson, head of ABB's Power Transformers Business Area. 'Our most important strength is that we have 25 factories around the world, each with its own president, design manager, marketing manager and production manager . . . we want to create a process of continuous expertise transfer.'

A further example of ABB's decentralised approach is provided by the recent creation of ABB–Daimler–Benz Transportation, aiming to establish world leadership in the supply of rail equipment. This venture is made up of about 50 companies, employing about 22,000 workers in 40 countries.

(Source acknowledgements:
a) Articles in *The Times,* 1. Peters, Tom (1992) 'ABB's prophet of smallness points the way to profit in the Nineties', 11 November, and 2. Narborough, Colin (1995) 'ABB and Daimler form rail venture', 17 March.
b) Articles in the *Harvard Business Review,* 1. Taylor, William (1991) 'Power transformers – the dynamics of global coordination', March–April, and 2. Ghoshal, Sumantra and Bartlett, Christopher (1995) 'Changing the role of top management: beyond structure to process', Jan–Feb.)

QUESTIONS FOR DISCUSSION

1. Is ABB's highly decentralised type of organisation structure only suited to heavy engineering industries, or can it be applied elsewhere?

2. Might this kind of organisation structure lead to a serious neglect of career planning and staff development?

3. Should a global business like ABB aim to achieve a common corporate culture, or should it aim for diversity?

Case study 4

Restructuring at Cheshire and Liverpool

Local authorities are as subject to pressures for change in the current decade as private corporations. These pressures include rate-capping, compulsory competitive tendering (CCT), education reforms, housing reforms, and changes in social services. Recognising the pace of change and the need to adopt appropriate policies, the Local Government Management Board recommended in their 1991 report 'Strategies for Success', that 'Authorities adopt a strategic approach . . . traditional structures, practices and procedures are being re-examined to find new ways of improving service to their communities.'

In the case of Cheshire County Council the process of major structural and cultural change commenced in the second half of the 1980s. In 1987 the authority adopted a new set of values, which in shortened form were:

- The purpose of the County Council is to serve the Cheshire people.
- Councillors and employees are accountable to the Cheshire people.
- The County Council will act with honesty, integrity and respect for the individual in its dealings with the public.
- The County Council is a partnership between councillors and employees.
- The County Council's most important resource is its employees.

Coopers and Lybrand were commissioned to undertake a review of its existing management and style. After twelve months of planning following this review, Cheshire implemented a radically new office structure and committee system in April and May 1989. In future the chief executive was to be responsible for the Council's strategic decisions, within objectives and strategies set by Council members. A management board was to be accountable collectively for planning policy and resource use. Each board member was also to have individual accountability for strategic management in defined service areas. Heads of service, not board members, were to be responsible for service delivery and quality.

In consequence the existing 21 services were collated into six groups:

- Education
- Environment
- Finance and management services
- Information and leisure
- Social services
- Support services

The net effect was to move from a structure which was vertical and based on homogeneous roles, reflecting a professional culture operating as top management, middle management, and service providers, a top down structure with a focus on inputs and budgets. In its place came a flexible structure, capable of functioning in the new era of direct service organisations, contractors, devolved management to schools, and so on. There are still three levels, but with a new purpose.

- Strategic management, who set overall direction and key issues.
- Service management, who set service objectives and specifications and ensure they are met.
- Service providers, who come in a number of forms, but all with the task of meeting the objectives and specifications

This approach switches the emphasis from inputs to outputs, whilst retaining responsibility for deciding what services are needed, and seeing that they are provided.

Liverpool City Council placed their recent reorganisation in the context of their strategic planning process and statement of values. Key elements included a vision of the city over the next 10 years, clear objectives based on an analysis of the needs of the city, a corporate strategy setting out the broad framework within which the council will operate, service and action plans, and a performance and review process. The statement of values refers to accountability, quality services, encouraging and developing staff, participation, equality of opportunity, integrity and respect.

The resulting reorganisation of their management and committee structure has involved moving from twenty-two departments to eight directorates responsible for groups of services.

- Development and environmental services
- Education
- Housing and consumer services
- Leisure services
- Operational services
- Personnel and administration

This new structure facilitates strategic management, which is the responsibility of the management team, comprised of the eight directors, the chief executive, and the assistant chief executive who heads up the Central Policy Unit.

(Source acknowledgements:
Stephenson, Tom (1989) 'Ensurers not enablers – the management response to change in Cheshire', *Local Government Policy Making*, 16(1) June: 3–8, and Chape, Alan and Davies, Phillip (1993) 'Implementing strategic management in local government: Liverpool City Council as a case study', *Local Government Policy Making* 20,(3) December: 3–8.)

QUESTIONS FOR DISCUSSION

1. What are the similarities and what are the differences in the approaches to reorganisation at Cheshire and Liverpool? Should there be such differences, and if so, why?

2. Both Councils refer to the importance of employees in their value statements. Is this right? How can it be made to sound convincing?

3. To what extent are models of strategic change developed in the private sector relevant in the public sector, particularly local government?

British Airways
Organisational turn-around and culture change

British Airways (BA) was formed from the merger of the two state owned airlines, British European Airways (BEA) (short haul) and British Overseas Airways Corporation (BOAC) (long haul) in April 1974. BA's aim was to create a worldwide network and achieve economies of scale. The merger created an airline with 50,000 staff and 215 aircraft, considered to be grossly overstaffed with several levels of incompatible management structure. Cultural differences between the merging airlines caused problems, with almost a 'class' type distinction between staff. BEA at the time was described as having a 'Grammar School' image whilst BOAC was described as having a 'Public School' image.

The Middle East Oil crisis resulted in the reduction of the market and left an already oversized BA with none of the proposed financial savings, but with massive losses, 20,000 potential redundancies and a very poor service reputation. The heavily unionised company made it very difficult for management to take positive remedial steps. By 1980, despite downsizing the fleet to 174 aircraft, the company was still losing money at the rate of £200 per minute. With the company supported by the government, there was a lack of internal urgency for the need to change and adapt to outside competition. The situation was similar to that of Air France today.

In 1980 the company still had many layers of hierarchical management, was bureaucratic and heavily influenced by RAF practices. The company was driven by operational considerations. Issues such as aircraft and crew availability, scheduling and engineering excellence dominated all discussions regarding the market place. The customer was not a high ranking priority. A survey carried out by the International Airline Passengers Association in 1980 revealed that 33 per cent of consumers wanted to avoid BA at all costs.

Whilst functionally fairly effective, the company lacked the 'marketing' and 'softer side' of the service in dealing with people.

THE CHANGE IN DIRECTION

In 1979 the election of the Thatcher administration, which adopted the policy of the 'privatisation' of nationalised undertakings, marked the start of preparing BA for eventual selling off. In 1981, Lord King a successful businessman and industrialist, was appointed as Chairman. His hard line, no nonsense management style forced through what many regarded as draconian measures in his determination to produce a leaner and fitter BA ready to compete and win against the world's airlines. Lord King moved firmly to achieve improvements in productivity – one of the two major factors in contributing to a profitable airline. However, higher loading, the other half of the equation, still needed to be addressed. This was not helped by the fact that following the implementation of Lord King's 'survival' strategy, morale of staff at BA was at an all time low; this would have obviously reflected badly in the market place in a service based industry requiring high levels of personal contact.

In 1983, Lord King appointed Colin Marshall as Chief Executive. His background was from service based industries, notably Avis and Sears, and he had very definite views that to survive and prosper, BA must reflect the needs of the market place. This approach was completely new to BA and did not fit easily with the airline's existing culture or structure. Marshall knew that BA could never be a small scale player like Laker, operating on low-cost, tight margins. He therefore decided to go for the opposite and make BA become the 'Harrods of the airlines of the world'. Marshall viewed the personal aspects of the service as being the key to providing a real competitive edge. His philosophy of service as the main industry critical success factor demanded a strategy of re-focusing the entire business on the customer. He knew however, that this could not be achieved by decree and that staff would need to share the vision, feel empowered to act and become accountable for their actions.

Marshall was not alone, or indeed first in his move to take BA towards a marketing orientation and 'brand' development. The previous chief executive of BA had already identified a marketing blueprint with a vision of 'internal appreciation' which included increases in productivity, no further new staff and categorising of passengers. Unfortunately as a result of union resistance and massive increases in the cost of fuel the strategy proved impossible to deliver. SAS chairman Carlsson had also recognised the importance of the personal aspects when he claimed that the success or failure of an airline hinges on the contacts made between the passenger and the airline staff. He calculated that with 10 million passengers each making five contacts with SAS staff for an overage of fifteen seconds, he had 'fifty million moments of truth' when the employee had the chance to convince the customer he was right to choose SAS.

IMPLEMENTING THE CHANGES

Having identified that the existing bureaucratic, inward looking rigid and complacent culture that prevailed in BA was particularly strong at the top of the management hierarchy, Marshall recruited a new top management team, whose values matched his own and were to underpin the new customer orientated culture. A two way audit was carried out by an external consultancy firm, covering customers' perceptions of service provided by BA, and customer-contact staff's perceptions of their jobs, their roles, and their relationship with customers and BA management. The audit highlighted many weaknesses in the company's customer service, primarily due to poor human resource management in BA, and to related major behavioural and performance problems among the contact staff.

Part of Marshall's plans necessarily included restructuring the company to provide the front-line employee with the information and authority needed to handle situations at the customer interface. The process began immediately and Marshall started removing layers from the management structure and changed the emphasis from a divisional to a functional structure. Many managers were thrown into the front line and forced, for the first time, to deal directly with the customer. Marshall restructured the personnel function and created the human resources department in preparation for the mammoth task ahead. Part of this restructuring included devolving the administrative functions to the line managers and streamlining the department with fewer but higher level consultants. The devolving of certain responsibilities forced managers into becoming accountable for staff performance and discipline.

The marketing function was significantly strengthened and a new department was created, Marketplace Performance, which was given equal status with existing established functions such as operations, finance, computing. Marshall's two main 'image' fronts, the company livery and the uniforms of customer contact staff, were given extensive face lifts to give a visible break from the old BA image. However as recognised by the audit, changing the external face of BA was not enough. Attitudes within the company would have to be changed in order to support the new customer orientation and this could only be achieved by extensive training events.

A training programme was designed by Time Management International, a consultancy firm who worked closely with BA's training department. The programme was a direct response to and answered the needs identified in the audit. A two day corporate-wide course was launched called 'Putting People First'. All 50,000 staff attended the course in the three years between 1983 and 1986. The course was designed to improve self-image, to change attitudes towards internal and external customers, and to achieve the highest possible standards of customer care. The courses led into quality circle team initiatives resourced by 'management workshops', and the new ideas generated for the company, as well as reinforcing the enthusiasm, commitment and positive attitudes of employees.

At the same time as initiating the 'Putting People First' another two-way audit was carried out. This time it covered the mutual perception of contact staff and their managers. This revealed exactly the same kind of tensions between staff and managers as had been identified between contact staff and customers. In response to these problems a series of courses 'Managing People First' were developed for all strata of management. The review of progress in 1983 also led to longer courses of training for managers and for professional and technical staff, focusing on team building, objective setting and other skills to produce across all of BA a more target-centred, efficient and productive organisation.

The final and logical step in this progression was to link performance with pay. The continued training and heavy support from top management (Marshall spent 20 per cent of his time attending the various staff and management programmes), softened the harsh impact of the organisational and cultural change being introduced as did enhanced communication procedures. Other supportive initiatives included updated performance management, action groups, educational seminars, the implementation of total quality management (TQM), and the staff newspaper 'British Airways News'. These latter factors have opened a debate as to whether

TQM, team work and excellent customer services are compatible with performance related pay.

The process implemented by Marshall to bring about his desired changes fits well with the 'textbook' approach to introducing organisational and cultural change. These included:

- Senior manager commitment and training
- Reorganisation of the personnel function to a human resource (HR) function
- Ensuring the involvement of all staff
- Improving communications
- Provision of training and education for all staff
- Introduction of performance appraisal
- Introduction of performance related reward systems
- Continual feedback, reassessment and consequent refinement of change programme.

THE RESULTS

By the late 1980s BA were a successful company but things were changing rapidly. The deepening recession and the Gulf War led directly to a new management initiative, 'Sustain Service Excellence'. This involved heavy commitment on training for supervisors and managers and spawned another corporate event, 'Winning for Customers'. Deregulation in the USA effectively meant that the fight for fewer customers had become even more cut-throat. BA was able to cut costs and put people on short time and long unpaid holidays in order to combat the new pressures. This would have been unthinkable for BA a decade earlier as a national company. BA's efforts to make each employee feel personally responsible for the success or failure of the company undoubtedly played a key role in helping the airline ride out the worst of the recession. The company now had a flatter structure and far greater flexibility enabling it to react more quickly to environmental changes.

APPRAISAL AND FEEDBACK

A correctly managed programme of change should always incorporate a monitoring, appraisal and feedback element, thereby ensuring that the original objectives have, and still are, being attained whilst assessing whether any changes are necessary to meet current requirements and allowing these changes to be fed back into the programme. Part of the 'Winning for Customers' initiative involved a staff survey to provide feedback on the success of the overall training and culture change programme. The results of this survey were published in 1992. The survey indicated that the majority of staff score the company well on being a 'safe, secure and financially successful company' but BA was rated poorly as an employer for 'sustaining a working environment that attracts, retains, and develops committed employees who share in the success of the company'. The survey showed that only 28 per cent of respondents felt the airline took notice of what its people said. The factors that made a good manager included 'letting me use my own initiative, recognising my achievement and giving honest feedback'.

Some writers have claimed that the results of this survey indicate that BA was only paying lip service to some of the initiatives and schemes they were introducing; and that they did not have total commitment to the new 'customer service' based strategy. However the results of the staff survey would appear to be consistent with the fact that the airline had undergone a massive change and was still in a state of flux as it sought to cope with its rapidly changing environment. All people dislike and resist change to a greater or lesser degree.

It would appear that what is actually happening is that staff are gaining more confidence and responsibility to use their own initiative. As this has been a progressive change, staff may not have fully appreciated the move forward and at the same time, having tasted some empowerment, feel frustrated because they now want more – hence the criticism. The target for future training events could therefore be the supervisor/first line manager who needs to be educated to delegate more responsibility and provide better feedback.

The action taken by King and Marshall fourteen years ago, first of all the rationalisation then the culture change, have placed BA in a very strong position in the market and ready to capitalise on the weaknesses of their rivals who had failed to act in a similar way with the same degree of foresight.

The company is now very competitive with committed staff. One must however ask whether King's aim to build 'the biggest, best and most successful airline in the world' together with the airlines' culture change of 'Winning for Customers' has actually resulted in an attitude in certain quarters of 'Winning at all costs' and hence resulted in the recent court case and on-going publicity brawl between BA and Richard Branson's Virgin Airline over 'dirty tricks'. Staff at BA consider it sad that BA had to reduce itself to such tactics over an airline that could not really be regarded as a threat. Branson will milk every piece of public relations advantage and public sympathy he can from the episode. If BA is to maintain its 'upper class' image and support its culture change internally then it must avoid reducing itself to what can be viewed as underhand tactics.

The appointment of Colin Marshall, who some say was the real architect of BA's success, to succeed Lord King as Chairman sent a direct message to the staff of the continuing direction of BA into the next century, which obviously helps to reassure staff, and consolidates the base from which to build. However, the type of programme of change which Marshall has driven through does not have an end, since it requires continuous reviewing and updating to ensure the delivery of what the marketplace wants. In this respect nothing will ever be static as the company continuously adjusts and adapts to a changing environment. In February 1995 BA reported record third quarter profits, giving a nine month profit figure of £443 million, with passengers totalling 23.7 million. Chairman Sir Colin Marshall commented that although the general prospects for 1995 were encouraging, competition within the industry would continue to put pressure on yields.

The biggest danger to BA now is complacency. They are in one of the strongest positions of any airline and with their continued aggressive acquisition programme and current success they must guard against losing momentum on their on-going internal culture change.

(*Source acknowledgements:*
Chick, Colin (1994) unpublished MBA assignment, Middlesex University.
Elliott, Harvey (1991) 'BA is the world's most profitable airline', article in *The Times*, 13 Nov.
Lauermann, Eva (1992) 'Miles-High on Quality', *Human Resources*, Winter 1991/2.
Lynn, Matthew (1993) 'BA flies above airline turmoil', article in *Sunday Times*, 23 May.
Personnel Management, January 1992 – Article 'BA not listening to staff, survey finds', p. 20.)

QUESTIONS FOR DISCUSSION

1. What were the likely advantages and disadvantages for BA in devolving many personnel responsibilities to line management?

2. How successful do you think BA has been in achieving successful turnaround, and do you think it has now become the 'Worlds' most successful' airline?

3. Evaluate the eight steps taken by BA in implementing organisational and cultural change. Were any steps omitted, and were some of the steps of greater significance than others?

Case study 6

Rover
Change on a 'brown-field' site

In the Spring of 1994, British Aerospace sold its 80 per cent share of Rover to BMW for £800 million. The sale of Britain's last volume manufacturer to a German company provoked an outcry, but this has begun to subside as BMW provide assurances as to the future of the Rover factories and the Rover badge, and settle their differences with Honda who owned the other 20 per cent of Rover. These events come at the end of a remarkable story of strategic change in a company written off just a few years ago as incompetent, out of date, riddled with bad industrial relations and poor working practices, and producing second rate motor vehicles. The chief trade negotiator for the MSF Union at Rover commented 'Over a decade ago, Rover managed workers by fear and intimidation'.

Rover manufactures cars at its principal sites at Longbridge and Solihull, near Birmingham, and at Cowley, Oxford. These sites were typical British 'brown-field' sites with competing unions and poor productivity, but with considerable engineering experience and innovation. The Cowley plant was opened by Lord Nuffield in 1913 to house Morris motors. Today 3500 workers at Cowley turn out the Maestro and Montego, former Austin models, an MG sports car (now being phased out), but more importantly, the Rover 800 and 600 saloons, of which 28,000 and 30,000 respectively were built in 1993, with sales of the 600 series targeted to rise. Annual productivity has risen to 34 cars per employee.

Land Rover is based at Solihull. Ten years ago it was a ponderous sprawling business, overmanned and inefficient, and with two products, the Land Rover and Range Rover, which were long in the tooth. Today Land Rover has also been transformed; it took 115.9 hours per man to make a Land Rover in 1991, and by 1993 this was down to 86.4 hours, and progressively reducing. A new model, the Discovery, is helping to push up sales. Remaining models, including the 200/400 series, are built at Longbridge, the former Austin car company headquarters.

In order to understand the culture change that has transformed Rover, it is important to understand its past history, and the transformation which has taken place. The Austin car company dates back to 1905, Morris to 1912, Rover to 1904, and Leyland to 1896. In 1968 British Leyland was created to run the British-owned vehicle industry, incorporating these and other once famous names. In 1975 the Labour government bought out British Leyland's private share holders. In 1977 Michael Edwards was appointed chairman to turn the company round. Edwards was successful in gaining new investment, taming the power of the union barons, and reforming working practices. However the company was still making losses, and producing cars with a quality inferior to the Japanese and Germans. In 1986 Graham Day was appointed chief executive. Under Day the car business was reshaped, cutting production to viable levels while moving the range upmarket with the help of Honda. Honda became the dominant partner in engineering design. BL, as British Leyland was now termed, was, sliced up – Trucks were sold to DAF of the Netherlands, buses to a management group, Unipart – the spare part operations, to a group of financial institutions, and the remains of BL, renamed Rover, to British Aerospace in 1989.

The degree of change since 1989 has been remarkable, given this past history, and a culture developed over many years embodying hostility between management and workers. Strategic change at Rover has succeeded in combining essential ingredients of social and technical change. Rover could only hope to survive if it adopted the 'lean production' methods of the Japanese successfully, and achieve a social change amongst its employees whereby they willingly contributed to the goals of the organisation of survival and profit, and adopted the new working practices now needed. Alongside with lean production had to come a commitment to total quality. The basic ingredients of the constituent human resource strategy had to include a change of culture, a shared vision for the future, a major investment in retraining, a customer focus, team working, flexibility and an end to demarcation, and continuous improvement.

In 1987 the Rover Group board and executive committee were trained in total quality. The group's managing director announced the launch of a total quality improvement programme. A total of 3,300 managers went through four days of training in TQI, plus a 'call back day' and this training was then cascaded to the remaining 40,000 employees through two and a half day sessions. Employees were issued with a handbook setting out seven basic principles of TQI:

- Prevention not detection
- Management-led
- Everyone responsible
- Cost of poor quality
- Right first time
- Company wide
- Continuous improvement

This handbook also explained that TQI required employees to understand that everyone has customers, whether internal or external, and managers had a responsibility for ensuring that workers had the right tools and training for the job, that machines work within tolerances, that documents and machines are available, and that systems should be designed to help, not hinder.

Rover employees were organised in teams under team leaders, with teams operating like Quality Circles. Previously spans of control had about 30 hourly paid employees under a foreman, who was in turn responsible to a senior foreman, who answered in turn to a superintendent. An assessment centre was used to select the new team leaders. The new teams consisted of about 40–50 employees. No extra supervising jobs were created, and ex-foremen not selected as team leaders became trained facilitators or took voluntary redundancy. On the production line teams were empowered to stop the process when a fault occurred, and to work out the best way to solve the problem.

The Rover staff suggestion scheme generates more than 40,000 suggestions a year, a participation rate of 110 per cent compared with the UK norm of 5 per cent. The originator's manager is required to research and implement the suggestions within 30 days, or inform the originator of progress, and Rover pay 10 per cent of any estimated savings, up to £5000, plus the gift of a camcorder or car. In 1972 £1.5 million was paid out, and an estimated £10.5 million saved.

In 1991 Rover management proposed a new industrial relations deal. This proposal was made two weeks before the implementation of the second stage of a two year pay deal, guaranteeing an increase in grade rates of 7.5 per cent at a time when inflation was 5 per cent and falling. These proposals included:

- single-status terms and conditions;
- greater emphasis on team working and continuous improvement;
- full flexibility;
- streamlined trade union arrangements, and
- an updated procedure agreement.

Following negotiation with the unions and a ballot of workers, the agreement accepting these principles took effect in April 1992. As a result 'clocking' has been abolished, single status has been implemented, regular health checks are provided and payment is by weekly credit transfer. In the event of lay-offs, for so long the bug bear of the car industry, all employees continue to be paid their standard salary, provided they undertake other work. The grading structure comprising a five-grade hourly and six-grade staff structure is being replaced by a scheme with a reduced number of occupational classifications. Teams are now responsible for quality, routine maintenance, house keeping, plant and office layout, process improvements, cost reduction, control of tools and materials, work allocation, job rotation, and training each other.

The new working practices are supported by a major investment in training. This is exemplified by their continuous professional development (CPD) scheme, spearheaded by Rover Learning Business (RLB) a wholly owned subsidiary. RLB has three distinct missions – to educate the company's dealers, to facilitate the management of change within the company, and to support general management development. A two year part time course, the Integrated Manager Learning Programme (IMLP) is run by Warwick University for Rover, embarked on by over 700 staff. In all some 1500 of Rovers 4000 managers have taken some sort of course at Warwick University. Around 70 per cent of all the 33,000 employees have a personal development file, a comprehensive set of documents allowing them to map out their own career progress plans. The Rover Employee Assisted Learning (REAL) scheme allows every Rover employee to claim a £100 subsidy towards tutored learning in any subject. All this costs the company around £35 million a year in direct charges and time lost from work. This accords with the company's Corporate Quality Strategy Document, which specifically identifies 'learning' as a fundamental activity.

In conclusion, one can argue that the turnaround at Rover and the cooperation of the unions only came about because Maggie Thatcher made it quite clear that she was not going to bail the company out again. Faced with the prospect of massive unemployment and lay-offs, a sense of realism took over. However, to achieve levels of quality and productivity which match the Japanese and Germans, as Rover has done, required a change in attitudes and working practices of major proportions. The human resource strategy was an essential ingredient in the total corporate strategy, and the turnaround at Rover. In 1993 Rover sales rose 9.7 per cent to 363,890, the only mass car producer in Europe to show any growth in that year, and a further rise in 1994 to 478,000 vehicles. Rover is back in profit.

Rover is now owned by the German firm BMW, who have undertaken to maintain the momentum for change. Time will tell whether this interesting fusion of German leadership and British manufacturing can succeed.

(*Source acknowledgements:*
Farish, Mike (1994) 'Back to the school desk with Rover', article in *Financial Times*, 25 March.
Eason, Kevin (1993) 'Rover's tale of remarkable revival', article in *The Times*, 16 July.
IRS Employment Trends 514 'Lean production – and Rover's "New Deal"', June: 12–15.
Eason, Kevin (1993) 'Land Rover', article in *The Times*, 12 November.)

QUESTIONS FOR DISCUSSION

1. In what respects does a strategy for human resources pose different problems on a 'brown-field' site, compared with a 'green-field' site?

2. To what extent is it necessary to include training in total quality in major change programmes, such as Rover's?

3. Compare the approach taken to employee relations at Rover with that taken by Ford, as described in case study 12. What are the similarities, and what are the differences?

Komatsu
Culture and change on a 'green-field' site using Japanese methods

It is frequently argued that it is easy to develop an appropriate culture on a new 'green-field' site. Because all the employees are new, they can be carefully selected to ensure that they have favourable attitudes. Human resource strategy then becomes simple and straightforward, so this argument goes. Recruit selectively, train systematically, reward good performance, and all will be well. This argument is superficial and of course neglects the problems associated with recruiting employees in an area where there may have been a history of management–worker conflict, poor industrial relations, and frequent business failures. Creating success in such an economic and social environment represents a major challenge to general managers and human resource professionals. When the companies concerned are Japanese, suspected of importing an alien culture and repressive ways of working, the challenge is even greater. Yet in the North East of England a number of success stories exist, of which Nissan and Komatsu are probably the best known. The Nissan story has been well told by Peter Wickens in his book *The Road to Nissan* (Wickens, 1987).

Perhaps less well known is the story of Komatsu. This may partly be because manufacture of earth moving equipment is less well publicised than the manufacture of cars, and because it is more recent. Komatsu came to County Durham in December 1985, in the wake of the closure of Caterpillar's troubled plant on the same site. Caterpillar manufactured construction equipment at Chester le Street, but in 1983 had been forced to close down the very factory which Komatsu subsequently acquired for £3 million. Caterpillar had become paralysed by bad industrial relations, with eleven different trade unions competing with each other and with management. When Caterpillar finally closed its doors, 1500 people were made redundant.

Komatsu set up its manufacturing plant in order to make medium-sized wheel loaders and hydraulic excavators in a location which would give it access to European markets. One of their first appointments was a personnel director, a clear indication of the priority given to human resource strategy by the Japanese owners. They appointed Clive Morton, in February 1986. He had been trained as an engineer, but subsequently gained experience in industrial relations at a senior level.

The approach to recruitment was meticulous. 'We haven't necessarily taken on the most skilled people, but the ones who have the right attitude to teamworking and flexibility' commented Morton. Some 3,500 people applied for the first 70 shop-floor positions, and many more have applied subsequently. By the end of 1987 some 270 staff were in post, of whom only 12 were Japanese. A single union agreement was drawn up with the Amalgamated Engineering Union (AEU), giving the AEU sole bargaining rights and sole representation of employees. Single status for all employees was the rule from the start; all staff, including directors, wear the same uniform, and commence work at the same time, and use the same canteen and car park. An advisory council was set up, consisting of senior managers plus nine elected representatives from the constituent parts of the company. It meets once a month. Initially staff were expected to join in physical exercises prior to commencing work (termed *Taiso* in Japanese), but this requirement has now been dropped.

Today Komatsu UK employs about 450 people, produces six basic machines, but can offer up to 16 variations on each of its core modules. The company is one of the biggest manufacturers of excavators in Europe, and exports 70 per cent of its products, with a turnover in excess of £100 million a year. The company's working philosophy is based on team building, total quality, a single union agreement, single status, continuous development, and enhancing the role of supervisors. Supervisors at Komatsu receive training in basic management, make recruitment decisions (assisted by the personnel team) and train and appraise team members. A performance related (PRP) scheme is also in operation. In this respect Morton decided to deviate from the pure Deming-Japanese model of quality management. 'I'm a believer in PRP' he is quoted as saying

Objective	Policy	Method
High Quality	Best employees Development TQC	Thorough selection Training Quality circles Motivation
Cost reduction	Continuous improvement Reduce inefficiencies	Involvement 'Bottom up' ideas 5'S' System
Reliable delivery	Uninterrupted production Constructive supervision	Single-union agreement Authority and reponsibility
Safe working	Responsibility of each person	Good protection Education
Technical development	Close to customer Design development	High tech Engineering Close communications

Figure CS 7.1 Komatsu UK employment policies
Source: Adapted from Morton, 1994

'but as a reward system. I don't believe money motivates, but you sometimes need it to provide a stimulus.'

The Japanese cite three basic problems with the traditional attitudes of British workers, which needs to be overcome. Kagao Murato, managing director of Yuasa Battery in South Wales described these as:

- Work attitudes: 'I will produce a given amount and no more';
- There are company rules, but they are not followed, and enforcement is not strict;
- Improvement in working practices and productivity is not my business, but should be left to experts.

The key to achieving the right culture and high productivity at Komatsu can be found in employment policies. As indicated in figure CS7.1, these lay emphasis on quality, cost reduction, reliable delivery, safe working, and technical development. Employment policies are integral to the production policies.

The emphasis on team working has underpinned the total quality culture. Team working has been successful, in spite of a history in the region of demarcation disputes, particularly amongst shipbuilders. The selection process aimed to recruit team orientated people, and teamworking and flexibility were constantly encouraged by training, appraisal, and trained supervisors.

Even so, there were problems, largely because of cultural differences between Japan and Britain, and not because of the attitudes of the employees. Japanese decision making by consensus is time consuming and frustrating for British managers who are used to speedy decision making. But to the Japanese management meetings are part briefing, part fact finding, and part reporting. The aim is to achieve '*namawaski*', or consensus building. These seemingly inefficient meetings are essential to understanding and commitment by all involved.

The tangible results for Komatsu UK are demonstrated by its record in becoming the largest producer of hydraulic excavators in the UK, accreditation for BS5750 and Investors in People, the Queen's Award for Export, and survival of the deep economic recession of 1991–2.

(*Source acknowledgements:*

Broad, Geoffrey (1987) 'Shaping up under Japanese Management', *Personnel Management*, August.

Gabb, Annabella (1988) 'Komatsu makes the earth move', *Management*, April.

Harris, Derek (1991) 'Japanese construct success', article in *The Times*, April 22.

Morton, Clive (1994) *Becoming World Class*, London: Macmillan.

Pickard, Jane (1992) 'Profile of Clive Morton', *Personnel Management*, September.

Wickens, Peter (1987) *The Road to Nissan*, London: Macmillan.)

QUESTIONS FOR DISCUSSION

1. Why have Japanese companies been successful in building and operating engineering plants in the UK?

2. To what extent was Kagao Murato correct in his comments on

the problems stemming from traditional attitudes amongst British workers? Does the Komatsu formula provide a general solution?

3. Consensus decision making takes time. Can strategic decisions be made on these lines in Western companies, or should it be restricted to shop-floor type problems, or avoided altogether?

Human resource planning at ICL

ICL employs some 24,000 people. In 1993 it achieved sales of 4.3 billion pounds and pre-tax profits of 23.4 million pounds and was Europe's only profitable maker of mainstream computers, a record unmatched by IBM, Siemens Nixdorf, Olivetti or Bull. Human resource planning, a major investment in training, career planning, a decentralised structure, a positive corporate culture, and a policy of continuous improvement have made a major contribution to financial targets and to the human resource strategy of the enterprise.

ICL was formed in 1968 from the merger of ICT with English Electric Computers. In 1976 it took over Singer Business machines and in 1984 merged with STC. In 1991 it was sold to Fijitsu of Japan, providing it with the backing of the second largest technology company in the world, and giving Fijitsu a foothold in Europe. Subsequently ICL purchased Nokia Data, the Finnish computer group. Today it operates in seventy countries with 40 per cent of its turnover based on overseas business.

Today ICL is increasingly a software and services business. Sales of mainframes and associated equipment account for just 10 per cent of revenues, against almost a third when Fijitsu took over, and 70 per cent a decade ago. The company now derives more revenue from computing services than from hardware manufacture.

STRAGETY AND STRUCTURE

Competition amongst computer manufacturers and service providers is ferocious, and the problems experienced by IBM have been well publicised. In the mid-1980s when almost all the world's big computer companies were dedicated to selling proprietry hardware, ICL broke away from the mould. Under the leadership of Peter

Bonfield, it targeted itself at five 'vertical' markets – retail, financial services, local and central government, manufacturing and defence – and focused on 'open systems' that allowed networking customers to link ICL products to those of other manufacturers. Today, targeted marketing and open systems have become the industry norm.

Five years ago the company enjoyed gross margins of 50 per cent. Subsequently gross margins have dropped drastically in a very competitive market. 'We need' commented Peter Bonfield recently, 'to be able to make a profit at margins below 30 per cent. We had to make the company move faster, and with much greater flexibility.' To help achieve this, the company sought the advice of C.K. Prahalad, professor of management at the University of Michigan. He advised that the company needed a structure which would enable it to coordinate across businesses, while creating the agility of a small company. In order to achieve this, Bonfield has shaped the company into three business streams – industry systems (for the five target markets), technology (comprising computer hardware, from mainframes to PCs) and ICL Enterprise (computer services). Executive responsibility has been devolved to the managing director of each of the 26 business units. Overheads have been slashed from 27 per cent of sales to 17 per cent.

THE ORGANISATION AND MANAGEMENT REVIEW (OMR) PROCESS

Human resource planning in ICL has been principally conducted through the annual cycle of the Organisation and Management Review. As shown in figure CS8.1 below, this commences with the development of five year strategic plan guidelines at the end of the calendar year. This is then taken on board by line units in January for further development and subsequently reviewed and finalised in April. These reviews of the strategic plan form the basis for the operating plan guidelines for the next company year which are converted into budget guidelines in June. Line units respond to these by September, and an organisation budget is then agreed by October, thus completing the annual cycle.

The OMR mirrors this process. In July the first implications of the budget guidelines for organisation and human resource levels are considered. Each unit's budget implications for human resources are subsequently considered in detail in September and October. In

Date	Activity	QBR Focus*	OMR Focus+
Nov. Dec.	5 year strategic plan guidelines		
Jan. Feb.		End of year actual	Individual development
April	5 year strategic plan complete	Strategic plan	Organisation strategy
June	Budget guidelines		
July Aug.		Mid-year review	Organisation SWOT and initial view of plan to delivery of budget
Sept.	Budget reviews		
Oct.		Forecast/Budget	Organisation for budget year

Figure CS 8.1 The business planning cycle at ICL

* Quarterly budget review
+ Organisation and management review

February the development needs of senior managers are considered individually, with the personnel director sitting in on meetings between managing directors and their direct reports. This OMR process is 'owned' by line management, and not personnel.

Using a company wide categorisation of skills, units carry out their own manpower planning, looking forward two years, assessing the developments in skills required by their business plans. At the centre of the company an across the board review takes place, considering productivity indices, skills mix, the overhead to direct ratio, and overall productivity improvements. The company view is that whilst manpower planning can never be an exact science, by integrating it with the business planning and review cycle, shifts in skill can be detected and appropriate plans formulated.

CAREER PLANNING AND CAREER MANAGEMENT

Career management is seen as 'making sure the organisation will have the right people with the right skills at the right time'. Its task is to understand the implications for human resource development of the strategies and objectives of the organisation and the external trends in the environment. Four key areas influence career management policies:

- Organisation structure: this determines the number of promotion steps, the types of jobs etc;
- organisation culture;
- Manpower needs;
- Knowledge and skills needed.

ICL tries to ensure 'career bridges' are in place to facilitate movement across functions; one of the weaknesses of the 'self development' approach is considered to be that individuals on their own are confined to vertical career moves within their exisiting function. Development into general management however requires horizontal movement. ICL produces booklets on career structures for all the main streams, and tries also to show how jobs can be interconnected. Career guidance centres help managers to recognise opportunities for growth in their job through special assignments, projects and secondments.

For each individual, ICL aims to have a:

- Chosen career direction
- Current perception of potential
- Career plan
- Development action plan

The key link between the individual and the organisation is seen as the appraisal and development discussion. ICL recognises that career counselling by line managers is often done very badly. Therefore providing their own managers with assessment and counselling skills is taken very seriously.

MODELLING MANPOWER FLOWS

Key questions in human resource planning at ICL, as in most large organisations, include the following:

- What is the state of succession, both short and long term?
- What are our loss rates, particularly of good people?
- What is the balance between internal and external resourcing?

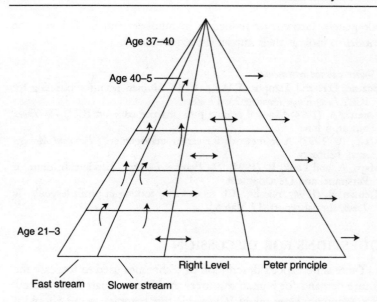

Figure CS 8.2 Providing different career paths at ICL

- How many young entrants should we be recruiting and training?
- How many high flyers are we able to accommodate?

In the world of computing, real high flyers make the top level before 40; the average age of ICL's board is well under 50. The slower stream may reach the level below the board by about 45, where they 'top out'. It is company policy to promote from within in the majority of cases, but still to allow for up to 20 per cent of managers to be recruited externally. This situation is depicted in figure CS 8.2.

These factors of loss rates, resourcing ratios, numbers at each level, and speed of progression combine to produce a mathematical model which tells the company how many upwards potential people are needed at each level to provide adequate cover for succession into more senior positions. Experience within ICL indicates a ratio of about 30 per cent upwardly mobile managers, with about 10 per cent as high flyers. This model also indicates the number of young entrants to be hired each year in order to staff the organisation adequately. Growth or reduction in numbers can be fed into the model to look at their impact on requirements.

(*Source acknowledgements:*
Beattie, D.F. and Tampoe, F.M.K. (1990) 'Human resource planning for ICL', *Long Range Planning* 23: 17–28.
Lorenz, A. (1994) 'Radical regime puts sharper edge on ICL', *The Times*, report, 6 June.
Mayo, A. (1992) 'A framework for career management', *Personnel Management*, February.
Mayo, A. and Lank, E. (1994) *The Power of Learning*, London: Institute of Personnel and Development.
Tieman, R. (1994) 'Nimble ICL retains sole footing in profit league', *The Times*, special report, 17 March.)

QUESTIONS FOR DISCUSSION

1. There is no explicit description of techniques used to forecase the future demand for human resources in this case, apart from succession planning. How might ICL tackle this complex issue? Should it be left to the line units?

2. Ten per cent of ICL's managers appear to be 'high fliers'. Is this a sensible figure, and might it lead to a loss of motivation on the part of other managers?

3. Will the provision of training in assessment and counselling to line managers be sufficient to ensure they carry out these roles successfully? What support could the personnel department supply?

Case study 9

Strategic selection at Nissan

The Nissan organisation provides an opportunity to examine a major success story in recent times, namely, the Japanese organisation, and its use of strategic selection among other human resource management practices.

Japanese companies in Britain have been practising what has become known as lean production methods (LPMs). These involve flexible working practices, team working, multi-skilling, and operation of production on just in time principles.

Researchers, Garrahan and Stewart (1991), investigating the Japanese sector in north-east England, argue that instances of innovation in the labour process must be seen within the social and political context in which this takes place. In their view there is a vital reciprocal relationship between the external and internal environment of current changes in working practices.

In a study of the Nissan plant in Sunderland, they conclude, from their analysis of how LPMs work, that the relationship between the internal and external environments of the plant is crucial. The imbedding of the corporate human resource strategy in the plant depends upon this relationship.

The company is an excellent example of how an organisation 'strategically' recruits and orients employees so that they match the 'Nissan Way'. Moreover, the collectivist, team working, company image is nurtured in the external community where the first phase of the strategic acquisition of employees actually commences.

The organisation, when it was preparing to set up operations in the UK selected a greenfield site in Sunderland and negotiated a single union agreement. The area is one in which there is higher than average unemployment and low pay levels.

Nissan's recruitment process has two distinct features that have significance for the success of the company. One is concerned with the cognitive appropriateness of all employees. The second is to ensure that the appropriate psychological–ideological characteristics are identifiable and can be harnessed to the requirements of the organisation. In this manner, candidates unsuitable to the 'Nissan Way' can be eliminated. This latter aspect is explored in an interview which focuses on attitudes to participation and dissent. The mix of questions is designed to define the kind of collectiveness that any future employee might espouse. Numerical, fluency and mechanical comprehension tests are also administered. There is a probationary period of 3 months and about 9 per cent turnover in this period. This is a costly first phase and it has to be judged against the benefits that accrue from successful completion of the second stage which consists of a sustained process of individual and social induction into the 'Nissan Way'.

The recruitment process actually commences in the community environment of the organisation, where it engages in external cultural activities which project an image of the company which reinforces its culture, for example, its commitment to team working.

The continued success of Nissan indicates that it has, undoubtedly, created a 'winning' HRM strategy.

(*Source acknowledgements:*
Garrahan, P. and Stewart, P. (1992) *The Nissan Enigma: Flexibility at Work in a Local Economy,* London: Mansell.)

QUESTION FOR DISCUSSION

Identify the core effectiveness criteria by which Nissan is linking its selection strategy to organisation strategy. In your view how should these criteria be linked to assessment, training, rewards and employee relations to provide an integrated HRM support system.

Organisational learning at Hitachi-Seiki

Japanese organisations know that by expanding their range of manufacturing capabilities, they also increase their range of strategic options. Few however have created strategies which address the issue of which capabilities should be developed to enhance strategic flexibility. An exception is Hitachi-Seiki. By the 1980s the organisation had risen, from being a relatively obscure manufacturer of machine tools in the 1950s, to become a leading world supplier of flexible manufacturing systems, computer-controlled equipment that can perform a variable sequence of machining tasks.

As early as 1952, when the first numerically controlled machine tool was developed at MIT, Hitachi-Seiki set for itself the ambitious goal of developing the capabilities required to become a leader in computerised automation. It started this process by undertaking basic research in automated production, some of which was carried out in collaboration with other Japanese manufacturers through a consortium organised by the Ministry of International Trade and Industry. When the consortium was disbanded, Hitachi-Seiki persisted in building its knowledge base, even though most companies had decided to continue with traditional manufacturing processes because of the problems with the new technology.

One of the first things the organisation realised was that successful automation would require that mechanical design (traditional machine tool technology) and electronics would have to be integrated. It began to recruit electrical engineers and in 1967, set up a new engineering discipline, named 'mechatronics'.

The organisation's first project in flexible manufacturing systems failed. This first system developed in 1972 only slightly improved productivity in relation to traditional machinery and had reliability and coordination problems. Nevertheless, in building that system, capabilities for future projects were established, for example, it brought together top engineers from different disciplines to write software. As a consequence the organisation was able to develop engineers with broad skills and perspectives.

The second project incorporated lessons learned from the first. Results were slightly better but the goal was still not achieved. Productivity was not high enough to represent an adequate return on investment. There were several critical learning lessons. The organisation found that it was mistaken in viewing flexible manufacturing as a set of purely technical problems to be solved with technical expertise. It realised that it would be necessary to take a systems approach to development that combined manufacturing and engineering perspectives.

The third project brought a development team together from a range of functions, including manufacturing, machine design, software engineering, and tool design. The project leader was a mechanical engineer who had also experience in tool design and manufacturing. Learning from the prior projects was utilised. They realised that it would be difficult to develop one system that could achieve all the required performance targets which included: automatic tool changing, flexible fixtures that could hold materials of different sizes, and the ability to operate untended. The team decided to develop three systems and they created separate teams to tackle each. All three systems were finished on time within their financial and performance targets.

After developing the organisation's first commercially successful flexible manufacturing system, many of the project team members were transferred to the customer service department, where they designed and built systems for customers.

(*Source acknowledgement:*
Hayes, R.H. and Pisano, G.P. (1994) 'Beyond World-Class: The New Manufacturing Strategy', *Harvard Business Review,* 72(1) p: 85.)

QUESTION FOR DISCUSSION

The lesson from Hitachi-Seiki is 'If at first you don't succeed, try, try, try again'. The organisation had the goal of developing flexibility capabilities to increase its strategic options. As it made successive attempts to achieve this, what learning insights were gained and what principles of a learning organisation were applied? What advice would you give to an organisation, in a similar position to Hitachi-Seiki, to assist it in becoming a 'fully-fledged' learning organisation.

Performance management and strategic change at ICI Pharmaceuticals

In the late 1980s many large organisations underwent extensive restructuring exercises in order to match rapid change in their environments, and the major European chemical companies were no exception. In 1990 BP, Hoechst and ICI announced major restructuring programmes. All these programmes aimed for further decentralisation and an improved management of performance.

ICI was facing major challenges both at home and abroad, including the expiry of patents, competition for resources to support existing products, and a highly competitive market. Within the pharmaceutical division a review of its organisation revealed a task-orientated culture in which employees felt disconnected from the business, people management skills were undervalued and under-developed, and decisions were taken at a high level. A performance improvement strategy was initiated, based on a new performance management system aiming to achieve better communication of company objectives, developing individuals to help them achieve agreed targets, and fostering closer relations between staff and line managers. A booklet termed 'Towards a healthy future' was used to communicate strategic objectives throughout the business.

Five guiding principles underpinned the new performance management programme:

- Facilitate best management practice
- Remember individuals work in teams
- Address performance in the current job
- Accommodate local variation
- Accountability lies with managers

The performance management process as a whole was developed in accordance with the integrated structure depicted in figure CS11.1.

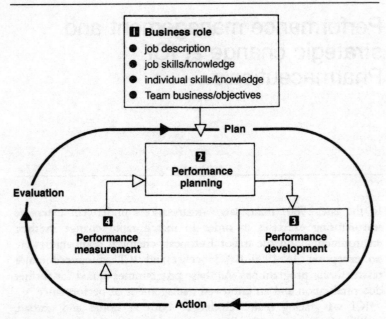

Figure CS 11.1 Performance management system at ICL Pharmaceuticals

Senior managers were asked to work on their own objectives, linking them to the business's strategic objectives. This process was cascaded down through directors and general managers to heads of department. Departmental objectives were agreed for up to two years ahead. Individuals were able to see how they and their departments contributed to business results. A company wide initiative on the 'development of people, work, and reward' (DPWR) provided a set of guiding principles covering the organisation of work, communication, training and development, and the reward of staff. A single job evaluation scheme for all monthly paid staff linked to a simpler grade structure was introduced. The job description of line managers included their people management responsibilities. Benefits claimed for managers included the following:

- Individuals linked into teams
- Performance evaluated objectively
- Development in current job encouraged
- Rewards linked to performance

and the following benefits were claimed for individual members of staff:

- Clear understanding of the job
- Basis created for regular discussion of tasks
- Agreement on development needs
- Feedback given on performance

It is important to stress that line managers were heavily involved in drawing up and steering the performance management programme. A group of senior experienced business managers formed the steering group, and the job of introducing and integrating performance management in departments was given to line managers. Each function and department develops its own reward plan which reflects business goals and priorities. Implementation is managed locally within previously agreed budget constraints. Heads of department are provided with guidelines for measuring performance and a recommended process for evaluating performance. They have at their disposal a portfolio of reward options, including intrinsic rewards. Non-financial rewards include the following:

- Recognition of achievement
- Additional responsibility
- Greater autonomy
- Involvement
- Career development

The verdict of one head of department, previously sceptical about performance management, provides a useful comment on this major initiative. 'When I walk around I find people are clear about what is expected of them, how they are contributing to projects, and why. There is less moaning, turnover has reduced, and people recognise that there are opportunities for development for everyone'.

(*Source acknowledgements:*
Lester, Tom (1992) 'A structure for Europe', *Management Today,* January.
Sheard, Angela (1992) 'Learning to improve performance', *Personnel Management,* September.
Sheard, Angela to IPM Annual Conference, October 1992.)

QUESTIONS FOR DISCUSSION

1. Compare the approaches to performance management in this case study company with the one being used in the company

described in figure 9.2 in chapter 9. What are the similarities and differences, and can both approaches be applied with commensurate success in the majority of large organisations?

2. Is there not a danger of wide variations in rewards across the company as each function and department develops its' own reward schemes? How might this danger be monitored and controlled?

3. The views quoted in this case generally reflect management attitudes. Is performance management likely to appeal as strongly to non-managerial staff? How can the motivation of non-managerial staff be ensured?

Moving from control to consent at Ford

The Ford Motor Company has traditionally utilised a highly bureaucratic, centralised and functional style of management. In the field of
industrial relations this style has historically been associated with an
approach to work design based on the fragmentation of job tasks
and hence the minimisation of worker discretion; an emphasis at
plant level on the preservation of managerial prerogatives; and the
existence of often highly conflictual relations with trade unions.

At the end of the 1970s senior management, in the face of
growing product market competition, notably from Japanese car
manufacturers, concluded that the company's existing patterns of
management–worker relations were not compatible with its required
need to increase productivity, cut costs, improve quality and develop
more flexible methods of product design and production. It consequently decided that urgent steps had to be taken to develop more
consensual labour relations as a route to achieving improvements in
each of these areas.

At first this change of strategy took the form of an initiative called
'After Japan' (AJ), which was intended to move the company's style
of management towards that of its Japanese competitors. In particular, and more specifically, it sought to place more emphasis on
management by consent rather than control and to shift the
company's approach to job design away from reducing worker
discretion to one which emphasised the need to more fully utilise
worker knowledge and skills.

In pursuance of these objectives Ford of Europe decided in 1979
to introduce quality circles into its operations. However, in the UK
this did not prove to be possible as a result of trade union
opposition – this opposition reflecting union fears that quality

circles would be used to by-pass existing collective bargaining institutions. Ford UK was therefore forced to abandon the AJ initiative, and the broader ambition of wholesale 'Japanisation' which underlay it, and to instead adopt a more pragmatic, long-term approach to organisational change. That is an approach which took greater cognisance of its history of adversarial, low-trust relations, and focused greater attention on obtaining workforce support for change.

This new strategy has incorporated two distinct initiatives. First 'Employee involvement'(EI), and second, ' Participative management'. The first of these was originally conceived as a long-term trust-building exercise under which management and unions would agree to the introduction of various types of cooperative programmes designed to reduce absenteeism, and improve efficiency and quality. The second was intended to develop more devolved and cooperative systems of management.

In the UK the new EI imitative again fell victim to the low levels of trust that existed between management and unions. Thus while the staff unions agreed to the proposed programme, the manual ones rejected it. Faced with this situation the company decided to continue to pursue its objectives, but in a more ad hoc and opportunistic way.

This approach has nevertheless enabled significant changes to be obtained. For example, unions at national level have agreed to allow more scope for local plant agreements on work reorganisation. They have also accepted a breakdown of craft demarcations; a dramatic reduction in the number of production grades – a change which has significantly expanded the roles and responsibilities of production operators; and the introduction of team working involving maintenance craftsman working alongside production staff.

Overall there is no doubt that the EI and PM initiatives represent a 'quiet revolution' in Ford's management strategy and a significant reversal of the fragmentation rationale which has informed the company's policy towards job design since its foundation. At the same time the process of moving towards management by consent remains an uneven process and one which might even be reversed.

(*Source acknowledgements:*
McKinlay, A. and Starkey, K.(1992) 'Between control and consent: corporate strategy and employee involvement in Ford UK', in P. Blyton, and J. Morris (eds) *A Flexible Future?*, Berlin: de Gruyter.)

QUESTIONS FOR DISCUSSION

1. What lessons concerning strategic employee relations emerge from a comparison of the Ford case with the two earlier cases (6 and 7) on Rover and Komatsu?

2. In what ways can the frames of reference adopted by Fox and Edwards, described in chapter 10, be applied to Ford? Will a 'Unitary' perspective ever be possible or desirable at Ford?

3. What advice would you give Ford on a strategy of change that would develop higher levels of trust between management and workers, whilst strengthening Ford's competitive position?

Index